MW00647354

PLAYS AND PLAYWRIGHTS

2008

edited and with an introduction by

Martin Denton

This collection copyright © 2008 by The New York Theatre Experience, Inc.

Introduction and Appendix copyright © 2008 by Martin Denton

All rights reserved. Except for brief passages quoted in newspaper, magazine, radio, or television reviews, no part of this book may be reproduced in any form or by any means, electronic or mechanical, including photocopying or recording, or by any information storage and retrieval system, without permission in writing from the publisher.

CAUTION: These plays are fully protected, in whole, in part, or in any form, under the copyright laws of the United States of America and of all countries covered by the International Copyright Union (including the Dominion of Canada and the rest of the British Commonwealth), and of all countries covered by the Pan-American Copyright Convention and the Universal Copyright Convention, and of all countries with which the United States has reciprocal copyright relations, and are subject to royalty. All performance rights, including professional, amateur, stock, motion picture, radio, television, recitation, and public reading are strictly reserved. Please refer to Permissions, beginning on page i, for information concerning such inquiries.

Published by The New York Theatre Experience, Inc.
P.O. Box 1606, Murray Hill Station, New York, NY 10156
www.nyte.org
email: info@nyte.org

ISBN-10: 0-9794852-1-5
ISBN-13: 978-0-9794852-1-3
ISSN 1546-1319

 Plays and Playwrights 2008 is made possible, in part, with public funds from the New York State Council on the Arts, a state agency.

Plays and Playwrights 2008 is made possible, in part, with public funds from the New York City Department of Cultural Affairs.

Plays and Playwrights 2008 is made possible, in part, by support from the Peg Santvoord Foundation.

Book and cover designed by Nita Congress

PERMISSIONS

The Telling Trilogy copyright © 2007 by Crystal Skillman. Amateurs and professionals are hereby warned that *The Telling Trilogy* is fully protected by copyright law and is subject to royalty. All rights in all current and future media are strictly reserved. No part of this work may be used for any purpose without the written consent of the author. All inquiries concerning production, publication, reprinting, or use of this work in any form should be addressed to the author in care of The New York Theatre Experience, Inc., P.O. Box 1606, Murray Hill Station, New York, NY 10156; by phone: 212-217-9627; or by emailing the author directly at: crystalskillman@gmail.com.

What Happened When copyright © 2006 by Daniel Talbott. Amateurs and professionals are hereby warned that *What Happened When* is fully protected by copyright law and is subject to royalty. All rights in all current and future media are strictly reserved. No part of this work may be used for any purpose without the written consent of the author. All inquiries concerning production, publication, reprinting, or use of this work in any form should be addressed to the author in care of The New York Theatre Experience, Inc., P.O. Box 1606, Murray Hill Station, New York, NY 10156; by phone: 212-217-9627; by email: info@nyte.org.

Antarctica copyright © 2007 by Carolyn Raship. Amateurs and professionals are hereby warned that *Antarctica* is fully protected by copyright law and is subject to royalty. All rights in all current and future media are strictly reserved. No part of this work may be used for any purpose without the written consent of the author. All inquiries concerning production, publication, reprinting, or use of this work in any form should be addressed to the author in care of The New York Theatre Experience, Inc., P.O. Box 1606, Murray Hill Station, New York, NY 10156; by phone: 212-217-9627; by email: info@nyte.org.

Cleansed copyright © 2006 by Thomas Bradshaw. Amateurs and professionals are hereby warned that *Cleansed* is fully protected by copyright law and is subject to royalty. All rights in all current and future media are strictly reserved. In its present form, the play is dedicated to the reading public only. The amateur live stage performance rights to *Cleansed* are controlled exclusively by Samuel French, Inc., and royalty arrangements and licenses must be secured well in advance of presentation. Stock royalty quoted upon application to Samuel French, Inc., at 45 West 25th Street, New York, NY 10010. Royalty of the required amount must be paid whether the play is presented for charity or gain and whether or not admission is charged. For all other rights than those stipulated above, apply to Beacon Artists Agency, 120 East 56th Street, Suite 540, New York, NY 10022, attn: Pat McLaughlin.

Linnea copyright © 2007 by John Regis. Amateurs and professionals are hereby warned that *Linnea* is fully protected by copyright law and is subject to royalty. All rights in all current and future media are strictly reserved. No part of this work may be used for any purpose without the written consent of the author. All inquiries concerning production, publication, reprinting, or use of this work in any form should be addressed to the author in care of The New York Theatre Experience, Inc., P.O. Box 1606, Murray Hill Station, New York, NY 10156; by phone: 212-217-9627; by email: info@nyte.org.

...and we all wore leather pants copyright © 2007 by Robert Attenweiler. Amateurs and professionals are hereby warned that *...and we all wore leather pants* is fully protected by copyright law and is subject to royalty. All rights in all current and future media are strictly reserved. No part of this work may be used for any purpose without the written consent of the author. All inquiries concerning production, publication, reprinting, or use of this work in any form should be addressed to the author in care of The New York Theatre Experience, Inc., P.O. Box 1606, Murray Hill Station, New York, NY 10156; by phone: 212-217-9627; by email: info@nyte.org.

Marvelous Shrine copyright © 2007 by Leslie Bramm. Amateurs and professionals are hereby warned that *Marvelous Shrine* is fully protected by copyright law and is subject to royalty. All rights in all current and future media are strictly reserved. No part of this work may be used for any purpose without the written consent of the author. All inquiries concerning production, publication, reprinting, or use of this work in any form should be addressed to the author in care of The New York Theatre Experience, Inc.,

P.O. Box 1606, Murray Hill Station, New York, NY 10156; by phone: 212-217-9627; by email: info@nyte.org.

In Our Name copyright © 2007 by Elena Hartwell. Amateurs and professionals are hereby warned that *In Our Name* is fully protected by copyright law and is subject to royalty. All rights in all current and future media are strictly reserved. No part of this work may be used for any purpose without the written consent of the author. All inquiries concerning production, publication, reprinting, or use of this work in any form should be addressed to the author in care of The New York Theatre Experience, Inc., P.O. Box 1606, Murray Hill Station, New York, NY 10156; by phone: 212-217-9627; by email: info@nyte.org.

Universal Robots copyright © 2007 by Mac Rogers. Amateurs and professionals are hereby warned that *Universal Robots* is fully protected by copyright law and is subject to royalty. All rights in all current and future media are strictly reserved. No part of this work may be used for any purpose without the written consent of the author. All inquiries concerning production, publication, reprinting, or use of this work in any form should be addressed to the author in care of The New York Theatre Experience, Inc., P.O. Box 1606, Murray Hill Station, New York, NY 10156; by phone: 212-217-9627; by email: info@nyte.org.

Fall Forward copyright 2007 © by Daniel Reitz. Amateurs and professionals are hereby warned that *Fall Forward* is fully protected by copyright law and is subject to royalty. All rights in all current and future media are strictly reserved. No part of this work may be used for any purpose without the written consent of the author. All inquiries concerning production, publication, reprinting, or use of this work in any form should be addressed to the author in care of Mark Subias, Mark Christian Subias Agency, 331 West 57th Street, No. 462, New York, NY 10019; by phone: 212-445-1091, by email: marksubias@earthlink.net. Inquiries can be also be addressed to New Dramatists at newdramatists@newdramatists.org.

TABLE OF CONTENTS

FOREWORD vii

    Mark Blankenship

ACKNOWLEDGMENTS ix

INTRODUCTION 1

    Martin Denton

THE TELLING TRILOGY 13

    Crystal Skillman

WHAT HAPPENED WHEN 41

    Daniel Talbott

ANTARCTICA 53

    Carolyn Raship

CLEANSED 73

    Thomas Bradshaw

LINNEA 89

    John Regis

…AND WE ALL WORE LEATHER PANTS 129

    Robert Attenweiler

MARVELOUS SHRINE 163

    Leslie Brumm

IN OUR NAME.. 197

    Elena Hartwell

UNIVERSAL ROBOTS 209

    Mac Rogers

FALL FORWARD 275

    Daniel Reitz

APPENDIX: NEW AMERICAN PLAYS IN NEW YORK... 289

FOREWORD

Mark Blankenship

Let me say it up front: I didn't see any of the plays included in this edition of *Plays and Playwrights*. Before I read the table of contents, I hadn't even heard of them.

That wouldn't be surprising if I were a stock trader, or a baker, or say, a resident of France. But I'm a New York theatre critic. I'm in an audience almost every night, and I'm usually seeing the type of underground work this book preserves. Despite my best efforts, though, I can't notice everything, and when these shows sprang up, I was unaware.

In a way, that's comforting. I want the theatre to bulge with excellent work. I want to be overwhelmed by the vigor of my community.

But eventually, I want to catch up. For instance, I've never seen a production of *Signs of Life*, a play by Joan Schenkar that premiered in the early eighties, but after I read it in 2004, it became one of my favorites. I'm grateful it was published, or else it never would have snared me.

After they close, too many plays are denied that chance to make new fans. Without a permanent record, they evaporate, and we are robbed of something before we realize we have it.

That's why this book is so important.

Personally, I like to think about the people who will find this collection in five years, or ten, or twenty. Maybe they'll read it and be shocked, discovering a script that inspires them. Maybe they'll pick it up because one or more of its plays has become famous. Maybe they'll buy it because it's on a syllabus.

Whatever happens, these ten plays will have permanence. They won't be lost to anyone they might inspire.

As I write this, a new farce by Mark Twain, *Is He Dead?*, is about to open on Broadway. No one thought about it for over a hundred years, and then a Twain scholar unearthed it from a university archive. Now we all can experience a show that would have been terrible to lose.

What an excellent reminder that we always need someone digging through the archives, rescuing what might otherwise be abandoned. Once again, Martin Denton and his team at The New York Theatre Experience have done us that service. No one can see everything, but their efforts make it easier not to fret about it. Thanks to them, we have the chance to catch up.

Mark Blankenship is a theatre critic and reporter. A regular contributor to Variety, *he also has written for the* New York Times, American Theatre, *and the* Village Voice.

ACKNOWLEDGMENTS

For the ninth year in a row, a new *Plays and Playwrights* anthology is about to go to press. Like its predecessors, this book would not be possible without the contributions of many talented and dedicated people.

First and foremost are the ten playwrights who are sharing their work here: Robert Attenweiler, Thomas Bradshaw, Leslie Bramm, Elena Hartwell, Carolyn Raship, John Regis, Daniel Reitz, Mac Rogers, Crystal Skillman, and Daniel Talbott—thank you for your trust and fellowship.

I would not have discovered some of these plays and playwrights were it not for some generous colleagues who urged me to check them out or made their work possible in the first place. And so major thanks to Julie Kline, Ken Urban, Elena K. Holy, Ron Lasko, Peter Dobbins, Erez Ziv, Morgan Lindsey Tachco, Natasha Yannacanedo, Lanie Zipoy, and James Comtois, each of whom helped me locate and/or learn about one or more of the pieces herein.

Michael Criscuolo compiled the authors' biographies and edited the appendix, and he has done—and continues to do—much behind the scenes to make this book and the rest of the *Plays and Playwrights* series possible. Thank you, Michael.

Rochelle Denton, managing director of NYTE, makes the creation and production of this book possible in just about every way imaginable.

Nita Congress is our copy editor, book designer, and life force of the whole project—without her, there would be just empty air where this book is.

Finally, a dedication. In my line of work, it is my good fortune to rub shoulders with people whose artistry, passion, commitment, and brilliance variously thrill, awe, and inspire me. Actor, director, and longtime NYTE intern Julie Congress is about to begin her final semester of college and is poised to join this remarkable group. *Plays and Playwrights 2008* is for her.

Martin Denton
December 31, 2007

INTRODUCTION

Martin Denton

This is a book about ghosts.

Now, when we select the pieces to be included in a volume of *Plays and Playwrights*, the goal is to represent all of the currents of contemporary American drama—to be as inclusive and comprehensive as possible in terms of genre, form, style, and so on. So when I look back, once the selections are made and the production work is finished, and find a common theme where I didn't expect one—indeed, where I purposefully tried to omit one!—well, that says something significant about what's on the minds of people working in the world of indie theater.

So this year, it's ghosts and specters. A subconscious or unconscious looking backward and inward, trying to figure out what's keeping us up at night: the path we took that we shouldn't have taken; the bump in the road ahead that we need to swerve to avoid. There are plays here that confront the sickening decay that's rotting away at the American Dream—Leslie Bramm looks at hero worship in *Marvelous Shrine*, Robert Attenweiler at materialism in *…and we all wore leather pants*, and Thomas Bradshaw tackles insidious black-on-black racism in *Cleansed*. The impact of the current war in Iraq on the folks here at home is the starting point for Elena Hartwell's *In Our Name*, while the escalating dehumanizing effects of unchecked technological advancement underlie *Universal Robots* by Mac Rogers.

More personal specters from their own childish pasts haunt the main characters in Carolyn Raship's *Antarctica* and John Regis's *Linnea*, both of which are wise plays looking back on coming-of-age foolishness. And there are ghosts here of the most classical and traditional variety as well, i.e., the recently departed—they figure prominently in *The Telling Trilogy* by Crystal Skillman, *What Happened When* by Daniel Talbott, and *Fall Forward* by Daniel Reitz. The last of these is perhaps the most evocative and mature 9/11 play yet produced by an American author.

Behind these ghosts are ten remarkable playwrights who collectively represent what's best, freshest, and most vital in twenty-first century American drama. Don't let the spirits on these pages fool you: theatre writing is very much alive right now, and thriving. Whittling the many great scripts that graced NYC's indie stages during the 2006–07 season down to just ten was a supreme challenge (and that embarrassment of riches is one reason why this year we once again include an appendix providing a comprehensive list of more than seven hundred new American plays produced in New York during the period covered by this book). It's a privilege to present these ten plays and playwrights to you.

✔ ✔ ✔ ✔ ✔

Crystal Skillman was a photographer before she was a playwright, and a strong visual sense of composition, location, color, and light is evident in all of her work for the theatre. You'll certainly notice it in *The Telling Trilogy*, which was written for Rising Phoenix Repertory over a period of a year and a half to be staged in specific areas of an East Village restaurant. (None was a traditional theatre space; indeed one of my most memorable theatre experiences was seeing the second part, *The Ride*, in a dim, narrow hallway with seating for no more than a dozen people—talk about a great way to experience a ghost story!) Though each of the component plays of *The Telling Trilogy* stands on its own, we present them here as one entity and hope that directors and producers will want to mount all three parts of this play cycle as a single unified evening of theatre.

This is a quirky, challenging piece, full of riddles and enigmatic twists and turns and disparate supernatural phenomena. Together, the three linked stories depict the deep and irredeemable loss that comes when we lose our bearings and our connectedness. There's a family at the root of *The Telling Trilogy* and it's their unraveling that threads through the piece. The first part, *The Reaching*, introduces us to two estranged sisters (the one who stayed and the one who came back, in Skillman's economical phrasing):

> VIC: I don't exactly know how to…I don't exactly know what to say to you.
>
> TY: You can tell me why you're here.

VIC: Don't start that. Don't ask a whole lot of questions you know the answer to.

TY: Now that he's gone you're here. To take care of things.

VIC: He wanted me to sell it.

TY: You never asked me.

VIC: I don't need to—the decision's been made, alright.

TY: You made the decision to sell it.

VIC: It's the last night, I've got to make sure this place is cleared out tonight.

Skillman gets the cadences of loss achingly right here and throughout the trilogy, knowing just what to put in and just what to leave out as her characters try to articulate things they cannot understand. Hers is a singular and important voice, and it will be exciting to see where it takes her—and us—in the future.

❧ ❧ ❧ ❧ ❧

The director and producer of *The Telling Trilogy* was Daniel Talbott, a founder and the artistic director of Rising Phoenix Repertory. Talbott is one of the most versatile and talented artists working in the theatre today (witness the Caffe Cino fellowship that his young company received from the New York Innovative Theatre Awards this year), and he's represented as a playwright in this volume with his New York debut work, *What Happened When*. It was presented at HERE Arts Center in a finely realized production directed by Brian Roff and featuring the excellent actors Jacob Fishel and Jimmy Davis.

This is a taut, spare one-act about two brothers who reunite for what we understand will be the very last time, to reminisce about their shared past and to try to heal some shared wounds so that both can move forward. I don't want to say too much more for fear of giving some important secrets away. The surprises at this play's climactic moments are breathtaking, and all the more so for being deliberately subject to more than one interpretation: this is a short but very full, very nourishing work.

Talbott's voice is distinctive, economical, and loaded with emotions that are specific, unstated, just below the surface, and ready to explode at any moment.

BROTHER 2: Dad hated snow.
Used to say his cousin was Cuban.
Used to cut out all those travel magazines. Tape them to the
    bathroom mirror.
Trees. Fish. Towels.

> Fucking nets.
> Shells.
> *(Beat.)*
> He wanted to take us to Hawaii.
> Buy stupid fucking shirts.
> Go whale watching.
> Scuba diving.
> Eat pig.

Talbott, in addition to working in indie theater as producer, director, and writer, makes his living as an actor (see his bio for some recent credits); his experience on the stage informs his writing invaluably. In *What Happened When*, he gives us two eminently playable roles that young actors are going to want to sink their teeth into for years to come. As playwright, actor, director, and producer, Talbott looks to be one of the bright lights of his generation of American theatre artists, and it's exciting to introduce his work to a broad audience here.

❦ ❦ ❦ ❦ ❦

When I saw Carolyn Raship's *Die Like a Lady; or What Barbara Got* at the 2002 New York International Fringe Festival, I wrote "somehow it's harrowing and breezy and cynical and affecting all at the same time." That same kind of ambivalence and paradox infuses *Antarctica*, the next produced play by Raship and the next piece in this volume. It's a fantasia about two high school girls who set out on a journey to the South Pole (the true magnetic pole, mind you, not just Antarctica in general). One of them is the dreamy, obsessive, fitfully bossy, perpetually out-of-place and out-of-joint Magda; the other is the less complicated, more "normal" Winnie.

Raship introduces her singular yet archetypal characters with brilliant economy:

> MAGDA: Meticulous records must be kept of all we see and do. On our return we will be fêted and toasted as Great Explorers. Posterity will be grateful for the knowledge bestowed to humanity by the first successful expedition to the true southern Pole by American Girls.
>
> WINNIE: I saw polar bears at the zoo once. They looked really bored.
>
> MAGDA: My life will be perfect.

They're the only two characters in this remarkable nonlinear sort-of travelogue, unless you count the White Bear, a variation on Red Riding Hood's Wolf whom they encounter at the Pole and elsewhere; Raship smartly equivocates on exactly how he needs to be depicted in production, the better to engage the imaginations of future directors and actors of this piece as well as of the characters themselves.

Everything's finally up for grabs in this play. Do Magda and Winnie really go to Antarctica? Are they really best friends? By theatricalizing so effectively the turmoil of a young girl on the brink of womanhood, Raship accomplishes something very special—*Antarctica* is a contemporary fairy tale, or myth, wrought larger than life on stage.

Antarctica premiered, in a slightly different form, at the San Francisco Fringe Festival in 2005, and was then presented in the version included here at the 2007 New York International Fringe Festival. Anchoring both productions as Magda was Raship's frequent collaborator Maggie Cino, a very fine actor/creator whose work has been featured in this series already (her solo play *Ascending Bodily* was part of *Plays and Playwrights 2003*). Raship directed both productions, and her fluid staging was exemplary. She's provided terrific user notes to guide newcomers into *Antarctica*'s unconventional world.

❦ ❦ ❦ ❦ ❦

Thomas Bradshaw is just twenty-seven years old, yet in a very short span of time he's become one of indie theater's most controversial figures. His first produced play, *Strom Thurmond Is Not a Racist*, explores the seeming paradox of the country's foremost segregationist also being the apparently loving father of an illegitimate daughter (from a liaison with his black maid). His next piece, *Prophet*, deals with a white man named Alex who claims that God has commanded him to spread a gospel of enslavement of women. *Purity*, which followed, is centered around a very successful African American English professor at an Ivy League university who is working out issues of entitlement and self-hatred; it also features a notorious scene in which said professor and an associate gang rape a nine-year-old girl.

Is Bradshaw simply courting controversy in his career? I don't think so, and that's why his fourth produced play, *Cleansed*, is included in *Plays and Playwrights 2008*. The plot of this drama sounds like a media-grabbing sensational high concept: a teenage girl in Indiana, daughter of a black man and a white woman, becomes a skinhead. It sounds like satire, but there's really nothing funny about *Cleansed*. Watch how quickly the playwright turns the tables on his characters (the father, Vernon, and the daughter, Lauraul) and his audience in the first scene:

> LAURAUL: My favorite color's blue!
>
> VERNON: I thought your favorite color was yellow! Are you telling me a fib?
>
> LAURAUL: I changed my mind. It's blue now. I love you Daddy.
>
> VERNON: I love you too. *(Kisses her on the forehead.)*
>
> LAURAUL: Daddy?
>
> VERNON: Yes?
>
> LAURAUL: *(Cheerful.)* Are you a nigger?

It's clear that there's more going on here than a playwright simply trying to get our attention; rather, here is a playwright desperately trying to make us pay attention to problems that have been with us for decades and that, despite some improvements, refuse to go away. Putting issues like racism and sexism front and center inside his jolting, in-your-face plays, Bradshaw is only the newest practitioner of a healthy tradition of shaking up the masses with art that's rude and unpredictable.

Cleansed debuted, by the way, at the Brick Theater in Williamsburg, Brooklyn, which has lately emerged as one of the go-to venues for interesting, cutting-edge theatre in New York. It was paired with *Strom Thurmond Is Not a Racist*, on a bill mounted by director Jose Zayas, who is, like Bradshaw, an up-and-coming force in American theatre.

✔ ✔ ✔ ✔ ✔

Playwright John Regis is one of the growing number of theatre artists who excel in many disciplines: besides writing plays, he frequently directs them—including, in 2007, a fascinating production of *Job* by Karol Wojtyla (Pope John Paul II)—and acts in them; his day job is teaching drama and video making at a New York City school. He's also a cofounder of the Storm Theatre, and that's where I first got to know his work; I saw and greatly admired his one-act play *Stavrogin's Confession* back in 1998, before the *Plays and Playwrights* books had even begun.

Stavrogin was based on Dostoyevsky's *The Possessed*, which somewhat foreshadows the Regis play in this volume. *Linnea* is inspired by *The Idiot*, with a love triangle at its center involving an earnest but naïve writer-in-training, an older and much more dangerous artist, and the beautiful and irresponsible exotic dancer they both love. Regis has observed that if he'd written *Linnea* fifteen years ago, when he was about the same age as the play's protagonist Danny, it would have been a much different piece—more strident and effusive, perhaps. As it is, *Linnea* is wistful, melancholy, and gratifyingly mature: the reflections of a settled mind looking back on an untethering (but necessary) coming of age.

One of the neat things about this script is the way it plays fast and loose with naturalism. It constantly feels like it's going to tell its story realistically, but then there'll be this absurd twist here or that surreal touch there, and we realize that we're actually watching someone else's half-remembered dream. It's also very funny; here's one of Regis's most inspired creations, the Beggar King, introducing himself to Danny:

> BEGGAR KING: My friend, you see before you a truly broken man. A broken down bit of Fifth Business. But I was not always as I am now. Oh no, dear friend, no! *(Pulls an old headshot out of his cart.)* I was an actor who could sing! *(Chuckles.)* Once I played the great stages of the world: the Lyceum, the Old Vic…the Burt Reynolds's Dinner Theatre! Why was my head so big? BECAUSE IT WAS CHOCK FULL OF DREAMS! But, that was then, this is now…Conspiracies were hatched. Equity Warmongers held my career at bay! In fear and loathing, I gnashed my teeth, and cried out: why? Why! WHY JERRY ORBACH AND NOT ME!

Director Peter Dobbins brought just this magic quality to the premiere production at the Storm; it will be exciting to see how other artists capture *Linnea*'s splendid ephemeralness.

❧ ❧ ❧ ❧ ❧

…and we all wore leather pants is set in a small town in Ohio in the '80s and concerns a dysfunctional American family in the midst of a meltdown. But lest you think this is a Sam Shepard retread, know that those other great Midwestern theatre poets, Williams and Inge, are equally antecedents to Attenweiler's singular style; and so are the South American magic realists and the mid-century European absurdists. His is a genuinely original voice.

…and we all wore leather pants introduces us to the Sturgess clan: the opportunistic patriarch Blanton; the elder son Jagger, who thinks he might be a car mechanic; the younger son Krank, who lives in a car up on cinder blocks in the driveway; and Jagger's sort-of nymphomaniac wife Mary, who makes a habit of losing her children (as in, she can't find them). All of them are looking for something that's been eluding them all their lives, and when

a mysterious stranger drops (literally) into their house during a storm that might be a cyclone or might be a meteor shower, all are convinced that he's their deliverer/redeemer.

But the plotting is less important here than the astonishing poetry that Attenweiler puts into his characters' mouths. The rhythms and cadences of the language constantly surprise, as do the (often bitingly pointed) sentiments:

> BLANTON: I am recently turned a serious religious man. Not in the way where I'm good to people or nothin', but I heard talk on the radio the other day 'splained Jesus in a way I finally get it. Said he's comin' an' the time a comin' is soon so I figure I got to put a good face on my situation 'fore he comes and starts pickin' the wicked and the virtuous out of the flocks. Way I see it, I ain't the wicked and I ain't the virtuous—an' if I can keep a low profile when he comes 'round—nose clean and everything—I'm hopin' to fly total under his radar an' I'll wake up one day and won't be no one on this world but me and then I will have the life I always should have.

Attenweiler's work is produced by Disgraced Productions, for which he is artistic director; he's blessed with many simpatico collaborators in the company, including director John Patrick Hayden and actress Rebecca Benhayon, who created the role of Mary in the New York production of *leather pants*. Other actors and actresses will be clamoring to play these eccentric characters in the future, and I look forward to what Attenweiler comes up with next.

❦ ❦ ❦ ❦ ❦

Leslie Bramm's *Marvelous Shrine* also takes place in a small town in the United States (in New Jersey), and gives us a more naturalistic look at a family in crisis. Marvelous is a seventeen-year-old boy whose passion is the heavy metal of Kurt Cobain and others. At the moment he's trying to figure out whether or not he's gay; his mother, would-be socialite Bobbie (an alcoholic), is urging him to come out, but his father Peter (a petty officer in the Coast Guard, separated from Bobbie) is determined to turn his son into a man.

The foregoing simply sets the stage and barely scratches the surface of the raw emotional drama that occupies *Marvelous Shrine*. Bramm explores here the nature of heroism and family pride and, not at all incidentally, the tragic effects of war. But at its core, the play is perhaps most concerned with the dynamic of the father-son relationship, from both angles:

PETER: Because I am the "nothing man"! Because my wife, in the midst of yet another Cosmo blur half sings and half says "Really Peter, you've done nothing you've ever wanted, nothing you've ever planned, you've turned yourself into a nothing man." And she says it casually, matter of fact. Like a ticked-off list of things to do…Maybe for a lot of things in my life, it's already too late. But not for Junior. Not for my son.

Bramm has said that *Marvelous Shrine* owes its genesis to this question: If a young man dies in combat, "would the hero's medals, the letter from the President, the flags and ribbons fill the space left by a dead son?" He gives us some highly resonant food for thought in this play.

Bramm's frequent collaborator (and wife) Pamela Butler directed the original production at the 2007 New York International Fringe Festival, which was brilliantly acted by Jack Halpin as Peter, Sara Thigpen as Bobbie, and newcomer Paul Hufker as Marvelous. (Halpin and Thigpen have figured in previous *Plays and Playwrights* volumes: both were in the original cast of 2003's *Last Call* and Thigpen was also in 2006's *Burning the Old Man*.) Bramm himself has been an important fixture of the indie theater scene for more than a decade, writing socially and politically conscious works like *Big Ball* and *Leo Oscar's Backyard*, which, like *Marvelous Shrine*, hold a perhaps too-honest mirror up to contemporary American mores and values.

❧ ❧ ❧ ❧ ❧

The war in Iraq is now in its fifth year, yet to date there has been shockingly shallow treatment of it in American drama. Elena Hartwell, a Seattle-based playwright who runs a company called Iron Pig, has provided perhaps the most direct and honest response to the war so far in her triptych of short one-acts called *In Our Name*. Two of these three plays are monologues, while the third features just two characters. These are compact, intense, timely, and necessary works that look at the very real and personal effects of a war that still feels very "foreign" to many Americans.

I love the bravery and balance of these plays. *The Unraveling* is about a college professor whose daughter has returned from Iraq badly wounded. *The Things He Carried* depicts an expectant mother talking to her unborn child about her husband, who has been at war. And *Waiting for the Light* juxtaposes a Bush supporter with a Recordkeeper tracking the casualties of the current conflict.

None of these pieces is even remotely polemical: they're all richly human and complex, as they consider aspects of a policy (or set of policies) that has taken us in directions that perhaps were never foreseen. Here, for example, is the wife in *The Things He Carried*:

> WIFE: I was proud when he signed up for the National Guard. After seeing what that flood did to some of our neighbors ten years ago he wanted to be a man that helped. A man that stepped up when people were in need.
>
> One weekend a month, two weeks a year, that seemed so…manageable. He's been in Iraq for seven months now. We certainly know when you were conceived, the night before he left. We weren't really trying, we just weren't trying not to. You'll understand that difference some day.

Hartwell performed *In Our Name* with Iron Pig's cofounder Rebecca Nachison at the 2007 New York International Fringe Festival, in a production notable for its simplicity and truth. (As we go to press, they're getting ready to reprise their roles in an engagement in Seattle.) The three pieces that comprise this play are ripe for broader exposure and offer strong, challenging roles for actresses hungry for smart, pertinent material.

❦ ❦ ❦ ❦ ❦

Mac Rogers made his *Plays and Playwrights* debut in last year's volume; he played the title role in James Comtois's *The Adventures of Nervous-Boy*. Rogers is yet another of the indie theater scene's great "hyphenates": an actor-playwright-director-producer whose work, over the past five or six years, has become more and more well known as both consistently entertaining and challenging. Rogers won the playwriting award at this year's FringeNYC festival for *Hail Satan*; just a month before that piece premiered, he knocked our socks off with *Universal Robots*, presented for just two short weeks at Manhattan Theatre Source in a production Rogers directed himself.

Universal Robots has two sets of antecedents. It is inspired by the play *R.U.R.* by Karel Čapek, a cautionary fable about a company that creates "robots" (the term was coined by Čapek's brother, Josef); these eventually threaten the very continuation of life on earth. Yet it also owes much to the world of science fiction and alternative history. An intensely thought-provoking and even philosophical work, it is also an extremely well-made yarn, the kind that keeps you on the edge of your seat waiting to find out how it will all turn out.

Rogers takes considerable liberties with the facts of *R.U.R.*'s creation, to the point that Čapek's brother Josef is here reimagined as a sister, Josephine, whose fondness for a humble barkeep becomes one of the pivotal linchpins of the story, thematically and dramaturgically. Real historical figures such as Czech president Tomáš Masaryk are mixed with purely fictional creations such as the singular eccentric Rossum, the brilliant but clearly off-balance inventor of the robots of the play's title. And the grand pulpy tradition of sci-fi storytelling (will the robots take over the world?) constantly gives way to unexpected social/moral conundrums, like the chilling one posed by this gentleman, writing a letter to Čapek:

> LETTER 6: I am a lonely man, possessed of an unspeakable desire, one that is very difficult for me to control. No remedy I have attempted has extinguished the desire, or even decreased it. But you can help me, Mr. Čapek. You can help me, and others like me. All I ask is a robot the size and shape of a child. A boy or a girl. Either will suffice. One of the newest models, with the skin and the hair that feels almost real. Since the robot will not be human, there can be no harm, and indeed much harm may be prevented. Please write back to me soon.

❧ ❧ ❧ ❧ ❧

Plays and Playwrights 2008 ends, as it begins, with a piece from Rising Phoenix Repertory. *Fall Forward* by Daniel Reitz was written for Sitelines '07 in Lower Manhattan Cultural Council's River to River Festival; like *The Telling Trilogy*, it was written to be performed in a specific locale (and also like that play, will work beautifully in a traditional theatre space or elsewhere).

The site of the original *Fall Forward* was very particular: the John Street Methodist Church, which is the oldest Methodist church in the United States and which is located about two blocks from the site of the World Trade Center. The play that Reitz has written for this place is a remarkable exploration of many of the questions that the catastrophe that was 9/11 was supposed to have drawn into sharp focus. His protagonist is a young stockbroker who, after spending half of his lunch hour in empty pursuits on his high-powered cell phone, encounters a stranger inside the church. Their conversation, and what follows it, touches at the core of what's fundamental in life: love, honesty, self-fulfillment, happiness. The two earlier works Reitz created for Rising Phoenix (*Three Sisters* and *Rules of the Universe*) demonstrate his ingenuity, intelligence, and social conscience. In this remarkable play, we see revealed his great humanity and wisdom.

It starts, so gloriously mundanely, with the anonymous young man negotiating with his girlfriend over the phone:

MAN 1: No. Not Saturday. Because Saturday is dinner with
my mom, I told you this. *(Beat.)* It isn't that you're excluded,
you're just not invited. *(Pause.)* A. You don't like to eat. And
B. She likes to cook. And she'll watch you not eat and it will
annoy her.

And then Reitz pulls us up short when the man meets an older
lady inside the church:

MAN 1: Broker. I'm a broker.

WOMAN 1: Do you enjoy it?

MAN 1: Sure. *(With more conviction.)* Yes. Absolutely. *(Looks
at her.)* What do you do?

WOMAN 1: For sanity or money?

MAN 1: Uh…money.

WOMAN 1: Ah, that's the easy one. I live off my dead
husband.

Daniel Talbott directed the exquisite original production of *Fall
Forward* at the church, with a sterling cast (Joel Johnstone as the
Man, Jan Leslie Harding as the Woman, and Julie Kline and Dean
Imperial as the play's other two characters, whom I leave for you to
discover). It now awaits the interpretations of many, many others;
it's very much a play for our time—and for all time.

᾿ᾨ ᾿ᾨ ᾿ᾨ ᾿ᾨ ᾿ᾨ

Fall Forward, as one of the most moving and mature plays written about 9/11, has its ghosts, of course, bringing this essay full
circle. The specters that occupy our imaginations and our hearts
inspire us to all kinds of activities, and certainly the creation of
art is one of the most important. I hope that *Plays and Playwrights
2008* inspires readers, actors, directors, playwrights, producers,
designers, and audience members everywhere to go to the theatre,
to make theatre, to support theatre, and very specifically to bring
these ten plays and their ten authors to stages across the country
and around the world. The goal of this volume, as with its eight
predecessors, is to try to bring attention to some of the remarkable
but not-quite-heralded talents in the indie theater sector. Crystal
Skillman, Daniel Talbott, Carolyn Raship, Thomas Bradshaw,
John Regis, Robert Attenweiler, Leslie Bramm, Elena Hartwell,
Mac Rogers, and Daniel Reitz give voice to some of the spirits that
haunt humanity in these early years of the twenty-first century. I
hope you enjoy listening to them!

THE TELLING TRILOGY

Crystal Skillman

CRYSTAL SKILLMAN is a playwright. She was born in San Diego in 1974, and was raised both there and in Wappinger Falls, New York. She graduated from the New School with a degree in theatre studies, and studied at the Hartford Art School and Parsons School of Design. She also studied playwriting with Mac Wellman at The Flea Theater. She is the author of *Tooth* (Ensemble Studio Theatre, 2000), *In the Wild* (Perishable Theatre's Women's Playwriting Festival, Rhode Island, 2000), *Ballad of Phineas P. Gage* (Drama of Works, 2002), *Depth of Sight* (Avant-Pop Productions, 2003), *4 Edges* (Amphibian Productions, Fort Worth, 2004), and *Apocalypse Neo* (cowritten with Rob Neill and Justin Tolley, New York Neo-Futurists, 2007). She also wrote the screenplay adaptation of her play *7 Variations on the Same Lover*, which is currently in development with the Weird Sisters film production company. Her play *The Vigil or the Guided Cradle* was an award finalist for the 2007 Bay Area Playwrights Festival; *The Ride*, which is the second part of *The Telling Trilogy*, was nominated for the 2006 New York Innovative Theatre Award for Outstanding Original Short Script; her play *Warrior* received the award for Best Adaptation at the 8th International World Festival of Puppet Art in Prague, 2004. Another play, *Flow*, was commissioned by Ensemble Studio Theatre's Sloan Project in 2000. Skillman also wrote the song "Bow Down," sung by Dr. Doom in *Marvel Adventures Fantastic Four* #25. She is currently writing the book and lyrics for the musical *That's Andy* with composer Kevin Carter, and working on a new drama titled *The Sleeping World*. She lives in Brooklyn with her husband, Fred Van Lente, and their cats, Max, Ivan, and Zelda.

The Telling was first presented by Rising Phoenix Repertory (Daniel Talbott, Artistic Director) on October 23, 2005, at Seventh Street Small Stage at Jimmy's No. 43, New York City, with the following cast and credits:

Vic ....Addie Johnson
Ty...Samantha Soule
Harry Price...Sturgis Warner

The Ride was first presented by Rising Phoenix Repertory (Daniel Talbott, Artistic Director) on February 1, 2006, at Seventh Street Small Stage at Jimmy's No. 43, New York City, with the following cast and credits:

Will..Denis Butkus
Linn .... Julie Kline

The Reaching was first presented by Rising Phoenix Repertory (Daniel Talbott, Artistic Director) on June 4, 2007, at Seventh Street Small Stage at Jimmy's No. 43, New York City, with the following cast and credits:

Kay Davern ....Samantha Soule
Patience Worth..Elizabeth West
The Man .... Spencer Aste

All three were directed by Daniel Talbott.

www.risingphoenixrep.org.

Special thanks to:

All the amazing actors listed above and the incredible Daniel Talbott for all his time and dedication to making this work a reality; the Rising Phoenix Rep family who are a constant source of inspiration especially Artistic Associates Denis Butkus, Addie Johnson, Julie Kline, Brian Roff, and Samantha Soule; Artistic Advisors Jack Doulin and Stephen Willems; all the Rising Phoenix Rep Company Members and Bailey. Many thanks to Martin and Rochelle Denton and the entire New York Theatre Experience family for this great publication, Christopher Borg and the NYIT Awards for their encouragement, the MCC Theater Playwrights' Coalition for their support, Jimmy of Jimmy's 43 for giving us such a cool space to work in (while eating his great food!), and of course the love of my life Fred Van Lente for being there every step of the way.

For John Belluso

AUTHOR'S NOTE ABOUT PRODUCTION

When Rising Phoenix Repertory was asked to stage new work at Jimmy's 43, a wonderfully eerie bar/restaurant on the Lower East Side, Daniel Talbott, RPR's artistic director who would direct the pieces, commissioned me to write three plays that were in essence related ghost stories. One play a year was produced in different seasons (*The Telling* in fall, *The Ride* in winter, *The Reaching* in summer). As a playwright, I was very excited to be writing my own series of chilling tales for, in most cases, specific actors Daniel had in mind. All those working on the project agreed that the writing must take into account the seasons, the actual structure of the space, and any ambient noise or lighting that might appear to give an authentic sense of place. If a scene was in a bathroom, it would be in the actual bathroom, etc.

After coming up with the basic idea for a story and then sending a blurb on to Daniel to get his thoughts, I would go off and write for a few days. We would hold internal readings of the work (for the first two plays, Daniel and I lived right around the corner from each other in Boreum Hill, Brooklyn). After these readings, Daniel and I would meet. Then I would go away and write some more, and most likely in just a few days, we'd read the piece again and go into rehearsal, where there would be further minor cuts/ rewrites. After a rehearsal period of about four to six days, the show would open.

The seating for the audience was limited and intimate. The largest number of people who could see *The Telling* or *The Reaching* at one time was about thirty, sitting in the back space of Jimmy's. Only ten audience members at a time could see *The Ride*, the second piece, which took place in a hallway.

After the first two plays were written, I knew that with the last story, *The Reaching*, I wanted to really bring the trilogy to a close. While the other pieces took a relatively short time to write (about five days each), *The Reaching* took several months. As I wrote, the back room to Jimmy's was upgraded and modernized, so the fictional location became New York City, taking us from the more rural setting of the other plays and bringing us to a more urban but still ghostly landscape.

Those who wish to stage the piece are welcome to perform the separate pieces, produce them over a period of time as they were originally or let them unfold in one night.

AUTHOR'S NOTE ABOUT RESOURCES

Notable sources of inspiration for me included the cases of Ed Warren (a ghost hunter who, with his wife, investigated the "real" Amityville house), and his essay, "The Dangers of Ghost Hunting," for the ghost hunter Harry Price in *The Telling*. A wonderful book called *The Supernatural*, published in 1965 by Douglas Hill and Pat Williams, which I picked up at the Strand ages ago, was very inspirational in researching unexplained phenomenon as I wanted each play to touch on a different aspect of the unknown (haunting/ ghost hunting, possession, psychics/mediums). It was a great source for names as well—Harry Price was named for an actual famous ghost hunter from Britain, and Worth was named for Patience Worth, an alter ego of automatic writer Mrs. Curran.

TIME AND PLACE

The Daverns Inn, a bar and guest house on the edge of a small dying town—*The Telling* takes place in the basement; *The Ride* takes place twenty years later in a hallway at the inn. *The Reaching* takes place in the back room of a small pub in New York City, another seven years later.

SET

Minimal.

1.
THE TELLING

CHARACTERS

VIC, the sister who has come back
TY, the younger sister who stayed
HARRY PRICE, the ghost hunter

A wooden space. Curved archways. A dank richness. More specifically: the dimly lit basement of the Daverns Inn. The light doesn't reach the edges. In the center is a small sealed box. VIC stands over it, runs her hand across it. The sound of footsteps. TY appears, standing there. VIC stares at her. A long silence.

TY: We shouldn't be down here.

VIC: What are you…

TY: But I heard so I came down here so…

VIC: So?

(Pause.)

VIC: I couldn't stay after.

TY: But you came back.

VIC: Yes. *(Pause.)* You…

TY: What?

VIC: You look like a kid just standing there, you look like…

TY: Like?

VIC: You look like…

TY: Your sister.

VIC: But not a kid really, all grown up. Different but the same.

TY: I haven't…I haven't seen you.

(Pause.)

TY: Not in a long time.

VIC: It's been a while.

TY: Since we were kids.

VIC: That long?

(TY nods.)

VIC: Yeah, I guess that's why you look that way.

TY: Same but different. You look that way too.

VIC: Right. I guess I would.

TY: Tired?

VIC: What?

TY: You seem tired.

VIC: Well, considering that it's god knows when at night…

TY: *(Gesturing to door.)* You came in this way?

VIC: I was in a hurry. It's late and I just wanted to get in here.

TY: They told us not to come down. Not here.

VIC: That's what you came to tell me? What our parents said.

TY: The door is locked for a reason.

VIC: Upstairs. Obviously not here, you should look into that.

TY: You should listen to them.

VIC: We're not kids anymore. Not theirs. *(Pause.)* Dad's…

TY: I know.

VIC: I just came from there so…

(Pause.)

VIC: It was peaceful.

TY: What?

VIC: How he went. Peaceful.

TY: That's what people say when they don't know how else to describe it.

VIC: I don't exactly know how to…I don't exactly know what to say to you.

TY: You can tell me why you're here.

VIC: Don't start that. Don't ask a whole lot of questions you know the answer to.

TY: Now that he's gone you're here. To take care of things.

VIC: He wanted me to sell it.

TY: You never asked me.

VIC: I don't need to—the decision's been made, alright.

TY: You made the decision to sell it.

VIC: It's the last night, I've got to make sure this place is cleared out tonight.

(TY looks at the box, the only thing in the room.)

TY: Then what's that?

VIC: You tell me.

TY: I don't go down here anymore.

VIC: You're telling me you haven't been down here in all this time?

TY: I don't have to tell you where I go.

VIC: No, no but you're here now so.

TY: I heard you. I came down. I think the boy, he comes down to get some things now and then. But no one since Mom and Dad double locked the door. No one comes down here.

(Noises upstairs are heard.)

VIC: What's that?

(Pause. TY doesn't answer.)

VIC: Who's up there?

TY: The same.

VIC: You're kidding me.

TY: They heard you were selling. They wanted to say goodbye to the Daverns Inn.

VIC: I guess you've only got two choices in this town, right? Johnnie's Diner across town or here.

TY: I guess.

VIC: All three of them. They're up there? The toothless blind man, the old hag with that brown wandering eye, and that guy with the thick glasses and the stained tie with his old dog, that red hound. The same ones drinking here since we were ten.

TY: Aren't you going to open it?

(Silence. VIC stares at the box.)

TY: What?

VIC: Grinning at me in the light.

TY: Mom and Dad wanted to keep us out of here. Always worried about what we'd find.

VIC: Well it looks like I found it.

TY: Weird, isn't it.

VIC: Well, yeah. It is. It's all kind of unreal, right?

TY: I think you're frightened.

VIC: Frightened of what?

TY: You tell me.

VIC: This coming from the one who stayed.

TY: I didn't have a choice. You took off, then come back like you don't remember any of this, us.

VIC: I just don't think like that.

TY: Like what?

VIC: Remembering all the time—I can't like you. It hurts my head.

TY: Are you going to open it?

(VIC still stares at it.)

TY: It has your name on it.

(A moment.)

TY: It's addressed to you. Vic Davern.

VIC: In your handwriting. So out with the gag. What's in it?

TY: I don't know.

VIC: You don't.

(Lights go out on VIC and TY as the bathroom door in the back of Johnnie's Diner bursts open, slamming the door against the wall with a clang. Light bursts forth from the bathroom. The white tiles gleam. PRICE pisses, talking to himself in the mirror.)

PRICE: New truths, new discoveries can only be found through danger. Dangerous encounters. You take your chance. Carefully. We as hunters of ghosts are visible. The ghost has the upper hand for it can see what we do not. It can hear what we cannot. It can perform feats we cannot. It is an unexpected thing. But there are choices they've got to make in how they'll spend their time here. For let's be clear, there is only so much time. Each ghost's time is numbered differently and each of their times must be measured correctly. Because there comes the time when their time runs out, just like everyone else's. They can't stay in this ghost state forever. And when the time comes you've got to make sure they know it. Every ghost tries their best to forget that, get lost here. That's why it's up to you. You follow them, keep your night watch, get to know your prey. Where they've been and why and most importantly where they'll be going. If you want to hunt ghosts you must know your opponent. You must respect their powers as they have to respect you. The person who says he's not afraid of ghosts had better think twice about hunting one. The person who says he's not afraid of anything is an uneducated asshole. Don't be an asshole. Be a survivor, an intelligent researcher. Set the clock, get your gear, heed the call, and close in for the pickup. Don't let shit get out of hand. Chomp your chili dog, slurp down your beer, piss your brains out. Leave the diner. *(Flushes.)* Head out to your destination. Keep it simple. *(Washes his hands.)* Clean.

(PRICE hums as he prepares to leave—a strange, haunting melody. Turns out the light.)

VIC: What's in it, Ty?

TY: All I remember is that it has something to do with your stories.

VIC: Mine?

TY: One of your stories. One of the ones you'd tell.

VIC: This is, this is…

TY: So maybe if you told them like you used to—

VIC: Crazy. Why the hell would I want to do that? I break my neck to come back here, stay up all night with Dad, watch him…And then what? Come here to tell stories?

TY: You didn't come here to see me but here I am.

VIC: Yes but—

TY: Besides, that's how we did it then. Psyched ourselves to open the door down here. Though it was locked. Though they told us not to.

VIC: And look, here we are down here, Ty.

TY: Nobody calls me Ty since I was a kid. Not since you left.

VIC: No? God, it's so hard to remember all the in between for some reason.

TY: I'm not in between. I'm here, I'm telling you—

VIC: What you put in a box to give me. And my telling some story is going to help that?

TY: What person do you want to use?

VIC: What does that matter?

TY: We always asked that. You used to say, "There's a lot of ways to tell a story, but there's only one way to—"

VIC: "—tell it right."

TY: And that's in *how* you tell it. Choices. Didn't you say that?

VIC: Yes, I did.

TY: First. Second. Thi–

VIC: Right. Third. No omniscient. Real far out. Like a real story where you can go into everyone's thoughts. So what—the one about the severed bloody ghost hand and its deadly five fingers?

TY: What's the one with the book? Price.

VIC: That one? How does it start— There was a book…

TY: There was a book. When it was made nobody knew and nobody…

VIC: Remembered, right. It sat for years among many shelves, unnoticed, wrapped in brown paper, waiting. Until the day it was picked by a boy, Harry Price, as he was known in town. Harry loved books more than anything, so that year for his birthday his father had taken him to the bookseller. Harry picked a wrapped one, not knowing what book was inside but he was curious. When he opened it, later, alone, he found it was a black book with a long, thin spine but the pages were blank. There was nothing in it. When the father saw that after weeks the book remained empty, he chided his son for not filling what he took to be a journal. Harry told him he had nothing to write. So the father told him to write down his one greatest wish—what he wanted more than anything in the world. Harry did. "I want to live forever," the paper scratched with the thick lead Harry held as he scrawled his wish. And though "live" could barely be read on the page and "forever" was missing the first R, Harry felt better than he ever had before. He closed the book and went to bed, dreaming of great things he could do with his long life—reading stories, writing new stories, telling them. He couldn't wait for morning when he opened the book to write all of these things. But there was already something else written in a handwriting different than his own. Underneath Harry's wish to live forever was a question: "How much?" It was a question for him and his eyes only. Harry wrote back—

TY: "More than anything I love."

VIC: Right—this is stupid—I'm not going to.

TY: You've got to finish.

VIC: We're not kids anymore, Ty.

TY: Then open it.

VIC: You said you'd tell me.

TY: You didn't finish.

VIC: Why? There's no point.

TY: You're frightened. You're shaking.

VIC: And what about you?

TY: I don't know but I'm not scared.

VIC: No? Then I'll make you.

TY: How?

VIC: Angelina.

TY: Stop it.

VIC: Angel-ina.

TY: There was nothing wrong with my doll. Stop freaking me out.

VIC: You noticed your doll started changing rooms.

TY: You were moving it!

VIC: And the messages? "Help us Tyler."

TY: You left them.

VIC: And you wanted to help whoever needed help.

TY: You made it up.

VIC: Notice I'm using the second person. I've progressed.

TY: Stop making it up.

VIC: No, this story, this story, it's true.

TY: No!

VIC: You asked if there was a spirit that needed help. And what did the spirit say—Tyler?

TY: "Yes."

VIC: The spirit went on to confide in you it was of a small child who had died young. The poor child whose name was Angelina wanted to live in the doll, wanted nothing more than to be loved and squished and held. It asked you if it could live there. And you, being the sweet, giving girl you are, said…Tyler? You answered—

TY: "Yes."

VIC: So the doll became…

TY: Angelina.

VIC: And one night after this all happened you fell into the deepest sleep you had ever had. You could feel yourself wake up in the dream, only to watch Angelina walking up your body, sliding up your body—

TY: No!

VIC: That little doll's plush self at the top of your chest reaching out its chubby cloth arms and there was nothing you could do to stop Angelina's little glove hands from closing in around your throat.

TY: Stop it.

VIC: Shush…You couldn't speak. You couldn't move. Your doll was choking you, the air being drained out of you.

TY: "Angelina…"

VIC: You sputtered out. But the doll only turned its head. "There is no Angelina. I am something else and you invited me in and I'm killing you." It was a ghost demon that you had invited in and it was the ghost demon that took you with its tiny, stitched cloth hands that very night.

TY: It's an awful, terrible story. A doll can't kill people.

VIC: It wasn't the doll—it was the demon, wasn't it?

TY: You think of yourself like that?

VIC: I'm up all night holding Dad's cancer-weak hand. All the time he thinks I'm Mom, right. He's calling me Mom. So when I come back here to a prank like this and a sister who won't even say what she really means at practically three o'clock in the morning. Won't even tell me what's…so fine, I should just— *(Goes to throw the box out or destroy it.)*

TY: Vic—don't!

(VIC picks up the box, holds it out to TY.)

VIC: Why? What's in it? A demon? Whatever's in it you put it there, so tell me.

TY: You didn't even finish telling me the Price story.

VIC: I don't need to because it doesn't mean anything. It's just a story.

TY: That's not true. You said you liked making those stories up. You said that's what you'd do, what you wanted to do.

VIC: And you expect me to believe you cared about what I wanted? You didn't even like me, Ty. That's the truth. I didn't like you much either. So…

TY: You really think that's true?

VIC: We never even talked other then to tell these stupid stories and we told them to—what? To just frighten the shit out of each other. Do you think that shows how much we loved each other? Ty? Are you crazy? Shit, maybe I am. Maybe it's me.

TY: It's a gift.

(Lights go out on VIC and TY. PRICE appears outside the field, the lost grave-yard.)

PRICE: Ghosts only know so much but you—you've got to know everything. And the most important thing to know is that one of the main reasons for ghost hunting is to have encounters with ghosts. Sometimes, though, the hunter can become the hunted. And that sucks because as much as you try, shit can never be planned just the way you want it. Because you never really know what's going to happen. It's unnerving. Graveyards are one of these places where you just don't fucking know what's going to happen. And this one's even worse because it's been lost, forgotten. It's a field now, markers grown over. But you know the dead are there. You can feel them prick your skin. So before you go in, prepare yourself, ask yourself why you're doing this. You ask yourself all the questions the other flesh sacks ask each other smiling like apes on late-night talk shows. "Are ghosts the spirit of the dead that are buried here?" Fuck yes. Don't be a shitface. Don't be stupid. Just because people write books that make a lot of money about this shit doesn't mean it's not true. "Do spirits hang around, waiting to reenter the physical life?" Absolutely. But that's nasty. That's undead, possession, black magician stuff. You've got to stop any of that before it starts. These guys are drawn to where human suffering has occurred. These areas are full of the vibrations of torment, people who've lost their loved ones, can't let go of something, have something left to say. Spirits, good, bad, whatever their intention, revel in the deterioration of human bodies. But they lose track of time and what the hell they're hanging around for in the first place. They are the dangers in the exploration that the living must encounter. You get your head straight. Set your traps, pique their curiosity, and you let yourself in. You go on and when you start walking you don't stop. You don't. Your only goal is to get closer, faster. Go in. *(Goes into the fields.)*

VIC: Well, thanks for the gift—it really livens up the place, doesn't it?

TY: It won't have to for long.

VIC: What's that supposed to mean?

TY: You don't come back in all this time. Not until now, to…

VIC: You're angry because…God. You want…You want to stay here?

TY: No.

VIC: But you did stay. For what?

TY: You don't understand.

VIC: Don't tell me you stayed for me.

TY: What if I did? This town, there isn't much to it. The diner, the lake, cross the field, and you're here. Not much to stay for. But I did. Because this, this place it means something…

VIC: To you.

TY: And it should to you too. It's not like I wanted to stay here forever or anything but I did.

VIC: Then what do you want. Huh? Ty? You never told me.

TY: I'm trying to tell you now.

VIC: I'm all ears.

(TY is silent.)

VIC: You waited for me to come back. And then what?

TY: No—you tell me. What you did while you were away. I bet you learned so much. I bet you could teach me.

VIC: It doesn't work like that.

TY: What?

VIC: You have to go through it. Experience things. Live them. That's what being away taught me.

TY: So?

VIC: So that's not something I can tell you.

TY: Try. Tell me. What you did out there while I, nothing of a thing, stayed behind? Stayed *here*. What did you do out there, Vic? Tell me.

(VIC is silent.)

TY: But you can't. You can't tell me because there's nothing to tell. You did nothing. You just wandered around like some lost kid. You act like you forgot it all, here, this place. But you didn't. You left but you couldn't stop thinking about what happened. You left but you were always here. I wasn't stuck, not like you. I chose to be here, I chose to stay, to…

VIC: What?

TY: Well I'm here now, aren't I? Talking to you? Or maybe I'm the one going crazy trying to tell you…

VIC: You shouldn't be…

TY: What?

VIC: Shouldn't even be talking to me.

(Silence.)

TY: It doesn't matter if you blame me or yourself. That doesn't matter now.

(Long silence.)

VIC: It's dry down here. Wouldn't think that down here. There's a dank richness to it. All this curved archway stuff. Makes you think you're in England or somewhere eating dumplings or exotic fruits. Didn't Mom and Dad want something like that? Like we were full of high breeding. Like we were English. Like a real English pub or something. *(Finds a piece of an antler on a mount.)* See—they even kept these antlers around. Didn't they want to call it Hunter and the Hare or something like that?

TY: Hart and the Hound. Like a…

VIC: Hart's like a big stag, I think, a red deer.

TY: I know a real hunt story.

VIC: I never told…

TY: You didn't tell it to me. Someone else told me. Animals. When they're hunted—the point isn't that the prey is

snuck up on. The prey knows it's being hunted.

VIC: So the prey runs away.

TY: It doesn't work like that. Not when there's nothing to run to. But the prey, this deer in the case of this story, can outsmart the hunter.

VIC: How's a deer going to outsmart a hunter?

TY: There's two of them, really. Two deer.

VIC: Sisters, I assume.

TY: Brothers, actually, the way it was told to me. They were all that was left of their family. The hunter had killed all the rest. He had a calling, you see, something in him that made him believe they were better off really. He didn't really care for the living. To him it was some kind of mission, setting souls free. When he came you could hear him coming because he had a song he'd sing, real low as he followed you. I can't do it just as he'd sing it but…

(TY sings softly "The Telling Song," a strange, haunting melody, as VIC watches her.)

TY: STARS DIM
THE NIGHT GROWS
AND I FOLLOW
ON MY WAY

AFTER HIM
THE LIGHT SHOWS
BY THE HOLLOW
ON MY WAY

THE TREES SWAY
UNDER THE WEIGHT OF CROWS

DEEP IN THE THICK
WHERE THE DANGER GROWS
MY SONG'S THE TRICK

THAT YOU HEAR IN THE FRAY
THE TELLING THAT
TELLS I AM ON MY WAY

VIC: Where'd you hear that? I never heard that song.

TY: I told you, this isn't your story, Vic.

VIC: I didn't say it was.

TY: *(Forcefully)* It's mine.

VIC: Alright.

TY: One of the brothers heard him singing and raced back to their place in the thicket—only to discover his brother had already been killed, hit deep and hard in his flesh. And the brother could run no further, he laid there, beside his brother, waiting to die. To feel the steel of the hunter's gun. But instead he felt the prodding of upright horns in his side, fur against his and heard hooves digging into the ground. His dead brother had risen himself up, his body matted red against his skin. His eyes were black and hard, empty like the eyes of the crows dotting the trees. His breath was white upon the air and his nostrils were wide and fuming. He dug at the ground again and a twig snapped. The hunter, who had been waiting, had sprung up but was now frozen in fear as the phantom stag approached him, stood on the back of his legs and raced through him. The hunter disappeared with him. The brother stood up, trembling like he had never been before. Alone but alive.

VIC: Coming back tonight. It was strange, weird. It's freezing like snow's coming.

(Lights out on VIC and TY. In the fields, PRICE stands, a great light shining behind him. Wind whistling through the reeds.)

PRICE: In the thick of it, in territory like this, you must be extremely careful of not becoming the hunted. How do we accomplish this? By using the knowledge that the enlightened ghost hunter, me, must know. The enlightened ghost hunter, again me, envisions himself in a bright white glowing holy light of protection before he or she ever enters any haunted place. He or she, in this case he, me, asks for the protection of those higher-ups. But these protective measures are only as effective and as powerful as the ghost hunter's belief in them. Until the gift turns to shadow. Until it's time.

(PRICE turns to face the light, which fades.)

VIC: I got dropped off on the road across from the field. My head was aching so bad from the cold I could barely remember who I was. All I had to do was cross the field but I couldn't budge. Then I heard you telling me, "Imagine what's scarier is behind you not in front."

TY: Yes, yes.

VIC: And I saw it, a hulking figure, a dark thing, watching me—and everything shifted in me from past to present. I wasn't frozen anymore, I was alive, and I looked up in the light, the moon, and I felt like all of this was new. New in a way I had never seen before. The whipping leaves and weeds, the sound of the wind, the moon shining down on me. You know what they said about the field? Dad told us—the cemetery isn't where it is now. On the map, back in those days, it was underneath where I am now, in the fields. Dad would tell us it was a lost graveyard and we believed him, didn't we?

TY: You believed him.

VIC: Well, it's true I think. Because if you listen hard there's thoughts in that wind. There's thoughts that don't belong to you. It's like a beckoning call, it makes you shiver like crazy and you feel like you're going crazy and you're alone and if you stop in the middle, and—you don't know where you are. All direction seems gone. You're lost, hearing those lost cries underneath, a dark thing behind you, following you, until you, until you…

TY: Run.

VIC: I don't stop until I'm opening that door. Until I come here to see this. This, with my name scrawled on it in the middle of the floor. In your handwriting. And you. You. Just standing down here after all this time. It makes me think of all those times, us together, telling stories just to tell them…but it doesn't matter, Ty. Not now.

TY: You didn't have to come back to see Dad.

VIC: No.

TY: You didn't have to come back to sell it either.

VIC: No I didn't. Getting dropped off in the middle of the night to be scared to death. Walking in to see this, this box or porthole to some other world or whatever shit it is and it's dark and it feels like there are furry catlike things at my legs which I guess are spiders or something like that or god knows what and I'm thinking why the fuck did I come back here? Why the fuck did I come back here to this shit town for this?

TY: For me. You came back for me.

VIC: What's in it, Ty?

TY: It's not something I can tell you.

VIC: I don't understand why you won't just—

TY: You have to go through it, experience it.

VIC: I'm tired of this. I'm fucking tired of this. You know what? I don't need to ask you because I know what's in it.

TY: Tell me.

VIC: Nothing. There's nothing inside because it's meant to be filled up. That's what you've got to do. That's why you came down here. It's a game. It's just a stupid tea party. Like when we'd play tea party or something.

TY: We never played tea party. We weren't like that.

VIC: No.

TY: We weren't sisters like that.

VIC: We were the sisters who would sneak into the guest rooms, set traps for each other. You'd hide in the closet, bounce out.

TY: You'd hide under the bed, you'd grab my ankles when I walked past.

VIC: Why did we like to scare each other so much?

TY: It wasn't the being scared.

VIC: Then what was it?

TY: It was the stories. How we told them. How you told them. Christ you were good, Vic. I loved to listen to the way you'd tell it.

VIC: What?

TY: Anything. Because when you were telling me, just telling me, I believed…

VIC: What?

TY: That you wanted to tell them to me. Just to me. Like a secret. Like something we shared.

VIC: Why'd you ask me to tell about Harry and the book? Why that one?

TY: I don't know…I always thought— you and Harry. You were like the same really.

VIC: You want what happened to him at the end to happen to me.

TY: No—it's just—you wanted the same things. In choosing how you wanted to live forever. In what could live forever.

VIC: What are you talking about?

TY: You said you were going to go away to be a writer.

VIC: I went away.

TY: And did nothing. All you do is think of yourself, how alone you are but you don't see—

VIC: What do you care?

TY: What do you mean "what do I care"?

VIC: Someone like you.

TY: And who is someone like me?

VIC: Someone who can't even tell me what's in a box she wants to give to me. Like it's something else, like it's a trap.

TY: "There's lots of ways to tell a story, but there's only one way to tell it right." And I want this to be right. And you should too.

VIC: Fine, if it upsets you that much just tell. Tell me what you want me to—

TY: I told you. Open it.

VIC: I can't…

TY: Why?

VIC: Who cares? We'll clear out, we'll leave, leave it here.

TY: *(Forceful—scary.)* No. You can't leave this unfinished. You went and I stayed. I stayed. Don't tell me I've waited for nothing.

VIC: I'm not going to open it.

TY: But it's yours.

VIC: Look, I'll tell you the end of the Harry story, then you can cut all this and tell me what's in it, which is the same thing as me opening it really and then…and then it'll be over, okay?

(TY is silent.)

VIC: Okay. I left off where…yes. When Harry opened the book the next day to what he wrote—his wish to live forever—there was written a question in a handwriting different than his own—

TY: "How much?"

VIC: Right. It was a question for him, for his eyes only, which grew wide. Harry wrote back, "More than—"

TY: "Anything I love."

VIC: Right, yes. And suddenly Harry's hand shook with excitement as story upon story came to him. So fast he couldn't help but write and write until he dug himself deeper and deeper into the paper, until his hands had been taken in, then his arms, his head, his body, and so he disappeared through the book itself which closed for good to live forever in his stories.

(We hear PRICE approaching, singing his song, "The Telling." The song grows and grows.)

TY: I have a story to tell you. A dream. I dreamed that I died.

VIC: Now you're just fucking with me. Right. Stop making it up.

TY: No, Vic. I'm not.

VIC: People, they dream of things that never happened, that are never true.

TY: We were telling stories, we stole the key, we were going down to where we were never allowed to, I had already come down here, all by myself and I wasn't scared. You didn't know but I had already come down here and left something for you. I got you, I started to drag you down here to show you, to tell you what I left but you were scared, frightened. I told you I'd show you I wasn't. I ran down the stairs first. I ran down the stairs and then there was a sound of tumbling and I had to raise myself off the floor to see. I was lying in a stain, my blood was spreading. You were calling my name but I couldn't tell you, Vic, I couldn't tell you. It was lying right there but you wouldn't come down. You were afraid to come down.

(PRICE's song is tremendously loud now. He is nearly upon them.)

VIC: I don't want to be afraid.

(VIC and TY look to each other. The lights go out. The singing grows even louder, and in the darkness appears a sliver of light that grows and grows, the opening of a door.

Then the sounds of a door slamming shut. The lights return to find VIC, alone, with the box. TY is not there. A moment. VIC is overcome, almost crying, then she steadies herself. VIC goes to the box, goes to open it but can't. A moment. PRICE appears in the fields, on the next job.)

PRICE: I've been in this line of work, this exploration, for more years than I'd like to say. And what's important is not just that the job is done, but that it's done right. Short, quick, effective. A flash of light, you're in and then…No one ever wants to go. Still once in a while one of them reminds you there's been a price to it all. You look at her and know that time for us can't be measured by anything but what you believe, right then, a dream, a shadow in the night, a song you half remember—that's the story underneath. The one we forget to tell, what we can't remember. You can't count the years by looking at my face, so don't waste your time. I'll never stop what I do. It's been exciting, frightening, but never boring. Anyway, I do it because I have to. That's how it's written. I don't always like it, but that's not what counts. The truth is, the real secret? When we survive to what many believe to be the end, in reality that is just the beginning. Or that's what they tell me. That's the story I've been told.

(The lights have grown very dim on PRICE. He shimmers for a moment, then walks into the fields.)

2.
THE RIDE

CHARACTERS

WILL, the man who was called
LINN, the girl who was waiting

Twenty years later. A long hallway in the Daverns Inn. Dark, wooden, and empty. An endless feeling to it. But there is an end: the door with a tiny window up top where fading light streams in from the outside. The sound of keys being jingled; after a moment, the sound of a lock being turned; the door opens. WILL stands there wearing his hat and heavy overcoat, holding his bag, his hair a little out of place, just as he looks, as usual, a little out of place. WILL steps inside, closes the door. There is the faint sound of music.

WILL: Hello? Hello?

(No response.)

WILL: Hey.

(Pause.)

WILL: Is anyone…?

(Nothing. One light in the hallway abruptly turns on, startling him—a girl is there underneath the light, with headphones on, listening to music. WILL stares at her. LINN takes off her headphones.)

WILL: What are you—What are you doing here?

(Pause.)

WILL: You're not supposed to be in here.

LINN: I'm just waiting.

WILL: For who?

(She doesn't respond. Looks at herself in a mirror hanging in the hall, running her hands through her hair.)

WILL: Guests are supposed to wait in the lobby.

LINN: Too many people in there. Just listen to them. It's better in here, right?

WILL: In the dark?

(She doesn't respond.)

WILL: Look, if you don't want to wait in the lobby, you can wait outside.

LINN: It's freezing. The ice's sticking to the ground. You should know, you drove up the hill.

(WILL gives her a look.)

LINN: I saw you come up. Burst in last night. The lights going on and off like crazy. Because of the storm.

(WILL looks through his bag, checks out one of the lights in the hallway.)

LINN: The blackout last night because of the storm?

(WILL pauses, doesn't answer for a moment, then:)

WILL: It's all fixed. All except here. You know Johnnie wouldn't want you here. That's why he locked it.

(Silence.)

LINN: Will? You're Will, right? I heard last night when they called you.

(WILL stares at her.)

LINN: It'll be like…You won't even notice me.

(WILL goes to work, tries to ignore her. LINN leans against the wall, hears the commotion in the lobby through the wall.)

LINN: You hear that! They're playing games in there. Like parlor games. You should have seen them when the lights first went out. Panic. Everyone freaking out. *(Laughs.)* Some holiday celebration. A party for old, fat people and babies. Tons of crusty food. An avalanche, punch and pinwheel cookies, deer as decoration.

(WILL looks at her. She pauses, then continues:)

LINN: Dried fruits, fruitcake. Carved roast beef, chocolate-covered stuff, cakes. All neat in a row, circles, in piles. Then boom—lights out! Other places the lights just came back on. Not here.

WILL: Nope.

LINN: Why they called you.

WILL: Why they called me.

LINN: All the old folks huddled together, scared of the dark—with candles and then when you slammed the door open, I thought they'd jump out of their

skins. Your hair was white because of the snow. I thought you were like fifty.

WILL: Thanks.

LINN: When I first saw you.

WILL: And now?

LINN: Seventy.

WILL: You're funny.

LINN: No. I'm hilarious.

(WILL can't help but laugh a little.)

LINN: He laughs, he breaths—he's alive.

WILL: *(Looks at her, smiling. Then more curiously:)* I didn't see you.

(LINN doesn't respond.)

WILL: I didn't see you when I came in, at the party.

LINN: No? Then why'd you look at me…Like you knew me.

WILL: I don't.

(Pause.)

LINN: I'm Linn.

WILL: If you'd just let me—

LINN: Concentrate?

WILL: I'll be in and out. *(Realizes the awkwardness of what he's just said, but recovers.)* And you can go back to hiding out here by yourself.

LINN: I'm waiting.

WILL: Right.

LINN: There's no place to hide here. Not really.

(WILL goes to the end of the hall, turns, disappears for a moment.)

LINN: All those grown-ups, scared out of their wits.

(All the lights in the hallway come on; the hallway is still dim by most standards, but brighter than it once was.)

LINN: Even Johnnie. He practically owns everything in this town, right? He sweats all the time. He doesn't think anyone can see it but I do. He's afraid.

(Pause.)

LINN: When it's dark, quiet, you can hear things. The wind, crows flying from branch to branch. The crows—you saw them when you came up? You go by the weed fields last night, past the lake? Bet it was frozen. Bet it just froze. You get out and walk across it? I'd love to. Feel my boots on the ice. I do that, I used to. Build forts. Make traps, just in case. "Keep out. Danger!"

(WILL comes back out into the hallway.)

WILL: In case?

LINN: I knew how to take care of myself. I know a lot of things.

WILL: Like?

LINN: I knew that it was frozen, before you told me.

WILL: How'd you know that?

LINN: I knew because last night when I heard the wind—I heard the center of it. And it crackled. At night when the wind's like that, when it moves it sounds like that...

WILL: Crackling?

LINN: It only does it when it comes across the lake when it's...

WILL: It's?

LINN: Real late, at the end. The end of the day.

(A moment.)

WILL: So you hear all that last night?

LINN: Didn't you?

WILL: I was...I just went to sleep.

LINN: I couldn't. I just kept thinking about today...The trees, the birds. Etched in my mind. You really didn't hear anything?

WILL: I was out.

LINN: Gone.

WILL: Dead to the world.

(Pause.)

WILL: Look, I don't mean to be...But if you are waiting, shouldn't you be looking out *(Gestures to the window in the door.)* for...

LINN: I'll know.

WILL: Okay.

(Pause.)

WILL: Lonely, just waiting here.

LINN: It's okay. Truth is, I don't like many people.

WILL: That's why you keep talking to me.

LINN: I like you.

WILL: Alright.

LINN: You don't like people either.

WILL: You can tell.

LINN: I can.

WILL: Then why don't you tell me my life's story?

LINN: There's not much to tell.

WILL: That's...

LINN: Don't take it—

WILL: I mean Christ. Who do you think you are?

LINN: You're not—

WILL: You think this is all I do?

LINN: You're not listening. I didn't mean it like that.

WILL: You're the one who should be careful. Should be looking out.

LINN: Stop it. It's not mean, it's just true, right?

(Slight pause.)

LINN: You're not pissed off because of what I said?

WILL: I'm not, no. It's just...you look just like this girl...Back in high school. You look like her.

LINN: And something happened to her.

WILL: Why'd you say that?

LINN: They never found her.

WILL: One day she was just...gone. *(Shakes his head.)* I'm sorry, it's crazy.

LINN: Could you show me?

WILL: I don't...

LINN: How I look like her.

WILL: *(Stares at her a moment.)* I shouldn't—

LINN: No one's here but us.

WILL: I'm just. I'm tired.

LINN: You said you fell asleep last night. Dead to the world.

WILL: Right.

LINN: No?

WILL: Yeah. Almost.

LINN: You heard something?

WILL: There was this strange sound.

LINN: Like...

WILL: Like I don't know if I really heard it...It was faint, just a...inside the walls. Like a scraping, something crawling out.

LINN: Like a mouse or something.

WILL: Whatever it was, it gave me some crazy dreams.

LINN: About?

WILL: Just dreaming, you know. I keep saying.

LINN: What?

WILL: I keep saying. I keep saying the stupidest things. "I had a bad dream." I mean, c'mon. I don't... *(Pause.)* Look, I don't even know you.

(Pause.)

LINN: But you knew I'd be here.

(WILL stares at her.)

LINN: Sometimes that happens, right? Like a premonition. I read that somewhere.

(Pause.)

WILL: Sometimes what you say, I don't get how...

LINN: It's a feeling. You get that. Feelings.

WILL: Yeah, right.

LINN: I think you want me to go with you. I can't stay here. Like that crazy old man, on the third floor. They say something happened to him. He got soft. Gave up what he was born to do. Now he's just wasting away.

(A long pause. WILL looks at her.)

WILL: I'm not going like that.

LINN: No?

WILL: Not in a place like this, getting old like you said, dying here.

LINN: I wouldn't like that.

WILL: What?

LINN: Wouldn't like to see you dead.

WILL: People make up stories about this place, doesn't mean they're true.

LINN: But they tell them.

WILL: Look, I worked here back then when all the rumors started, helped out as a kid before the place...but I didn't see anything.

LINN: But people still believe they're here.

WILL: What, ghosts?

LINN: I don't like to say it like that. People think— *(Imitates ghosts.)*

WILL: Well, whatever it is, it's—

LINN: Right. I know.

WILL: You get that out of that book they sell in the lobby? That Davern sister book?

LINN: It's not something you think happens.

WILL: No.

LINN: But you know when it gets dark here, the thing is I can hear voices. There's something...

WILL: Something?

LINN: There's something. You hear it. And when you reach out to whoever's there, even though you don't see what you're reaching out to, you become...something else.

WILL: Linn, who's coming for you?

LINN: I don't know. I don't care. But I know you do.

(Slight pause.)

LINN: Because I look like that girl.

WILL: No, I shouldn't have said, it's just when I dreamed—

LINN: She was in your dream.

WILL: No. I mean, it wasn't like a dream.

LINN: Then what?

WILL: It was like she was here. I don't know, don't know why. Back then, she wouldn't have ever seen me, she wouldn't have noticed. Truth is, when it happened, when she didn't come back and no one found her I thought about her a lot. Maybe it was because whatever happened to her even though it was bad, at least...at least something happened. I used to have nightmares. Imagining what happened to her. What something, someone did to her but last night, she was...she was here and she saw me and she told me. She told me to....

LINN: Wait.

WILL: It was part of what I saw, dreamt, whatever you want to call it. Here in this dark place. You.

LINN: And.

WILL: And how I came here and how we…

LINN: We.

WILL: Left together.

LINN: That's it?

WILL: That's it. Us leaving.

LINN: Out, over the snow.

WILL: The frozen lake.

LINN: Past the fields.

WILL: Gone.

(Moment.)

LINN: I'd like that.

WILL: It's okay because I know, I knew from when you told me. No one's coming.

(She doesn't respond.)

WILL: But me.

LINN: Yes.

WILL: You will…you want to.

LINN: I do.

WILL: Okay. I'll finish up, I'll finish up and…

LINN: And.

WILL: *(Picks up his equipment, going to the back.)* I just have to check one more. Then I'm done.

LINN: Right.

WILL: Just a minute.

LINN: That's okay.

WILL: It'll go dark.

LINN: I'll wait.

(WILL goes in the back. He's turned the corner, gone. The lights go out. Darkness. LINN slowly walks to the back in the dark, turns the corner after WILL. A long moment in the dark. The lights turn abruptly back on. A moment. WILL walks into the hall; he puts his tools back into his bag. Puts on jacket. He runs his hands over his hair, just like LINN in the mirror. He looks sad for a moment, then laughs, a sort of sad laugh—just like LINN. He grows somber. Almost nervous. Takes out LINN's headphones from his pocket, puts them on. Faint music is heard as he presses play. He takes out his keys and goes to the door. He looks back at the hallway for a moment. Then feels the wind from the outside, shivers. Turns into the wind, closing the door, slams it shut. The light that comes in through the door dies out, fades.)

3.
THE REACHING

CHARACTERS

KAY DAVERN, the daughter seeking answers (played by the same actress as Ty in *The Telling*)

WORTH, the medium asking questions

THE MAN, the stranger who answers back

Now, seven years later. The dimly lit back room of a small pub in New York City. Small dusty black tables. The smell of cigarettes, beer, dirty cat. A sliver of daylight. On the walls are some oddities: tiny tin lanterns hang as well as framed pictures, a bone sits on a dusty shelf, a mounted deer head stares at a stuffed raccoon cringing on the opposite wall. A small stage in the corner is piled with flowers, cards, books—perhaps a framed picture of a much older Vic. There is a sense of a void, of an emptiness that seems to fill the room, but the room is far from empty. WORTH, an older woman who stares straight ahead, sits in the center. THE MAN sits in a corner, twirling a cigarette case in his hands. A humming is heard. Low, soft, growing louder. It is "The Telling Song" Ty once sang. KAY comes in through the red curtains. She looks exactly like Ty. She sees THE MAN, then WORTH.

KAY: *(Surprised, scared.)* Hi.

WORTH: Hi.

(THE MAN stops twirling the cigarette case, then begins again. KAY watches him. WORTH gestures to a seat. KAY stands there, silent. She notices the empty coffee cups on WORTH's table.)

KAY: You look. You look like you've been waiting.

WORTH: It's good to see you. I haven't...

KAY: Since. Right. A long...It's been a long time.

(Silence.)

WORTH: You sound tired.

(Pause.)

KAY: It's. It's so quiet here. The city—it's different than I. Than what I remember.

WORTH: You weren't as skinny. What I remember.

(Pause.)

WORTH: Last time I saw you, going off to school.

KAY: I was like what, thirteen when I left.

WORTH: You had braces.

KAY: God. I must've. I must've looked hideous. *(Slight pause.)* You still live here?

WORTH: 181 West—

KAY: 83rd Street.

WORTH: *(Smiling.)* I'm impressed.

KAY: I'd hear her say it. When she'd call a car for you if it was late at night. Across the park. You used to walk there with her sometimes.

WORTH: I did.

KAY: When she was working on something. On something new.

(Pause.)

KAY: I haven't been to the hotel. It's been the plane, the taxi. We drove by our old building. It's the same. Red brick, iron gate. I could see that suncatcher. The guy driving. Must have thought I was insane. Me staring up there. There were still news vans. Even now, after. After weeks you'd think.

WORTH: Your mother's work touched a lot of people's lives.

KAY: I mean all these calls. Interviews, lawyers, agents. I don't listen. I just try...

WORTH: It's a lot to—

KAY: It's not that. It's just. It's how. On the news people still call the police. They've seen her at some diner or ATM or in some store. They think they. But she was never there.

WORTH: Leaving like this, it can be the most. *(Pause.)* Difficult.

KAY: So people feel they have to come together, to gather. *(Stares at the flowers, cards addressed to her mother, photographs still piled on the stage from the gathering.)*

WORTH: It was nice.

KAY: Nice.

(Pause.)

WORTH: They read from her. *(Pause.)* Selections. People brought food, pic-

tures, spoke. There was a book with her name written out on the front, people could sign it, could give their thoughts. When I heard I wrote you. They kept a spot, just in case.

KAY: I'm sorry I couldn't. All of it. Just.

(Silence.)

KAY: I'm still just.

(Pause.)

WORTH: Still...

KAY: No it's not like that. I'm not.

WORTH: Alright.

KAY: I don't want you to think. I'm...I'm okay.

(Pause.)

WORTH: Must have been a long flight.

KAY: That's the thing about being overseas. Coming back it's...It's harder.

(Pause.)

WORTH: You like it?

KAY: What?

WORTH: College.

KAY: It's alright.

WORTH: And you're studying...

KAY: Literature.

WORTH: I didn't know you wanted to write.

KAY: I don't. Not like.

WORTH: You don't?

KAY: I don't like. Fiction.

(Pause. KAY looks over to THE MAN in the corner.)

KAY: You don't mind it. Him....

WORTH: You get used to it.

(Silence. KAY looks back to THE MAN; WORTH does not, looks straight ahead at KAY.)

WORTH: Some stay. Even after.

(A moment. KAY turns away from them, stares at the mounted deer head and stuffed raccoon on the wall.)

KAY: She liked it here. When I was little I used to pretend they could speak. That only I could hear them.

WORTH: And they'd tell you.

KAY: Stupid things. What I wanted to hear. What a kid wants to hear.

WORTH: Like.

KAY: I told you it was stupid. It's just seeing everything again, it's… *(Trails off.)*

(Silence.)

WORTH: Your mother told me she was just walking past one afternoon when she first saw this place. She had just moved, she was pregnant, was expecting you. Even after she published, everything taking off for her, she'd still come here to work.

KAY: It'd be like this real quiet, middle of the day, the light from the door. I used to fall asleep. She'd sit for hours, drinking coffee, writing. To come in here, to see him…And you here, sitting right where she'd.

WORTH: I didn't mean to upset you.

KAY: No, I'm just. I'm trying to figure it out. I mean all the times I've seen you. I don't think we've. Ever really talked. *(Short pause.)* We've barely spoken.

WORTH: What your mother went through.

KAY: Right.

WORTH: It was.

KAY: So you're saying it's—

WORTH: I'm not saying it's right. What I'm saying is so you understand.

(Beat.)

KAY: "The Reader will see you." I remember. No names. Like a summoning. "The Reader." Their laughter would stop. You'd be staring straight ahead. You'd sit there. Silent, speak in a whisper, soft, so only they could hear. They looked like they believed you could. You'd sit on the bed, on the edge. Your feet on the ground, planted. Like you are now. Waiting…Waiting. Is that why you've come? To make me understand?

WORTH: I don't consider it waiting.

KAY: Why?

WORTH: Because.

(Short pause.)

KAY: I mean you were close to my mother but she wasn't. She wasn't a kind woman. She wasn't nice.

WORTH: No.

KAY: Not even to you.

WORTH: She had difficulty with letting things be, yes.

KAY: I mean my mom said your books were shit.

(WORTH is silent.)

KAY: I mean someone who treats you like that.

WORTH: It wasn't easy.

(Pause.)

KAY: You've got to admit, your books they. They ask you to believe a lot.

WORTH: Most don't until.

KAY: Until.

WORTH: It happens to them.

(Pause.)

KAY: On the way over, in the cab. There were tons of birds, black like crows. "They were thick on the trees like leaves and when we came by they took off into the sky." Just like in her book. I thought for a moment it was like some kind of sign. It's insane, I mean. I'm…

(Short pause.)

WORTH: Making sense of it… *(Trails off, is silent.)* It doesn't always come when you want it. My mother when she passed—

KAY: My mother isn't dead.

(Pause.)

KAY: She's missing. That's what they said. No one knows. What happened, how she…So we don't. We don't know. This thing it's, it's normal, this feeling. This being alone. There's nothing different about it. She barely spoke to me before I left. Her and I. C'mon. You read it, everyone did. *(Quoting the title of the interview:)* "How the Magic Happens?" How does she come up with so much fucked-up shit? And then they ask about me. "I don't have a daughter, I had a sister."

(Pause.)

WORTH: The little things that come into your head, the feelings I get it's not like. I told you, you don't choose when.

KAY: So you're saying you don't know. You don't…You're saying. You're in the dark. *(Stares off again at the gathered flowers, pictures.)* What did you have them read?

WORTH: Selections, pieces.

KAY: The man in the hallway who disappeared, the story about Price. Wanted to live forever. Got swallowed up…

WORTH: The ghost hunter walking in the fields.

KAY: It's a fucking game. When they called me I thought—it's a joke. This is. It's crazy. Some kind of stunt, she's looking for material, another story.

WORTH: You know she didn't work like that.

KAY: Then writer's block. She was at her worst when she couldn't write.

(Pause.)

KAY: When I came in, I saw you and I thought…

WORTH: Thought?

KAY: My mother wouldn't go near me. She wouldn't look at me. She wouldn't touch me.

WORTH: No.

KAY: I don't look anything like my mother.

WORTH: No.

(Pause.)

WORTH: We met right here, your mother and I. I heard her read, just a story. The way she spoke, the way she phrased things, the way she told it. I was impressed. She'd heard of my work, seen my books. You were with her. But even then I could see. I could see that with you she was not…Was not prepared.

(Silence as KAY stares at WORTH. THE MAN looks up at KAY directly, still turning the cigarette case in his hands.)

MAN: You don't feel it, do you?

(KAY looks at him.)

THE MAN: When he fucks you with it. That man of yours.

(KAY is silent.)

THE MAN: You know what it's like. To be like. To be…Not feeling anything, what goes right through you. *(Stares at her, silent. Then:)* I had a man. There was a man. His eyes, round, the white. *(Pauses. Leans in a bit, talking.)* Up alleys, backyards, up broken concrete, sidewalks. I followed. Him letting me. The wind, his coat blowing through the streets. The winter night. Knuckles freezing in my gloves. Breathing heat. Keeping pace. Getting faster. Watching street lamps as we go, bare trees, crooked fence. Over the gate, he looked back, looked at me in the light. Followed him in. The trees. Hate places like that. Too much emptiness. Too much green. No moon, no stars, just black. The dark. Cold. Frozen. Stiff. He was breathing out hard, white. Went to him. His eyes two pins in the dark. Like an animal. There was something that repulsed me. But something sweet too. He let me touch his face, his arms, his hands…It was like moving toward myself. I took off his clothes, he was shivering, naked. Body skinned, young. Smoothed down. A rabbit. I was in hard. The trees moving. Over us. Fucking him. 'Til there was nothing, blackness, until all things that hurt, could reach me were…When it was over, I try to turn him to me. I see something sharp. He goes toward me, into me. When he cut, I felt my skin unpeeling, a wrapper. He disappears, tracking snow behind him. Empty. The green gone. White.

(Pause. Silence.)

KAY: That was my mother's.

THE MAN: I found it.

(Brief pause.)

KAY: *(Terrified.)* This is crazy. This is fucking crazy. You don't know. Both of you. You don't know shit.

THE MAN: Black coat, green threading around the edges, grey pants, red scarf, black shoes. What she was wearing when she went out. And then.

(THE MAN is silent. KAY looks to him. THE MAN makes a "poof" gesture and sound. KAY stares at him.)

WORTH: No one's asking you to believe.

(KAY turns away. WORTH is strong with her, firm.)

WORTH: Sometimes you don't. You don't know. What's unexplained. What's buried within you. You don't want to face it, hear it. But something in you does. Something in you pulls it out. Something tells you to come. To come here. You get up, pack, get on a plane. You arrive. You face it. You face it to become something else.

(Pause.)

KAY: The thing inside me, that thing that others have, what tells you to…When they called me at school to tell me. That no one knew where she…I didn't cry. I didn't…*(Grows silent, overcome.)*

(WORTH is still, she waits. KAY turns to her.)

KAY: She called me before it happened. There's no way she could have known I skipped class that day. I mean I never. But I was feeling really bad. I couldn't do anything. Couldn't listen to music, read, watch anything. Usually—when I need to just forget, I turn off the phone, get in the bath you know, just try to get it all out. That's what I kept thinking I was going to do but I just sat there and waited. When it rang it didn't even startle me. I picked up. I picked up and I knew weirdly that it was my mom. She never calls. She hadn't called me since I started school, not in like years and she, she was so silent. I mean we both were. We didn't know what to say. And then she asked out of nowhere how I was. She'd never done that. I said I don't know. There was silence. Then. She asked. Asked if I was happy. Actually asked if I had anyone in my life, that has ever stayed or wanted to be there. For me. Touching me, wanting me. Out of nowhere. It's long and awkward. And then she asks. Asks if I forgive her. The phone is silent. So much that I ask if she's still there. And then I hear her, hear her open her mouth. "I'm sorry, Ty." She called me Ty. And I don't even miss a beat, I tell her, "Yes, Vic, yes." I let her.

(A long silence.)

WORTH: The last time I saw her. She walked in. She spoke before I'd even had a chance to speak. She was rambling, it was hard to follow even for me. She wanted to remember all the old times, back to the Inn. About selling it and moving here. When she was pregnant with you. She told me it was after you were born, after she saw you that she started writing it down, all of it. And then she told me. She told me she was scared. That she was afraid of…She was quiet for some time. And all I sensed I knew it was true. Because what I saw—it frightened me too.

(WORTH stares ahead at KAY hard, speaks in a low, intent voice.)

WORTH: She said she was alright now. That she was. That she'd spoken to…her sister. That she was…Prepared.

(A moment. KAY looks at WORTH, she slowly gets her bags, looks to THE MAN,
walks out. WORTH and THE MAN remain still. Silent, then:)

THE MAN: You didn't want to frighten her. Sharing, putting it into words, it's. *(Pause.)* I saw her—the one who read. Who reads. She had a cigarette while she spoke. I had my eye on the case beside her. I wanted it. When she said the last word, she put it in her pocket. Closed the book, smiled, looked down. Everyone clapping. Past the red curtains, the hallway, the curved archways. The woman, the one serving, behind the bar. Smiled. Waved. The fan above her circling, casting shadows. I was behind her. Following. The heat, the lights, candles flickering. She opened the door and we were out. The sky heavy, rain falling. A storm. The light. Rumbling. Up the steps, she reached. Walked past the gates into the night. And I heard. The ones I'd never go near. Those that stay, that want so badly to live, the ones that whispered to her, told her stories, kept close, kept her away. She was coming apart. Breaking the surface of her. From the inside. From the inside they were…It was a devouring. How they went in and out. Took her. It was. I had to look away. *(Short pause.)* And when I did. Nothing. Not a trace. Just… *(Looks at case.)* It's all that was left. I put it in my pocket and I didn't. I didn't tell her.

WORTH: No.

THE MAN: No one. No one but you. I told you.

(Pause. A painful expression crosses WORTH's face. It's all more to take in than she can bear but she does. She responds.)

WORTH: Yes.

(Silence together. Blackout.)

(END OF PLAY.)

WHAT HAPPENED WHEN

(A Memory Play)

Daniel Talbott

DANIEL TALBOTT is an actor, director, playwright, and artistic director. He was born in the Bay Area and moved around the country with his family before landing back there for high school. He trained as an actor at the American Conservatory Theater's Young Conservatory, Solano College Theatre, and The Juilliard School. His work as a playwright and director has been seen at HERE Arts Center, the Lower Manhattan Cultural Council's Sitelines series, Singularity, Synapse Productions, Six Figures Theatre Company, Expanded Arts, Ensemble Studio Theatre, Rattlestick Playwrights Theater, Soho Rep, the New York International Fringe Festival, the Royal Court Theatre, and The Side Project. Talbott's most recent acting credits include *Tartuffe* (McCarter Theatre/Yale Repertory Theatre), *Marat/Sade* (Classical Theatre of Harlem), *Progress* (Immigrants' Theatre Project), and the workshop of *Passion Play* (The Goodman Theatre). His most recent film and TV work includes *Law & Order*, *Buffalo Girls,* and *Pretty Bird*. He is the recipient of two Dean Goodman Choice Awards for his performances in *Eurydice* (Berkeley Rep, 2004) and *3F, 4F* (The Magic Theatre, 2005), a Drama-Logue Award for his performance in *Fortune and Men's Eyes* (The New Conservatory Theatre, 1996), and a 2007 New York Innovative Theatre Award for Outstanding Direction for *Rules of the Universe* (Rising Phoenix Repertory). Talbott was also named one of nytheatre.com's 2006 People of the Year. He is the artistic director of Rising Phoenix Repertory and lives in Brooklyn with his wife, Addie, and son, Bailey.

What Happened When was first presented by Rising Phoenix Repertory (Daniel Talbott, Artistic Director) on July 5, 2007, at HERE Arts Center, New York City, with the following cast and credits:

Brother 1 .... Jimmy Davis
Brother 2 .... Jacob Fishel

Director: Brian Roff
Stage Manager: Bertie Michaels

BIG HUGE THANKS LIST

- Brian, Bertie, Jacob, and Jimmy
- Kristin Marting, Noah Diamond, and everyone at HERE Arts Center
- Stephen Willems and Jack Doulin
- Martin and Rochelle Denton, Michael Criscuolo, The New York Theatre Experience, and nytheatre.com
- Shay Gines, Jason Bowcutt, Nick Micozzi, and the New York Innovative Theatre Awards
- Jay Catlett and timessquare.com
- Robert and Louise Rosen
- Wendy vanden Heuvel and the JKW Foundation
- Heidi Riegler and Riegler Communications
- Bill Timms, Michelle Arst, Jeffrey Lockhorn, Peter Strain, and Peter Strain & Associates
- The Juilliard Drama Division, Kathy Hood, Joe Kraemer, and Michael Kahn
- Amy Potozkin and George Maguire
- Berkeley Rep, Solano College Theatre's Actor Training Program, A.C.T.'s Young Conservatory, and Craig Slaight
- Adam Webster and the Side Project
- The McCarter Theatre, Yale Rep, Daniel Fish, and the entire cast and crew of *Tartuffe*
- David Van Asselt, Lou Moreno, Sandra Coudert, and everyone at Rattlestick Playwrights Theater
- Seth Numrich, Kirsten Kelly, and Brian Smith
- All the Rising Phoenix Repers and Group 31ers
- Julie Kline, Samantha Soule, Denis Butkus, and Sarah Wilson
- My mom Denise, and Darlene, Jan, Jean and Susie Pral, Grandma Mattie, and all my brothers and sisters
- Dean Goodman, Richard Ramos, Sarah Fox, Caitlin Clarke, John Seitz, and John Stix
- And, of course, Addie and B.

NOTE ABOUT "........."

This indicates that the character has something specific he'd like
to say or wants to continue to say, but he can't say it, either emo-
tionally or because he chooses to keep it a secret. It's something
specific that might add to the train of thought, but the character
lets it sit there and decides not to say it.

Darkness.

Moonlight.

Snow and wind.

A farmhouse and wind chimes.

*A window, a twin bed, and a dresser with a
lamp, an antique toy fire truck, and a vase
of limp, store-bought roses on it.*

A chair in the corner.

A radio alarm clock.

BROTHER 1 awake in bed in the dark.

*BROTHER 2 sitting in the chair, fully
dressed, with worn-out baseball cap and
Converse hightops.*

Silence and the sound of breathing.

BROTHER 1: You're not supposed to
    be up.

BROTHER 2: I'm not tired.

(Silence.)

BROTHER 1: Mom fell asleep on the
    couch.
I carried her to bed.
She's gotta get up early tomorrow.

BROTHER 2: She's got work.

BROTHER 1: Yeah.
We both do.

(Silence.)

BROTHER 2: You get your car fixed?

BROTHER 1: No.

She drives me.

BROTHER 2: Dad's pickup.

BROTHER 1: No engine in it.

(Short silence.)

BROTHER 2: We used to sleep back
    there.
When we were kids?
Go fishing.
Have Grandpa drive us around.
It's a good truck.

(Short silence.)

BROTHER 1: Mom keeps it locked up.
She sits in it.
Sometimes I find her out there.
By herself.
Asleep.
Up on the seat like a cat.

(Silence.)

BROTHER 2: The horses are gone.

BROTHER 1: She sold them.
A few months ago.
Nice couple with a daughter lookin'
    to ride.

BROTHER 2: Cute?

BROTHER 1: Okay.
Big tits, weird teeth.
Kind of shy.

(Short silence.)

BROTHER 2: Still bowling?

BROTHER 1: Sometimes…
Sometimes with Robby.
We'll go down, throw a few games.
Get some nachos and cheese fries.
Some Cokes.

BROTHER 2: He still with Linda?

BROTHER 1: No.
Not after he found out you fucked her.

BROTHER 2: She fucked everybody.
She was a fucking hole.
She used to suck guys off at the truck
    stop for money.

(Short silence.)

BROTHER 1: Her dad was a trucker.
Used to beat the shit out of her mom.
Used to arm wrestle for money.
(Beat.)
She still comes into work sometimes,
    says "hi."
I think she misses Robby.
I think she's lonely.

BROTHER 2: He's a good guy. He could
    do better.

BROTHER 1: He's alright.

(Silence.)

BROTHER 2: It's cold.

BROTHER 1: The heat's off.

BROTHER 2: I can hear the TV.

BROTHER 1: She leaves it on.
Likes the noise.
Sounds like there's people.

(Short silence.)

BROTHER 2: Still a virgin?

BROTHER 1: Still a faggot?

BROTHER 2: (Laughs.) You naked?

BROTHER 1: Boxers.

BROTHER 2: Still piss like a girl?

BROTHER 1: Sometimes.
When I'm tired.

(Silence.)

BROTHER 2: My bed's not made.

BROTHER 1: It's the same.

BROTHER 2: It stinks.

BROTHER 1: It hasn't been cleaned.
She left it.

BROTHER 2: You take my money?

BROTHER 1: No.

BROTHER 2: You should take it.
See a movie.
(Short pause.)
Ever wear my stuff?

BROTHER 1: Your socks sometimes.
    Your deodorant. Your jacket.
Sometimes your hat.
I borrowed your Nirvana CD.

BROTHER 2: You sleep in there?

(BROTHER 1 shakes his head.)

BROTHER 2: You should open the
    window.

BROTHER 1: I can't.
Mom nailed it shut.

(Silence.)

BROTHER 2: I used to jerk off in your
    shoes.
When we were little.

BROTHER 1: Why?

BROTHER 2: 'Cause.

BROTHER 1: 'Cause?

BROTHER 2: Yeah 'cause.
(Beat.)
To fuck with you.
Be a dick.
I used to rub it in so you couldn't tell.
(Short silence.)
I fucked your bear too.

BROTHER 1: I thought I lost it.

BROTHER 2: I fucked it.

(Silence.)

BROTHER 1: Amber's pregnant.

BROTHER 2: Yeah?

BROTHER 1: Yeah.

BROTHER 2: Tommy's?

BROTHER 1: Think so.
She's moving back to Wyoming.
Wants to be closer to her mom and her sister.
They seem happy.

(Beat.)

BROTHER 2: It's snowing.

(They watch the snow.)
(Silence.)

BROTHER 1: It's been too cold.
It hasn't in days.

BROTHER 2: Dad hated snow.
Used to say his cousin was Cuban.
Used to cut out all those travel magazines. Tape them to the bathroom mirror.
Trees. Fish. Towels.
Fucking nets.
Shells.
(Beat.)
He wanted to take us to Hawaii.
Buy stupid fucking shirts.
Go whale watching.
Scuba diving.

Eat pig.

(Silence.)

BROTHER 2: Ever think this place is haunted?

BROTHER 1: ………

BROTHER 2: I used to think I'd hear shit when I was a kid.
When I was little.
When I was by myself.
When they were gone.
(Short silence.)
Why didn't you play basketball?

BROTHER 1: Not tall enough.

BROTHER 2: But you're fast.

BROTHER 1: Not fast enough.

(Short pause.)

BROTHER 2: I used to fuck Coach Lachey's daughter.

BROTHER 1: Which one?

BROTHER 2: Brenda.

BROTHER 1: Yeah?

BROTHER 2: Yeah.
Wanted to fuck Stacey but she wouldn't let me.

BROTHER 1: She died.
(Short silence.)
A car crash in May.
Her boyfriend too.
Was pregnant with their first kid.
Fell asleep behind the wheel.
(Beat.)
Her mom had a breakdown, moved to Florida.
(Beat.)
Coach just kind of pretends it didn't happen.
Like it's not there.

Hangs out at school a lot.
Eats in the cafeteria with us.
Got DirecTV so he wouldn't be so
lonely.

(Short pause.)

BROTHER 2: You remember Tony
    LaVito?
That fucking ugly bitch with long hair?
Dated that cunt with the chipped
    tooth?

BROTHER 1: Yeah.

BROTHER 2: He was in a convertible
    junior year.
Flipped it.
Found his head in a pumpkin patch.
Knocked the fucker right off.
Some dog carried it three miles down
    the road.

(Short silence.)

BROTHER 2: Ever measure your dick?

BROTHER 1: Yeah.

BROTHER 2: How big?

BROTHER 1: A little over six.

BROTHER 2: Seen others?

BROTHER 1: Yeah. Yours.
Robby's a few times.

BROTHER 2: You measure up?

BROTHER 1: About the same.

BROTHER 2: Ever been in love?

BROTHER 1: Don't think so.

BROTHER 2: Ever want to?

BROTHER 1: Haven't really thought
    about it.

(Short silence.)
(Wind.)

BROTHER 2: Old man Keith used to
    pay me.
Used to have me sit on his bed and jerk
    off while he watched.
Gave me fifty bucks every time I did it.
Told me he'd give me a hundred if I
    brought a friend.

BROTHER 1: Did you?

BROTHER 2: He used to tape it.
Had them organized next to his bed.

(Short silence.)
(Snow and wind.)

BROTHER 2: I miss pussy.
I miss the smell.
Getting down there.
Getting my face in it.
Rubbing it around.
(Short pause.)
You ever go down on a girl?

BROTHER 1: No.

BROTHER 2: You should find some
    really fat chick and muff dive her till
    she passes out.

(Short pause.)

BROTHER 2: I can't feel my legs.
It's like there's nothing there.
Just wind.
I can feel my face and hands but I can't
    feel my feet.

(Silence.)

BROTHER 2: You remember hunting?
When we were kids?
With Dad?

BROTHER 1: ....

BROTHER 2: That game we played?

(Slight pause.)

BROTHER 1: No.

BROTHER 2: Liar.
Counting?
In the woods?
Taking turns by ourselves?
With him.

BROTHER 1: ....

BROTHER 2: You remember.

(Silence.)

BROTHER 2: What's that song Mom
    used to sing?
The Bonnie Tyler song?
She used to rewind it in the car?

BROTHER 1: ....

BROTHER 2: Did she ever tell you how
    her and Dad met?

BROTHER 1: No.

BROTHER 2: She found him in a park-
    ing lot with no pants on.
He couldn't remember how he got
    there.
Couldn't remember where he lived.
Felt sorry for him.
Had his address written on his hand.
Like he knew he'd forget.
Like he knew he'd be there.
Lost.
In the dark.

BROTHER 1: I thought he played
    football.

BROTHER 2: He did.

BROTHER 1: I thought they listened
to "Crimson and Clover."

BROTHER 2: They did.
It was her favorite song.

(Short silence.)

BROTHER 1: Do you think they
    smoked pot?

BROTHER 2: All the time.
They were fucking drug addicts.
Then they found God.

BROTHER 1: And each other.

BROTHER 2: And us.
(Beat.)
Why don't you have any friends?

BROTHER 1: I have friends.

BROTHER 2: Not Robby.
Like real friends.
Friend friends.
Like guys you hang out with and go
    camping and get stoned and shoot
    things and shit.

BROTHER 1: I don't like hunting.
Don't like killing things.

(Beat.)

BROTHER 2: I saw you.
With Robby.
When you were like ten.
(Beat.)
You like that?

BROTHER 1: ....

BROTHER 2: You like that stuff?

BROTHER 1: What?

BROTHER 2: Don't fucking "what?"!

BROTHER 1: No.

BROTHER 2: Did he make you?

BROTHER 1: No.

BROTHER 2: You sure?

BROTHER 1: Yeah.

BROTHER 2: On your knees.
Like a little girl.
(Beat.)
You fucking swallowed.

BROTHER 1: I did not.

BROTHER 2: I didn't see you spit it out.

(Short pause.)

BROTHER 2: Is that why you don't like girls?

BROTHER 1: I do.

BROTHER 2: You've never fucked one.
I never see you with one.
You never go the movies or take anybody out.

BROTHER 1: I just don't…
I just don't know anybody.
I don't know what to say.
(Short pause.)
There's no one who likes me.
I don't…
I don't know how you know.

BROTHER 2: You just know.
They…
They send it out.
They give you signals and shit.

BROTHER 1: Like what?

BROTHER 2: I don't know, you just know.
They let you know.

(Beat.)

BROTHER 2: You ever let him fuck you?

BROTHER 1: No.

BROTHER 2: You sure?

BROTHER 1: Yeah.

BROTHER 2: You lying?

BROTHER 1: No.

(Short pause.)

BROTHER 2: Your hair tucked behind your ears.
Fucking eyes open.
Fucking makes me sick.
Thought I was going to throw up.

(Silence.)
(Snow.)

BROTHER 2: What you have for dinner?

BROTHER 1: Pizza.

BROTHER 2: What kind?

BROTHER 1: Pepperoni and sausage.

BROTHER 2: Gino's?

BROTHER 1: Yeah.

BROTHER 2: They still have those balls?

BROTHER 1: The dough balls?

BROTHER 2: Yeah.
With butter and garlic?

BROTHER 1: Yeah.

BROTHER 2: I used to hang out there.
Play Galaga.
Fuck around as a kid.
They used to give me free refills on Coke.
(Beat.)
Used to steal quarters out of Mom's underwear jar.
Walk there.

(Silence.)
(Snow and wind.)

BROTHER 2: They ever find those kids?

BROTHER 1: The Barretts?

BROTHER 2: Yeah.

Went fishing Old Stones Bridge.
Disappeared.

BROTHER 1: No.

(Short pause.)

BROTHER 2: Mom used to work with
    their mom.
At the chiropractor's office.
They used to trade days.
Used to give her a ride home on Satur-
    days when they worked together.
(Beat.)
She said she was nice.
That she was obsessed with animals.
Had like ten dogs when you'd go up the
    driveway.
Used to keep a picture of them on their
    desk at work next to ours.

(Short pause.)

BROTHER 2: Remember Dad and
    those puppies?

BROTHER 1: No.

BROTHER 2: Fucking bag and the
    shovel?
The snow?

BROTHER 1: ....

BROTHER 2: Carried them over his
    shoulder.
His gloves.
Cigarette in his mouth.
Behind the barn in the woodpile.
(Short pause.)
Made me hold you so you wouldn't
    run away.
Made me hold your head.
Make you look.

BROTHER 1: ....

BROTHER 2: Fucking took a piss.
Finished his cigarette.
Kicked the snow off his boots.

Walked home.
Made us clean 'em up.

(Short pause.)

BROTHER 2: I used to steal shit out
    of his truck.
Bury it in the backyard.
Tie notes on it.
Like, "if you find this know what a piece
    of shit you are."
Piss on his toothbrush.
Wipe my dick in his mug.
Move his shit around.
Drive him crazy.

(Beat.)

BROTHER 2: What happened to your
lip?

BROTHER 1: I cut it.

(Beat.)

BROTHER 2: You jerk off tonight?

BROTHER 1: No.

BROTHER 2: Why not?

BROTHER 1: Not horny.

BROTHER 2: You take a bath?

BROTHER 1: No.

BROTHER 2: I used to...
I used to go in there.
Turn off the lights.
Put a towel under the door.
Lock it.
Leave the window open.
Make it really hot.
Hold my breath.
Sink into darkness.

(Silence.)

BROTHER 1: You ever talk to Kim?

BROTHER 2: ....

BROTHER 1: Mom says you see her.
That you get to see her now.
That you hang out.
That you're together.

BROTHER 2: ………

BROTHER 1: That you probably don't spend a lot of time with Dad, but…

(Silence.)

BROTHER 1: I have her ring on my pinky.
They gave it to her…
To Mom when…
I have her camera in my drawer.
I take it out sometimes.
Clean it.
Don't know how to use it but…
(Short pause.)
They said she was playing the butt game.
That she was sliding on her ass to the edge.
Hands up.
Flipping onto the branch.
Climbing back to safety.
Everyone laughing.
(Short pause.)
That she just sat there.
Let go.
Relaxed.
That she didn't even try to hold on.
That she just…

(Silence.)

BROTHER 2: Remember the pond?
The rope swing when we were kids?
Barbecues?
Bandanas? Roach clips with Indian feathers on 'em?
Taking the raft around the island?
Keeping watch while we kissed girls?
(Short pause.)
First time I saw pussy hair?

Got so hard I jerked off in the bushes.
(Short pause.)
Playing catch.
Frisbee.
Pink Floyd. The Allman Brothers Band.

BROTHER 1: I remember the rides home.
The three of us asleep in the back of the car.
Sleeping bags and jackets.
The window down.
Mom and Dad holding hands.

BROTHER 2: Smoking cigarettes.
Laughing.

(Snow and wind.)

BROTHER 2: I asked him to go the store with me.
Said I needed cigarettes and Coke.
That I'd buy him another six-pack so I didn't have to drive alone.
(Short pause.)
He wanted to take the van.
Said my tires were bald. My seatbelt was broken.
I lied.
Told him there was no gas in it.
That I wanted to, but couldn't find the keys.
(Beat.)
Grabbed my hat.
Kissed Mom's head.
Turned down the TV.

BROTHER 1: ………

BROTHER 2: We listened to music.
A mix tape from when I was a kid.
Guns 'N' Roses.
"Patience."
"One in a Million."
"Rocket Queen."
Smoked cigarettes.
The front window kept fogging up so we had to keep the windows down.

You could see our breath.
The moon.

(Snow.)
(Ice.)
(Trees.)
(Short pause.)

BROTHER 2: I kept hoping it would just happen.
That it would sneak up on us.
Be a surprise.
Come out of the darkness…

BROTHER 1: ………

(Silence.)

BROTHER 2: What happened to Mom's hand?

BROTHER 1: She broke it.
Fell on the front steps with a bunch of groceries.

BROTHER 2: Where were you?

BROTHER 1: By myself. At work.

BROTHER 2: Who gave you the flowers?

BROTHER 1: No one.
I bought 'em.
At Safeway.
By myself.

(Wind and wind chimes.)

BROTHER 2: I heard him.
With you.
Dad.
The night before.
In the bathroom.
Grunting like a pig.
His zipper.
The sink.
Clearing his throat.
Flushing the toilet.
Washing his hands.
(Silence.)

The showers as kids.
Line up.
Soap.
Tape measure.
Shoestrings.

BROTHER 1: Haircuts.
In the summer.
Three-quarter inch, close to the scalp.
Trim.

BROTHER 2: Pushups.
Sit-ups.
Staying hard.
Thin.
(Short pause.)
He taught me how to throw a baseball.
How to align my knuckles when you swing.

(Silence.)

BROTHER 2: She should sell this place.
Move back to Florida.
Pack up our things.

(Short silence.)

BROTHER 1: I applied to college.
Community college.
Night classes in the spring.
Study English. Writing.
Go there a couple years.
Transfer.
Save some money.
After high school.
Do something.

(Snow.)
(Short pause.)

BROTHER 2: I sat there waiting.
His door open.
Music still playing.
The windshield cracked.
My legs crushed.
The horn stuck.
The car up on a tree.
(Short pause.)

He looked like he was sleeping.
His mouth open.
Eyes up.
Forehead caved in.
At ease.
(Short pause.)
I felt happy.
I felt relieved.

(Silence.)
(Snow and wind.)

BROTHER 1: Remember the field?
In winter?
Late at night when we were kids?
All three of us?
The fort?
Kim, you, and me?

BROTHER 2: *(Nods.)* ………

BROTHER 1: Planning.
Digging.
Building.
Waiting.
(Short pause.)
We'd always crawl backward.
To the back.
(Silent.)
No words.
Flashlights on.
(Short pause.)
Together.
Asleep.
Warm.
Under the snow.
Just us three.

(Short pause.)
I would dream.
Long car rides in the summer.
The Snake River.
Trips to the beach.
(Beat.)
I used to think it meant he loved me.
That we were close.
That it was our thing.
(Beat.)
I loved feeling held.
Wanted.
His needing me.
(Short pause.)
I thought it's what I could do.
What I could give.
Could bring.
(Short pause.)
He'd be so still.
His mouth in my hair.
Eyes closed.
His body limp.
Breathing.
(Beat.)
He was like a little kid.
Embarrassed.
By himself.
Alone.
Lost.
Hiding.

(Silence.)
(They watch the snow.)
(Snow and wind.)
(Blackout.)

ANTARCTICA

Carolyn Raship

CAROLYN RASHIP is a writer, director, and illustrator. She has written and directed *Penguins* (Theatrix, 1998), *Angry Little People* (co-created with Maggie Cino, 2000 New York International Fringe Festival), *Another Glamorous Historical Footnote* (Reverie Productions Reading Series, 2001), and *Die Like a Lady; or What Barbara Got* (2002 New York International Fringe Festival). She is also the author of *Sex: One Girl's Story of Heaven and Hell, Leo and Rowsby Ruff Ruff Ruff* (both at Two Boots Den of Cin, 1997); *The Kane Mutiny* (Screaming Venus Productions, 1999); and the screenplay for the film *Carefully* (cowritten with Daniel McKleinfeld, Injury to the Eye Productions, 2003). For the past ten years, she has held various positions with the New York International Fringe Festival. She lives in Brooklyn and is currently working on a novel and the grown-up picture book version of *Antarctica*.

Antarctica's New York premiere was presented by Fevvers Productions as part of the New York International Fringe Festival (Elena K. Holy, Producing Artistic Director) on August 11, 2007, at The New School of Drama, New York City, with the following cast and credits:

Magda.. Maggie Cino
Winnie.. Jessi Gotta
The White Bear, et al. ....Christopher Lueck

Director: Carolyn Raship
Production Stage Manager: Simon Bogigian
Rehearsal Stage Manager: Leslie Nevon Holden
Set Design: Daniel ZS. Jagendorf
Sound Design: Daniel McKleinfeld
Lighting Design: S. Ryan Schmidt
Costume Design: Martha Sullivan
Slide Illustrations: Jennifer Daltry
Production Goddess: Alexa Shaunghnessy

Song "Till Antarctica" by Elisa Korenne
Produced by Jon Margulies at Tribeca Recording

Antarctica premiered at EXIT on Taylor on September 9, 2005, as part of the San Francisco Fringe Festival with the following cast and credits:

Magda.. Maggie Cino
Winnie.. Robin Reed
Voice of the White Bear..Fred Backus

Director: Carolyn Raship
Set and Lighting Design: Daniel ZS. Jagendorf

At rise: In blackout. Music fade up. Music fade down. Wind sounds.

MAGDA: Winnie? Winnie?!

(Pause.)

MAGDA: Hello?

(Pause.)

MAGDA: I'm sorry I swear to God I'm so sorry I promise I'll fix everything if you answer scout's honor but Jesus I was never a scout I swear to God I'm so sorry are you there Winnie oh Jesus just answer don't leave me here alone I know everything is all my fault just answer…

(Wind cuts out. Lights up.)

WINNIE: Winnie first met Magda when they were fifteen years old.

MAGDA: Magda was sitting near the window.

WINNIE: It was history class.

MAGDA: Seventh period. And it was called social studies.

WINNIE: Whatever.

MAGDA: Mrs. Walden's class.

WINNIE: Winnie was late—

MAGDA: Magda was looking out the window—

WINNIE: Winnie was—

MAGDA: She was poking her finger with a well-sharpened No. 2 pencil and—

WINNIE: She was late because in her previous class, Ms. Margolis's Trigonometry 2, she got this unbelievably impressive nosebleed and—

MAGDA: Magda would hear about Winnie's legendarily gory nosebleed and how the spurting blood hit Jake Minas

right in the face from many students in the coming weeks.

WINNIE: No one in Ms. Margolis's trig class ever forgot it.

MAGDA: But back to Mrs. Walden's social studies class. Magda sat staring pensively out the window. During her silent ruminations, she had managed to smear pencil across her cheek, lending her an unusually scholarly air for a fifteen-year-old.

WINNIE: Winnie was wearing the T-shirt she wore in gym because she got blood all over the halter-top she wore to school. It totally sucked, actually, because Winnie had only worn it once. And she was really worried that the gym shirt smelled. So anyway, when she went— late, to social studies she pretty much felt like crap.

MAGDA: This was Magda's first day of school here. But she was used to being the new girl. She looked out the window and thought the campus looked like a high school on television.

WINNIE: Winnie walked into class with a note from the nurse.

MAGDA: Mrs. Walden was talking about penguins.

WINNIE: Again.

MAGDA: It was the first time Magda had heard it.

WINNIE: When she was young Mrs. Walden had visited Antarctica with her explorer husband and she never stopped talking about it.

MAGDA: Magda suddenly sat up very straight. She listened very intently to Mrs. Walden for the first time since she arrived in class. She heard about penguins and frostbite and maps. About ships crushed by the force of the ice as the men who had journeyed in them stood and watched. About icy cold adventure and glory—

WINNIE: Until Mrs. Walden told Winnie—Why don't you take that empty seat right there are you—

MAGDA: —are you sure you're feeling alright? And then she went right back to the penguins.

WINNIE: The penguins and Antarctica.

MAGDA: Emperor! Gentoo! Adélie! And chinstrap!

WINNIE: This is so shitty.

MAGDA: What?

WINNIE: Do I have blood on my face?

MAGDA: Huh?

WINNIE: Blood, hello. On my face? Is there any.

MAGDA: I don't see any.

WINNIE: This is so shitty.

MAGDA: What?

WINNIE: Oh God. Don't worry. You'll hear about it. From everybody. This fucking sucks.

MAGDA: Yeah.

WINNIE: Who are you? Are you new?

MAGDA: Um.

WINNIE: What's your name?

MAGDA: Today's my first day here.

WINNIE: Do you like have a name?

MAGDA: And that was the momentous and earth-shattering beginning of the most important friendship of Magda's

life. Magda felt the connection between Winnie and herself immediately. The protons crackled in the air between them.

WINNIE: Do protons crackle?

MAGDA: Winnie was much better at science than anyone might have expected.

WINNIE: Or is that like neutrons?

MAGDA: Magda looked around at the other students in class and their faces looked alternately bored or cruel. They were faded out, dimly colored, barely alive. Only she and Winnie had red blood flowing through their veins. Magda had no desire to have them as friends.

WINNIE: Jimmy Ferguson is a dick. You will totally want to stay out of his way. Jenny, over there in the striped sweater? She's okay, kind of annoying, we were friends in middle school. Jared is, as you can see, totally hot, but he's like aware of it so it's kind of gross…

MAGDA: If she were to be perfectly honest, Magda had to admit that cruel experience had taught her that she wasn't very good at remaining aloof, above the alliances and battles of will that formed such a large part of teenage life. Magda liked to think she didn't care. But she did.

WINNIE: Kelly Kuckler's parents are in Cancun, so she's having some people over. You should totally come.

(WINNIE is at the party. Music. It begins in blackout. Flashes of light up in a series of tableaux. Fun and hilarity turning to teenage badness. Scenes of WINNIE alternate with scenes of MAGDA standing around uncomfortably. Maybe THE WHITE BEAR is there, in teenaged boy form, or at least the actor who plays THE WHITE BEAR. Lights up for the last time *on WINNIE by herself. MAGDA standing awkwardly.)*

WINNIE: I fucking hate everyone.

MAGDA: What happened?

WINNIE: Nothing. It's fine.

(Pause.)

WINNIE: You came.

MAGDA: I usually don't like parties.

WINNIE: I fucking hate Jimmy.

MAGDA: What did he do?

WINNIE: I'm such a moron.

MAGDA: You should just stay away from him. It's just so not worth it.

WINNIE: Uch. I wish we had a car. I want to just—I don't know—drive. I look so fat in these jeans shorts.

MAGDA: I don't know why I came. I don't know anyone here but you.

WINNIE: Where should we drive to?

MAGDA: Everywhere is exactly the same.

WINNIE: Do you smoke pot?

MAGDA: I've lived in so many different places, and they are all exactly the same.

WINNIE: That is a really depressing thought. Maybe we could drive to the beach.

MAGDA: We don't have a car. Or driver's licenses.

WINNIE: We could try to make someone drive us. But that would be like bringing all the same old bullshit to the beach with us.

(Pause.)

MAGDA: We could go to Antarctica.

WINNIE: What, like Mrs. Walden?

MAGDA: Yeah. You want different, right?

(Pause.)

WINNIE: Okay.

MAGDA: Really?

WINNIE: Sure.

MAGDA: We'll travel to Antarctica. It will change everything!

(Music. Transition. MAGDA is in bossy, lecture mode.)

MAGDA: Before leaving on any expedition, great attention must be paid to the subject of packing.

WINNIE: We went shopping. We had this whole argument about whether we should bring tuxedos or not. Apparently, there's this whole thing where people go to Antarctica, put on tuxedos, and have their picture taken with the penguins.

(Pose. Penguin puppet. FLASH! Resume play.)

MAGDA: Specifically, emperor penguins.

WINNIE: Whatever. I think it would be fun. I mean, yeah, it's kind of cheesy, but we could use the pictures for Christmas cards for like ever.

MAGDA: I have no problem with taking pictures with penguins—

WINNIE: They're so cute.

MAGDA: Yes, very cute, but—

WINNIE: We'd wear lots and lots of black eyeliner and white ties—

MAGDA: Important calculations have to be made. We need formulas and spreadsheets. How much food we'll need balanced by how much we can transport.

And there is the possibility, remote as it may be, that we could be trapped over the winter, frozen in—

WINNIE: Are there polar bears?

MAGDA: Goggles. Parkas. Specimen cases. Journals. Dogs?

(WINNIE is flipping through magazines, trying on pairs of sunglasses, etc.)

MAGDA: Should we bring dogs? The dog question is really what seems to make or break an expedition.

WINNIE: I'd like to see polar bears.

MAGDA: That's the Arctic. Not the Antarctic.

WINNIE: Oh. That sucks.

MAGDA: Lots of Antarctic explorers ate penguins.

WINNIE: Ew. I'm not going to eat a penguin.

MAGDA: Or used their blubber as fuel. I don't think I could kill a penguin. They're so helpless. But then, so are we, really. And, I guess, they aren't exactly running out of penguins in Antarctica.

WINNIE: That's just—Ew.

MAGDA: Meticulous records must be kept of all we see and do. On our return we will be fêted and toasted as Great Explorers. Posterity will be grateful for the knowledge bestowed to humanity by the first successful expedition to the true Southern Pole by American Girls.

WINNIE: I saw polar bears at the zoo once. They looked really bored.

MAGDA: My life will be perfect.

(Big production number! Musical packing extravaganza starring WINNIE and MAGDA!)

(They are on the boat.)

MAGDA: To reach Antarctica one must journey south to Tierra del Fuego in Argentina. From there, one can simply hop an ice breaker and set course for the Bottom of the World!

(WINNIE laughs. She and JOSH (BEAR) are flirting. MAGDA looks out at the sea, taking notes.)

MAGDA: Look! Whales.

WINNIE: *(Crosses to MAGDA.)* I don't see anything.

MAGDA: Not there. There!

WINNIE: That is so cool. Whales, like flocks of them.

MAGDA: I don't think whales travel in flocks.

WINNIE: So, I was talking to Josh before—

MAGDA: Schools? Anyway, there are a *lot* of whales. Herds, do they travel in herds?

WINNIE: What I was saying—I was hanging out with—

MAGDA: Note for later: Look up whale, collective noun.

WINNIE: You know the second mate?

MAGDA: Bjorn?

WINNIE: No. Bjorn's the one with the fucked-up teeth who looks like a giant walking fish head. I mean Josh.

MAGDA: I don't know him.

WINNIE: Yes, you do. Josh, the second mate. The cute one.

MAGDA: I never met him.

WINNIE: You totally did, but whatever. Anyway. He told me he had weed and would smoke us up if we wanted. Him and his friends hang out by the lifeboats. If the captain caught them he'd be so pissed.

MAGDA: Magda began to think that Winnie had lost sight of why they had embarked on this journey to Antarctica.

WINNIE: Josh has this friend, Andrew. He's really nice. And smart. I told them we'd hang out tonight.

MAGDA: I can't.

WINNIE: Don't be like that. I said we'd go.

MAGDA: Stop it. I can't go smoke pot with you and Josh, the cute second mate, okay?!

WINNIE: Are you mad? Don't be mad.

MAGDA: I just have a lot to think about right now. We didn't bring the dogs because I wasn't sure how we were going to feed them and now I think it might have been a giant mistake and I'm really worried. I have to stay on top of so many things right now.

WINNIE: Don't freak out. It will be fine.

MAGDA: It's all heavier than I thought. I'm just really scared—not scared—concerned that I've made all kinds of fatal errors.

WINNIE: Josh is really cute. I think he's from Finland.

MAGDA: I have to recheck our supplies.

WINNIE: And Andrew is so nice.

(Pause.)

MAGDA: Is he cute?

WINNIE: Um, not in an obvious way, but he is so nice. And really smart. He showed us Cassiopeia last night.

MAGDA: We're in the southern hemisphere. You can't see Cassiopeia.

WINNIE: Oh.

MAGDA: You should go.

WINNIE: I mean, if you want to do something else…

MAGDA: I'll be fine. I promise. I have lots to do.

WINNIE: Are you sure?

MAGDA: Go. I'll be fine.

(MAGDA writes in her journal. WINNIE is with JOSH.)

MAGDA: The night before the real journey begins. Everything is packed away and triple cross-checked. Any mistake can mean an icy, unmarked grave. Oh look—whales do travel in schools!

WINNIE: Oh my God, Josh, Bjorn was so fucking seasick! Is there anything grosser than Bjorn barfing overboard?

MAGDA: I am still uncertain I made the correct decision regarding the dogs. I believe I finally decided against bringing them because so many explorers who brought sled dogs wound up eating them.

WINNIE: Do you have any like chips or something? I like so have the munchies.

MAGDA: I am a little concerned about Winnie. She doesn't seem to be regarding this journey with the seriousness with which it is due.

WINNIE: Oh my God get the fuck out of here Bjorn!

MAGDA: Two lone American girls battling the elements. Fighting against the most inhospitable environment imaginable to girlkind. I know I can prevail, but

I begin to think that Winnie might not be strong enough to withstand the rigors of Antarctic travel.

WINNIE: I can't believe he told the Captain on you guys.

MAGDA: I must look after her carefully to ensure no harm befalls her.

(Traveling sequence.)

(Music. Slides. Increasingly ominous penguins.)

MAGDA: There are penguins everywhere.

WINNIE: I knew we should have brought the tuxes.

MAGDA: It would have been too cold.

WINNIE: We would have blended better.

MAGDA: There are penguins everywhere.

WINNIE: It's kind of scary.

MAGDA: They're looking at us.

WINNIE: I knew we shouldn't have brought the lox.

MAGDA: Maybe we should just, I don't know, hand over the fish.

WINNIE: If this turns ugly we are seriously outnumbered.

MAGDA: There are penguins everywhere.

WINNIE: Come on. Let's back away very, very slowly.

(They back away very, very slowly and then RUN. They travel.)

WINNIE: When we get back to school, I'm going to do a MASSIVE extra credit project on this.

MAGDA: I'm going to present our findings to the Mid-Atlantic Democratic Geographic Society.

WINNIE: I'm going to have like this slide show presentation. It will be awesome.

MAGDA: Winnie's slide show presentation on "Magda & Winnie's Journey to Antarctica: Continent of Ice."

WINNIE: Slide number one:

(Picture of a penguin.)

WINNIE: Slide number two:

(Blank white.)

WINNIE: Slide number three:

(Blank white.)

WINNIE: Slide number four:

(Blank white.)

WINNIE: Slide number five:

(Blank white.)

WINNIE: The end.

(More traveling. They are getting weary.)

WINNIE: I'm hungry.

MAGDA: Have a peanut.

(MAGDA hands her one peanut. WINNIE eats it.)

WINNIE: I'm still hungry.

MAGDA: I know. Me, too.

WINNIE: I want pizza.

MAGDA: French toast.

WINNIE: Mallomars.

MAGDA: Ring Dings.

WINNIE: What are they?

MAGDA: You've never had a Ring Ding?

WINNIE: No.

MAGDA: I guess they're an East Coast thing.

(They set up camp, i.e., open the umbrella, and sit down.)

WINNIE: I want a Sno Ball.

MAGDA: We ate them all.

WINNIE: I'm really hungry, Magda.

MAGDA: I know. Me too.

(They are under the umbrella. MAGDA writes in her journal; WINNIE is curled up asleep.)

MAGDA: Everything is white, silver, blue, or black. It is beautiful and terrible beyond imagining. Never dark, always shining, it pounds through my eyes, into my skull. I cannot sleep. Winnie does. She sleeps like a child as I write in my journal in what would be night if the sun would ever go down. Our tent is red. I can't decide whether it looks beautiful against the white and blue, or if it just looks dirty and wrong.

(THE WHITE BEAR enters. Knocking!)

WINNIE: What is it?

MAGDA: Just the wind.

WINNIE: Shut up. I hear something.

(They peer out of the tent, i.e., over the top of the umbrella.)

WINNIE: It's a bear.

MAGDA: It's huge!

WINNIE: I thought you said there aren't any polar bears in Antarctica!

MAGDA: There aren't!

WINNIE: Why don't you go tell that to the big white bear that's outside of our tent.

MAGDA: We could be hallucinating.

WINNIE: Maybe.

(They look outside again, i.e., above the umbrella.)

WINNIE: Okay.

MAGDA: Not hallucinating.

WINNIE: You said there were no bears.

MAGDA: There aren't supposed to be people either and we're here.

WINNIE: What is he then, an explorer bear? A representative from the Royal Exploring Bear Society?

MAGDA: I suppose I'd better go outside and see what it wants.

WINNIE: Be careful!

(They lower the umbrella as MAGDA slowly stands to face THE WHITE BEAR.)

MAGDA: Magda stepped outside the tent and faced the bear. He was enormous, his fur shone silver white, and she looked into his eyes. They were intelligent and deep, but very wild. Only a fool would think he was a tame bear. He continued to look at Magda and she got very uncomfortable.

MAGDA: Hello? Hi.

(THE WHITE BEAR sighs.)

MAGDA: What do you want from us?

(Pause.)

THE WHITE BEAR: You're going to die, you and your friend.

MAGDA: What?

THE WHITE BEAR: Without my help. You will both die.

MAGDA: Leave us alone.

THE WHITE BEAR: The bear turned and walked off into the bright Antarctic night.

MAGDA: In the morning, they packed up their tent and trekked across the frozen wilds. Another night was passed with Winnie asleep and Magda writing in her journal.

(THE WHITE BEAR enters. Knocking!)

WINNIE: It's back.

MAGDA: I should go outside and see what it wants.

WINNIE: Be careful!

(They lower the umbrella as MAGDA slowly stands to face THE WHITE BEAR.)

MAGDA: Magda stepped outside the tent, and once again faced the bear.

MAGDA: Why have you come back? I asked you to leave us alone.

(THE WHITE BEAR sighs.)

MAGDA: What are you doing here? Bears don't live in Antarctica.

THE WHITE BEAR: People don't either, and you're here.

MAGDA: What do you want?

THE WHITE BEAR: I want to help. You will both die out here, in the wilds, unless you accept my aid. I will make sure you survive. And more. When you get back to where you came from, you will be given honor, riches, glory.

MAGDA: What would I have to give you in return?

THE WHITE BEAR: You will be noticed, admired, loved.

MAGDA: What is the price?

THE WHITE BEAR: You will have everything you ever wanted.

(Back under the umbrella.)

MAGDA: If you don't go with him we'll die.

WINNIE: I can't believe you want to sell me to a bear for some frigging Spam.

MAGDA: He seems like a very civilized bear.

WINNIE: Shut up.

MAGDA: I don't want to die.

WINNIE: What did he promise you?

MAGDA: He said we'd die without his help.

WINNIE: Is this like some kind of bear-Antarctic-extortion racket?

MAGDA: No. No, I don't think so.

WINNIE: What did it say?

MAGDA: He said you should meet him outside of the tent tonight.

WINNIE: There isn't any night here.

MAGDA: At eight o'clock.

(MAGDA takes the umbrella from WINNIE.)

MAGDA: He said he wouldn't hurt you.

WINNIE: That's what they all say. *(Stands.)* Winnie was never really sure why she agreed to step out of the tent to go with the bear. Maybe she was scared of dying, cold and hungry on the endless white plain. Maybe she wanted to see what would happen. She stepped outside and she saw the bear.

MAGDA: Winnie was right.

THE WHITE BEAR: Hello. It's Winnie, right?

WINNIE: Yes. Hi.

MAGDA: We got Spam.

WINNIE: Winnie followed the bear out across the great southern white waste.

MAGDA: But not just Spam.

WINNIE: When she got tired, she rode on his back.

MAGDA: After Winnie went off with the bear, I had dogs and a sled.

WINNIE: As he moved swiftly over the ice they talked. Winnie told the bear about school and her friends.

MAGDA: The dogs seemed to know the way without my having to consult my instruments or calculations.

WINNIE: When the bear told her about himself, she felt vaguely embarrassed. It all seemed so small.

THE WHITE BEAR: I have a king-dom, away up north. I'm just as much a stranger here as you are.

MAGDA: I had a warmer and well-provisioned tent.

WINNIE: After they had traveled for many miles, Winnie saw what looked like a large black dot on the whiteness ahead. As they got closer, she saw it was the entrance to a cave.

THE WHITE BEAR: This is where we'll spend the night.

WINNIE: Really?

THE WHITE BEAR: But, you know, no pressure.

(WINNIE and THE WHITE BEAR exit.)

MAGDA: It was lonelier, now that Winnie was with the white bear.

(MAGDA travels. Dogs bark.)

MAGDA: My instruments tell me I'm getting very near the true magnetic Pole. The very end of the earth. I don't know if it's because I'm alone now a lot of the time, but I feel strange. My eyes are playing tricks on me. Maybe it's just from staring at the white so long, but I swear I could see the wind. It was made of colors and I think it had a face. And then, far away in the distance, I thought I saw a woman on a sleigh. I know it sounds crazy, and I won't show anyone this part of my journal when I get back. But she was there. When she appeared on the horizon, the dogs got very, very quiet, as if they didn't want her to know we were here. The compass says I'm heading due South, but I really have no idea where I am anymore.

(THE WHITE BEAR and WINNIE enter.)

THE WHITE BEAR: If you wish, I can return you to Magda in the morning and you can come back to me at night. On one condition:

WINNIE: Winnie must never tell Magda what went on between them or it would bring destruction down on them all.

(THE WHITE BEAR exits. WINNIE and MAGDA are sledding.)

MAGDA: Wait. Stop.

WINNIE: What is it?

MAGDA: Just—Ow.

WINNIE: What?

MAGDA: My eyes.

WINNIE: Let me see.

MAGDA: No—

WINNIE: Let me look. Here.

MAGDA: Stop. Ow.

WINNIE: Let me see. Okay.

MAGDA: What?

WINNIE: Can you see at all?

MAGDA: Not really.

WINNIE: How long has this been going on?

MAGDA: I've been letting the dogs guide us.

WINNIE: Jesus.

MAGDA: They seem to know where they're going.

WINNIE: You should have told me.

MAGDA: I'll be okay.

WINNIE: Look. The white bear told me what to do. Here. *(She puts her goggles over MAGDA's eyes.)*

MAGDA: The white bear told you what to do in case of snow blindness?

WINNIE: Uh huh.

(Pause.)

MAGDA: What else do you talk about?

WINNIE: *(Looks uncomfortable.)* I don't know. Like, different things.

MAGDA: Like what?

WINNIE: Nothing.

MAGDA: Why don't you want to tell me?

WINNIE: Can we just like change the subject okay?

MAGDA: Okay. Fine.

(They sled on in silence.)

WINNIE: Winnie decided that this was going to be even more awkward than she initially thought. It was really weird. You see, everything had changed for Winnie and she wasn't allowed to tell Magda, which was really hard, because ever since they had become friends she had told Magda everything.

MAGDA: So where do you go each night when you go off with the bear?

WINNIE: Winnie bit her lip and looked nervously away, but said nothing.

MAGDA: Are you hiding something from me?

WINNIE: No.

MAGDA: Did you and the bear find the Pole?

WINNIE: No. I don't think so. I wouldn't know if we did.

MAGDA: Do you really think you can trust him?

WINNIE: Yes, I really do, okay?

(WINNIE exits. MAGDA stands on chair.)

MAGDA: My goal is finally in sight! The true Southern Pole is finally within my grasp. I really want to pause and eat a Sno Ball, but I think I must soldier on until the Pole is mine. *(Leaps triumphantly off chair. As she lands:)* I thought it would be more exciting to find the absolute Polar South. Actually, it's a little anticlimactic. I'm looking at my compass and it points north in all directions. I am the first American Girl to stand EVER on the Southern Pole. It's really vast and impressive and all, but it's kind of lonely. I miss the penguins. It's nice having the dogs here but they aren't that friendly, they're kind of aloof. I guess it's because they're enchanted. I wish Winnie was here.

(MAGDA plants her flag and walks off. The dogs bark.)

MAGDA: Winnie hadn't returned for many days. Magda knew she was safe, but wished she had someone to talk to. Finally, one morning she saw a speck on the horizon. Magda thought at first it was that woman in the sleigh, but the dogs barked louder than ever.

WINNIE: Magda! It's me!

(WINNIE hugs MAGDA.)

WINNIE: Oh my God, I missed you so much!

(Pause.)

MAGDA: Hi.

(WINNIE is dressed more glamorously than she was before.)

WINNIE: I am so sorry I was gone for so long.

MAGDA: It's fine.

WINNIE: Really? You don't look fine.

MAGDA: No, I'm fine. I found the Pole.

WINNIE: That is so awesome. I'm so sorry I missed it. Tell me about it.

MAGDA: It was great.

WINNIE: Okay, what's the matter?

MAGDA: Nothing.

WINNIE: Yes, there is. You are obviously upset with me. What's up?

MAGDA: I told you, nothing.

WINNIE: Fine, be that way. I'm going back to the bear.

MAGDA: Wait.

WINNIE: What?

MAGDA: It's just—I thought we were doing this together, and then you go off and leave me to travel through Antarctica all by myself, I mean it's not like I know anyone here.

WINNIE: Magda?

MAGDA: What?

WINNIE: What's the deal?

MAGDA: What do you mean?

WINNIE: Do you have like amnesia?

MAGDA: No.

WINNIE: Because you were the one who told me to go off with the bear. You said we would die if I didn't. It's not like I met a new guy and stopped hanging out with you for two months. I hate girls who do that. So tell me what you are so upset about.

MAGDA: I don't know. I mean, it's not so much that you spend all your time with the bear, but you won't even tell me what's going on.

WINNIE: I know. But I can't.

MAGDA: Just tell me.

WINNIE: He told me I shouldn't tell you.

MAGDA: Okay. Think about that for a minute. I mean, isn't that kind of controlling?

WINNIE: I guess, but—

MAGDA: But what? This is so not like you. I mean who is he to say what you can tell and what you can't.

WINNIE: It didn't seem like that. He said something really bad would happen if I told.

MAGDA: Winnie. Now I'm not at all mad, just really worried. What is going on?

WINNIE: Nothing.

MAGDA: Secrets are bad. They'll just blow up in your face eventually. Tell me.

WINNIE: This is going to sound really weird.

MAGDA: Magda felt ferocious. All her explorer's instincts were telling her there was something here worth knowing. She wanted to think, she had almost convinced herself even, that what Winnie would tell her would be the linchpin to this entire journey.

WINNIE: Every night, when I'm with the white bear—

MAGDA: That Winnie, and it did almost kill her to think this, with the white bear's guidance, had—had—

WINNIE: We go off to where he is living, to this cave, it's not where he's from or anything—

MAGDA: That she had found something worth finding, and Magda was determined to know what it was. It was unfair. She was the one leading this expedition. She was the one who had done all the work and planned so carefully. She was the one who knew all about Poles and pack ice and penguins. And for Winnie—who really when it was all said and done, was really a, a passenger—for Winnie to be the one who made some glorious discovery—Magda just—

WINNIE: It's just beautiful, Magda.

MAGDA: The cave?

WINNIE: It's all ice white, but really warm, but not at all stuffy. All the furniture is so comfy, and really pretty. Way nicer than Erika Pascal's house, even.

MAGDA: Wow.

WINNIE: And the white bear and I eat dinner together, the food's really good, but it's weird. It all just seems to show up, and then at the end of the meal, all the plates vanish. It's startling at first, but you get used to it.

MAGDA: Wow. I knew there was more to the Pole. I mean, finding it—

WINNIE: I'm sure it was the most exciting thing. Like ever.

MAGDA: Oh, it totally was. But, I just kind of wished it were a little more distinguishable—

WINNIE: From everywhere else for a thousand square miles around it?

MAGDA: So what else happens in the bear's cave?

WINNIE: After dinner we talk, or watch movies and stuff.

MAGDA: You watch movies? He has electricity?

WINNIE: Again, I'm not so sure how it works.

MAGDA: Tell me, what else? What happens after you watch movies or whatever?

WINNIE: Then we go to bed.

MAGDA: Yes?

WINNIE: Nothing.

(Pause.)

WINNIE: Are your eyes feeling better? Want me to take a look at them?

MAGDA: They're fine. Tell me everything.

WINNIE: We go to bed in a room. With very soft sheets, and it's entirely dark. And we, you know, go to bed.

MAGDA: You and the bear?

WINNIE: I can't explain this, but he's human. I can't see anything because it's so dark, but he's human, a person.

MAGDA: Are you sure?

WINNIE: Magda, just take my word for it. I'm sure.

MAGDA: You have to find a way to see him.

WINNIE: I asked. He said I couldn't.

MAGDA: He could be anyone. He must be hiding something.

WINNIE: He loves me.

MAGDA: I have a plan.

WINNIE: I'm actually happy with him.

MAGDA: The next time you go to bed—

WINNIE: I don't know if it's going to be forever. I'm not stupid. He lives in a cave in Antarctica and takes the form of a polar bear during the day, which, in his defense, he clearly can't help.

MAGDA: Bring a flashlight into the bedroom with you and hide it.

WINNIE: No.

MAGDA: And when he's asleep, point it at his face, switch it on, and take a good long look.

WINNIE: I said, no. He trusts me.

MAGDA: And you trust me, right? I'm the one who wanted to come to

Antarctica, right? And I'm the one who said it would be fine if you went with the white bear, right? Hasn't everything I've asked you to do on this expedition turned out for the best? He could be anyone. He could be a monster.

WINNIE: He could be famous.

MAGDA: I just want to make sure you're safe.

WINNIE: Winnie lay in bed with the white bear, her smuggled flashlight hidden under the covers, and for the first time in that room she was unhappy.

MAGDA: Magda lay in her overstuffed down sleeping bag, half-awake. She shut her eyes and saw a beautiful woman in a fancy old-fashioned dress. She had blonde hair and looked like this French actress she had seen once in a movie her parents were watching on TV. A small golden key was tied to her wrist with a red velvet ribbon. She stood in front of an open door, and she screamed. Magda wasn't sure if she herself screamed, or if it was the beautiful movie star who was staring at the unspeakable carnage beyond the unlocked door.

WINNIE: Bear?

MAGDA: Magda turned over, and saw a beautiful girl entwined with a snake.

WINNIE: She ran her finger along his jaw, down to his Adam's apple and across his chest.

MAGDA: Jewels dripped from her ears and her neck and she had a look of pure joy on her face. The scene then shifted, and she saw a second girl, who looked so much like the first, Magda knew they had to be sisters. She was being devoured by a snake from the feet up, her arms pinned to her sides. The girl was screaming, or the screams might have belonged to Magda herself, she wasn't sure.

WINNIE: Winnie raised the flashlight and hoped the white bear would wake up and stop her because she knew she wouldn't stop herself.

MAGDA: I placed a flag on the South Pole. The true geographic South. I stood in a field of hundreds of thousands of penguins.

WINNIE: Winnie kissed him on the lips.

MAGDA: I packed all the supplies.

WINNIE: She clicked on the flashlight.

MAGDA: I planned it all.

WINNIE: At the sound of the flashlight's click, he opened his eyes.

(WINNIE removes THE WHITE BEAR's mask.)

THE WHITE BEAR: What have you done?

WINNIE: I just wanted to see your face.

THE WHITE BEAR: You talked to Magda about me, didn't you?

WINNIE: I couldn't help it. I mean, I owed it to her to tell.

THE WHITE BEAR: I'm not mad.

WINNIE: You look mad.

THE WHITE BEAR: Well, I'm not.

WINNIE: Okay then. What's the big deal?

THE WHITE BEAR: It's over.

WINNIE: What?

THE WHITE BEAR: All of this. I'm living under an enchantment. And as is usual with enchantments, there are rules.

WINNIE: So you're really not a bear.

THE WHITE BEAR: Of course not. There aren't any bears in Antarctica.

WINNIE: So I've heard.

THE WHITE BEAR: You see, the Snow Queen wanted me for herself. She saw me—

WINNIE: Where did she see you?

THE WHITE BEAR: I did this Burger King commercial and it went national—

WINNIE: Oh that's so cool.

THE WHITE BEAR: As if I can get my residual checks sent here. Anyway, the Snow Queen wanted to marry me. I didn't want to marry her, so she made me a white bear by day and a man, I mean myself, at night. If, during the year of my enchantment, I could find someone who would love me and stay with me, without ever seeing my true face, the enchantment would be broken.

WINNIE: I'm assuming the enchantment kept you from explaining all this so I wouldn't screw everything up.

THE WHITE BEAR: It's really not your fault.

WINNIE: Can I ask you a question?

THE WHITE BEAR: I have to go.

WINNIE: Did you ever really love me or was I just a very convenient enchantment breaker?

MAGDA: And the bear—I mean the handsome young actor—vanished in a very cinematic puff of smoke.

WINNIE: Winnie felt a cold blast of wind on her face.

MAGDA: Magda woke up with a start.

WINNIE: Winnie saw the cave was gone and that she stood alone in the bright white snow.

MAGDA: Magda shivered. It was perfectly quiet.

WINNIE: The lovely warm clothes the bear had given her were gone, and she was again wearing the parka she had bought at Marshalls before journeying south.

MAGDA: She was sleeping in the old red tent she had brought from home. She stepped outside and the dogs and the sleigh were gone.

WINNIE: All Winnie wanted was to find Magda. And, you know, she actually felt a little guilty. I mean, maybe she did behave like one of those girls who get a new boyfriend and then neglect their girlfriends.

MAGDA: Magda knew she had to find Winnie. She looked for tracks, but they had all blown away during the night.

WINNIE: Of course she knew all this hardly mattered in the face of starving and freezing to death. Her nose began to spurt blood. The red looked magnificent on the white snow, she thought, I have to sit down, she thought, her head swam, and all she could see finally was white.

(WINNIE lies crumpled in a heap on the ground. MAGDA stands, panting. She cannot see WINNIE.)

MAGDA: Winnie? Winnie?!

(Pause.)

MAGDA: Hello?

WINNIE: *(Sits up.)* Tragedy.

MAGDA: Romance.

WINNIE: Adventure.

MAGDA: This could really end one of three ways.

WINNIE: You first.

(WINNIE lies crumpled in a heap on the ground. MAGDA stands, panting. She cannot see WINNIE.)

MAGDA: Winnie—

WINNIE: Wait. Does this look okay?

MAGDA: It's good. Very dramatic.

WINNIE: Cool.

(WINNIE lies crumpled in a heap on the ground. MAGDA stands, panting. She cannot see WINNIE.)

MAGDA: Winnie? Winnie?!

(Pause.)

MAGDA: Hello?

(Pause.)

MAGDA: I'm sorry I swear to God I'm so sorry I promise I'll fix everything if you answer scout's honor but Jesus I was never a scout I swear to God I'm so sorry are you there Winnie oh Jesus just answer don't leave me here alone I know everything is all my fault just answer…I'm so sorry. I was so jealous. And this is all my fault you see I lied to you, I did and I know there's no excuse, but I was scared. The bear didn't ask for you, he asked for either of us, he said he was lonely, and I was too scared to go and so I told you he wanted you, can you forgive me?

WINNIE: And then all Magda could see was white, and then she was very warm, and she thought to herself—

MAGDA: I knew it would work out—

WINNIE: Magda had told Winnie to trust her—

MAGDA: And Winnie did, and she looked at the blood on the snow, and then she too felt warm—

WINNIE: And that was the last thing—

MAGDA: —either of them remembered.

(Ending music. Lights begin to dim.)

MAGDA: Wait!

(Lights back up.)

MAGDA: You next.

WINNIE: I looked at my blood falling onto the white snow—

MAGDA: Nosebleed blood.

WINNIE: That makes it sound so much yuckier.

MAGDA: Sorry.

WINNIE: And in the spot where the blood fell grew a tree—

MAGDA: With silver leaves and golden apples.

WINNIE: That sounds so gay. Whatever. Fine. So what do the apples do again?

MAGDA: They give you strength and make you warm.

WINNIE: Oh, right.

MAGDA: Do you want me to tell this?

WINNIE: So I ate the apples, which made me strong and warm, found the Snow Queen's palace, and rescued the prince—

MAGDA: Actor—

WINNIE: Prince, and we both became movie stars and lived happily ever after. The end.

MAGDA: So much for romance.

WINNIE: That leaves adventure.

MAGDA: Magda struggled nearly blindly through the snow. Nothing but white as far as she could see—but wait!

WINNIE: What?

MAGDA: Were her eyes playing tricks on her, or did she see teeny tiny droplets of blood? Yes, there was definitely something there! Now splattered blood is rarely a sign of hope or of imminent safety, but Magda believed this was the rare exception. She followed the path of blood, hope welling up inside her. Until—

WINNIE: Until she saw Winnie, huddled on the ground. Now Winnie was entirely pissed off at this point. Her, as it surprisingly turned out, totally hot boyfriend was gone, and she had no idea whether she had been played, or if it was in fact, true love.

MAGDA: Winnie?! I knew I'd find you.

WINNIE: I have a nosebleed.

MAGDA: Here's a tissue.

WINNIE: Thanks.

MAGDA: Okay. I have a plan!

WINNIE: Good. Because beyond freezing to death, I'm kind of at a loss.

MAGDA: First we'll make a fire.

WINNIE: You have fuel?

MAGDA: I'm sure we have something that will burn.

WINNIE: Everything is like flame retardant.

MAGDA: So after a long, and very frustrating process—

WINNIE: A pair of snowshoes did the trick. I bet the tuxedos would have burned if we had brought them.

MAGDA: A helicopter saw the smoke. Amazingly enough, it was a helicopter from the Mid-Atlantic Democratic Geographic Society.

HELICOPTER PILOT: We were out looking for you and fearing the worst, but when we were on our way back to the base station we saw smoke. Lucky for you those snowshoes went up like kindling!

MAGDA: And we went home.

WINNIE: Back to high school.

MAGDA: As promised, Winnie had a kick-ass extra credit project.

WINNIE: Magda never did publish.

MAGDA: I'm still revising.

WINNIE: They grew up and neither ever went back to Antarctica.

MAGDA: They stayed in touch, but weren't very close.

WINNIE: We lived in different parts of the country.

(Phone rings.)

WINNIE: Hello.

MAGDA: Winnie, that you?

WINNIE: I just got back from the Yucatan.

MAGDA: Did you see the Daily Beagle this week?

WINNIE: I haven't seen the Daily Beagle in like ten years.

MAGDA: Remember Mrs. Walden?

WINNIE: Of course. Social studies. Penguins. I remember.

MAGDA: Well she died.

WINNIE: Oh, that's too bad. How old was she?

MAGDA: I don't know. In her eighties, I think.

WINNIE: Huh.

MAGDA: But that's not what I called you about. You see—there's a picture. You just really have to see it.

WINNIE: What is it?

MAGDA: She's wearing a tuxedo.

WINNIE: Let me guess, standing surrounded by penguins.

MAGDA: And looking surprisingly glamorous for an eleventh grade social studies teacher.

WINNIE: White tie?

MAGDA: Of course.

WINNIE: No bears though?

MAGDA: Haven't we been over this? There are no bears in Antarctica.

(Blackout.)

(THE END.)

ANTARCTICA: A USER'S GUIDE

1. When embarking on any theatrical endeavor, be sure to remember that telling stories and playing parts should be an actual good time.

2. Please note that the stage directions included with the text are really just an indication of what we did in our production and include jokes that we thought were funny. Please feel free to be as creative as you wish, make stuff up, find ways of telling this story that work for you, do things that make you laugh, etc.

3. Musical and dance numbers are always fun.

4. The White Bear can be played in many different ways. In our first production he was a voiceover. Onstage, when he was speaking to Magda, the actor playing Winnie wore a mask, and the opposite was true when he was speaking to Winnie. In the FringeNYC production he was played by an actor who also played all the boy characters mentioned in the text. This worked very well, but there are lots of other possibilities.

5. Read about legendary Antarctic explorers Shackleton and Scott. It's some really fascinating stuff.

6. Lots of this play is based on the fairy tale "East of the Sun and West of the Moon." I first read it in Andrew Lang's classic collection *The Blue Fairy Book*.

7. Please take a look at Kay Nielsen's illustrations for "East of the Sun," as they are really haunting and unspeakably beautiful. You can find them on the Internet. If you find any of his illustrated books in real life, they tend to cost hundreds, if not thousands, of dollars. If you have a spare copy of any of them just, you know, sitting around gathering dust, feel free to send me a copy. You can reach me through the contact information at the front of this book (hey, it can't hurt to ask, right?).

8. I would be really intrigued to see a production where The White Bear was a puppet.

9. I would also be really interested in seeing someone try using a White Bear chorus. The staging could be really interesting.

10. Don't forget that when leaving on any expedition, you must, in addition to making lists and packing well, be nice to the people you are working with. Adventures should be fun, and hard, but if done correctly, you will learn many new things, and remember: you never return from any expedition worth embarking on as precisely the same person you were when you set out.

CLEANSED

Thomas Bradshaw

THOMAS BRADSHAW is a playwright. He was born in Summit,
New Jersey, on March 18, 1980, and grew up in Orange, New
Jersey. He graduated from Bard College, where he studied with
Chiori Miyagawa, with two BA degrees: one in playwriting and one
in sociology. He received an MFA in playwriting from Brooklyn
College, where he studied with Mac Wellman. He is the author
of *Prophet* (P.S. 122, 2005), *Purity* (P.S. 122, 2007), and *Strom
Thurmond Is Not a Racist* (Brick Theater, 2007; Blank The Dog
Theatre Company, Los Angeles, 2008), all three of which have
been published by Samuel French, Inc. He has also performed in
Richard Maxwell's *End of Reality* and *Pullman, WA* by Young Jean
Lee. *Strom Thurmond Is Not a Racist* won the American Theater
Coop's 2005 National Playwriting Contest. Both *Cleansed* and
Strom Thurmond Is Not a Racist were nominated for the 2007
New York Innovative Theatre Award for Outstanding Full Length
Script. Bradshaw has been a member of both the Lincoln Center
Writer/Director Lab (2005) and the Soho Rep Writer/Director
Lab (2006), and was a 2006–2007 Playwriting Fellow at New
York Theatre Workshop. In 2006, he received a Jerome Grant, was
named one of *Paper Magazine*'s Beautiful People, and was featured
as one of *Time Out New York*'s Ten Playwrights to Watch. *The
Village Voice* named him Best Provocative Playwright in 2007. He
is also a New York Theatre Workshop Usual Suspect, and has been
commissioned by Soho Rep to write an adaptation of *The Book of
Job*. Bradshaw is a playwriting professor at Brooklyn College and
also teaches playwriting at Medgar Evers College. He lives in Park
Slope, Brooklyn, with his wife, Roxane.

Cleansed was first presented by the Immediate Theatre Company
(Jose Zayas, Artistic Director) on February 8, 2007, at the Brick
Theatre, Brooklyn, New York, with the following cast and cred-
its:

Vernon ....Derrick Lemont Sanders
Carolyn ....Carleigh Welsh
Lauraul.. Barrett Doss
Mitch ....Joseph Carusone
Grandmother .... Suzan Perry
Kim.. Siho Ellsmore
White Supremacist #1 .... Bobby Moreno
White Supremacist #2 ....Matt Huffman

Director: Jose Zayas
Sets: Ryan Elliot Kravetz
Costumes: Mel Haley
Lighting: Jim French
Sound: Jeremy Wilson

CHARACTERS

VERNON, black, a heart surgeon in his late thirties/early forties
CAROLYN, white, his wife
LAURAUL, their daughter
KIM, Asian, Lauraul's best friend
GRANDMOTHER, Carolyn's mother
MITCH, the leader of the white supremacists
WHITE SUPREMACISTS #1 and #2

TIME AND PLACE

The setting is a small town in Indiana. The time is the present.

SCENE ONE

At rise, VERNON has just walked in the door of his house. CAROLYN is in the kitchen. Their daughter LAURAUL is on the floor in the living room playing with toys. She is eight years old.

VERNON: How's my sugar plum doing today?

LAURAUL: Fine Daddy.

(CAROLYN enters the living room and kisses VERNON.)

CAROLYN: How did the transplant go?

VERNON: Went off without a hitch. What's for dinner?

CAROLYN: Your favorite! Steak au poivre with foie gras for an appetizer.

VERNON: That's sweet of you.

(They kiss, and she exits the living room. VERNON goes over to LAURAUL and picks her up.)

VERNON: How was school today?

LAURAUL: *(Happy.)* Good.

VERNON: What did you learn?

LAURAUL: We learned the difference between Cows and Horses.

VERNON: Oh yeah? What's the difference?

LAURAUL: Cows have milk and horses don't.

VERNON: Is that the only difference?

LAURAUL: Uh-huh.

VERNON: Are you sure?

LAURAUL: Yes I'm sure silly!

VERNON: Did you learn anything else?

LAURAUL: I learned—um—I learned that red and blue make purple.

VERNON: Purple's my favorite color.

LAURAUL: My favorite color's blue!

VERNON: I thought your favorite color was yellow! Are you telling me a fib?

LAURAUL: I changed my mind. It's blue now. I love you Daddy.

VERNON: I love you too. *(Kisses her on the forehead.)*

LAURAUL: Daddy?

VERNON: Yes?

LAURAUL: *(Cheerful.)* Are you a nigger?

VERNON: What? Where did you learn that word?

LAURAUL: Bobby at school told me that you and I are both niggers and that Mommy's a traitor bitch.

VERNON: *(Doesn't really know how to respond. Pause.)* Nigger is a very bad word Lauraul, and Bobby was mean and nasty for calling you and I that. No one here is a Ni—is a Nigger. If anybody ever calls you that again, I want you to tell the teacher. Do you understand?

LAURAUL: *(Shakes her head yes.)* Is Mommy a traitor bitch then?

VERNON: No. Mommy's not a traitor. And don't ever use the word bitch. It's very bad. Your mommy's the most wonderful woman in the world. Remember that. I love you.

(They hug.)

VERNON: I don't want anything bad to ever happen to you.

LAURAUL: I love you too Daddy.

CAROLYN: *(Returning.)* Dinner's ready.

SCENE TWO

At rise, VERNON and CAROLYN are in the bedroom after dinner, putting on their pajamas.

CAROLYN: What's wrong honey? Didn't you like your dinner?

VERNON: Dinner was great. *(Pause.)* It. It's happening.

CAROLYN: What's happening?

VERNON: A kid named Bobby said something to Lauraul at school today.

CAROLYN: I know Bobby. What did he say?

VERNON: He told her that she and I are niggers and that you're a traitor bitch.

CAROLYN: *(Shocked.)* Bobby said that? I wonder who taught him that kind of language?

VERNON: I'm sure he heard it from his parents.

CAROLYN: He seems like such a sweet little boy.

VERNON: Little kids don't come up with stuff like that by themselves.

CAROLYN: What are we going to do?

VERNON: What is there to do?

CAROLYN: We could send her to another school.

VERNON: That won't do anything. Everybody around here is the same. She'd be around the same type of people.

CAROLYN: *(Getting offended.)* What's that supposed to mean?

VERNON: You know damn well what it means. Everybody around here is a piece of white trash.

CAROLYN: I hate when you get this way.

VERNON: I fucking told you we shouldn't have moved to redneck Indiana with these pickup-truck-driving, sister-fucking, Confederate-flag-flying, shotgun-toting white trash hicks! But no, you wanted to live near your white trash family, so here we are!

CAROLYN: Don't you dare try to blame this on me.

VERNON: Oh I'm sorry! Who should I be blaming this on?

CAROLYN: How could I have foreseen this?

(LAURAUL enters, but they don't see her.)

VERNON: I told you this would happen. I wanted to move to New Jersey with nice, rich, mild-mannered, liberal-minded white people—

CAROLYN: There would be racism there too!

VERNON: Yes! But the racism would consist of people inviting Lauraul on ski trips, to fancy dinners, and trying to get their sons to date Lauraul to prove that they aren't bigots. That's the racism in white-rich-liberal America! Being extra nice to black people to show how unracist they are. Those are my type of bigots and I wish that my daughter was going to school with them right now.

CAROLYN: *(Crying.)* You're not being fair! Can't you understand that these are the type of people that I grew up with? When you insult them you insult me. I know they're ignorant, and it makes me ashamed sometimes. But my father's dying, and I feel that I should be near him right now.

(VERNON goes and puts his arm around her.)

VERNON: I'm sorry honey. I'm sorry for blowing up like that.

CAROLYN: We can move to New Jersey or wherever you want after my father—after this is all over. Okay?

VERNON: Okay. I just don't want Lauraul to have to deal with these types of problems.

CAROLYN: I know. It shouldn't be long. The doctor only gave him six months.

VERNON: But that was over two years ago and he keeps on ticking.

LAURAUL: Are you finished fighting now?

CAROLYN: We won't fight anymore. Come here honey.

(LAURAUL climbs in her mother's lap and they all hug as the lights fade to black.)

SCENE THREE

At rise, LAURAUL and CAROLYN have just shown up at LAURAUL's mother's house unexpectedly.

GRANDMOTHER: This is a surprise!

(GRANDMOTHER picks up LAURAUL.)

GRANDMOTHER: How's my apple pie?

LAURAUL: Fine Grandma.

GRANDMOTHER: How's school?

LAURAUL: Wonderful!

CAROLYN: Why don't you go in the den and play your video games so Mommy and Grammy can talk.

LAURAUL: Yaay! Video games! *(Runs off.)*

GRANDMOTHER: She is the sweetest child.

CAROLYN: She's a dream come true.

GRANDMOTHER: What's wrong dear? Why do you seem so sad?

CAROLYN: Lauraul's having problems at school.

GRANDMOTHER: What kinds of problems?

CAROLYN: She's been getting called names.

GRANDMOTHER: What kinds of names?

CAROLYN: Nigger. And a little boy told her that I was a white traitor bitch. I don't know what to do.

GRANDMOTHER: Well, Lauraul seems okay. That's what's important.

CAROLYN: She's not affected because she doesn't know what those words mean.

GRANDMOTHER: There's really nothing to get upset about. Kids will be kids. We all get called names in school.

CAROLYN: This is different Mom! This is just the beginning. These kids barely know what race is right now. The racism is only going to get worse as these kids get older.

GRANDMOTHER: You don't know that. You're overreacting.

CAROLYN: How can you say that? Are you saying these people aren't racists? You've lived here for forty years. You should know that they are better than anyone!

GRANDMOTHER: You should be ashamed of yourself! Generalizing like that! Your neighbors are good Christian people! You may think that they have some outdated views, but they have god in their hearts, and that's what matters.

CAROLYN: These people are racist trash!

GRANDMOTHER: Don't you dare speak that way in this house. You get this nasty talk from your husband! That's where you get it from. Him and his fancy schools and his snobbish city

ways have taught you to look down on your heritage! That man has taught you to look down on your own parents! *(Starts to sob.)* You obviously think that your mother and your dying father are trailer trash too.

CAROLYN: I'm not going to let you do this to me. I love you and Dad very much. But I need you to recognize that we have a problem with Lauraul's classmates and something needs to be done about it.

GRANDMOTHER: *(Accusing.)* He's trying to get you to move away from me! That's what this is about. Vernon's filling your head with this nonsense so that he can raise Lauraul around a bunch of citified snobs!

CAROLYN: Stop it Mom! Just stop it! Vernon's not trying to move us away from here.

GRANDMOTHER: It'd be a sin to leave your dying father. I can't believe you're trying to leave us alone in our old age.

CAROLYN: We're not going anywhere Mom.

GRANDMOTHER: Promise?

CAROLYN: I promise. *(Pause.)* You're right Mom. I'm probably overreacting.

(They hug.)

SCENE FOUR

It is six years later. LAURAUL is fourteen and in high school. The grandfather still has not died. At rise, LAURAUL and KIM, who is also half-white, have been thrown against a wall by WHITE SU-PREMACISTS at their school, MITCH and his gang. LAURAUL and KIM are dressed in all black with spikes, like rebellious punk rockers. MITCH Shouts at LAURAUL and KIM while WHITE SUPREMACISTS #1 and #2 pin them against the wall.

LAURAUL: Get off of me! *(Struggles.)*

MITCH: You fucking half-man half-monkey nigger-mutt! Why don't you go to the ghetto where you belong? You should go deal drugs and get shot like the rest of your people do.

(She elbows him and WHITE SUPREMACIST #1 restrains her harder. He then licks her face.)

MITCH: I should fuck your ass good and hard for elbowing me like that. A good drilling would teach you that your place is beneath the white man, to submit to his every desire.

KIM: Why don't you say something creative. You always say the same boring shit!

(MITCH slaps KIM.)

MITCH: Shutup you stupid slant-eyed gook. Your people shouldn't be allowed to drive because you can't see straight.

WHITE SUPREMACIST #1: Why don't you go back to the rice paddy where you belong.

KIM: Shutup.

MITCH: Tell me what this means you stupid chink: Bong Chong Ding Dong Bing Bang Bong Dang Dong.

KIM: It means you've got a small dick and you fuck your mother.

SCENE FIVE

At rise, KIM and LAURAUL are walking home after school.

KIM: I'm sick of this shit. Every day it's the same.

LAURAUL: I hate those motherfuckers.

KIM: Don't they have better things to do than to follow us around saying: "Nigger."

(They start imitating Mitch to each other.)

LAURAUL: "Gook."

KIM: "Half-breed mutt."

LAURAUL: Who are you calling a half-breed mutt!? You're a half-breed mutt you slant-eyed chink!

(They laugh, and their act stops.)

KIM: What do you want to do?

LAURAUL: This town sucks. There's nowhere we can go around here without getting made fun of or beat up.

(Pause.)

KIM: I've got some weed at my house.

LAURAUL: Why didn't you say that before? Let's go!

SCENE SIX

At rise, LAURAUL and KIM are in KIM's room smoking a joint.

LAURAUL: I hate being black.

(KIM starts laughing.)

LAURAUL: What?

KIM: *(Very amused.)* What do you mean by that?

LAURAUL: I mean that I hate being black.

KIM: *(Laughs harder this time.)* What kind of thing is that to say?

LAURAUL: I mean it. I wish I was one-hundred-percent white like my mother.

KIM: *(Amazed.)* I can't believe you just said that!

LAURAUL: What's so hard to believe?

KIM: Can I tell you a secret?

LAURAUL: Yeah.

KIM: I feel the same way.

LAURAUL: Really?

KIM: Yeah. I hate not being able to see straight.

LAURAUL: *(Busts out laughing.)* I hate the fact that *(Makes quotation marks with her fingers.)* "My People" are a bunch of poor, uneducated monkeys, who do nothing but wear baggy clothes and deal drugs all day. *(She starts to imitate a homeboy from the ghetto. To KIM.)* "Yo my nigga. You a fine lookin ho! I'll buy you a Happy Meal baby, then we'll go back to my crib for a little bump and grind."

KIM: *(Laughing.)* At least your people know how to eat with forks and knives. My people still eat with wooden sticks! My people all work in prostitution, dry cleaning, and nail salons. *(Heavy Asian accent.)* Would you like the egg foo young or the mu shu pork? *(Acting like a prostitute.)* Me love you long time. Me fucky fucky real good.

(They laugh. Pause.)

LAURAUL: I mean, why did my mother marry my father? That's what I can't figure out. If she had just married a white guy instead of that nigger then I wouldn't have all of these problems.

KIM: On some level I wish that my father had married a white woman instead of a Korean, but on the other hand, if he hadn't then I wouldn't be me. I'd be someone completely different. You know?

LAURAUL: I know. But I don't really like being me. *(Pause.)* I wish I had long flowing blonde hair, ivory skin, pink lips, and light blue eyes.

KIM: We all dream about that sometimes. But this is the hand that we've been dealt. I love you just the way you are.

LAURAUL: I love you just the way you are too.

KIM: Best friends forever?

LAURAUL: Best friends forever.

(They hug.)

SCENE SEVEN

At rise, CAROLYN and VERNON are sitting in their living room when LAURAUL walks in the door.

CAROLYN: Hey honey.

LAURAUL: Hey Mom.

(She goes over and hugs her mother.)

VERNON: How was school today?

(LAURAUL quickly runs up the stairs without saying anything to her father.)

VERNON: Why won't she talk to me anymore?

CAROLYN: She's fourteen Vernon. Teenage girls are very temperamental.

VERNON: She talks to you.

CAROLYN: Yes, because she's turning into a woman. She just identifies with me more at this stage of her life. She's going through a lot of changes like discovering boys and getting her period—

VERNON: I don't think I need to hear about that.

CAROLYN: I'm just saying that I acted the same way towards my father when I was her age.

VERNON: Are you sure that I haven't done anything to upset her?

CAROLYN: Trust me. In a couple of years you'll be her best friend again. *(She kisses him on his forehead.)*

VERNON: I guess you're right. I just miss my little girl.

(The phone rings, and VERNON answers it.)

VERNON: Hello. Uh-huh. Okay. I'll be right there. *(Hangs up the phone.)* I've got an emergency at the hospital.

CAROLYN: How long will you be gone?

VERNON: Don't know. A couple of hours.

(They kiss, and he walks out the door. Then LAURAUL walks down the stairs.)

LAURAUL: Where'd he go?

CAROLYN: To the hospital. Can I talk to you for a moment?

LAURAUL: Sure.

CAROLYN: Why won't you talk to your father anymore?

(Silence.)

CAROLYN: You're really hurting him. He loves you very much.

(Long pause.)

LAURAUL: Why did you marry Dad?

CAROLYN: I married your father because I love him.

LAURAUL: Did it bother you that he was black when you first met him?

(Pause.)

CAROLYN: No. Well. I knew there would be some problems.

LAURAUL: Like what?

CAROLYN: I really don't want to talk about this.

LAURAUL: Fine. *(Gets up and starts to leave.)*

CAROLYN: Come back Lauraul.

(LAURAUL comes back.)

CAROLYN: I just don't like to think about those times. I was a different person when I met your father. I grew up in this town. People are good here, but they have some ignorant and outdated views. I was one of them. When I fell in love with your father in college it surprised me. I didn't want it to happen and I resisted it at every turn. I don't like to think about those days because I treated your father very poorly at times, because of my prejudice and ignorance. It wasn't fair to him. But no matter how hard I fought I couldn't shake the love I had for him. Your father taught me how to let go. He taught me not to care about what other people thought about us. That the only thing that matters is the love we have for one another. Your father has made me the happiest woman alive. I hope you meet a man just like your father some day.

LAURAUL: I don't.

CAROLYN: What's that supposed to mean?

LAURAUL: *(Angry.)* Did you ever think about what your decision would do to your children? About what that decision has done to me?

CAROLYN: What decision?

LAURAUL: Your decision to marry a fucking nigger!

CAROLYN: Lauraul! What on earth do you mean? How can you talk about your father like that?

LAURAUL: Your selfish decision to marry that man has ruined my life!

CAROLYN: *(As if she's not sure who she's speaking to.)* Lauraul?

LAURAUL: Yeah. You heard me. I wish I was never born. I'm a fucking monster! I'm half-woman half-beast. Why couldn't you have married someone white so that I would be normal?

(CAROLYN is speechless. LAURAUL runs out of the room.)

SCENE EIGHT

At rise, LAURAUL is late to class and MITCH is skipping class. They are alone in the hallway. LAURAUL tries to run away from him, but he throws her against the wall.

MITCH: Where do you think you're going mutt?

LAURAUL: Get off of me asshole!

(MITCH pushes his pelvis against her.)

MITCH: Where do you get off talking to a white man like that? I should stick my dick in your mouth and shoot my cum down your throat! Then you might learn how to shut up when your superiors are speaking to you.

(The sexual tension is thick and obvious between them. He has her pressed against the wall and their mouths are practically touching.)

MITCH: What do you think about that?

LAURAUL: *(Pause. Hesitant.)* I—I think I'd like that.

(He rubs his pelvis against her, and she moans.)

MITCH: What did you say nigger bitch?

(He pushes his pelvis against her, and she moans again.)

LAURAUL: I said I think I'd like for you to stick your dick in my mouth and shoot your cum down my throat.

(They kiss uncontrollably. Then they stop and look around for a private place. They go into a janitor's closet where the audience is still able to see them.)

MITCH: You want the white man's dick inside you?

(LAURAUL shakes her head lustfully.)

MITCH: Say it! Say: "I want the white man's dick inside me."

LAURAUL: *(Takes off her underwear. She is still wearing her skirt.)* I want the white man's dick inside me.

(She unbuckles his belt, and he pushes her against the wall, and they start to have sex.)

LAURAUL: The white man's dick feels so good.

MITCH: Your nigger pussy is tight!

LAURAUL: I love the white man's dick. He can do what he wants with me any time!

MITCH: Nigger-mutt.

LAURAUL: I love the—

(The sex has ended and they are both panting heavily.)

SCENE NINE

At rise, MITCH and LAURAUL walk on stage hand in hand. He has brought her to a meeting of his white supremacist group. The other members of the group are looking at MITCH like he's lost his mind.

MITCH: She's cool guys.

WHITE SUPREMACIST #1: What do you mean she's cool?

WHITE SUPREMACIST #2: She can't be cool she's a fucking nig—she's black Mitch!

LAURAUL: *(As if ready to fight.)* You call me black again and I'll bite off your testicles, chew them up, then spit them down your fucking throat.

(WHITE SUPREMACISTS #1 and #2 are taken aback. MITCH comes between them.)

MITCH: She's not black, she's half white. She's one of us.

LAURAUL: That's right. I'm renouncing every drop of black blood in my body. I'm purging myself of the evil within. I hate niggers.

WHITE SUPREMACIST #1: Why should we believe you?

WHITE SUPREMACIST # 2: This is fucking weird. This has got to be some sort of fucking trick.

LAURAUL: Don't fucking doubt me! You think you hate black people? You think you hate black people? You don't know the first thing about hating them! You can't truly hate black people, until you've been one of them. Till you've walked in their shoes. Only then could you start to understand. I understand because I'm infected with their disease. Their dark disgusting dirtiness covers my body and their animal-like wool infects my hair! I'm cursed with being related to every welfare ghetto in this country! But I fight it. I fight it every day, and I hate my father more than anything for infecting me with this disease! So don't talk to me about hating niggers! You have no authority. You don't know the first thing about hating them. The hate you feel pales in comparison to mine. I have a wealth of wisdom that you can't even begin to understand. You will learn a lot from me.

(They're all speechless.)

WHITE SUPREMACIST #1: I'm convinced.

WHITE SUPREMACIST #2: Me too.

MITCH: You're in.

(Lights dim, and they perform their induction ceremony, which includes giving her a tattoo and shaving her head. This should happen onstage and have the feel of a holy ritual from the Catholic church.)

SCENE TEN

At rise, LAURAUL has just entered KIM's house.

KIM: Lauraul!

LAURAUL: *(Coyly.)* What?

KIM: You don't have any hair!

(LAURAUL laughs.)

KIM: Did you shave it yourself?

LAURAUL: No. Mitch did.

KIM: Skinhead Mitch?

LAURAUL: Yup. He's my boyfriend now.

KIM: You're joking!

LAURAUL: I'm not.

(KIM is shocked and anxious to hear the details. They go into teenage girl mode.)

KIM: This is unbelievable! When did this happen? And how?

LAURAUL: I was late to class, and I guess Mitch was skipping class. Anyway, we were alone in the hall together and he threw me against the wall and started taunting me. He was saying things like: "You filthy nigger, I should stick my dick in your mouth and shoot my cum down your throat to teach you not to talk back to your superiors."

KIM: Had you said anything to provoke that, or was he just being himself?

LAURAUL: *(Thinks.)* I think I told him to get away from me after he threw me against the wall. *(Thinks again.)* Yeah, that's what happened. That's why he said that.

KIM: That makes sense. Go on.

LAURAUL: Anyway, the way he had me pinned against the wall was making me so hot. I was so turned on that my panties were completely soaked and cum was beginning to run down my leg.

KIM: Oh my god! This is making me hot. Keep on going!

LAURAUL: Then he started rubbing his boner up against me as he called me nigger and mutt. It was out of control.

KIM: How big is his dick?

LAURAUL: Huge! *(Shows KIM how big his dick is with her hands.)* Anyway, suddenly we start making out.

KIM: In the hallway?

LAURAUL: In the hallway. But then we went into this janitor's closet and he fucked me.

KIM: *(Goes wild over this.)* Oh my god! You lost your virginity in a janitor's closet! That's so exciting!

LAURAUL: Yup. It was crazy.

KIM: I can't believe you lost your virginity to skinhead Mitch. I guess he really doesn't hate black people as much as he claims to.

(They laugh.)

KIM: Did it hurt? Did you bleed?

LAURAUL: I bled a little, and it hurt when he first stuck it in, but then it started to feel alright. Maybe it didn't hurt because I was super wet.

KIM: That's probably the reason. I hear most girls hurt a lot. How long did it last?

LAURAUL: Not long. Maybe a minute. Two minutes.

KIM: That's it?

LAURAUL: Time didn't matter. For those few moments Mitch and I were one. We melded into one another.

KIM: Did you use protection?

LAURAUL: There wasn't time for that. I'll just get the morning-after pill tomorrow. I hear it's no big deal. *(Pause.)* I joined his group.

KIM: That's weird.

LAURAUL: I know. I want you to join too.

KIM: Do you think they'd let me?

LAURAUL: Sure. As long as I vouch for you.

KIM: I don't know. Something about a black chick and an asian chick joining a white supremacist group doesn't seem right.

LAURAUL: What about our conversation the other day? You said that you wished you were all white too.

KIM: I know. But I'm not. I feel like I'd be betraying my mother.

LAURAUL: You have to forget about her. You have to act as if she doesn't exist.

KIM: I can't do that.

LAURAUL: Yes you can. I did it with my father. You must turn your back on the blood that taints you.

KIM: Let me sleep on it. Okay?

LAURAUL: Okay. But I really want you to do this. I need you.

(They hug.)

SCENE ELEVEN

At rise, LAURAUL is at her GRAND-MOTHER's house. They are eating cake.

LAURAUL: This is the best cake I've ever had.

GRANDMOTHER: It's your grandfather's recipe.

LAURAUL: Really? I didn't know Grandpa could cook.

GRANDMOTHER: Of yes. He did all the cooking before he got sick.

LAURAUL: How long has Grandpa been sick for?

GRANDMOTHER: It's been about ten years. He was diagnosed with cancer when you were just a little girl. *(Pause.)* You and your parents moved here because your mother wanted to be near your grandfather when he died.

LAURAUL: No one ever told me that.

(GRANDFATHER moans in back room.)

GRANDMOTHER: That's because it's a sore spot in your parents' relationship.

LAURAUL: Why is that?

GRANDMOTHER: Your father never wanted to live here. He didn't believe that a child should be with her father while he's on his deathbed. He wanted to raise you in New Jersey around a bunch of elitist snobs. If he's so unhappy here, he should move to snobland all by himself. *(Pause.)* I like having you and your mother around. I don't want to be all alone after your grandfather passes. *(Long pause.)* Are you upset that your parents didn't move when you were a child?

LAURAUL: No. Why would I be upset?

GRANDMOTHER: Because you get made fun of. No one likes getting made fun of.

LAURAUL: *(Getting suspicious.)* Why are we talking about this?

GRANDMOTHER: Your mother's very worried. She told me about the conversation you had with her.

(Pause.)

GRANDMOTHER: About how you feel about your father.

(Pause.)

LAURAUL: So what?

GRANDMOTHER: So. Can I tell you something?

LAURAUL: Sure.

GRANDMOTHER: You have to swear to secrecy.

LAURAUL: *(Intrigued.)* I swear.

GRANDMOTHER: I think you're right.

LAURAUL: Really?

GRANDMOTHER: Yes. Your mother should never have married that nigger. It's been nothing but problems since she met him. When you were a child she came crying to me about the fact that kids were making fun of you. What did she expect? Everyone could see that coming a mile away. But what really upset me was the fact that she had the nerve to blame it on your classmates and their families! She called them ignorant and racist! I have lived in this town for forty-six years and I can assure you that the people in this community are neither ignorant or racist! They're just good Christians. And all good Christians know that the mixing of races is a sin. Your mother and father are the ignorant ones.

LAURAUL: Do you think that I'm a sin?

GRANDMOTHER: *(Hugs LAURAUL.)* Oh no honey. Your parents' sins are not your fault. I'm just sorry that they didn't consider your feelings before they had you. It's not fair that you've been treated this way all these years. And it makes me love you even more to know that you're rejecting the culture and the blood that your father infected you with.

LAURAUL: Thank you Grandma. I'm so glad that someone understands.

GRANDMOTHER: But you know that you must fight hard every day to resist your tainted blood. It's very powerful, and can sneak up on you when you least expect it. So I'm giving you something to help you to resist it. *(Takes out LAURAUL's grandfather's grand wizard Klan hood.)*

LAURAUL: What's this?

GRANDMOTHER: Your grandfather was a grand wizard in the Klan before he got sick. This is the hood he wore.

LAURAUL: *(Overwhelmed with emotion.)* This is the most beautiful thing that I've ever seen.

GRANDMOTHER: It will give you the strength to eliminate the poison which infects your blood.

LAURAUL: I will eliminate it. I promise. *(Pause.)* I love you Grandma.

GRANDMOTHER: I love you too.

SCENE TWELVE

At rise, LAURAUL, MITCH, and GANG are at KIM's house. LAURAUL knocks on the door, and KIM answers it.

LAURAUL: You ready?

KIM: I'm not going.

LAURAUL: Why not? You said you wanted to.

KIM: I changed my mind. I don't agree with what you're doing, and I don't want to be part of it.

LAURAUL: I can't believe you're doing this to me.

MITCH: (To LAURAUL.) Never trust a chink. I told you she wasn't cool.

KIM: I'm not going to turn my back on who I am. You can't just ignore your culture and who you are because it sucks sometimes, or because it's inconvenient for you. I like being me, in spite of the fact that people make fun of me and give me mean looks. I'm proud of who I am and I wouldn't change that for the world. Please don't do this Lauraul!

(MITCH gives a signal, and WHITE SUPREMACISTS #1 and #2 restrain her.)

MITCH: Shut the fuck up! You better not say a god damn thing to anyone. You understand me?

(She shakes her head yes, and they let her go.)

LAURAUL: (To KIM.) Mitch is right. I should never have trusted a fucking chink.

SCENE THIRTEEN

At rise, LAURAUL, MITCH, and GANG are putting on Klan uniforms. LAURAUL wears her grandfather's. While they are getting dressed, we hear them saying: "This is so cool." and "This is awesome." Then they erect and light a burning cross on the lawn of LAURAUL's parent's house. They watch in amazement for a few moments. At this point, VERNON runs out of the house and starts running towards them, and they try to get away.

VERNON: You better run you cowards!

(LAURAUL can't run as fast as the others and is running last in the group. VERNON is running right behind her

and grabs hold of her arm. He pulls off her hood. He is shocked when he realizes it is LAURAUL.)

VERNON: Lauraul. My own daughter.

SCENE FOURTEEN

At rise, LAURAUL and CAROLYN are sitting. VERNON is pacing. An uncomfortable amount of time passes before he speaks.

VERNON: I can't believe the level of disrespect you've shown me. Do you have anything to say for yourself?

LAURAUL: Fuck you!

CAROLYN: Lauraul!

(CAROLYN smacks LAURAUL.)

CAROLYN: How dare you speak to your father that way!

LAURAUL: Fuck you too you white traitor bitch!

(CAROLYN starts to hit LAURAUL again, but VERNON catches her hand.)

VERNON: That's not going to help. (He kisses CAROLYN on the forehead.) I think I need to talk to Lauraul alone.

(CAROLYN nods her head yes, and they kiss. Then she walks up the stairs.)

VERNON: (Sincerely.) Your mother told me about the conversation that you and she had the other day, and it hurt me very much.

LAURAUL: You've hurt me more!

VERNON: I know you feel that way but I don't understand why. I don't understand why you never tried to reach out to me. Why you never told me how you were feeling. Don't you know that we've had many of the same experiences? That I've been made fun of. That I've been discriminated against too?

(Silence.)

VERNON: Do you know how hard it is for a black man to become a doctor? You can't comprehend the obstacles I faced. *(Pause.)* I have broken my back to provide for you. I've done everything in my power to make sure that you wouldn't have to face the obstacles that I faced. So that your life would be easier. So that you won't have to work a full-time job to put yourself through college like I did. It amazes—

LAURAUL: I don't give a damn about what you've been through! I don't give a fuck about what you think you've done for me.

VERNON: *(Angry.)* What the hell has gotten into you? You speak to me as if I'm a stranger! As if I'm not the man who gave you life.

LAURAUL: You seem to think I owe you something! Well guess what? I didn't want this life! I wish I was never born! But since I have this life I'm going to live it as I see fit.

VERNON: You burned a cross on your own father's lawn and you're hanging out with skinheads! That's how you see fit to lead your life?

LAURAUL: I am a skinhead.

VERNON: Do you really think those racist motherfuckers are your friends!?

Don't you see a contradiction with a black woman being a skinhead?

LAURAUL: They understand how I feel! They are my heritage. Mom's dad was a Grand Wizard in the Klan.

VERNON: That may be true. But my father. Your other grandfather would turn over in his grave if he could hear you speaking right now! Don't you understand that the burning cross was a symbol used by the Klan to oppress you ancestors for over a hundred years?

LAURAUL: Shutup! I'm sick of your fucking lectures about my ancestors! Those niggers you talk about are not my ancestors. I don't want anything to do with them. You can have them if you want. *(Runs out of the house.)*

VERNON: Don't leave Lauraul. I love you.

SCENE FIFTEEN

LAURAUL walks into her house the next morning. VERNON is alone in the living room reading the newspaper.

VERNON: *(Sweetly.)* Hey Lauraul.

(LAURAUL pulls a gun out of her bag and shoots him twice.)

LAURAUL: I hope you burn in hell nigger! *(Pause. She goes and stands over his body.)* I hope you burn in Nigger Hell.

(Blackout.)

(End of play.)

LINNEA

John Regis

JOHN REGIS is an actor, a director, a teacher, and a playwright.
He was born in Marblehead, Massachusetts, on July 4, 1958,
and raised in both Peabody, Massachusetts, and Hampton, New
Hampshire. He received a BA in communications from Fordham
University, and studied with Stella Adler and Mario Sileti at the
Stella Adler Conservatory. He is the author of *St. Vitus' Dance*, an
adaptation of Dostoyevsky's *The Idiot* (also director: Theater Off
Park, 1993); and *Stavrogin's Confession*, adapted from Dostoyevsky's
The Possessed (New York International Fringe Festival, 1998; The
Storm Theatre, 1999; Three River Arts Festival, Pittsburgh, 2005).
His adaptation of William Tenn's science fiction novella, *Winthrop
Was Stubborn*, was commissioned for the 2006 Three River Arts
Festival. He is a founding member of The Storm Theatre, and has
directed its productions of Jean Anouilh's *Eurydice* (2000), Luigi
Pirandello's *Henry VI* (2001), and *Job* by Karol Wojtyla (2007).
He has also directed nearly forty Shakespeare productions with
students at both the Bank Street School and the Calhoun School
in New York City. Regis teaches drama and video making at the
Bank Street School, is a lifelong Red Sox fan, and lives in New
York's West Village.

Linnea was first presented by The Storm Theatre (Peter Dobbins, Artistic Director; Chance Michaels, Producing Director) on January 11, 2007, at The Storm Theatre, New York City, with the following cast and credits:

Danny...Josh Vasquez
Susan.. Jenn Zarine Habeck
Beggar King .... Ken Trammell
Maggie ....Benita Robledo
Cody Marlin ....Jamil Mena
A Waitress ....Christy Linn
Red .... Stephen Logan Day
Slim ....Gabe Levey
Clown ....David Bodenschatz
Linnea...Benita Robledo

Note: The original production included the nonspeaking characters "A Waitress" and "Clown."

Director: Peter Dobbins
Assistant Director: Rachel Mudd
Stage Manager: Michelle Kafel
Scenic Design: Todd Edward Ivins
Costume Design: Jessica Lustig
Lighting Design: Bill Sheehan/Matthew Gordon
Sound Design: Scott O'Brien
Composer: Jeremiah Lockwood
Choreographer: Enrique Cruz DeJesus
Associate Lighting Designer: Sandy Paul
Program Designer: Philip Raiten

> *I dreamt a Dream! What can it mean?*
> *—William Blake*

CAST

(In order of appearance.)

DANNY: A young writer
SHADOW DANCER
BEGGAR KING/MAN: A homeless person
MAGGIE: A student and bookseller
CODY MARLIN: A painter
SUSAN: A waitress
RED: A clown
SLIM: A clown
LINNEA: A stripper

TIME AND PLACE

The action of the play takes place in real and imagined places in Park Slope Brooklyn, the East Village, and the Lower West Side of New York City in a spring, summer, and fall in the early 1990s.

ACT ONE. SONGS OF INNOCENCE.

Prologue. Danny's just-below-street-level-apartment in Park Slope. Dawn.

Scene 1. A park bench in Tompkins Square Park, evening of the same April day.

Scene 2. The Grassroots Tavern, later that night.

Scene 3. Fallen Angels, a fictional topless bar in Lower Manhattan, a few hours later.

Scene 4. The Blue and Gold, a Ukrainian bar on East Seventh, a few hours later.

Scene 5. Tompkins Square Park, dawn.

ACT TWO. SONGS OF EXPERIENCE.

Scene 6. Danny's "Funk Cell," an early morning in May.

Scene 7. Tompkins Square Park, a week or so later.

Scene 8. Cody's loft in Alphabet City, late afternoon, two months later.

Scene 9. Fallen Angels, a few nights later.

Epilogue. Tompkins Square Park, the next morning.

ACT ONE
(SONGS OF INNOCENCE)
Prologue.

*DANNY's just-below-street-level apart-
ment in Park Slope, Brooklyn. Dawn.
DANNY lies asleep on a futon, a beat-up
thrift store overcoat for a blanket.*

*Music up: A siren song. A shadowy figure,
female in form, enters the dark room.
She beckons the dreamer with a strange,
Balinese-like motion. She leans down to
him, whispers in his ear, and then kisses
the top of his head. DANNY stirs. The
SHADOW DANCER exits. The music
echoes out.*

*Lights rise. It's early morning. DANNY
awakens. He kicks off his overcoat and
swings his feet onto the floor. DANNY's
twenty-six or -seven, with large, gentle,
dreamer eyes. He's dressed in an old flannel
shirt and wrinkled chinos. He shakes out
the cobwebs, looks about the room. The futon rests in one corner—in the other, there's
a bureau. In the middle, against the wall,
there's a writer's desk with a manuscript
and electric typewriter. DANNY crosses
to the back wall of the apartment, and
opens three wooden-shuttered, iron-barred
windows that look out onto a courtyard,
and, just beyond that, a quiet city street.
The brilliant morning light floods into the
room. Outside, birds chirp.*

*From beneath the futon, DANNY
produces a notebook and pen. He sits
on his bed and writes. Outside, church
bells chime.*

*DANNY closes his notebook. He puts on
some workboots, as well as the overcoat, and
a well-worn Boston Red Sox cap which was
jammed into the coat's pocket. He replaces
the cap with his notebook and pen and exits
the room. Lights fade out.*

Scene 1.

*Lights rise on a park bench in Tompkins
Square Park. It's now evening of this same
April day. Behind the bench, a street lamp
filters light through overhanging tree
branches. DANNY sits on the park bench
writing in a notebook. Offstage, the sound
of squeaking wheels. Enter BEGGAR
KING, a grandiose homeless person pushing a battered shopping cart filled with his
belongings. DANNY pauses in his work.
BEGGAR KING positions the cart near the
bench and begins his spiel, gesticulating in
the "old style."*

BEGGAR KING: My friend, you see
before you a truly broken man. A broken
down bit of Fifth Business. But I was not
always as I am now. Oh no, dear friend,
no! *(Pulls an old headshot out of his cart.)* I
was an actor who could sing! *(Chuckles.)*
Once I played the great stages of the
world: the Lyceum, the Old Vic...the
Burt Reynolds's Dinner Theatre! Why
was my head so big? BECAUSE IT WAS
CHOCK FULL OF DREAMS! But,
that was then, this is now...Conspiracies
were hatched. Equity Warmongers held
my career at bay! In fear and loathing, I
gnashed my teeth, and cried out: why?
Why! WHY JERRY ORBACH AND
NOT ME! But, it was and is a question
without an answer. A question blown to
the wind (so to speak). So what remains?
Inexplicable dumb show? TV naturalism?
I SLEEP ON A FUCKING SUBWAY
GRATE! I WANT A HANDOUT,
NOT A KING'S RANSOM! My friend,
I have now reached the final humiliation.
I needs must stand before you...head
bowed...arm extended...palm up-
turned. I have not asked to drink from
this cup; it has been thrust upon me (so
to speak). Therefore, I must beseech
you: please...please...please: help out

an old player who's fallen on hard times. I thank you.

(Pause.)

DANNY: I, eh, I'm afraid I haven't any change.

(BEGGAR KING visibly deflates.)

DANNY: But…

(BEGGAR KING perks up.)

DANNY: I do have this pint of brandy. Would you like a nip?

BEGGAR KING: Fair enough, old boy.

(He sits down on the bench. DANNY hands over his pint.)

DANNY: Here, put the quietus to it.

BEGGAR KING: Cheers. *(Drains the bottle, hands it back.)* For this relief, much thanks.

DANNY: Don't mention it.

BEGGAR KING: So my boy, what brings you out so early in the season?

DANNY: The promise of spring.

BEGGAR KING: Oh yes. Still, this April chill's rather daunting.

DANNY: That's where the pint comes in, eh old man?

(They both laugh.)

DANNY: No, I love to come to the East Village this time of year. Sit in Tompkins Square Park. Write down what I hear, see, and feel.

BEGGAR KING: Yes, well this was once a wondrous place. Do you remember the old band shell?

DANNY: Yeah, sure.

BEGGAR KING: The old band shell was sanctuary for our kind. Many a long, cold night, by way of diversion, I would perform for the unfortunates huddled there: IF THERE BE CHORDS OR KNIVES, CATARACTS OR HURRICANOES…But then, the tractors came and tore it down, and the police came and hustled us out. Now our kind pass through this park like shadows in the Elysian Fields.

DANNY: For a shadow you do all right. Look what I jotted down as you came up to me. *(Holding up his notebook.)* Read that.

BEGGAR KING: "Enter the Beggar King." Hmm. Beggar King! I like that. Once it was even true.

DANNY: It's still true. Your monologue attests to undiminished powers.

BEGGAR KING: It really did *play* tonight, didn't it? You should see when it's performed on the Broadway Local: pure gold!

DANNY: I can imagine.

BEGGAR KING: *(Stands.)* You were right, dear boy: your brandy worked wonders. That and your kind words. Until the next. *(Exits.)*

(DANNY returns to his notebook. Enter MAGGIE, pulling a child's red wagon loaded with cardboard boxes and a sheet of plywood. She crosses down right to a trash barrel, where she creates a makeshift book table out of the plywood sheet, stocking it with books contained in the boxes. MAGGIE is in her early twenties, has a cheerful, sometimes mocking countenance—wears a grey Fordham sweatshirt and fingerless gloves. Her setup catches DANNY's eye.)

MAGGIE: Wanna buy a book?

DANNY: You're off the beaten path.

MAGGIE: I've lost my spot on St. Marks. Thought I'd try here. So, wanna buy a book?

DANNY: Depends. Whatcha got?

MAGGIE: Well, come over here and see.

DANNY: *(Crossing.)* I'm a sucker for street books.

MAGGIE: I'm banking on that.

DANNY: How so?

MAGGIE: I have you pegged as the aspiring young writer-type.

DANNY: Am I that obvious?

MAGGIE: You might as well put it up in lights!

DANNY: Oh yeah? What are some of the telltale signs?

MAGGIE: Let me count the ways.

DANNY: Please do.

MAGGIE: First, you're alone in the park, writing away in your little notebook.

DANNY: Couldn't that just as easily peg me as an NYU undergrad?

MAGGIE: Couple it with the ratty over-coat...the flannel shirt—did you sleep in that thing, boy?—In fact, your overall *slightly* unkempt appearance. The *slightly* part is extremely significant.

DANNY: *(Holding up the empty pint.)* You've forgotten the concealed pint.

MAGGIE: Thank you. After all, what could be more romantic than equating alcoholism with creativity?

DANNY: *(Laughing.)* The defense rests! I'm every inch the pretentious young writer.

MAGGIE: I didn't say "pretentious," I said "aspiring."

DANNY: Right. Anyway...'bout dem books. *(Begins to study the titles of books.)*

MAGGIE: See anything you like?

DANNY: I dunno. How about Henry Miller?

MAGGIE: How about Henry Miller? Are you into sexist pigs?

DANNY: And you would have me read, what? Susan Sontag? Jane Austen?

MAGGIE: Read anything you want, my dear!

DANNY: Call me Danny.

MAGGIE: Read anything you want, Danny.

(Slight pause.)

DANNY: And you are?

MAGGIE: I won't tell you unless you buy a book.

DANNY: Now, there's an inducement! *(Looks some more.)* Nothing's jumping out at me. Do you have a book by Dostoyevsky?—

MAGGIE: Add that to the list under "pseudo-intellectual literary heroes"!

DANNY: *(Ignoring.)* I've forgotten the title, but I do know it's out of print.

MAGGIE: *The Insulted and Injured.*

DANNY: Yes!

MAGGIE: No! I don't have it.

DANNY: That's too bad. Now I'll never know your name.

MAGGIE: Hold on, hoss…tell ya what we're gonna do. Buy a book. Establish a line of credit with me and I'll promise to get my hands on *The Insulted and Injured*. Deal?

DANNY: Deal. Let's see…I'll take… *(Picking a paperback.)* This.

MAGGIE: *The Idiot*?

DANNY: Contrary to popular opinion, not my autobiography!

MAGGIE: More Dostoyevsky?

DANNY: I congratulate you on your powers of observation.

MAGGIE: But you've read it.

DANNY: Yes, yes I have. How did you know that?

MAGGIE: Elementary, dear Danny. You were asking me to locate one of his rare, out-of-print books. Certainly you've read one of his most famous.

DANNY: Certainly.

MAGGIE: What's this: a token purchase to learn my name and pester me with dates?

DANNY: You see right through me. *(Indicating the book.)* This also happens to be a different translation from the one I've read.

MAGGIE: What's with you and Dostoyevsky? Into suffering?

DANNY: Well, I am a long-time Red Sox fan!

(No reaction.)

DANNY: Actually, I'm trying to adapt *The Idiot* into a play.

MAGGIE: My, aren't we ambitious!

DANNY: Not really. I'm isolating one story line. Do you know the book?

MAGGIE: Uh-huh.

DANNY: I'm revising the love triangle between Prince Myshkin, Rogozhin, and Nastassya Filippovna.

MAGGIE: Sounds like a plan.

DANNY: If it's not, I've been pining away all winter for nothing.

(Slight pause.)

DANNY: Well…what do I owe you?

MAGGIE: Three dollars.

DANNY: *(Takes out his wallet and hands over the money.)* Three dollars.

MAGGIE: Need a bag?

DANNY: Nah. *(Puts the paperback in his coat pocket.)* Well, I—

MAGGIE: My name's Maggie.

DANNY: Well, Maggie, I guess our transaction's complete.

MAGGIE: I guess so.

DANNY: I hope this sale is the first of many tonight.

MAGGIE: Thanks. Maybe this spot will work out.

DANNY: It's a nice spot.

(Slight pause.)

MAGGIE: Give me a week to find *The Insulted and Injured*.

DANNY: Oh…right.

MAGGIE: Come find me. If I'm not here, I'll be on St. Marks.

DANNY: Okay. See you then.

MAGGIE: You promise?

DANNY: Sure. *(Exits.)*

(MAGGIE goes back to stocking her table. The lights fade out.)

SCENE 2.

DANNY sits reading The Idiot *at one of the old, initial-carved tables in the Grassroots—a turn-of-the century tavern on St. Marks. Laid out on the table: a pitcher of beer and a half-filled mug. Up left, half hidden in the darker recesses of the tavern, is another table. There CODY sits, sketching DANNY (something he's presently not aware of). CODY could be anywhere between thirty-five and forty, with piercing eyes deeply set upon a broad forehead. The eyes presently affix on DANNY. Sensing he's being watched, DANNY pauses in his reading. With that, CODY springs up, sketchpad in hand, and approaches DANNY's table. CODY's dressed in a leather jacket, jeans, and biker boots. He arrives at the table, pauses for effect, then with a quick flip, opens his sketchpad. Revealed: a decent likeness of DANNY.*

CODY: Ta-da!

DANNY: Hey, all right!

CODY: You like?

DANNY: I like.

CODY: Could you tell I was sketching you?

DANNY: I knew something was going on. I could…feel your eyes upon me.

CODY: A little creepy, huh?

DANNY: It was a little…strange. *(Laughing.)* Oh, don't get me wrong. I'm flattered you chose me as a subject.

CODY: Hey, you have an interesting face.

DANNY: Oh yeah?

CODY: Very childlike. Sorta like a clown out of makeup.

DANNY: That's funny! In college, my nickname was Jocko.

CODY: Jocko, huh?

DANNY: Yeah, he was like this alter ego of mine. A clown-saint, Fifth Marx Brother type of character I would assume somewhere between my third and fourth pint.

CODY: I never much liked the Marx Brothers. I was more of a Three Stooges fan.

DANNY: With Curly or Shemp as the third stooge?

CODY: Do you even have to ask! Anyway, Jocko me boy: I answer to Cody. Cody Marlin.

DANNY: Cody Marlin.

(They shake.)

DANNY: Wanta help me finish this pitcher, Cody?

CODY: I'll go get my mug.

(He crosses back to his table. In his absence, DANNY flips through the sketchpad. CODY quickly returns, mug in tow.)

DANNY: *(Indicating the sketchpad.)* I hope you don't mind?

CODY: Not at all.

DANNY: *(Indicating the pitcher.)* Help yourself.

CODY: *(Fills his mug, touches up DANNY's.)* Here's to chance encounters.

DANNY: Cheers.

(They clink mugs. CODY downs his in a gulp.)

CODY: Oh yeah! Just what the doctor ordered! *(Refills his mug.)* So, Jocko, what's your road?

DANNY: My, like, Jack Kerouac road?

CODY: Yeah, that works.

DANNY: Holy Boy Road.

CODY: How so?

DANNY: I work at a private school on the Upper West Side.

CODY: With kids?

DANNY: Yep.

CODY: You're a teacher?

DANNY: Of sorts.

CODY: Any other aspirations?

DANNY: Lately, I've been trying my hand at writing. But…

CODY: But?

DANNY: What did Kerouac say? Walking on water doesn't happen overnight.

CODY: Stick to it. You wanta write, write. Me, I aspire to paint. It's my road. But sure as hell not holy!

DANNY: Oh? What road is it then?

CODY: You tell me. See, I live in a loft on Seventh Street—between Avenue D and Loisaida. The kind of neighborhood where ya have ta shoo the crack addicts away at night. Anyway, I spend my time there painting. I'm one of the bright lights of the East Village Jailbird Junkie School of Modern Art. Problem is, Mr. Soho Natural and his Yuppie Mistress—you know, the one he lets run the gallery—THEY JUST DON'T GET IT!—so, like, my phaser's set on Survival Mode. This mode you don't want getting back to the kids. It's based on Cody Marlin's law of the quick score. There are two ways to make a quick score. Number one: the drug trade—if you can't beat the crack addicts, deal to 'em. Number two: the, eh, adventures in the skin trade. You dig?

DANNY: I do, daddy-o! You're on a long-gone, Mad Boy Road!

CODY: *(Laughing.)* Ain't it the truth! Ain't it the truth!

DANNY: So, you don't make any kind of a living as an artist?

CODY: Actually, yeah, I do. Here. *(Takes back the sketchpad, flips through to a new page.)* These buxom biker chicks…they're illustrations I did for *Screw* magazine. I'm also a tattoo artist.

DANNY: Skin trade indeed!

CODY: *(Flipping through the sketchpad.)* I freelance at Smokey Joe's. Right here on St. Marks.

DANNY: I remember walking past it.

CODY: *(Handing back the pad to DANNY.)* Here are samples of my tattoos.

DANNY: *(Perusing.)* I like this one.

CODY: Oh yeah?

DANNY: The way the dragon and the plant life and the buxom biker chicks all intertwine. Reminds me of some of William Blake's engravings.

CODY: You like it? Then come up and see me and I'll put my mark on you.

DANNY: You'd give me a tattoo?

CODY: I won't give you a tattoo. I'll give you a good deal on one—'cause you're my drinking buddy. Interested?

DANNY: Oh, I don't know.

CODY: Come on, Jock: I'll make a man of you yet!

(DANNY grins a goofy grin. CODY roars with laughter, pours himself another drink. DANNY flips to the next page and fixates on the representation there.)

DANNY: Who's this?

CODY: Linnea—she's a stripper who works at Fallen Angels. Do you know it?

DANNY: No.

CODY: It's a downtown dive, on Vestry Street—by the waterfront. One night, I was out on a jag, and stumbled into it. This skinny-legs-and-all chick named Linnea stepped out from behind a screen, and, I mean, mister, I was annihilated. Right then and there, I did her portrait.

DANNY: I can see why: she has a striking face.

CODY: You should see her in the flesh!

DANNY: (Examining.) But she's been through a lot, hasn't she? Look at those eyes. There's a great and terrible pride in those eyes.

CODY: A great and terrible pride. Hmm! That's good.

DANNY: But not original.

CODY: Oh?

DANNY: (Holding up his paperback.) It's from The Idiot.

CODY: Well, original or not, it's true. I'll give you an example. When I showed her this drawing, she was furious. "You may think you captured me—but you didn't! Next time, ask my permission!"

DANNY: That's a strange reaction!

CODY: Same one you'd get in some fuckin' jungle if you tried to photograph the tribal chief.

DANNY: I don't understand.

CODY: Well, there they believe the photographer is tying to steal the chief's soul.

DANNY: I see. Was Linnea right to feel that way about you?

(A slight pause.)

CODY: I think women have great instincts about such things! (Roars with laughter.)

(A pause.)

CODY: You're staring at me, Jock!

DANNY: I'm sorry. It's just—you, you spoke of my face, but yours is fascinating. Sometimes it's mad and gleeful, like a naughty child's. Other times it's quite frightening.

CODY: Have you ever stared at your face in the mirror for a long time? Stared and stared to the point of hallucination? Your face changes. It turns into something demonic, like a gargoyle or a monster.

DANNY: Yes, yes I have!

CODY: Well, Jocko, I'm the fella ya see when you stare too long in the mirror.

(A pause.)

CODY: (Suddenly bursts into laughter.) Just fuckin' with ya! (Takes a final swig of beer.) Anyway, bo, gotta go.

DANNY: Oh?

CODY: Yeah, I got this mark lined up—this Hell's Angel with a back like a Coney Island sideshow! But hey, it pays the rent! *(Stands.)* Jocko, look me up when you decide on that tattoo.

DANNY: Sure thing.

CODY: And, put in a good word for me with Linnea.

DANNY: What? I didn't say anything about going there!

CODY: *(Smiling a gargoyle-like smile.)* Are you kidding me! I saw your face as you gawked at her sketch—you'll go…with my blessing. Just remember: she's mine!

(Roaring with laughter, he crosses back to his original table, gathers his belongings, and strides out of the bar. DANNY is left to ponder CODY's parting remarks. The lights slowly fade to black.)

SCENE 3.

Music up: hard driving and raunchy. Upstage left: a DANCER dances behind a scrim, creating a silhouette. We're in the lounge of Fallen Angels, a (fictional) topless bar near the waterfront in Lower Manhattan. The back wall of the lounge is painted black and scarred with graffiti. Against this back wall, some circular tables and chairs. Two CLOWNS sit at one of the tables drinking boilermakers. RED is short and stocky, and wears a brilliant red wig and "flasher" raincoat. SLIM is tall and thin, in baggy pants with suspenders…a little Stan Laurel hat. SUSAN (a waitress) leads DANNY through some black curtains into the lounge. SUSAN is twenty-four or -five—sports a nose ring and tattoos. She seats DANNY near the two CLOWNS.

The music and the shadow play upon the scrim slowly fade.

SUSAN: There you go. Welcome to Fallen Angels.

DANNY: Thanks.

SUSAN: What can I get you?

DANNY: A pint of whatever you have on tap.

SUSAN: Coming up. *(Exits.)*

(A one-beat pause.)

RED: *(Indicating the silhouette that has just faded from the scrim.)* Say, dat was one swell-looking doll!

SLIM: You can say dat again!

RED: Say, dat was one swell-looking doll!

(Rim shot.)

RED: I haven't used dat gag in twenty years!

SLIM: Just our luck!

(Rim shot.)

RED: Ya know, I was thinking of askin' her out.

SLIM: You?

RED: Yeah.

SLIM: You?

RED: Yeah!

SLIM: YEAH!

RED: YOU!! *(A one-beat pause.)* Dat can't be right!

(Rim shot.)

SLIM: With a mug like yers, ya better have money!

RED: Hey!

SLIM: Well, ya got any dough?

RED: Nope. Not one thin dime!

(SLIM shakes his hand.)

RED: What was dat for?

SLIM: Red, I just shook hands with yer date tonight!

(Rim shot. RED takes out an Elizabethan-type bladder and bops SLIM on the head. Three Stooges sound effects.)

SLIM: *(Dazed and confused.)* Nice comeback!

(Rim shot.)

RED: I'll show you! *(Crosses to the blank scrim.)* But soft! What light through yonda winda breaks?

(On the scrim: the silhouette of the DANCER.)

RED and SLIM: Va Va Va Voom!

RED: Hey, doll-face! How's about you 'n' me goin' out 'n' shakin' our tootsies?

(Scrim blanks out. From behind it, RED is doused with a bucket of water. Dejectedly, he crosses back to SLIM.)

SLIM: Nice play, Shakespeare!

(Rim shot.)

RED: *(Miserably.)* I'd like to see you do betta!

SLIM: Step aside, son! *(Crosses to the scrim.)* It's all in de approach. Hey, doll-face: rise 'n' shine!

(Lights up on the scrim and the same sil-houette. SLIM goes behind the scrim and enters into the shadow play. The sound of a fly unzippering. SLIM's silhouette produces

a gargantuan phallus. The effect is comic. Think Aristophanes, not John Holmes!)

RED: *(Aside.)* I had no idea Slim was so…talented!

(Suddenly: BANG! The phallus explodes like the giant balloon it really is…was. SLIM howls in pain. RED gesticulates in mock horror. Blackout, everywhere on stage, except DANNY's table. SUSAN stands there with his pint.)

SUSAN: Your beer.

DANNY: *(Paying for his drink.)* Keep the change.

SUSAN: Thanks.

(Lights back to normal. The two CLOWNS have now returned to their table and grimly sit over their drinks.)

DANNY: Interesting place.

SUSAN: The lounge here has been dubbed "Shadow Land," or "the Shadows" for short. I guess because it's located behind the dancer's stage. It feels a bit like being back of a movie screen.

DANNY: Or through the looking glass!

(Rim shot. The lights lower on the CLOWNS' table. Music up: The siren song of the Prologue. The silhouette of the DANCER plays upon the scrim, which is now backlit in blue. She beckons DANNY with the identical Balinese-like motion from the Prologue's shadow play. He gets up, crosses to the scrim, and gazes upon it. With his fingertip, he reaches up to touch the fingertip of the SHADOW DANCER. Still behind the scrim, the silhouette be-gins to move stage left. DANNY follows. Suddenly, LINNEA pokes her head out from behind the scrim.)

DANNY: *(Involuntarily.)* Linnea, it's you!

(The music and the light upon the scrim fade. Simultaneously, the lights rise on the CLOWNS' table where RED and SLIM are laughing at DANNY. LINNEA has entered, and now stands surveying the scene. She is in her early twenties, but seems older—a tall, linear girl, with cat-green eyes and a sallow tomboyish face and smile. Her nearly platinum blonde hair is streaked with dark roots. She wears a red minidress and heels. DANNY stares blankly at her.)

LINNEA: Don't mind them. They're a couple of clowns.

DANNY: I—I don't.

LINNEA: I saw you watching me as I danced.

DANNY: Yes. I, eh…I'm sorry.

LINNEA: Don't apologize. We do it to be watched.

DANNY: Yes…it's just…I couldn't not watch.

LINNEA: I know.

DANNY: I—I felt drawn to you. Like you were beckoning me.

LINNEA: *(Laughing.)* Maybe I did beckon you. *(A slight pause.)* What's your name, honey?

DANNY: Danny.

LINNEA: Danny, will you buy me a drink? That way we can sit and talk?

DANNY: Sure.

(LINNEA offers him her arm. DANNY escorts her past the now-quieted CLOWN table. SUSAN, in the know, exits back through the curtains. The two sit. LINNEA lights a cigarette. She will chain-smoke one cigarette after another in the scene. After a moment of silence:)

LINNEA: So Danny—

DANNY: Yes?

LINNEA: Why did you cry out when I appeared?

DANNY: I was surprised to see you.

LINNEA: But you knew my name. How is that?

DANNY: Cody Marlin told me about you.

LINNEA: Cody Marlin! Are you a friend of Cody's?

DANNY: Not really. I just met him this evening. He showed me the sketch he'd done of you. I was very struck by it.

LINNEA: Were you? So you decided to come have a look for yourself?

DANNY: *(Embarrassed.)* Well, I…

LINNEA: And now that you're seen me, what do you think?

DANNY: *(Quietly.)* No drawing could have prepared me for this.

LINNEA: Why, that's very sweet of you, Danny. You know, I feel like I've seen you somewhere before. Is this your first time here?

DANNY: Yes.

LINNEA: So, drawings aside, we've never actually met?

DANNY: *(Laughing.)* I didn't say that!

LINNEA: What, we have met? Where? Perhaps the East Village?

DANNY: *(Almost inaudible.)* Perhaps in a dream.

LINNEA: A dream? *(Laughing.)* Why, Danny, you're a madcap!

DANNY: A what?

LINNEA: A madcap little dreamer with pixie dust in his eyes!

DANNY: *(Laughing.)* It's true. I know so little of real life; I can't help living my life as if it were a dream. Tonight, in particular, I've felt that way. But, even in my wildest dreams, I never thought I'd be here, talking with you.

LINNEA: There's a reason for that, Danny.

DANNY: Oh?

LINNEA: *(Leans in closer to him.)* Yes. You see…I'm a madcap too.

(The two stare at each other. SUSAN returns with LINNEA's drink. DANNY pays for it.)

LINNEA: I just had an idea, Danny.

DANNY: What?

LINNEA: Well, it's very slow tonight. Hardly worth the effort. I mean, I'd really rather sit and talk with you. Get the chance to know you. Of course, once I finish this drink, I have to go back on the floor.

DANNY: Oh…I see.

LINNEA: So, what I'm thinking of doing is blowing off the rest of work. I'll tell them—I don't know—I'll tell them I'm not feeling well. That way I'll be free the rest of the night. Get my drift, Danny?

DANNY: Not really.

LINNEA: Then I'll spell it out for you. I like you, Danny, and I think you're cute.

I think it was fated we meet. I mean, we're madcaps, aren't we?

DANNY: Y-yes.

LINNEA: Now, don't get the wrong idea. I've never done this before. I mean, I wouldn't dream of doing this with any of the other clowns here. But you're different, Danny, I sense that.

DANNY: Doing what, Linnea?

LINNEA: Look, I'll just come out and say it. Would you like to go out with me? Maybe go back to the East Village and hit some bars, play some pool? It will be fun. What do you say, Danny? Two madcaps out on a tear?

(Pause.)

DANNY: All right.

LINNEA: You will?

DANNY: Yes.

LINNEA: You're sure?

DANNY: I'd love to.

LINNEA: Great!

(A pause.)

LINNEA: Now, look Danny, I'm going to ask you to front me some money. Say, eighty dollars? Now, it's not what you think! It's just, you know, I'm not working the rest of my shift, and I'm a little short. Look upon it as a loan. I mean, the next time will be my treat.

(A pause.)

DANNY: I, eh…I'll have to find a bank machine.

LINNEA: There's one near by. Here's what we gotta do. We can't just walk out together. That's frowned upon.

DANNY: I...I understand.

LINNEA: I'm going to get up now. I'll go tell them I'm leaving. They may ask me to dance one final dance. Meantime, finish up your beer. Walk out of here, cross back over the highway, and then go up two blocks on Twelfth Avenue. There's a Chinese takeout on the northeast corner. Wait for me there. I'll come by in a cab in ten minutes. Okay?

DANNY: I just have to make sure and find a bank machine.

LINNEA: We'll find a bank machine. *(A slight pause.)* You promise to wait for me?

DANNY: I promise.

LINNEA: Good man! See you in ten minutes. *(Exits.)*

(A pause.)

RED: Hey Slim?

SLIM: Yeah?

RED: What time's it gettin' to be?

SLIM: My watch died.

(A tugboat is heard in the distance.)

RED: Ya know, sometimes I feel like we're in exile.

SLIM: Who am I drinkin' wit' here, Albert Camus?

(A rim shot.)

SLIM: Dat was a question, not a laugh-line!

RED: Be serious, Slim. What I mean is, here we are exiled on de outskirts of town. Banished to de back room. Nobody knows 'n' nobody cares. No gurls come 'n' sit wit' us. No waitresses check on our drinks.

(A pause.)

SLIM: You know what we are?

RED: What?

SLIM: We're Lost in de Shadows.

RED: Yep.

(Music up. LINNEA's silhouette appears on the scrim. She silently beckons with a Balinese-like motion.)

RED: You wanta get outta here?

SLIM: Yeah, let's go.

(They stand.)

RED: Ya know, I always come in here with such high hopes. 'N' always leave sick to my stomach.

SLIM: I know whatcha mean.

(SUSAN enters as they stroll out through the curtains.)

SUSAN: See you boys tomorrow.

BOTH: You bet!

(A rim shot. The CLOWNS exit. SUSAN crosses to the CLOWNS' vacated table and begins to clear it.)

SUSAN: Can I get you another?

DANNY: No, I have to go.

SUSAN: So soon?

DANNY: Yeah. *(Takes a final sip of beer and heads for the curtains.)* Goodnight.

SUSAN: Come again.

(He exits. SUSAN crosses to DANNY's vacated table and begins to clear it. The lights fade on the circular tables. A slow fade to black upon the scrim.)

SCENE 4.

The Blue and Gold, a Ukrainian bar on East Seventh, a few hours later. DANNY

*and LINNEA sit in a booth, a couple of
bottles of beer in front of them. Behind
them: a faded lacquered mural depicting
a pine forest. LINNEA has changed into
a peasant blouse, blue jeans (torn at the
knees), a navy pea coat, and a floppy hat.
She wears John Lennon glasses.*

LINNEA: *(Lighting another cigarette.)*
How about it?

DANNY: What?

LINNEA: One more round and one
more game of pool.

DANNY: Oh, I don't know.

LINNEA: What don't you know? Come
on, Danny, we can take them this time!

DANNY: It's just…I'm fading fast.

LINNEA: Not an option! You promised
to stay out with me until sunrise!

DANNY: I know.

LINNEA: Come on. You'll get your
second wind. Besides, I've never beaten
the bartender in eight ball. Tonight's
the night!

DANNY: Not with me as your partner.

LINNEA: Stop with the negative vibes!
Your game's been improving as the
night's gone by. Like it or not, you're my
partner—so stop whining and get your
head together.

DANNY: *(Laughing.)* Yes ma'am.

LINNEA: That's more like it.

DANNY: It will cost you a cigarette.
(Reaches for her pack.)

LINNEA: Hey, that's my last one! Bad
luck, you know.

DANNY: It's all right. I'll make a run.

LINNEA: Fine, fine. *(Lights his cigarette.)*

DANNY: Thanks.

LINNEA: So…I'm glad we did this.

DANNY: Me too.

LINNEA: You know, I wasn't entirely
sure you'd be standing at that corner
when my cab pulled up.

DANNY: And I wasn't entirely sure your
cab was going to pull up!

LINNEA: *(Laughing.)* It's kinda a spooky
spot to have to wait all alone.

DANNY: Yeah.

LINNEA: Well, I hope it was worth it.
I mean I hope you've had fun.

DANNY: Oh yes!

LINNEA: I'm glad. You strike me as
someone who could stand a little fun
now and again.

DANNY: Oh? Why do you say that?

LINNEA: I don't know…there's, there's
something about your eyes.

DANNY: *(Defensively.)* What's wrong
with my eyes?

LINNEA: There's nothing wrong with
your eyes. They just seem a little sad.

DANNY: That's funny, that's what I first
thought of your eyes.

LINNEA: Really?

DANNY: Not so much when I first
met you, but when I looked at Cody's
picture.

LINNEA: Yeah, well Cody has a way
of making everything seem sad or
psychotic.

DANNY: Of course, now that I've spent time with you, they don't seem sad at all. They seem joyous and full of mischief. In fact, your whole face seems much younger than you were at the club.

LINNEA: That's because I'm playacting there. Away from work, I'm a complete child and always will be.

DANNY: There's nothing wrong with that. Years spent watching children has made me realize that play is serious work.

LINNEA: Huh! I bet you're great with kids.

DANNY: I love being with them. Trouble is…these days they're the only ones I feel comfortable with. That's why, away from the kids, I spend all my time alone.

LINNEA: What do you do with yourself?

DANNY: I don't do anything! I lie around dreaming. Lately I've taken to writing my dreams down.

LINNEA: Tell me: was I really in one of your dreams?

DANNY: Uh-huh. *(Takes out his notebook.)* Here. *(Hands the notebook to her.)* I wrote this as soon as I awoke this morning. You see, essentially I've been following a dream's shadow all day and night until it led me to you.

LINNEA: *(Finishes reading the entry. Hands the notebook back.)* Be careful, Danny.

DANNY: Why?

LINNEA: Because the shadow of a dream led you to Shadow Land, not to me.

(A pause.)

DANNY: You've changed again.

LINNEA: Have I?

DANNY: Yes you have. You suddenly seem older and sadder.

LINNEA: *(Laughing.)* Do you always say whatever comes into your mind?

DANNY: Pretty much.

LINNEA: I'll drink to that! *(She does.)* Why don't you go make that cigarette run? While you're gone, I'll get the next round and put our names on the board.

DANNY: Sure. Where's the nearest deli?

LINNEA: Around the corner to the left.

DANNY: I'll be right back. *(Exits stage left.)*

(A pause.)

LINNEA: All right Cody, you can come out now!

(Out of the blue, CODY appears.)

CODY: One night and already so well trained!

LINNEA: How long have you been lurking?

CODY: Not long. Glad to see me?

LINNEA: Relieved.

CODY: Oh?

LINNEA: Yeah. A pall had descended on the evening. At least now I know why.

CODY: Nice!

LINNEA: So why are you stalking me?

CODY: I'm keeping an eye on you, Linnea. There's a difference.

LINNEA: Thanks for the clarification, but I don't need any looking after.

CODY: Actually, I'm thinkin 'bout waiting for my new bud Jocko to return.

LINNEA: Jocko?

CODY: Yeah, he's the Fifth Ritz Brother or something. Anyway, I thought the three of us could get better acquainted—you know—sit down, have a drink…talk.

LINNEA: What do the three of us have to talk about?

CODY: Oh, I don't know: happy times!

(A pause.)

CODY: You two seem to be hitting it off.

LINNEA: We are.

CODY: How sweet!

(A slight pause.)

LINNEA: Why did you do it?

CODY: Do what?

LINNEA: Send that little pup my way?

CODY: Are you kidding me? I showed him your picture, and it was a done deal! I, eh, may have dropped a hint, I don't remember.

LINNEA: You don't remember!

CODY: Hey, even if I did, what's the big deal? We've played this con countless times before—for pleasure and for profit. Why should it be any different with him?

LINNEA: Geez, I don't know, Cody! Maybe because he's a true innocent?

Maybe because he's a part-time teacher who couldn't afford it!

CODY: Hell, just because I sent him your way doesn't mean you have to go ahead and fleece him.

LINNEA: And how do you know I did?

CODY: Stop it! I talked to Slim earlier this evening—as he was leaving the Shadows. Seems he was listening in on your foreplay! Granted, it was only eighty bucks, but eighty bucks is a lot for "a part-time teacher."

LINNEA: I guess I wanted you to see how low I could stoop.

(A pause.)

CODY: Look, put the eighty bucks underneath the ashtray, and let's get the hell out of Dodge.

LINNEA: Why the sudden need to make things right?

CODY: You said it yourself: tonight we've sunk to an all-time low.

LINNEA: Is it Danny's well-being you're concerned about or your own?

CODY: Who's Danny?

LINNEA: That's the name of your new drinking buddy.

CODY: You're asking me if I'm worried about him or about me?

LINNEA: That's right.

CODY: I don't understand.

(LINNEA appears amused.)

CODY: What's so funny?

LINNEA: Why don't you admit it, Cody?

CODY: Admit what?

LINNEA: You're scared of him.

CODY: I'm scared of that little mutt? Please!

LINNEA: You wouldn't be here otherwise.

(A pause.)

CODY: Okay, you win. Have it your way.

LINNEA: What way is that?

CODY: Spend the night with him. I give you that.

LINNEA: How kind of you!

CODY: But when the daylight comes…

LINNEA: What?

(A pause.)

LINNEA: What then?

CODY: I'll be at the Night Owl on First with Red and Slim. In case you need me.

LINNEA: Why should I need you?

(A pause.)

LINNEA: Answer me, Cody!

CODY: *(Looking offstage left.)* He's coming back. I'm outta here.

LINNEA: Goddamnit, answer me!

(He exits stage left. A moment later DANNY returns with the pack of cigarettes.)

DANNY: *(Handing over the pack.)* Here you are.

LINNEA: Thank you Danny.

(A pause.)

DANNY: Are you okay?

LINNEA: Yes, why do you ask?

DANNY: You look pale.

LINNEA: I'm just tired, that's all.

DANNY: The night air actually woke me up.

(A pause.)

DANNY: Are we up next?

LINNEA: W-what?

DANNY: Did you sign us up for pool?

LINNEA: I…forgot.

DANNY: Oh.

(A pause. LINNEA's hands tremble as she lights a cigarette.)

DANNY: Are you sure you're okay?

LINNEA: I'm fine. *(A pause.)* Fine.

(Lights fade to black.)

Scene 5.

Tompkins Square Park. Dawn. Two tattered feet protrude from the bushes behind the bench; BEGGAR KING's cart is nestled there as well. We hear the muffled sound of his snores. The street lamp snaps off. Morning birds are heard. DANNY and LINNEA enter.

DANNY: This is where the night began. What is it? Nine, ten hours ago? I sat here on this bench. *(Plops down wearily upon it.)* Drinking brandy and writing in my notebook. The light of this street lamp played upon the tree branches, turning green leaves to gold. A nice bit of alchemy, that! And you know, the whole evening's been like that—cast in the same fantastical light. I've met a Beggar King, a Bookseller, a Mad Boy Painter, two Clowns…and you.

LINNEA: *(Sitting beside him.)* And who would I be?

DANNY: The girl of my dreams.

(A pause.)

LINNEA: It will soon be morning. The sun will rise, and we'll go our separate ways. Then, and only then, will I be the girl of your dreams, because the whole night will seem like a dream.

DANNY: Will I ever see you again?

LINNEA: I don't know. Why?

DANNY: Because I love you, Linnea.

(A pause.)

LINNEA: You really do say whatever comes into your head!

DANNY: Yes.

LINNEA: Why, that's very sweet, Danny. But very, very silly.

DANNY: Why silly?

LINNEA: Because you don't even know me. And if you did, you wouldn't be saying those things.

DANNY: But I think I do know you, Linnea.

LINNEA: Do you really? Then you know this is not the first time I've asked someone out from the club. You must also know the eighty dollars wasn't a loan.

DANNY: I know.

LINNEA: You do?

DANNY: Uh-huh.

LINNEA: How did you know?

DANNY: I don't know...I just did.

(A slight pause.)

LINNEA: If you knew, then why go out with me?

DANNY: Because, I told you: you're the girl of my dreams. I know you—know what you've been through, what you've suffered. I also know that you're a very proud woman—that it cost you something to ask me out tonight. For my part, if it meant parting with eighty dollars, who cares? It was worth it.

LINNEA: You're a little nuts, Danny.

DANNY: No, I'm a madcap, just like you.

(A pause.)

LINNEA: It's true. Didn't I once dream of someone who was gentle, and decent, and kind...and ever so silly...someone who would come to me and help to ease my pain! But you never came. And now that I've finally met you, do you know what I feel, Danny?

DANNY: What?

LINNEA: Spite. Why did you wait so long? Who am I now worthy of but the likes of Cody Marlin? That's why I took your eighty dollars! It was my way of saying, "Look what I am! What I've become!"

DANNY: What have you become?

(A pause.)

LINNEA: You saw what I do for a living.

DANNY: Yes, but, I also saw you dance, and you know what? You're an artist, Linnea, you really are. There's something...profound in your dance.

LINNEA: Profound!

DANNY: Yes, it's a—a kind of penance! You dance at Fallen Angels, because you are trying to work things out. And you know what, Linnea? In time you *will* work things out!

(A pause.)

LINNEA: You know, I almost like that Linnea!

(A pause.)

LINNEA: Oh Christ! *(Standing.)* CODY!

(CODY appears with RED and SLIM. They all seem a little drunk.)

LINNEA: I need you, Cody! Take me away from here!

CODY: I knew it! I knew! Where to?

LINNEA: Anywhere, just get me the hell out of here—before I do something stupid like ruin this little pup's life!

CODY: My van's on Avenue A. Let's go!

DANNY: Linnea, wait!

CODY: *(Advancing.)* I told you before—she's mine!

LINNEA: Leave him alone, Cody! *(Turning to DANNY.)* Thank you for tonight. It was a beautiful dream. *(Turning to CODY.)* You knew all along I'd come running back to you! Of course, I don't think you realize just how hellish your life will be as a result! Now take me away! Before I change my mind!

(CODY stretches out his hand to LINNEA. She crosses to him.)

CODY: Sorry, Jocko, but all's fair in love and war!

LINNEA: Shut up and take me home!

CODY: Your wish is my command!

(Together they run offstage.)

DANNY: LINNEA!

(DANNY makes a move to follow them. SLIM stands in his way.)

SLIM: Not so fast, bub!

(RED has slipped up behind DANNY.)

RED: Yeah, where de hell do ya think you're going?

(DANNY tries to break away. The two begin to toss him around, back and forth between them, as if DANNY were a bouncy ball. Meanwhile, the BEGGER KING has roused himself from sleep. Seeing his young friend in trouble, he advances, brandishing an umbrella from his cart.)

BEGGAR KING: Unhand him, you curs!

(The two stop and stare with curiosity.)

BEGGAR KING: I said, unhand him you curs!

(The two CLOWNS begin to laugh uproariously.)

BEGGAR KING: Dare you insult the Beggar King! SMALL CURS ARE NOT TO BE REGARDED WHEN THEY SMILE!

RED and SLIM: Huh?

BEGGAR KING: *(Charging.)* NO PRISONERS!

(In the melee, BEGGAR KING is thrown to the ground, where he lies moaning. DANNY goes to his aid, as the two bullies exit laughing.)

DANNY: Are you all right?

BEGGAR KING: I think so.

DANNY: Thank you for coming to my aid.

BEGGAR KING: I'm afraid I rather bungled it.

DANNY: Not at all.

BEGGAR KING: *(Melodramatically.)* Beggar King indeed. I am a man of straw!

DANNY: Nonsense. I was in a tight spot and you bailed me out.

BEGGAR KING: Was this fracas over the girl?

DANNY: Yes.

BEGGAR KING: I know this type of woman and their strong hold. I myself was once laid low by a little chorine from Weehawken, New Jersey. This particular Jezebel's talent was her ability to inspire both feelings of eroticism and compassion. It's the strongest, most powerful type of love there is. My advice to you is, if it hasn't already happened, don't let it!

DANNY: Can one help who they fall in love with?

(A pause. Lights fade to black.)

ACT TWO
(SONGS OF EXPERIENCE)
Scene 6.

Lights slowly rise in DANNY's Park Slope "Funk Cell." It's an early morning in May. The sun's rays creep through the cracks in the wooden shutters deflecting down to the floor. DANNY, wearing a T-shirt and his wrinkled chinos, sits at his desk typing, a mug of coffee beside him. Outside we hear a tap, tap, tap upon his window frame. DANNY pauses in his work and crosses

to shutters and opens them. LINNEA is revealed kneeling outside in the courtyard looking in through the window bars.

LINNEA: Hi.

DANNY: Linnea!

LINNEA: I haven't been to bed yet. *(Giggles.)* I think I'm still a little drunk.

(A pause.)

LINNEA: Can I come in?

DANNY: Sure. Hold on. *(Exits stage left.)*

(We hear the sound of locks unlocking, of an iron door creaking open and slamming shut. DANNY reenters with LINNEA. Despite her lack of sleep, she's looking quite youthful and freshly scrubbed in a summer print dress and her John Lennon glasses. A canvas bag hangs from her shoulder. An awkward silence.)

LINNEA: I'm interrupting your work.

DANNY: That's okay. Can I get you some coffee?

LINNEA: I'm about to crash. Can I?

(A slight pause.)

DANNY: Sure.

LINNEA: Really?

DANNY: Of course.

LINNEA: I want to change first. Didn't I leave some clothes here?

DANNY: *(Indicating the bureau.)* Second drawer from the bottom.

(LINNEA crosses to the bureau, opens the second drawer, and begins changing into a T-shirt and cut-off jeans. DANNY returns to his seat and tries to make light of what

is becoming an increasingly uncomfortable situation for him.)

DANNY: Do you always leave behind a change of clothing?

LINNEA: Only in places I want to come back to. Cody calls them my "Linnea Droppings."

DANNY: "Linnea Droppings"! I like that.

(A pause.)

LINNEA: *(Bursts into laughter.)* It's all right, Danny, you can look at me while I change!

DANNY: W-what? Oh! I mean—

LINNEA: It's not like you haven't seen me this way before!

DANNY: I know. It's just—

LINNEA: What?

DANNY: This morning I feel like I'm seeing you for the first time.

LINNEA: There you go again!

DANNY: What?

LINNEA: Saying the first thing that comes into your mind.

DANNY: Oh, right!

LINNEA: It's funny you should mention it. Since last night, I feel like I've shed an old skin.

DANNY: Did, eh, you and Susan go out after work?

LINNEA: Oh, yes we did!

DANNY: Hoo boy! So, eh … how naughty were you?

LINNEA: Me, not very. Susan I can't vouch for. I left her at the Marriot

Marquis with this German guy who claimed to be an independent filmmaker. We'd spent the night doing lines, drinking beer. By sunrise I'd had a bellyful of them both! I decided to get in a cab and say good morning to you.

DANNY: There goes your chance to be in a German independent film!

LINNEA: I guess I didn't want it bad enough. By the morning all I wanted was sanctuary.

DANNY: Well, Brooklyn is the borough of cathedrals.

LINNEA: I like it here. It's peaceful and quiet. I feel safe. Here I can rest.

DANNY: *(Tapping the futon.)* So rest.

LINNEA: *(Crosses left, depositing her glasses on DANNY's desk, and plops down on the futon.)* What time do you have to be at work?

DANNY: Not until three. That's the upside of working in an after-school program.

LINNEA: Do you write the whole time prior to?

DANNY: I try to put in four hours a day.

LINNEA: I admire your discipline.

(A pause.)

LINNEA: Tell me a little about your play?

DANNY: The play? Well, it's based on Dostoyevsky's *The Idiot*.

LINNEA: Don't know it. I did once try to read *Crime and Punishment*. All the Russian names got to me!

DANNY: In *The Idiot* there's this love triangle I'm intrigued by and the woman involved particularly fascinates me: Nastassya Filippovna. Nastassya Filippovna's been seduced by this older benefactor and later she becomes involved with two men. One, Prince Myshkin, is a gentle, almost Christ-like figure—like Dostoyevsky, he's epileptic. Unlike Dostoyevsky, he's asexual. He loves Nastassya with a spiritual love. The other man, Rogozhin, is an obsessed merchant, who lusts after her, beats her, and finally ends up stabbing her to death.

LINNEA: Jesus!

DANNY: He loves Nastassya with a passionate love. She runs back and forth between the two, working the love triangle to its inevitable tragedy. While Rogozhin ends up committing the murder, it's implied that both men are responsible.

LINNEA: Huh! It's like you're playing my song!

DANNY: Gosh, I hope not!

LINNEA: So, is the play the reason you haven't called me? It's been a week.

DANNY: I don't know. I've been busy. I don't know.

LINNEA: You haven't been embarrassed?

DANNY: Why, just because the last time we were together we ended up running naked through Prospect Park? Because I woke up the next day to find you sleeping beside me? I mean, what's so embarrassing about all that?

LINNEA: *(Laughing.)* The park was your idea.

DANNY: I don't know what got into me!

LINNEA: About ten Yukon Jacks and lemon juice!

DANNY: Never mix, never worry!

LINNEA: Drunk or not, you were inspired. My own little Pan of the Woods! Of course, when I offered myself to you, you chickened out.

DANNY: Again, the ten Yukon Jacks and lemon juice!

LINNEA: Was it only the drink?

DANNY: What do you mean?

LINNEA: I don't know. I sometimes think I ruined any chance we might have had on our first night.

DANNY: We've gone out a number of times since.

LINNEA: Uh-huh. Of course, when push came to shove—

DANNY: I chickened out. No, it's true: our first night together was like a dream. But in the morning hour, you ran away. So I decided to pursue you. Not as some dream creature, some shadow of the night, but as a real person. And the person I've gotten to know fascinates me and excites me, but—

LINNEA: But?

DANNY: She lives in a different world than I do.

LINNEA: So, the other night, when it got a little too real, you became frightened and ran away and hid for a week?

DANNY: True Cancer that I am, I crawled back inside my shell.

LINNEA: Two things. One, even though you declined my offer to make love, I went back to your place and spent the night there—because I wanted to. Two, I ran away from you once, but today I came to you. Remember that.

DANNY: Just another drop-off post along the road?

(A pause.)

LINNEA: I suppose I deserved that.

DANNY: Tell me the truth about you and Cody.

LINNEA: What's to tell? I met Cody Marlin a couple of years ago. The competition began the minute we set eyes on each other. It's been going on ever since.

DANNY: Perhaps your coming here is part of that competition?

LINNEA: Perhaps it's my way of ending it.

DANNY: Cody won't quit easily.

LINNEA: I know.

(A pause.)

DANNY: I'm sorry about the drop-off crack.

LINNEA: Forget about it. Just—please—don't judge me. I couldn't take it if you did.

DANNY: Fair enough.

(A pause.)

DANNY: You okay?

LINNEA: Not really.

DANNY: What's wrong?

LINNEA: This life. It's slowly killing me.

DANNY: You're tired. Get some rest. You'll wake up with a better perspective.

(A pause.)

LINNEA: Tell me something, Danny. Do you think a person can really change their life...change it in ways that really matter?

DANNY: Sure. Of course—If they want to badly enough.

(A pause.)

LINNEA: Lay down beside me, Danny. Just 'til I fall asleep. I so need someone next to me.

(A pause.)

DANNY: All right.

(DANNY lies next to LINNEA. She puts her head on his shoulder.)

LINNEA: Thanks, sweetie.

(Outside, the church bells begin to chime.)

LINNEA: The borough of cathedrals.

DANNY: That's right. The borough of cathedrals.

(As the church bells fade away, LINNEA gently kisses him on the lips. DANNY responds in kind. Each kiss, each caress, grows more passionate. The two sad, lonely children of the night solemnize their love in the morning light as...The stage light discreetly fades to black.)

SCENE 7.

Tompkins Square Park, a week or so later. Another beautiful spring day. MAGGIE, dressed accordingly, puts the finishing touches to her makeshift book table. A moment later, DANNY enters somewhat tentatively.

MAGGIE: Saints preserve us! Look who's here!

DANNY: Hello, Maggie.

MAGGIE: Sir Danny of the Broken Vow—back from the Crusades! You're looking vanquished, pal!

DANNY: Comes from dragging my guilt behind me!

MAGGIE: Well, four weeks' tardiness is a hell of a lot of guilt!

DANNY: I know, I know! I come bearing apologies.

MAGGIE: I'd rather it was the spoils of war, but c'est la vie! You still want your book?

DANNY: But of course.

MAGGIE: *(Searching through her boxes.)* Now where did I put it? It's been so long, I should be charging you storage!

DANNY: That's it, play the guilt card for all it's worth!

MAGGIE: Here we go... *(Pulling out the book.) The Insulted and Injured*...vintage Black Cat Edition...circa 1962. *(Handing it over to DANNY.)* Yours for the low asking price of five dollars.

DANNY: *(Examining.)* The inside flap says three.

MAGGIE: The price includes a finder's fee.

DANNY: A late charge as well?

MAGGIE: Business is business. Now if you want to haggle—

DANNY: No, no, mine is not the strongest of bargaining positions.

MAGGIE: Good choice.

DANNY: *(Fishing through his wallet.)* Three, four...five dollars. *(Hands the money over to MAGGIE.)*

MAGGIE: Merci.

DANNY: No, thank you for finding it.

MAGGIE: So how's the play coming along?

DANNY: My play and I are presently engaged in a Texas Steel-Cage Death Match!

MAGGIE: Winner take all?

DANNY: Uh-huh.

MAGGIE: Hate to say it, but looks like the play is winning!

DANNY: That bad, huh?

MAGGIE: My friend, you look exhausted!

DANNY: Well, if the truth be known, my life has gotten a little...psychotic.

MAGGIE: Psychotic, huh? You must be dating an actress!

DANNY: Close... I've been seeing a...an exotic dancer.

MAGGIE: YOU'RE DATING A STRIPPER!

DANNY: A little louder! I don't think they heard you on Astor Place!

MAGGIE: Wow, Pinocchio's a real boy now! Come on, give me all the dirty details!

DANNY: Her name's Linnea and I met her the same night I met you. Remember it—clear and cool—a touch of winter, yet the unmistakable hint of spring?

MAGGIE: Seems so long ago!

(Noises off.)

DANNY: *(Freezing in his tracks.)* Holy shit!

MAGGIE: What? What is it, Danny?

(RED and SLIM enter.)

SLIM: Well, well, well! Lookey-here!

RED: Hey Pilgrim! Long time no see!

SLIM: We've missed ya at the House of Sodom and Gomorrah!

RED: Yeah. You was getting to be a regular *regular*!

SLIM: Right. We waz practically sizing you up for de act!

RED: What, we're turnin' into a three-some?

SLIM: Why not? Can't ya see him now in a pair of baggy pants?

RED: Some flop shoes!

SLIM: How's about a big red nose?

RED: Absa-fuckin'-lutely!

(RED tweaks DANNY's nose.)

RED: Honk, honk!

(The two CLOWNS roar with laughter.)

DANNY: W-what do you two want?

SLIM: Cody's been askin' for yaz.

RED: Something about welshin' on a debt.

SLIM: What, ya owe him dough? Or maybe it's, eh, some other valuable?

RED: Right! A crown jewel! Either way, peach fuzz—he wants ta talk to ya!

SLIM: Yeah. As we speak, he's at de Grassroots—waitin'!

(A pause.)

DANNY: All right. But I'm in the middle of something. Go back and tell him I'll be there.

RED: Ix-nay! He told us ta bring youz back wit' us!

DANNY: Well, that's too damn bad.

(A pause.)

SLIM: Tough guy! Have it your way.

RED: I dunno, Slim! I think he's tryin' ta pull a fast one!

SLIM: Hey, he can run, but he can't hide! Besides, we's only de messengers here!

RED: Yes, but, Slim, as Marshall McLuhan points out, in dese times it's not so much de message as de messengers dat is sent out.

SLIM: Point taken. But he also points out dat de present can only be viewed through a rearview mirror. Derefore, let us march backwards into da future.

RED: Where it will be Happy Hour!

SLIM: Correct!

(The two CLOWNS, having apparently forgotten about DANNY, exit merrily.)

MAGGIE: What was that all about?

(DANNY sits on the park bench with his head in his hands.)

MAGGIE: Danny, what's going on here? Danny?

(DANNY looks up.)

MAGGIE: Jesus, you're shaking! *(Sitting next him.)* What's wrong, dear? Who's this Cody character?

(A pause.)

DANNY: He's ... Rogozhin to my Myshkin! *(Bursts into laughter.)*

MAGGIE: What's so funny?

DANNY: *(Regaining his composure.)* Sorry! I just realized how absurd my life has become!

MAGGIE: Well it's not every day that a guy is leaned on by Tweedledum and Tweedledee!

DANNY: Their real names are Red and Slim. They hang out at Linnea's club—Fallen Angels. They're associates of an artist I know—Cody Marlin—who also just happens to be Linnea's onetime boyfriend.

(A pause.)

MAGGIE: Ah, the interconnecting threads! Let me guess: Cody's one of those super-macho predator types. His whole relationship with Linnea is one big psychosexual game and it's now spilled over to include you.

DANNY: You're good! You're very good!

MAGGIE: You know it! What are you, like, some kind of Method Playwright who has to live his play before he writes it?

DANNY: More like some kind of fool who's gotten in way over his head!

MAGGIE: And now that you're in the deep end...what are you going to do about it?

DANNY: What can I do? I have to go see him.

MAGGIE: Are you sure that's wise? I mean you're not going to have your legs broken or something?

DANNY: He's a painter, not a member of the Gambino Family! No, I'll be fine. I've been avoiding him for almost a month now. It's time I faced my shadow.

MAGGIE: Shadow in the Jungian— AKA "pretentious writer" sense of the word?

DANNY: Cut me some slack—I'm under duress here!

MAGGIE: *(Sighing.)* Oh, all right.

(Offstage, the sound of squeaking wheels. Enter BEGGAR KING. Seeing a captive audience, he strikes.)

BEGGAR KING: Dear sir, we meet again! Many a time and oft in the Rialto, yes? But what have we here? A fair maiden! Friends, I am happy to see you both—yes, very happy! Ah, the forest is deep and dark when one travels it alone! The shadow lengthens and the road is fraught with infinite peril! But the sight of the two of you—in the full bloom of youth (or so the old limerick goes!)—fills me with joy...and dare I say it? Hope. Hope that I might petition you for a small token...a mere bauble to send me on my way. But this time mine will not be the dark, dusty way of a down-and-out ham dedicated to destroying himself with demon drink! No, this time, mine will be the Artist's Way—that of a devout actor determined to drag himself out of the gutter! For hear this: I, the Beggar King, under the auspices of the good scribes at *Back Stage*, have finagled an audition for a featured role in an Off-Broadway production! *(Pulling out a dog-eared copy of* Back Stage *and handing it to DANNY.)* Here, dear boy, read it and weep o'er my glad tidings!

DANNY: *(Perusing the ad.)* But this is terrific!

(He shakes the old actor's hand.)

DANNY: Congratulations, old man, I'm very excited for you! Alas, I wish I could stay and chat, but, unfortunately, I have a pressing engagement.

MAGGIE: *(Standing.)* Danny wait—

DANNY: Now, now, Maggie, everything will be all right. By the way, Maggie, Beggar King—Beggar King, Maggie!

BEGGAR KING: *(Bowing.)* Charmed!

DANNY: Maggie, I'll have you know, is a seller of rare books. So, if there's anything you need in the way of an audition piece, I'm sure she can accommodate you.

MAGGIE: Hey—

BEGGAR KING: Excellent, excellent!

DANNY: *(Fishing through his wallet.)* Speaking of which…when is your audition?

BEGGAR KING: Tomorrow at one o'clock.

DANNY: Then we must act decisively! Here take this…*(Hands BEGGAR KING a twenty-dollar bill.)* A little starter-up stake!

BEGGAR KING: Dear sir!

DANNY: Now, now, no need to thank me. I look upon it as an investment.

BEGGAR KING: You take my breath away!

DANNY: Might I suggest a shave and a haircut? Perhaps a visitation to the Russian and Turkish Baths on Tenth Street where you can sweat out some of that road dust?

BEGGAR KING: A sublime notion!

DANNY: Break a leg! Maggie, see that my friend gets anything he needs! Put it on my tab!

MAGGIE: What?

DANNY: Talk to you later—ta ta! *(Hastens offstage.)*

MAGGIE: DANNY WAIT! DANNY?

(In his haste, DANNY has left behind his book.)

MAGGIE: DANNY YOU FORGOT YOUR BOOK! DANNY?

BEGGAR KING: *(Crossing over.)* A ploy on his part…gives the lad an excuse to come back! *(Nods and winks in a conspiratorial fashion.)*

(Sighing, MAGGIE picks up the book.)

BEGGAR KING: Now, dear lady, might I take a quick perusal of your playbooks?

(A slight pause.)

MAGGIE: Step into my office!

(The lights fade as the two cross to the book table.)

SCENE 8.

CODY's loft in Alphabet City. Late afternoon. Two months later. The loft is an artisan workspace, large and foreboding. Upstage left, a door leading to a landing. Right center, a workbench littered with paints, brushes, turpentine, and other tools. Downstage left, two beat-up wicker chairs and a crate that serves as a table. Down right, an easel with a work in progress: a portrait of LINNEA. The back wall of the loft is taken up with canvases of various sizes and shapes. Some are mounted on the wall, some simply lean against it. The bigger canvases are "Mad Boy" abstracts.

*All the others (save one) are studies of
LINNEA, including several nudes. The
one exception: a gargoyle-like self-portrait
of CODY hangs close to the center of the
wall. As the lights rise, CODY is behind
the workbench, cleaning brushes. A knock
comes from behind the door. CODY goes
to the door and opens it. DANNY stands
upon the landing.*

CODY: You're like the bad penny—you
keep coming back!

DANNY: Hello, Cody. Can I come in?

CODY: Sure.

*(He ushers DANNY in, letting the door slam
shut behind him. An awkward silence.)*

DANNY: I, eh, had an interesting walk
over.

CODY: You know what they say about
Alphabet City? "Avenue A, you're all
right. Avenue B, you're brave. Avenue C,
you're crazy. Avenue D, you're dead!" Of
course, all that's changing now. The yup-
pies are invading our territory. Soon we'll
be a nice respectable neighborhood!

DANNY: *(Indicating the portrait of
CODY.)* Is that—is that a self-portrait?

CODY: Yep.

DANNY: Did it come from staring at
yourself too long in the mirror?

CODY: Something like that.

DANNY: Surprised to see me?

CODY: Bowled over backwards.

DANNY: I thought I saw you earlier
this afternoon.

CODY: Oh?

DANNY: On St. Mark's standing in
front of the revival house.

CODY: Wasn't me, babe.

DANNY: Then you—you haven't been
following me around?

CODY: Now why would I be doing
that?

DANNY: I—I don't know.

CODY: Is that what you came here for—
to ask me that?

DANNY: N-no—not really.

CODY: What is it then? Afternoon tea?

DANNY: Is she…is she staying here?

CODY: What's it to you?

DANNY: I—I haven't heard from her in
a couple of weeks.

CODY: Coming to her rescue?

DANNY: Look, Cody, I—I thought
we cleared this up that afternoon in the
Grassroots. You know, when you called
for your Big Summit Meeting and had
your two goons come and fetch me? Back
then I truly believed things were over
between you two. In retrospect, I realize
I was being naive. When she came to me
in May, so open and honest, how could I
refuse her? She was so sad—so sad and so
tired—how could I not take her in?

CODY: That's all very touching, Jocko!

DANNY: The Cody I knew in the
Grassroots—he would have understood.
The one standing here now, staring
me down—Well, I won't bother you
again. Just know this: I regret the way
this all played out. I feel ashamed that I
avoided you for so long and, well, I—I
never meant to betray you. Take care of
yourself. *(Heads for the door.)*

CODY: Don't go, Jock. It's been a while.
Come—come sit down.

(CODY leads him to the wicker chairs. They both sit and are silent for a while.)

CODY: No, the trouble—it's not between you and me—it's you, the girl, and me. All that running back and forth between us—it's like she needs us both. Take the springtime—she quit her job— she was living a quiet life with you—then the panic set in. Back she comes asking me to marry her.

DANNY: W-what?

CODY: Didn't know that, did you? Oh sure, she wanted to get hitched. But not for the reasons people normally get married. It's because she didn't want to ruin your life! With me it's fine—but you she wants to protect!

DANNY: I—I don't understand.

CODY: It's because we love her in different ways, Jocko—and she becomes a different Linnea with each of us. With me she has no problem dancing at Fallen Angels and playing con games with the suckers there. But who knew that you'd bring out an entirely new Linnea—one who was horrified by the actions of the old Linnea and would try to clean up her act! But then, the old desires return and back she comes running to me.

DANNY: Only to return to me in two weeks' time.

CODY: Quite a fun-filled summer! I don't know…it's like she's split in two and no amount of attention or love from either of us can make her whole. For instance, the last time she lived with you, did you know she was still seeing me? Oh yeah, while you were off with the kiddies, she and I were playing hooky together!

DANNY: I knew.

CODY: Did you?

DANNY: She told me it was only one time—to see if there was anything left between you.

CODY: One time! And you believed that? Hell, even if it was only one time— why do it? Why sully her paradise on earth with a guy like me? By the same token, if I were suddenly to be removed from the equation—if I were struck by a lightning bolt or something—do you think it would be ukuleles in the sand for you and your Linnea? Please, in a day or two, she'd be seeking out the next Cody!

DANNY: Are you—are you really considering marriage?

CODY: Don't make me laugh! That was a whim of hers! Five minutes after bringing it up, she was onto something else!

DANNY: Listen to me, Cody: I only came here to see if you knew of her whereabouts. She left me so abruptly and for no apparent reason. It would be nice to know the reasons why—most of all, I want to see for myself that she's all right. I—I just want this to be over!

CODY: Have you—have you really stopped loving her?

(A slight pause.)

DANNY: The sad truth is I've stopped loving her *that way.*

CODY: What other way is there! No wonder she flew the coup! She takes tremendous pride in her sexuality.

(DANNY has been fixating on the portrait on the easel. A pause.)

CODY: What is it, Jocko? You keep staring at that painting.

DANNY: Sorry! It's just—well, I find it very interesting.

CODY: You like it, huh? I'm on the fence about it.

DANNY: No, no, it's good—very different from the others. Those are dark and filled with anger. This one—this one you really see the little girl lost—the Linnea who might have been.

CODY: You know what they say about art—it's the one place where you can get things right!

DANNY: Tell me, Cody: if you're able to paint with such…with such compassion…why aren't you capable of feeling it in real life?

CODY: *(Laughing.)* It's not that I'm incapable of it—it's just that—for me—desire negates everything else—including compassion. When Linnea's away from me, I can sympathize with her and her life. But when she's with me, the desire swells up and blots out everything else. Sometimes—sometimes, it frightens me.

DANNY: It frightens me too. Who knows? Someday you may do her serious harm.

CODY: Serious harm! What's that, a line out of a book—maybe your Russian play! *(Stands.)* You know what your problem is, Jocko? You should have never left your little hovel in the first place. Life on the outside is a little darker, a little dirtier, than anything you ever read about in your philosophy books. You're just begging to be hurt or disappointed. You want to learn about *serious harm*, hmm? Come here!

(CODY leads DANNY behind the workbench.)

CODY: One time Linnea was staying with me and we got into an argument. Surprise, surprise, huh! Anyway, we ended up standing as close to each other as you and I are standing now. I found myself with this edge cutter in my hand. *(CODY now holds a blade used for cutting canvas.)* I was holding it six inches from Linnea and my hand was shaking. *(Now holds it at a corresponding length to DANNY's navel.)* I swear to Christ, if at that moment, she had said the wrong thing—if she had uttered so much as one misguided syllable—well, who knows what serious harm might have befallen her? *(Bursts out laughing and just as suddenly turns sullen.)*

DANNY: P-please put that down.

(CODY tosses it back on the table. He leans over, elbows on the workbench, head in hands. A long pause. Finally, CODY turns back to DANNY.)

CODY: Show's over! It's time you left. Besides…you don't want to be in this neighborhood after dark.

DANNY: All right.

(CODY gently leads DANNY to the door.)

DANNY: Well I…

CODY: She's not living here. I have no idea where she's staying. I wouldn't sweat it though—our Linnea's a survivor. That's the one constant. This I do know: she's back at Fallen Angels. She couldn't stay away. Go to her. I won't interfere. You see, Jocko—I just want it to be over too.

DANNY: All right. Thanks.

(CODY opens the door. DANNY steps across the threshold.)

CODY: Ah, Jocko, Jocko me boy! What a pity. If it wasn't for a skinny-legs-and-all obsession, who knows? You and I might have ended up friends!

(He closes the door before DANNY can respond. He crosses to the table and resumes cleaning his brushes. On an impulse he crosses to the easel and paces back and forth in front of it—appears about to resume work on the painting. Instead, he kicks the easel over in disgust.)

CODY: Fuck it!

(Blackout.)

Scene 9.

Music up: something blue. Fallen Angels, a few nights later. The blue silhouette of the SHADOW DANCER grinding in time to the music. DANNY, looking disheveled, sits alone at one table, finishing up a beer and smoking a cigarette. To his upstage right, at another table, sits a dapper gentleman anywhere between fifty and sixty years old. MAN sips a whiskey and soda—an unaffected Alec-Guiness-out-of-makeup. (In reality, it's BEGGAR KING, out of costume and character.) RED and SLIM sit at their table. SUSAN is serving them another round.

SUSAN: That will be twenty dollars.

RED and SLIM: TWENTY DOLLARS!

SUSAN: Check. Two whiskey and beer chasers. Twenty dollars.

SLIM: How's our credit?

SUSAN: I beg your pardon?

SLIM: I SAID, HOW'S OUR CREDIT?

SUSAN: About as good as your chances of getting laid tonight!

(A rim shot.)

RED: Everybody wants ta get inta de act!

SUSAN: You paying or what?

SLIM: Hold your horses!

(SLIM nudges RED.)

SLIM: Pay her!

RED: What?

SLIM: It's your round—pay her!

(Muttering miserably to himself, RED fishes through his pockets, pulling out some loose change plus a never-ending stream of props, and placing them on the table. The collection should range from the profane—wind-up toys, chattering teeth—to the perverse—prophylactics and sadomasochistic sex toys. SLIM sits doing an Edgar Kennedy slow burn, finally interrupting.)

SLIM: NEVERMIND! *(Handing SUSAN a twenty.)* Here. Keep it.

SUSAN: Keep what? You owe twenty!

SLIM: And dere's a twenty—keep it!

(A rim shot. Defeated, SUSAN crosses to DANNY's table.)

RED: Nice save at de end!

SLIM: When dey's lookin' fer de fastball—slip 'em de curve!

SUSAN: *(Replacing DANNY's beer.)* Since when did you start smoking?

DANNY: Since the summer.

SUSAN: Go figure!

(The silhouette and music fade out.)

DANNY: *(Holding the money.)* Does she know yet?

SUSAN: I told her.

(He pays her.)

SUSAN: Thanks. If I were you, I'd nurse this one. You already seem three sheets to the wind!

DANNY: It's not the beer, Susan—it's this place. You see, a long time ago, I went through the Looking Glass. Now—now I'm trying to find my way back.

SUSAN: Well, sit tight. *(Exits through the curtains.)*

MAN: I dreamt a dream! What can it mean?

DANNY: Come again?

MAN: Blake. William Blake. I dreamt a dream! What can it mean?

DANNY: Do I know you?

MAN: As that Irish S.O.B. Peter O'Toole once said: "I recognize the name but not the face."

(DANNY laughs.)

MAN: May I join you?

DANNY: Why not?

MAN: *(Crossing.)* Do you really not know me?

DANNY: I'm not sure. This room works in strange ways. Maybe I'm drunker than I thought!

MAN: *(Sitting.)* What do they call this place? The Shadows?

RED: That's right: de Shadows!

SLIM: Udderwise known as de end of da line!

MAN: The only place for me! Here I can simply be.

RED: Is dat in de physical or de metaphysical sense of de woird?

SLIM: Don't start!

(A rim shot.)

MAN: What about you, laddie? What brings you here?

DANNY: How is it I think you already know?

MAN: Perhaps I do. I can see you're at a crossroads, laddie. Tonight can turn out one of two ways: you can walk out of here a free man or—

SLIM: Youz can end up here wit' us!

RED: Banished to de back room!

SLIM: Where no one will know 'n' no one will care!

RED: No gurls will come 'n' sit wit' youz!

SLIM: No waitresses will come 'n' check on yer drink!

RED: You'll be lost. Lost in de Shadows!

SLIM: Psst, kid: how's ya credit?

(A rim shot. Both CLOWNS laugh.)

MAN: Take heed, young man. Despite their foolish repartee, these two gentlemen know of what they speak. You suffer from a malaise very common to the younger generation. You are, as our friend here so blithely puts it, Lost in the Shadows—trapped between reality and dreams. You see, like the poet Blake, you were granted a Vision.

(Music up: the Siren Song.)

MAN: A Fallen Angel of the night came to you in an early morning dream. She sang her Siren Song and, like the hero of ancient lore, you followed her.

(The silhouette of the SHADOW DANCER appears upon the scrim.)

MAN: The road she led you on was dark. It wound with many twists and turns. But tonight it brings you back to this room. Tonight it all ends.

(The SHADOW DANCER beckons. Lights down on the tables as DANNY crosses to the scrim. There he pauses, gazing upon his Vision. With newfound resolution, DANNY bursts back behind the scrim. He begins to slow dance with the SHADOW DANCER—the perfect synthesis of life and art. The two silhouettes meld together—almost one. Eventually, the music and shadow play fade. Lights to normal levels as DANNY and LINNEA back out from behind the screen, still holding each other, staring into each other's eyes. LINNEA wears white.)

LINNEA: I saw you watching me as I danced.

DANNY: I couldn't *not* watch.

LINNEA: I know.

DANNY: My name is Danny.

LINNEA: I'm—

DANNY: I know who you are, Linnea.

LINNEA: How—how did you know my name?

DANNY: I've always known. You're the girl of my dreams, remember?

LINNEA: Buy me a drink, Danny? That way we can sit and talk.

SLIM: Don't do it, kid!

RED: Derein lies madness!

(A pause.)

DANNY: Sure.

(SLIM and RED groan. DANNY and LINNEA walk hand in hand to the table. The lights arise there; SUSAN has anticipated their round.)

SUSAN: These are on the house.

DANNY: Thank you.

(She exits. A pause.)

DANNY: I just realized something. You've been staying at Susan's.

LINNEA: Have Linnea Droppings will travel!

DANNY: So...let's talk.

LINNEA: You want to know why I left?

DANNY: Uh-huh.

LINNEA: I left you when I could. Before things got bad.

DANNY: Bad? In what way?

LINNEA: It's—hard to explain.

DANNY: Please try. I've been a wreck.

LINNEA: I'm sorry for that. But you see—one day—after you'd gone off to work—I read your play. It—it really freaked me out.

DANNY: How?

LINNEA: The girl in it—she was—just—so horrible! Running back and forth between the two guys like—like some kind of lunatic! And reading it, I realized that this was your take on me—this is how you perceived who I was—and it sort of pissed me off—but most of all, it really hurt me.

DANNY: Linnea, this was a character based on a book, adapted for a play started long before I met you! Perhaps, in retrospect, you overreacted a little?

LINNEA: I thought you just said you've always known me? If that's true, then you should have known this: the only reason the girl goes back and forth between the two is because *neither one of them gives her everything that she needs!*

(A pause.)

DANNY: I'm sorry, Linnea. I've been going around feeling sorry for myself—thinking I've been wronged in some way. I see now that it's me who's done you the disservice!

LINNEA: No you haven't, honey. Look, the reasons why I left you the first night are pretty much the same reasons why I left in the summer. But—but that doesn't mean that our interim together wasn't—wasn't special to me. There was a lot of love and a lot of shared experiences—and damn it—we had fun together! Admit it, I taught you how to have fun!

DANNY: You taught me a hell of a lot more than that. Some of it was—well painful—but, hey, that's the price of an education!

LINNEA: You were a teacher to me too, Danny. Remember our first night together—you said to me…you said—oh Jesus, I'm going to start to cry! You said, "There was something *profound* about my dancing." That I was working things out through my dance. Remember that?

DANNY: Of course.

LINNEA: It made such an impression on me. You see, Danny…I'm leaving the city. Susan and I have it all planned. We're buying a couple of bus tickets and heading out West. Our goal is to settle in Vegas.

DANNY: You're—you're leaving?

LINNEA: Uh-huh. I really have to get away from this circus. You see, I don't want to become the girl from your play! And—and the only way to do that is—is to make a clean break. If you're a dancer, Las Vegas is the place to be. I'll be able to find work there—in the desert I'll make myself pure again—and—who knows—make something of my life.

DANNY: Wow! *Viva Las Vegas!*

(LINNEA laughs despite herself.)

DANNY: So is this goodbye?

LINNEA: It doesn't have to be. Come visit me once we're settled. What do you say, Danny? Two madcaps on the Vegas Strip?

DANNY: Can you really picture me out there?

LINNEA: We won't know until we get you there! *(Leaning in seductively.)* Who knows, lover? With Cody out of the picture—maybe—maybe we can still make a go of it!

DANNY: Cody! Jesus, I forgot all about Cody!

LINNEA: W-what—what is it?

DANNY: *(Standing.)* Look, I'm pretty sure Cody's been following me around all evening!

LINNEA: What! W-why would he be doing that?

DANNY: Who knows? We're talking about Cody here! The point is I've led him right to your doorstep! We've got to get you out of here—and fast!

LINNEA: What?

DANNY: Don't you get it? You're leaving town tonight!

LINNEA: W-why?

DANNY: He's going to pop up here any minute now! You've got to get out of town! Just go out the back way, grab a cab, and hightail it to the bus station!

LINNEA: But Danny—

DANNY: There's no time for this! Have you got enough money?

LINNEA: I'm—I'm a little short.

DANNY: How short is short?

LINNEA: *(Weakly.)* E-eighty dollars!

DANNY: *(Fishing through his wallet.)* Look, here's a hundred bucks—take it.

LINNEA: Danny—I can't!

DANNY: *(Forcing it into her palm.)* JUST TAKE THE GODDAMNED MONEY!

LINNEA: All right…thank you. I—I owe you.

DANNY: Forget about it. Okay, now let's get Susan! *(Races to the curtains. Calling offstage.)* Susan? Psst! Susan! Come here!

(SUSAN appears at the curtains.)

SUSAN: What is it?

DANNY: I know all about your plans.

SUSAN: Y-you do?

DANNY: *(Taking her by the arm.)* Look I'm cool with it, Susan. But you two have to leave—now!

SUSAN: But what's the rush?

DANNY: There's no time to explain! Just go out the back door with Linnea!

LINNEA: Come on, Susan. I'll tell you all about it in the cab.

DANNY: Hurry!

(The two cross to the scrim. LINNEA turns.)

LINNEA: Goodbye, Danny! I'll—I'll be in touch. God bless you.

DANNY: Safe trip, kid. I'll—I'll see you in my dreams!

(The two exit behind the scrim. A pause. DANNY collapses in his chair.)

DANNY: Hoo boy! That sure sobered me up!

MAN: Well played, lad!

DANNY: Hey, the least I could do was give her a clean send-off!

MAN: Do you think you'll ever hear from her again?

DANNY: Hard to say.

RED: I'll tell ya one thing—you can kiss dat C-note goodbye!

SLIM: De price of an education!

DANNY: *(Springs to his feet and crosses to the CLOWNS' table.)* Now you listen to me, Bozo—we have to buy them some time! When Cody arrives, just play along with what I have to say—otherwise there'll be hell to pay! Get my drift?

(The two CLOWNS nervously look at each other.)

SLIM: We get ya!

(In the distance a tugboat sounds. CODY silently comes in through the curtains.)

DANNY: *(Turning.)* Hello Cody. I was wondering when you'd show up!

CODY: Where—where is she?

DANNY: She left.

CODY: What do you mean left?

DANNY: About an hour ago. Slim says she went home sick. Isn't that right, Slim?

SLIM: *(Nodding.)* Yeah. Sick.

(A pause.)

CODY: I get it. Off with a mark, huh?

DANNY: *(Standing.)* What can I say? You trained her well, my friend!

(RED lets out an involuntary giggle.)

CODY: *(Advancing.)* What is it? What's going on here?

(The two CLOWNS exchange glances.)

CODY: Well?

(CODY grabs SLIM by the collar.)

CODY: TELL ME GODDAMNIT!

SLIM: LINNEA'S RAN OFF WITH DAT DIKE WAITRESS!

CODY: *(Releasing him.)* What?

SLIM: DEY'S HEADIN' FER VEGAS! DEY JUS' BOLTED OUT DE BACK!

(A pause.)

CODY: Well now…we'll just see about that.

(He crosses toward the scrim. With lightning quickness, DANNY blocks his path.)

DANNY: Not so fast, Cody!

CODY: Get out of my way, Jocko!

DANNY: Let them go, Cody.

CODY: YOU LIED TO ME, JOCK! I'LL DEAL WITH YOU LATER! NOW GET THE FUCK OUT OF MY WAY!

DANNY: No.

CODY: I don't want to have to hurt you, Jocko!

DANNY: Cody, deep down you just want this to be over too! Now the only way you're getting past me is if you kill me or knock me out!

CODY: WHY YOU LITTLE MOTHERFUCKER! I SAID OUT OF MY WAY!

(In his fury, CODY hurls DANNY to the floor. He immediately springs up and tackles CODY before he can exit. The two begin to grapple. CODY initially gets the better of the skirmish, but DANNY shows remarkable resiliency. Blows are exchanged. Neither of the combatants appears willing to give quarter. The energy and passion of the fray dissipates; the fight begins to take on a comical, Three Stooges aspect. Both men are exhausted and past the point of inflicting any real harm. By this point CODY holds DANNY aloft and is shaking him, when:)

DANNY: *(Struggling for breath.)* Y-you want—want to—go get a beer with me?

CODY: *(Letting go of his former foe.)* Y-you—you want to go drinking?

DANNY: *(On the floor, gasping.)* W-why not? The—the Grassroots—w-we'll tie one on—f-for old times sake! We're drinking buddies aren't we?

CODY: *(Helping him to his feet.)* You buying?

DANNY: Unh-uh. You are. You owe me eighty dollars.

CODY: Huh! Getting pretty ballsy in your old age, ain't ya Jock!

DANNY: That's right.

CODY: Hmm! I finally made a man of you! So…what are we waiting for?

(The two head to the curtained exit, where DANNY pauses.)

DANNY: Thanks old man! We'll see you soon.

(He and CODY exit.)

RED: So long, sucker!

SLIM: Not ta worry—he'll be back!

MAN: No, I don't think he will. *(Raising his glass.)* Anyway, here's to our young friend! Tonight he earned his stripes!

(The two CLOWNS raise their mugs.)

RED and SLIM: Cheers!

RED: 'N' here's ta de act!

RED and SLIM: To de act!

(The two clink and drink.)

SLIM: Say, eh, Mister—ya ever considered burlesque?

MAN: Sorry, old boy—I'm strictly legitimate theater!

(A rim shot. Blackout.)

EPILOGUE

Tompkins Square Park. The next morning. A sleepless, somewhat hung-over DANNY sits on his fabled park bench, writing in his notebook. Enter MAGGIE pulling her red cart, looking rather radiant.

DANNY: Good morning, Maggie.

MAGGIE: Aren't you the early bird! Up early or out late?

DANNY: Need you ask?

MAGGIE: Looks like you closed a bar or two!

DANNY: Let's just say I watched the sunrise from the night owl's point of view!

MAGGIE: Young Hemingway! How are you otherwise?

DANNY: All things considered, I'm doing pretty well. Things have a way of working out.

MAGGIE: They do, don't they?

DANNY: Did you, eh, happen to retrieve my book?

MAGGIE: *(Sighing, fishes through her boxes and pulls out the book.)* I was told you'd be back! *(Hands it to him.)*

DANNY: Thanks. It won't happen again!

MAGGIE: It better not!

DANNY: So, eh, what are you up to on this beautiful Sunday?

MAGGIE: I was heading to a friend's loft. She's moving out and has a bunch of books she wants me to take a look at.

DANNY: I see. Is selling books your life's work?

MAGGIE: It's actually a front—I'm really a spy working for a secret government agency!

DANNY: Huh! Think you can take time out from your double life to go to breakfast?

MAGGIE: You asking me out?

DANNY: Well—I mean—only if you can spare the time!

MAGGIE: I can if the breakfast is at Veselka's!

DANNY: Think you can park the paddy wagon there?

MAGGIE: I might have some pull with the management.

DANNY: Veselka's it is!

(MAN—aka BEGGAR KING—enters, perusing a manuscript.)

MAN: Good morrow, dear friends, how do you both?

DANNY: Very well.

MAN: "You and I have heard the Chimes at Midnight"—eh, old boy!

DANNY: But what's that you're holding? Can it be?

MAN: It can, it can!

DANNY: Then you got the part?

MAN: *(Proudly displaying his script.)* I open in four weeks!

MAGGIE: Congratulations!

DANNY: Bravo, old man, bravo!

MAN: I couldn't have done it without the two of you. Please come and see the show.

DANNY: Of course!

MAN: There'll be two tickets left for you at the box office.

DANNY: *Mille grazie!*

MAN: No…thank you! *(Exits.)*

DANNY: Ready?

MAGGIE: Uh-huh.

(As they exit:)

MAGGIE: Danny?

DANNY: Yes, Maggie?

MAGGIE: You, of course, are free to do what you want. But after breakfast, might I suggest you head home and catch forty winks. Every time I see you, you look more exhausted than the last!

DANNY: Ah yes, sleep—I've heard of that! *Perchance to dream!*

MAGGIE: What you will, sir!

(The two exit the park together.)

(The End.)

...AND WE ALL WORE LEATHER PANTS

Robert Attenweiler

ROBERT ATTENWEILER is a writer and independent producer. He was born in 1975 and raised in Mansfield, Ohio. He received a BA in English from John Carroll University, where he studied Shakespeare with Dr. Chris Roark; an MA in English from The Ohio State University; and an MFA in dramatic writing from New York University, where he studied with Arthur Kopit, Neil LaBute, and Doug Wright. He is the author of *Places Like Here* (2005 New York International Fringe Festival), *Thick Like Piano Legs, Kansas City or Along the Way* (both at The Red Room, 2006), and *The Butterfield Tones* (2007 FRIGID New York Festival), all of which were produced by his theatre company, Disgraced Productions. From 2002 to 2004, he was the recipient of a full fellowship from New York University's Dramatic Writing Department. In 2006, he was named to indietheater.org's list of Who is Indie Theater in New York. Attenweiler has also been a theatre reviewer for nytheatre.com. Since 2004, he has been a member of the Lark Play Development Center. He lives in New York City's East Village with his girlfriend and frequent collaborator, Rebecca Benhayon.

...and we all wore leather pants was first presented by Horse Trade (Erez Ziv, Managing Director) and Disgraced Productions (Robert Attenweiler, Producing Director) on September 6, 2007, at the Under St. Marks Theatre, New York City, with the following cast and credits:

Mary ....Rebecca Benhayon
Jagger .... Danny Bruckert
Blanton ....Darren Ryan
Joanne...Ariana Shore
Krank.. Joe Stipek
Crumm/Bolt Bannister.. Ryan West

Director: John Patrick Hayden
Stage Manager: Lizz Giorgos
Lighting Designer: Justin Sturges

CHARACTERS

BLANTON STURGESS, male, thirty-eight. Patriarch of the Sturgess household.

JAGGER STURGESS, male, twenty-eight. He might be a famous heavy metal musician, he might be a local mechanic.

KRANK STURGESS, male, twenty-eight. A one-man hard-core punk band, estranged from his father and brother despite living in a car parked in their driveway.

MARY STURGESS, female, twenty-six. Jagger's wife. Mother of many, when she doesn't lose them.

JOANNE JONES, female, twenty-three. Local hottie. A mysterious note links her to Krank.

MR. CRUMM, male, thirties. A social worker assigned to the Sturgess case.

BOLT BANNISTER, male, late twenties. A mysterious visitor.

PLACE

An office, the inside of Krank's car and the living room of the Sturgess home. Ashtabula, Ohio.

TIME

The mid-1980s.

ACT I
SCENE 1

Lights up on an office. BLANTON sits in a chair. On the other side of the desk, MR. CRUMM sits reading through BLANTON's file.

CRUMM: I've heard all the stories.

BLANTON: Yes, sir, Mr. Crumm.

CRUMM: We don't keep to ourselves very much in this office. We want to help, do you understand?

BLANTON: I understand you laugh at us.

CRUMM: Laughing simplifies things. Simplifies people and their problems. Simple is easier to solve than difficult, do you understand?

BLANTON: I thought laughing was only for vascular health.

CRUMM: No, what I'm saying is that I work too hard already.

BLANTON: Then I'm allowed to leave.

CRUMM: Mr. Sturgess, it's probably no news that your case has been overseen by a record number of social service employees.

BLANTON: I'm familiar with the gaggle here.

CRUMM: And, while we've been observing your family since, it says here, November 1976—

BLANTON: That one was court ordered and my wife's fault. You can't blame me—

CRUMM: Yes, but in the last nine years there's been little, if any, improvement in your situation.

BLANTON: Nine years ain't that long a time.

CRUMM: Are you and your wife still together?

BLANTON: I don't remember.

CRUMM: When was the last time you saw her?

BLANTON: It's just me and the boys now.

CRUMM: And how old are your boys?

BLANTON: They're younger n' me, as nature deems it.

CRUMM: And is it true that one of your sons is living in a car outside your home?

BLANTON: Yeah, but it's not a worry. I put that thing up on blocks.

CRUMM: But that's no way for a child to live.

BLANTON: It's one way.

CRUMM: Have you done anything in the way of looking for a job?

BLANTON: I've had a lot of jobs. Just none right now.

CRUMM: What happened to your job on the farm?

BLANTON: Drought.

CRUMM: I don't remember any drought.

BLANTON: That's what we called it. So, I went to the steel mill.

CRUMM: After the steel mill?

BLANTON: Paper mill.

CRUMM: Reason?

BLANTON: Mill closed.

CRUMM: Paper mill?

BLANTON: Steel mill closed. Paper mill burned down.

CRUMM: So—

BLANTON: Auto plant.

CRUMM: And—

BLANTON: Everyone was squeezing through the door. One place left where you could work alongside big machines. That's all any of us really wanted. More an' more of us poppin' up at the plant every day 'til eventually me an' another guy both reach to put the same part in place. An' it was hot in there. You could feel the plant like a big belly getting overstuffed, distended and gassy. Then the belly burst and we spilled out onto the streets in bilious waves. I saw some sucked under but I grabbed hold of the chrome bumper I was working on an' I rode that wave. I surfed the foaming break of the industrial stomach juice 'til I grabbed hold of the low-hanging branch of a tree and pulled myself up and waited until it all receded. My bolt gun, they tell me, wound up in a puddle outside Mexico City.

CRUMM: And are you filling your free time constructively?

BLANTON: I watch football. I watch high school football on Fridays, the local colleges on Saturday, local pros on Sunday and spend the week filling notebooks with all I can remember. I try to completely recreate a game by remembering every single play.

CRUMM: So, you'd like to coach?

BLANTON: No. It's just good to remember, don't you think? Daddy was a big fan of the Cleveland team. He loved Jim Brown—big fan of the Cleveland team.

CRUMM: You've said.

BLANTON: Said there weren't nothing so beautiful as a black man running a football. Even times Daddy took baby pictures of Jim Brown and taped them over the face on my baby pictures. Mama told me he once did the same over her face in their wedding photo an' Daddy he looked at it and punched her pretty soft after. *(Pause.)* If that's not too much to say.

CRUMM: *(Consults the file.)* Are you still active in music?

BLANTON: Nah. That was back in my lean teens. Played in a surf rock group. But not much need for surf rock here in Ashtabula. Tried to reinvent ourselves as a motorcycle club—all decked out in leather—but Johnny kept his hair blond and we were transparent.

CRUMM: I wonder why we even bother. I really do. Your file's stayed in our system for years, but you just keep spinning our wheels.

BLANTON: That's a genuine concern of mine.

CRUMM: And I don't know what to tell you that will keep me from coming over to your home, putting your kids in foster care—and just blowing up the whole shit mess.

BLANTON: I'm sure you'll find us very happy.

CRUMM: I don't think that's enough.

BLANTON: I know what you're doin'. Takin' these shots—makin' a glass house outta me—but I will tell you one thing in me's changed: I am recently turned a serious religious man. Not in the way where I'm good to people or nothin', but I heard talk on the radio the other day 'splained Jesus in a way I finally get it. Said he's comin' an' the time a comin' is soon so I figure I got to put a good face on my situation 'fore he comes and starts pickin' the wicked and the virtuous out of the flocks. Way I see it, I ain't the wicked and I ain't the virtuous—an' if I can keep a low profile when he comes 'round—nose clean and everything—I'm hopin' to fly total under his radar an' I'll wake up one day and won't be no one on this world but me and then I will have the life I always should have. 'Cause right now I only got a couple a' good things in this world—

(A sound rises. A rattling. A rumbling. A little like an earthquake. Or a far-off crash.)

BLANTON: —but I will be goddamned if anyone—even Jesus Christ himself—is gonna get their hands—

(The noise keeps building and building. Everything in the office begins to rattle as the noise gets louder and louder until blackout.)

SCENE 2

Lights up on the living room of the Sturgess home. JAGGER STURGESS sits on the floor wearing only a work shirt, boxers, and work boots. He listens to a tape in a Walkman. He hears something, stops the player, rewinds, and listens again. MARY STURGESS enters.

MARY: *(Calling.)* Ruble? Where's my puddin' head? Oh. Jagger, what the hell?

JAGGER: Something was on this tape.

MARY: Where're your pants?

JAGGER: Something was on this tape.

MARY: Yeah, Journey. It was a dub.

JAGGER: Was I ever in a band?

MARY: No, dear. Baby, why don't you just have a drink? You're making less than no sense.

(She hands him a bottle of liquor.)

JAGGER: Then I think Steve Perry was sent to confuse me. I was going to put this on the big stereo, one speaker against each ear and just blast it with the idea that I'd become Steve Perry—concentrating him so much in the small space between my ears that I got more Steve Perry in there than Steve Perry does—just long enough to put a bullet through my head.

(MARY puts the liquor bottle to his lips and tips it way back—glug, glug, glug, glug.)

MARY: Journey's got nothin' for you, Jagger. And I won't have you hurtin' the father a' my babies.

JAGGER: I'm the father of your babies.

MARY: That's right. All I got in this world you put inside a' me. What'd you think Steve was trying to help you find?

JAGGER: I don't know. Just shapes. The ones that recede…

MARY: Christ n' crutch, Jagger.

JAGGER: I fix cars, right?

MARY: You sure do, my special man.

JAGGER: Normal family.

MARY: That's all I want. I've tried too many times before.

JAGGER: Who were you callin' after before?

MARY: I wasn't callin'.

JAGGER: We got a cat or some kinda hound?

MARY: You know we can't have no hound.

JAGGER: Wait. Ruble's that little one, right? I remember now. Where'd he get off to?

(No response.)

JAGGER: You didn't—

(No response.)

JAGGER: Jesus, Mary. You lost another one.

MARY: He's around here somewhere.

JAGGER: How many does that make? How many of our kids you gonna let slide off the radar?

MARY: I'll find him, alright?

JAGGER: And are you gonna find the others too? Ruble's sister. What was her name?

MARY: Manny.

JAGGER: And the other one. The one actually got to grow to be a boy.

MARY: Sissy.

JAGGER: They were good kids. What happens?

MARY: What happens is our cupboards go bare. So, I have to go out and get your Keystone Light and shells n' cheese an' white bread and Honeycomb cereal and iceberg lettuce and ranch dressing and number of pounds of chicken thighs think to sink a horse with to keep this family running. And Ruble's not for kee-pin' peace when I got mind on matters. He's carryin' on, eatin' all matter he can pull out his own head—eatin' what he pulls out his nose, what he scrapes out his ears, what's corner of his eyes, and what of these things might get stuck 'tween his teeth. An' I tell him, "Little precious, you a gift from the almighty—your in-nocence shows us scabs what it's like to wonder again an' I plan to make you so obese filled with my love that you'll get early-onset diabetes and every time you shoot yourself full of insulin that prick'll remind you of your mother's love every last day of your life." And that quieted him. I had a downright cheerful, even-tempered baby boy. On the way home in the car we had so much fun. I sang him all the children's songs I knew. And Ruble squirmed out his car seat and started crawling around our rapidly hurtling vehicle—*but it's okay*—it'd be fine on account of how good a mother I was. An' Ruble's climbing into each of the brown paper shopping bags, scattering the food all over the back seat. So, I say "Ruble, precious, calm down, you little shit. You wonderful, god-sent, little fucking shit," and soon he nodded off to sleep—twelve pack of hotdog buns for a pillow, nestled beneath a bright yellow box of Eggo waffles. I carried him inside, still tucked in the bag. Later, when I went to put away the groceries—and not hearing a peep from my adorable little monster all afternoon—I found his place in the brown bag occupied by a pineapple. It's a

downright cheerful, even-tempered fruit, but I ain' seen our boy since.

JAGGER: Did that happen with each of 'em? Turned to fruit?

MARY: It happened different but same, you know?

(*The rumbling begins. Same as the end of Scene 1. It keeps building and building. Everything begins to rattle as the noise gets louder and louder until blackout.*)

SCENE 3

Lights up on the front seat of KRANK's car. KRANK and JOANNE sit driver/passenger. KRANK drinks from a very large Styrofoam coffee cup from a gas station. JOANNE offers a drink from her flask. KRANK waves her off.

JOANNE: This is nice.

(*KRANK shrugs.*)

JOANNE: How long you been in here?

KRANK: On four years, close.

JOANNE: What about the wintertime?

KRANK: Yeah, winter comes.

JOANNE: I mean, does it get cold?

KRANK: As anywhere.

JOANNE: How do you keep from freezing?

KRANK: One night, pro'lly the coldest since I been out here, it was too cold to sleep. So I drove around, got this thing out onto a stretch of road can't see the end of. I tied the wheel tight so the car'd stay straight and nudged a half-empty two liter of Pepsi up 'gainst the gas. I leaned this seat way back and blasted the heater and fell sound asleep rollin' down stone cold interstate. Woke up and car's stopped in the sand 'long a Lake Erie beach, all gray, blue, and white on 'count a the cold. Now car's on blocks. So, you know, lots a' blankets.

JOANNE: Only time I ever been to the beach—they say how sand gets in everything you take—came home and found mouthfuls caught in my braces.

KRANK: How'd that pass through?

JOANNE: Ended up having to get them all removed 'cause the sand was in there tearin' up my mouth 'long the slow ways the braces were straightening. Now my teeth are gonna be fucked up—all outta place and sanded evil 'cause a' that one—

KRANK: Yeah—

JOANNE: Yeah. Why did you call me?

KRANK: Found this in my pocket the other day— *(Takes a note from his pocket.)* —got your name and number on it.

JOANNE: I give out notes with my name and number to lots of boys.

KRANK: But you didn't never give this to me, did you?

JOANNE: Did I? You got any food here?

(KRANK rustles through a crumpled-up McDonald's bag and finds a half-eaten sandwich.)

KRANK: Sorry. I was gonna save the whole thing for you. But that was a couple days ago. When I first found the note.

JOANNE: No, it's—It's okay.

KRANK: I like to have something to offer. But I don't get the callers.

(She leans in to kiss him. KRANK moves away.)

JOANNE: Why'd you call me?

KRANK: 'Cause I found your number.

JOANNE: An' you call every number you ever seen?

KRANK: Do you know who I am?

JOANNE: You're Krank Sturgess. You live in a car up on blocks.

KRANK: And do I know you?

JOANNE: Looks like you don't want to.

KRANK: I just—I'm not good at asking for help.

JOANNE: Why do you think I'd even be able to if you asked?

KRANK: 'Cause it says on here: "Joanne Jones can help you."

JOANNE: *(Looks at the note.)* That's not my normal line.

KRANK: What are you prepared to do?

JOANNE: What are you prepared to do?

KRANK: Can I get you a cup of coffee?

JOANNE: Sure.

KRANK: *(Pulls a pot from the backseat.)* Do you take it with blackener or with whitener?

JOANNE: Black better.

(He pours it into a Styrofoam cup, the same as his. She drinks.)

JOANNE: This is good. How do you keep it warm?

KRANK: Mix of carpet fibers and dried leaves keeps a good flame.

JOANNE: This thing is on fire right now?

KRANK: A very low fire. People tell ya shouldn't have fires inside a' cars, but they mean when you don't think n' crack a window.

JOANNE: Are you sure?

KRANK: *(Pulls out a Chips Ahoy cookie.)* They're good. Dip 'em in coffee. Too hard otherwise.

JOANNE: Thank you.

KRANK: They're good. Dip 'em. Decorated this place myself. Been doin' stuff by myself for a long time. Eat by myself. Got a kiddy pool in the trunk where I take baths.

JOANNE: See, I don't know no one got a place their own. Ingenuity's new to me.

KRANK: I got a band. Called "Me." That's what it is: me. Play the bass guitar. Sing. Write songs. Done it all myself. Carry all my equipment. Walk to shows 'cause my car's up on blocks. I never want to make any money doin' it. I'm not doin' it so someone'll say I'm talented.

JOANNE: Sounds you're pretty well set. That's the soil of a good crop a' life.

KRANK: Completely devoid of financial support, patronage, or public interest. My most original creative thoughts will be forgotten as soon as I forget them. That will be my legacy.

JOANNE: What am I to this?

KRANK: I thought you could tell me.

JOANNE: Me? No. I live in my grand-mother's basement and get two nights off from nursing school.

KRANK: So you got nothing for me? That's what you're hinting, right?

JOANNE: I don't know what you want.

KRANK: I knew it. Stupid calling you. All you gonna give me is nothing, I can do that well myself.

JOANNE: But—

KRANK: You may take one more Chips Ahoy if you like, but then I'm asking you to leave.

JOANNE: What if you tour?

KRANK: Flesh that.

JOANNE: Why not tour? Out on the road is when legends are made so, it stands, it might be where you can make people forget you entirely.

KRANK: Out on the road...

JOANNE: Out on the road. Except that you live on a car up on blocks.

KRANK: Then we'll have to make one stop first.

(JOANNE leans over to kiss KRANK. KRANK moves away.)

KRANK: What's with that?

JOANNE: You're not the only one found a note.

(She pulls out a note and hands it to him.)

KRANK: It reads: "Krank Sturgess will give you what you want." What do you want?

JOANNE: And baby makes three, right?

(The same noise starts up. Rumble, rumble, rumble.)

JOANNE: What's happening?

(Noise escalates. Blackout.)

SCENE 4

In black. The Sturgess living room. JAGGER and MARY wade about looking for flashlights.

MARY: Ruble? Ruble, if you can hear me: your daddy n' me right 'round the corner from finding you.

JAGGER: 'Less you might wanna find us first.

MARY: Baby, if you find us first—and if you can remember where Mommy put the flashlight—

JAGGER: That'd be a good boy—

MARY: Mommy's love for you a big ole pot a' steaming porridge I sit you down and make you eat every bite.

JAGGER: Ruble, you find us first, maybe just turn the lights back on if you can figure out the problem.

MARY: You there yet, baby doll? We don't know he's found the trouble. Don't even know he's in the house. Oh, here— *(Finds a flashlight and switches it on.)*

JAGGER: I was his age, I was pickin' locks to gun cabinets and whole lotta useful stuff help my parents pull weight. All I know is there are plenty a' people 'round here got kids sensible enough to be trusted with stuff. If I'm gonna be sittin' here in the dark, I'd like to think I could 'least send out my kid for a bucket a' chicken and a carton a' menthol cigarettes.

MARY: He once found me a MoonPie been dropped behind the fridge—

JAGGER: I just put high hopes on him, s'all.

(The rumbling noise starts again. MARY looks out the window. The noise builds and builds—then cuts out. The lights come back on.)

MARY: Are you gonna tease me if I tell you what I saw?

JAGGER: I'll tease you if it's stupid. I'll tease you if you're lyin'.

MARY: I looked outside maybe see that sweet, idiot munchkin a' ours. And while that noise goin', I looked up and the sky went from near black to purple, then orange, then red—like someone cracked the sky 'gainst a fryin' pan an' I was seein' what was behind it.

JAGGER: You're talkin' that way I don't understand.

MARY: I think the sky spit a gob a' meteor right down our shorts.

JAGGER: And if Ruble was out there—

MARY: You may have noticed that I am extremely weak in the knees.

JAGGER: And you're gonna tell me this the only one of our kids you ever got hit with a meteor—

MARY: Where's that bottle a' spirits?

JAGGER: Wait. Listen.

MARY: What?

JAGGER: You don't hear nothing, right?

MARY: No.

JAGGER: You don't hear nothing like what you think you'd hear after a meteor shower. What do you think you'd hear?

MARY: I don't know. Lot a' screamin'. Sobbin' and wailin' from those got limbs torn out down near point a' impact. Maybe a siren. Bunch, even more likely. Lot a' local hounds goin' at it. People blasting their car stereos to keep from thinking they might want to look in their rearview mirror and see what's become of the skin on their face.

JAGGER: And you don't hear any of that, do ya?

MARY: Not, like, really.

JAGGER: Okay.

MARY: Okay.

JAGGER: Maybe you should take a look.

MARY: Oh, but if Ruble's out there—and he seems the kind meteors would have a special taste for—I don't think I could bear to see him that way.

JAGGER: Well, our baby could just be a pineapple now. Right, Mare? A delicious fruit with that same spikey mop a' hair all the kids wearin' these days.

MARY: Yeah, I guess…

JAGGER: Well *I'm* sure as hell not goin' out there.

MARY: Why not?

JAGGER: Radiation, Mare? Think falling rocks bring with 'em a crock a pot roast? Radiation.

MARY: The kind I use to tan?

JAGGER: The kind goes straight for the hands. If I go out there, I could come back tan as tinkerbell—but radiation on me like a mess a' spiders—snackin', then dinin', then *cripplin'* my hands. And how am I s'posed to play guitar—

MARY: Fix cars—

JAGGER: Fix cars…

MARY: Jagger, listen to me, only time you ever picked up a guitar it made a noise so god awful you had to pick up all the dead birds fall from the sky. Remember?

JAGGER: I just…

MARY: Dead birds. An' what else? Maybe that's why I can't find the baby. Maybe that's you too.

(MARY exits. From offstage, someone starts pounding on the front door. Knock, knock, knock. JAGGER hides. Knock, knock, knock. KRANK peeks his head through the door.)

KRANK: Jagger.

(JAGGER tackles KRANK and pins him. JOANNE enters.)

JAGGER: Who're you?

KRANK: Jagger, it's me.

JAGGER: Who are you?

KRANK: It's Krank. Your brother.

JAGGER: I don't—

(MARY enters.)

MARY: Yes, you do. Remember Krank, your brother.

JAGGER: Oh, it's Krank, my brother.

KRANK: Shit, man.

JAGGER: Yeah. Sorry.

KRANK: You don't dress no more?

JAGGER: No pants a' mine feel right.

KRANK: You don't visit no more?

JAGGER: Well, I'm busy. I fix cars. Got several children all 'round here someplace. And you live so far away.

KRANK: I live in the driveway.

JAGGER: Her and I sleep on a foldout. *(To JOANNE.)* Who're you?

JOANNE: Jo Jones.

JAGGER: Yeah, I used to stutter too. Had problems with my s's.

KRANK: Where's Dad?

MARY: He had to meet with those people in town again. The social worker.

KRANK: They're not going to try to make me move back in here, are they? 'Cause I'll light them all on fire if I have too. I've done it before—

MARY: I know, I know. He should've been back by now—and then we heard the meteor shower—Is it bad out there?

KRANK: Whole world's a muddy shoe print.

MARY: Lots a' fire?

KRANK: Lot a' fires come an' burned out an' whole lot more 'fore everything's cleaned up.

MARY: Krank?

KRANK: Mmm-hmm?

MARY: You know I'm asking about literal fires.

KRANK: Oh, then, no.

JAGGER: What decent meteor shower don't bring fire?

MARY: Did you hear the noise? And feel everything shake?

JOANNE: Yeah. From under the ground, felt like.

MARY: No, not from under the ground. From the sky.

JOANNE: I know what I felt.

MARY: I know what I saw.

JAGGER: Maybe we're just talking about two different things.

JOANNE: I know that after, Krank had this soft white glow coming from behind his head—like maybe God had come from deep in the earth and was touching Krank, imparting a blessing on him saying "This is now a special time."

JAGGER: Well, that's a relief.

KRANK: I can't, you know, confirm that happened.

MARY: That's what you come to tell us? Hole yourself up in that car four years now—won't set a foot through this door—won't come see none of our babies—don't help us look when they go missin' and you come back n' tell us this is a special time?

KRANK: I need the tires.

JAGGER: Tires.

KRANK: I know Dad took 'em.

JAGGER: I know tires. Tires to what?

KRANK: I know Dad put that car up on blocks. And wager he's got 'em somewhere here.

MARY: What you need tires for? Tires gonna make that thing look busy.

JOANNE: We're settin' to tour. I'm gonna help Krank ruin his reputation and he's gonna give me what I want.

JAGGER: Sounds fair trade. Where ya gonna go?

JOANNE: Alliance, Ashland, Bedford Heights, Brecksville, Bucyrus, Chillicothe, Coshocton—

JAGGER: You're gonna tour alphabetical.

KRANK: Yeah, man. Think anyone ever has before?

MARY: So, Ashtabula's drippin' stomach juices and you think to high tail. *(Exits. Offstage.)* Ruble!

JAGGER: What about me an' the old man?

KRANK: Old man can go get himself stuck 'tween its teeth. Hope he does.

JAGGER: An' I'm not s'posed to keep goin' to my job at the garage?

KRANK: You don't have a job at a garage.

JAGGER: I fix cars. Don't I?

(MARY enters.)

MARY: Yes, you do fix cars. You have a nice normal job at the garage.

KRANK: That's what they're telling you?

JAGGER: Nice, normal job. What's wrong with that?

KRANK: Jagger, to my knowledge, you haven't left this house once in almost four years.

(JAGGER pauses.)

MARY: *(To KRANK.)* Look, I can help you leave. Just, please, shut your spring-loaded trap.

KRANK: Okay, fine.

(KRANK takes JAGGER to the window and points outside.)

KRANK: Yeah, you can fix cars. See there? You built that from the ground up. Thing was practically a push mower when you got it and now it's fine enough to call a home.

JAGGER: I put in those window treatments?

KRANK: Nah, that was me.

JAGGER: Flower box?

KRANK: Nah.

JAGGER: 'Cause I'll tell you right, flower box cause a hell a' lot of drag really piss away your miles per gallon.

KRANK: Yeah.

JAGGER: And I see that I'm saying that to you shows a level a' knowledge surely on par with a person who fixes cars.

JOANNE: A mechanic.

JAGGER: Yeah, I know that too.

JOANNE: I'm sure it's something on the road too.

JAGGER: Yeah, baby purrs. Got that staccato cough of a Harley bike spittin' down the Sunset Strip. Makes me want to get behind the wheel a' that beast I built and head back West to the angels.

MARY: Hey, baby— *(Holds up the liquor bottle.)* You wanna cheers?

JAGGER: Yeah, the life of a man who fixes cars—life of a mechanic—it's a good life—worth drinkin' to—

(MARY pours liquor down his throat.)

MARY: *(Looking out the window.)* The fog's rolling in. Let's take the flashlights up on the roof n' make sure your dad can find the house safe. *(To KRANK.)* You. Stay here.

(She takes JAGGER and exits.)

JOANNE: Is your brother all right? Seems like the crows got all the corn off his cob.

KRANK: You just shut up about him that way.

JOANNE: I didn't mean it in any a' the bad ways. Figure that's the type a' thing everyone gets said about them.

KRANK: Right, well he don't need it from you.

JOANNE: Why would your dad still have a set of old tires?

KRANK: He bought 'em first. Only part of the car he owned.

JOANNE: Out in the car—

KRANK: Yeah.

JOANNE: I said something.

KRANK: "Krank Sturgess will give you what you want."

JOANNE: Yeah. What I want. I'd lay wager I'm the only girl my age city wide ain' with a baby yet. Why is that?

KRANK: Luck?

JOANNE: And it ain't like there haven't been opportunities. I mean, people like me.

KRANK: Then it is luck.

JOANNE: I want to have a baby with you, Krank. You know how sometimes you see someone real nice, but you know there's something in 'em turn that baby in you ugly or pudgy or inept and you go and spit on their hand every time they extend it 'cause there's no way they're going to take that one part of you that's still beautiful in your own mind—the one thing that's still untouched—the one, last thing that might just work out. An' then there's people who can give you what you want.

KRANK: I don't—

JOANNE: Just think of us—a little boy n' little booties, a silk-lined blanket and tiny pink fingers like sensitive antennae.

KRANK: I—

JOANNE: We can do it now if you want.

KRANK: I can't—

JOANNE: Or go to your car for a little privacy.

KRANK: No, it's not that.

JOANNE: I don't get it.

KRANK: I don't, you know, touch women.

JOANNE: Nothing?

KRANK: Won't lay a finger. With all the ways out there you got women treated bad. I just don't want a part. So, I kind of leave that to everyone else.

JOANNE: What if I'm drowning? You won't—"Save me. Save me."

KRANK: Not if it furthers a previously held view of women as victims, no.

JOANNE: But don't you ever—

KRANK: Sure—

JOANNE: Don't you ever see a girl whose mouth you think would taste just right?

KRANK: With the smell a' perfume and cigarettes?

(She tries to kiss him. Again he moves away.)

JOANNE: Am I really…?

KRANK: What?

JOANNE: No. I was gonna say what I'm supposed to say right now when now is rejected and say "Am I really so ugly to you?" "Am I really so unappealing?" But that's not right. That's not the right question. The question is "Are you really so ugly?" So ugly you'd keep me back from realizing the only good thought I got left.

JAGGER: *(Offstage.)* He's here.

(JAGGER and MARY enter.)

MARY: Maybe he found Ruble.

JAGGER: I'll set the table for dinner.

KRANK: No. I'm not stayin' long enough to eat.

JAGGER: But Dad sometimes brings home chicken wings an' corn chips.

MARY: He's gotta be goin', Jag.

JAGGER: Huh? Oh, yeah. You 'least want me to take a look at your car before you go?

KRANK: That'd be fine.

(BLANTON bursts in.)

BLANTON: Alright, which of your goddamn hush puppies been tunnelin' under the yard again. Swear I got half a mind to stick a shotgun straight down into those holes and let rip.

MARY: Ain' our kids burrowin' under the yard.

BLANTON: Yeah, well somethin' is— An' you just breed ghastly monsters. *(Notices KRANK.)* Well, I'll be Lou "The Toe" Groza—

KRANK: Hey, Dad.

BLANTON: Come back now. My. Just said today to Mr. Crumm, the man most recent assigned our case. I said, "Sire, my family's the most important thing to me. From my two boys, whatever girls they might be bringin' 'round, to all my grandchildren—ghastly as they are. An'

while there may've been some mistakes made in the past—I been thinkin' nothin' but good thoughts 'bout keepin' all us together." An' someone said—think it may've been Jesus—that all you gotta do is put those good thoughts out there then sit back and reap returns. *(Notices JOANNE.)* An' who's this pretty?

KRANK: That's Jo Jones, sir.

BLANTON: Who?

KRANK: Jo Jones.

BLANTON: Now, I thought we got that stammer a' yours fixed. Who wants to make the Shake 'N Bake?

KRANK: I ain' stayin'.

BLANTON: Humm?

KRANK: I want the tires. An' I ain' 'bout to forgive on you just to get them.

BLANTON: You'll have to speak up, son.

KRANK: I want the tires. An' I ain'—

BLANTON: You'll have to speak up, son.

KRANK: I want—!

BLANTON: You'll have to, boy, please speak up! Sorry, it must be my creeping years.

JAGGER: Dad, I heard.

BLANTON: Did you?

JAGGER: Tires.

BLANTON: What about?

JAGGER: That's Krank's car out there in our drive. Up on blocks. Thinks you might have his tires up a sleeve.

BLANTON: Well, that's just puppy shit, ain't it? I'm sorry I ain' able to give you a home there ain' vandals around come an' steal the tires off your car. But there are. An' I'd appreciate it if you boys gave me more credit—people come from hard circumstances all the time and it makes them better people—hard circumstances make better people—now sorry I ain' gonna go out and get the high-powered with the company car and the salary the type I'd be puttin' away in a college fund for the two of you—apologize I want the best outta you two.

JAGGER: Sorry, Pop.

BLANTON: An' why ain' you no pants?

JAGGER: *(Beat.)* Did you make me cut off all my hair?

BLANTON: Shit. Mary?

MARY: *(Fetches the liquor bottle.)* He's been bad all day.

(She pours liquor into JAGGER's mouth.)

MARY: Here go, baby.

BLANTON: You don't wanna wear pants, son, that's fine. What was I sayin'?

JOANNE: Mr. Sturgess, please. I don't want to be here anymore.

BLANTON: Why come to me? Tires don't cost too much.

JOANNE: Everything costs too much.

MARY: Dad—

BLANTON: No. I know what's gonna happen. I'm not as simple as what's written. These two get their tires—however that happens—and then they peel away. They'll forget about Ashtabula, forget about all of this, all of us. This is my family and I want them to remember. I want them to have something to cling onto—someplace to say they've come

from, even if they think that place's just slime and vitriol. Because when I think back on my life, all I got is stories about the Cleveland Browns—not childhood thoughts, not high school memories— not thoughts 'bout who I am and from where I come 'cept stories 'bout the 1964 Cleveland Browns and a championship I ain' even lived through. I think about my own father and all I see is Jim Brown. That's all I come from. *(To KRANK.)* Now I'd apologize if I knew I'd done wrong. I got plenty to be sore with you 'bout too, but I'm willing to let that go. That enough to make you stay?

(JAGGER starts strumming an air guitar. It's a revelation. Bum-ba-da-dum. Bum-ba-da-dum.)

MARY: They're under his mattress. He's been sleeping on 'em for years.

KRANK: Thanks.

(KRANK and JOANNE exit to BLANTON's room.)

MARY: I'm sorry.

BLANTON: I'll send you back to your other home. They'll eat you alive yet.

MARY: It's not good for Jagger to have Krank around agitating things. I barely got him under control as is.

(She goes to him with the liquor bottle and makes him drink some. It calms him.)

MARY: Look, he's already forgot we're supposed to be looking for our baby.

(KRANK and JOANNE enter carrying four car tires.)

BLANTON: When you moved out of the house and into that car, I used to come out nights and watch you while you slept. Then one night you drove off and didn't come back. Thought you put a stamp on gone. So when you came back, I waited 'til night again and took those four tires to keep you close and maybe get you back someday.

KRANK: How didn't I wake up during any of that?

BLANTON: I'd hotwire the car and run a hose from the exhaust pipe to the crack in your window. You were a fussy sleeper as a baby and it was warming to see you down so sound.

(Nothing.)

BLANTON: Did you at least remake my bed after taking those?

(Nothing. BLANTON exits to his room.)

KRANK: Jagger, could you help me get these back on the car?

JAGGER: Maybe you could take me with you, Krank?

MARY: You gotta work tomorrow, hon. Can't go nowhere.

JAGGER: Well, 'least let me take a look at your car before you go.

KRANK: Sure, brother.

(JAGGER and KRANK take the tires and exit. The women, left alone, are silent for a bit.)

JOANNE: So—

MARY: So.

JOANNE: You got kids, yeah?

MARY: Some.

JOANNE: Got pictures?

MARY: They all button cute.

JOANNE: Sure. Jagger an' you both good lookin'.

MARY: They're not all Jagger's. How many you got?

JOANNE: Me? Oh, none yet.

MARY: Fucking princess.

JOANNE: What?

MARY: What? So you and Krank really gonna hit the way an' no lookin' back?

JOANNE: Yeah, I guess.

MARY: An' you're interested in the music business, is that it?

JOANNE: Not really. Just nothin' really for me here. Live with my grandma all my life but, you know, she's got knittin' so she doesn't really need me.

MARY: Well, this is a kinda celebration, ain't it? Fresh start to a brand-new life.

JOANNE: Yeah.

MARY: You don't seem too excited.

JOANNE: It might just be horrible. He's got some off-putting thoughts.

MARY: The whole "won't touch a woman" thing?

JOANNE: Not even if I was drowning.

MARY: And that's just the beginning of what he won't do.

JOANNE: No.

MARY: He's been on a bit of a kick since his mom went on.

JOANNE: I ask him don't he like it to see a pretty girl. He says he takes care of those things himself. What's that mean?

MARY: Why you think they call him Krank?

JOANNE: Huh?

MARY: Honey, surely you've noticed that he's an absolute magician of self-gratification.

JOANNE: I think I'm a page or two behind.

MARY: Listen, my husband don't satisfy me sexually. Pro'lly 'least a quarter my fault in how much booze I keep in him. But he's a good man—he's the man I chose to make it all work with—so I fully plan to wait it out 'til I don't have desirous thoughts no more then I can be really happy with him. But that don't mean my hips don't take to jigger from time to time. So, I'm walkin' about and thought I'd duck outside and see how Krank—

JOANNE: You were gonna make it with your husband's brother?

MARY: Huh? You know, I never thought that's how you could read that story. Maybe I was. I don't really know as, when I approach the car, I see it bouncin' the way those mechanical horses do on the outside walk at the supermarket. And I sneak up to take a peak, as I'd always been curious to see Krank naked. But he was all alone inside. He was all alone and going at himself like the angels must've gone at to drive the fallen out of heaven. And I saw things. And I watched and I studied and I learned. An' I now swear by goin' at myself 'least three times a day regular help make me a better person.

JOANNE: Really? I'd always heard the opposite.

MARY: What do *you* think?

JOANNE: Me? I never…

MARY: You never.

JOANNE: I'm a working parts kind a' girl.

MARY: Oh, dear, you have no idea how well these parts can work. You want my help?

JOANNE: I—

MARY: And I'm offerin' because I like you an' Krank together. Because I believe in the two of you and I agree that you should see what's out there for you elsewhere. But you cannot pin your hopes on his magically coming around anytime soon. Like I said, dear, life's about knowing how disappointing your situation is and also knowing how long you'll have to wait around 'til it changes itself.

JOANNE: What about your baby?

MARY: Hmmmm?

JOANNE: Shouldn't we be looking for him?

MARY: You know, I'd forgotten. How funny. But this is much more fun. Come on.

(*They start to leave. BLANTON enters with a pint of ice cream.*)

BLANTON: Care for butter pecan?

JOANNE: No, sir.

BLANTON: I'm gonna have some ice cream, I think.

JOANNE: Yes, sir.

BLANTON: You likin' on my son, JoJo?

JOANNE: I'm not fully sure, sir.

BLANTON: Well, he's an asshole.

JOANNE: Yes, sir.

(*MARY pulls her to exit. KRANK enters.*)

KRANK: (*Calling.*) Okay, Jo.

BLANTON: Where ya goin' first?

(Nothing.)

BLANTON: You like butter pecan, don't you?

(Nothing.)

BLANTON: You're getting your way. Maybe you can be two fingers worth a' civil 'til ya leave.

KRANK: *(Beat.)* Exact plans ain' been set.

BLANTON: An' you don't want me knowin'.

KRANK: We're just playin' it by our heads, is all.

BLANTON: I really want you to reconsider.

(Nothing.)

BLANTON: Can you tell me what was so wrong?

KRANK: They were Mom's sisters, Dad. All of Mom's sisters.

BLANTON: Yeah. Twelve, I think. And all looked just like your mother in one light or another. Identical, really. And your mother was so beautiful. Remember, I didn't yet have a whisker of face hair when your momma took me and made me head of a house. Those women were, all twelve of them, identical. Beautiful. I went into each one thinking it was your mother. They were terrible to each other, each one comin' after me. But it wasn't her used to pawn. I was the one deceived.

KRANK: Repeatedly.

BLANTON: Well, they exploited a weakness I never really got better at.

KRANK: And it drove Mom away.

BLANTON: Actually, I remember, it was you who drove her away.

KRANK: She wanted to leave. We made plans. I was gonna save her.

BLANTON: But you could have *driven* her across the Mexican border. You can do that, you know. Hell, you could have taken a boat over to Canada. You didn't have to shoo her under a fence and across a field so she'd get shot crawling on her belly going the wrong way 'cross a border.

(The sound of a motor turning over. A-voo-voo-voo. A-voo-voo-voo.)

KRANK: My car!

(He moves to the door. BLANTON throws him to the ground.)

BLANTON: No, you're not going—

(A loud explosion from outside. MARY and JOANNE rush back in. After a moment, JAGGER enters. He is singed and covered in soot.)

KRANK: What the hell?

BLANTON: What'd that drunk head a' yours do?

JAGGER: Turns out, maybe don't fix cars so well as told. But those shapes I see, they recede but it don't mean I can't still see 'em from far off, see what they are, what they were, what I was—

BLANTON: Shit.

JAGGER: —what I was and what you all made me forget.

MARY: *(Going for the liquor bottle.)* Oh, baby, just have a—

JAGGER: No. No drinks 'til I say what I say. 'Cause even if you force all this from my head, I need it clear a moment.

(Beat.)

MARY: You'd gone off, Jagger. That's what you're trying to remember.

BLANTON: Gone off and joined a rock n' roll band.

KRANK: An' come back when Mom died.

MARY: An' we just didn't want you leavin' again.

JAGGER: I can see them now. Five of us. Livin' in a two room where our filth was like turf over broken tiled floors. We behaved like all blessed with the mouth a' chimpanzees and we'd consume anything came an' stoke our way and spit the bones out, if could be made of bones, or spit the needles out, if could be made, or spit the pipes and we all wore leather pants an' everyone was naked waist up an' we didn't have to wait for something to come 'round and change everything 'cause we was that thing and we could just touch things and demons'd be planted at their core.

MARY: I couldn't bear you goin' back to that.

JAGGER: An' we were good.

BLANTON: Matter of opinion.

JAGGER: An' we were big.

KRANK: Not exactly.

MARY: But after you left, those guys you remember went on to form Mötley Crüe.

JAGGER: You think they'd let me back in?

(The noise from before starts up again—a slow rumbling that builds and builds. The noise gets louder, practically deafening. The

room shakes. The lights flicker on and off. Blackout. Lights back up to find BOLT BANNISTER standing among them. He is in athletic apparel—sweatpants, head- and wristbands. He's dripping in sweat and looks exhausted. Everyone just stands around staring at him. Finally—)

BOLT: Let me... Let me catch my breath...

(Blackout.)

ACT II
SCENE 1

Lights up on the Sturgess living room. BOLT sits tied to a chair with the rest of the FAMILY around as BLANTON dunks his head into a big bucket of water.

JOANNE: You sure this the best method?

BLANTON: These things you learn in the army.

KRANK: You never in the army.

BLANTON: But these are *things* you learn in the army. He's lyin', he'll eventually get tired a' this and talk. He's disoriented and not rememberin' straight, this'll wake him up. He's dehydrated, this'll quench. And so on.

(Pulls BOLT up.)

BLANTON: Now do you mind tellin'?

BOLT: You don't have well water. That must be nice.

BLANTON: I afford us a certain standard.

JAGGER: Askin' after our water, Pop? Been around long enough to know that a person knows to ask about a home's plumbing knows a lot more than just plumbing to start with.

BLANTON: What you think then?

JAGGER: You here to get me back in the band, isn't that right?

BOLT: Can you tell me where we are?

JAGGER: We ask the questions here.

(JAGGER charges BOLT and dunks him.)

JAGGER: You must think you're real quick, just appearin' from the blue.

BOLT: Quick…

(Dunk.)

JAGGER: Well, I'll believe you are who I say you are if you can produce the stretch limousine the band sent to chariot me.

(KRANK jumps in to restrain him.)

KRANK: More likely he's an insurance claims adjuster come to help us file a claim and get a brand-new car.

BLANTON: Or maybe you from the state. If so, I can assure you these are not the disciplinary measures I normally take on my boys—we are a happy family—

(The FAMILY descends on BOLT—each pulling him in a different direction. JAGGER dunks him.)

BOLT: Stop it! Don't you know who I am and how I came to get here? I ask this because I've come here from a very strange journey and I can only imagine that it's left me in the very pit of hell and, it's now occurring to me, that in hell you must be able to see people comin' a long ways off. So, you would have all been staring at me off in the distance knowing I was going to come to you while, to me, all of this is very new—so please answer for me if this is going to be my lot for eternity unless, of course, my lot is an eternity of not knowing the

answer to that in which case, I imagine, I'll just suffer.

BLANTON: Well, that was all a little too much to follow, wouldn't you say? If he moves a hair's length, start cutting off what he'll miss most. Me, I have my own time to shorten. *(Grabs the liquor bottle.)* See you on the other side.

(No response.)

BLANTON: I'm going to bed.

(BLANTON exits. As soon as he is gone, MARY rushes to BOLT and covers him with kisses.)

MARY: There's my baby. There's my sweet angel. Mama knew you'd come back to me, Ruble. Mama knew wherever you went, however hard it was, however it may have aged you terribly that you would find your way back home.

JAGGER: You stay away from him.

MARY: Look, Jagger. Ruble's come back to us. Not a pineapple at all—but some sort of man.

JAGGER: Boy here ain't no Ruble.

KRANK: This stretch limo my brother's talking about. It drive regular?

BOLT: I came here on foot.

KRANK: Give me the keys. I have a band.

MARY: Don't talk to your nephew that way, Krank. Ruble, when you were a baby—I don't know n' you remember as far back as yesterday—when you were a baby, you used to go fetch your daddy a bottle of whiskey when he got in a state like this.

JAGGER: I don't want any whiskey.

MARY: Honey, I think it might serve to calm you.

JAGGER: More n' deaden me. I got a list of your tricks runnin' now. I write things on the back of my hand—sayin' things like "she plies you with drink."

MARY: I only did it so we could be a normal family like the rest you see.

JAGGER: No matter I couldn't distinguish on a shirt which hole was for the head and which for the arms.

MARY: It was sweet you needed me like you did.

JAGGER: Well I got the clear vision now. Drink ain' touched my lips in goin' on an hour an' I never felt of sounder body—of sounder mind. This a new, pristine body standin' here—and I ain' gonna keep people around think to corrupt it.

MARY: You can't throw me out. Please. I'll pitch all the bottles and the cans and the prescriptions and the non-prescriptions and the flasks and the vials and the fixin's for intravenous.

JAGGER: You got another house to go to. I hope it swallows you in one gulp.

MARY: Ruble?

(BOLT shrugs.)

MARY: Then why did you even come back?

(MARY looks around and sees no one is going to help her. JAGGER throws her out.)

JAGGER: (To BOLT.) If you think to sing—or if you remember the number direct to the band's Malibu house—you call loud. A man a' my talents got a lot to offer to the scene. But now I need to find appropriate pants. (Exits.)

KRANK: You really don't have a car?

BOLT: I can't drive.

KRANK: Well ain' this shit thicker n' milkshake. (To JOANNE.) What's the plan, Jo?

JOANNE: Huh?

KRANK: You over there tackin' our next stop on the map.

JOANNE: I...I don't know.

KRANK: What if we travel Greyhound bus?

JOANNE: I don't...I just don't feel any of this, Krank. (Takes out the note.) This thing lied to me. Lied to me like a fish trombone. Like a sardine tambourine. You ain' ever gonna give me what I want.

KRANK: I just thought you believed in the music.

JOANNE: I thought you *didn't* believe in the music.

KRANK: This about that baby you wanted?

JOANNE: Mary tried to show me how you do what you do to yourself.

KRANK: Came to my attention she saw me once.

JOANNE: Well, I know all the tricks now. Tricks to keep me fast to you.

KRANK: Then why ain' we talkin' 'bout the Greyhound bus?

JOANNE: 'Cause it tore at me. Tore at my insides. Tore at my outsides. Every stroke or soft caress. Tore so much. Think I made myself unable for child.

KRANK: Sounds like she showed you wrong.

JOANNE: No. It's not her fault. It's you. I want to say it's my fault for believing any one person could be entrusted to give me so much. But when you get right down to it, it's your fault for just not doing it and watching as I go an' ruin myself.

KRANK: I think I'm going to be sick. (*Shudders—a retch in his mouth, maybe—and quickly exits.*)

BOLT: We all have a long way to go, you know.

JOANNE: Six feet down ain' so long.

BOLT: What's your name?

JOANNE: Jo Jones. What's yours?

BOLT: I'd like it a whole lot if you called me Bolt Bannister.

JOANNE: That's a funny name.

BOLT: Do you think it's too funny?

JOANNE: No, I'd say funny just enough. Are you the one caused the ground to shake—or the sky to open up?

BOLT: All that's in my head is pieces right now.

JOANNE: You got nothin' for me?

BOLT: Oh…Well…Okay, how about this? I can't yet say "This all started under the wide skies of Montana" or "I was birthed on a panhandle beach by a doctor who built a set of stirrups from catfish bones" but I know what all of those things are now, which is the ones and twos of it all. See, people always said I was slow so I wasn't allowed to do much. That's why I searched for the fleshy part of jogging's neck and got a good grip on it. I could do it whenever I wanted. And now I can *understand* that was all I did. While I normally took the same path, my most recent jog found me on a stretch of road I'd not come across before. It was a road I could not see the end of. It was, I thought at the time and still do, a jogger's perfection. So, I began at my normal pace—rarely did I ever break a sweat or breathe abnormally—but soon I noticed my legs moving almost without me and saw them jog faster and faster until what they were doing could no longer be properly considered a jog—more a sprint or a gallop and the lowlands butting against this road moved past me faster and faster. And I began to figure things. That's going on in my head right now. It's like all the information that was around me but just didn't stick, well, it's all finding a place. Which is why I know things like Montana, panhandle, and stirrups. But the slow wit isn't gone either. It's still in there, used to its world. And now I see things with two sets of eyes…two pairs, that is, four eyes. And I have one pair of thoughts. So as the world zoomed past and became gray and I could no longer make out anything I had a head that began working. And then I stopped. And I was here. Will you untie me now?

(*She tentatively touches his hands.*)

JOANNE: You know, everyone thinks you've been dropped from the blue to solve their problems.

BOLT: I'd think the same.

(*She unties his hands. They touch.*)

JOANNE: But that's thinkin' too much isn't it? Do you know what's happening here?

BOLT: I remember now that I've heard stories about poor people elsewhere who can turn into birds or cause an earthquake with a rumble of their tummy. And it seems to help.

JOANNE: Lotta help.

(They touch.)

JOANNE: It really don't hurt when I touch you soft like?

(BOLT kisses her. She returns it.)

JOANNE: Oh. Okay.

BOLT: Okay. *(Starts to leave.)*

JOANNE: *(Singing to herself.)*
OH, WE'RE HALFWAY THERE
OH, OH—LIVIN' ON A PRAYER

BOLT: *(Noticing—turns and sings.)*
TAKE MY HAND
WE'LL MAKE IT I SWEAR

BOLT and JOANNE: *(Singing.)*
OH, OH—LIVIN' ON A PRAYER
LIVIN' ON A—

(They kiss. JAGGER enters, wearing leather pants and carrying a dusty electric guitar. He slings the guitar over his shoulder and strums the guitar. It makes no noise, but a dollar bill falls from the strings to the floor. He strums again—no noise—another bill. What an interesting development. Strum—bill. Strum—bill. Strum—bill. Lights out.)

SCENE 2

Lights up—dim morning light—on JOANNE and BOLT. They lie peacefully in each other's arms. MARY enters. Her clothing's been ripped; she has bite and claw marks on her arms and face. She rolls JOANNE away from BOLT and takes him in her arms all sweet maternity.

MARY: *(Sings.)* HUSH LITTLE BABY, DON'T
    HAVE A…A FIT
MAMA'S GONNA BUY YOU A…A SHAVING KIT
AND IF THAT SHAVING KIT…PROVES DULL
MAMA WILL BANDAGE UP YOUR SKULL
AND IF ALL BANDAGED YOU CAN'T SEE

AND IF YOU WALK INTO A TREE
AND IN THAT TREE THERE IS A HIVE
'CAUSE BEES 'ROUND HERE ARE KNOWN
    TO THRIVE
AND IF THAT HIVE SHOULD DROP ON YOU
MAMA SHE WON'T KNOW WHAT TO DO

(He wakes—starts a little at the sight of her.)

MARY: I know you been away long 'nuff not to remember much 'a me. But I hope you'll forgive much of what I did to you.

(BOLT struggles to stand up but can't with MARY draped all over him. She fixes his hair, straightens his outfit. She wraps a rope around his wrists.)

MARY: What is it I done so bad to you? When you a baby I put you in diapers, 'cause that's what I seen the babies wearin', but that ain' good enough. When you turned a pineapple, did you know I had to go back out to the store for maraschino cherries 'cause that's topped all the upside-down cakes I can remember. And so I never change the diapers or don't take the cake out the oven—but where am I supposed to stop? How far do I go to not get looks from people tellin' me what's fallen outta me ain't different than any other dropping on the ground.

JOANNE: *(Wakes up.)* What are you doing?

MARY: Shut up! This is between me and my son.

BOLT: I can see you pause when looking over my face knowing that it's not how your son's would have turned out.

(She slaps him. She pulls back to slap him again, but stops.)

MARY: Then where is he? Where's my Ruble?

BOLT: Have you also been transported elsewhere?

MARY: Went back home.

(*She pulls BOLT to the window. Points out.*)

MARY: That's me there. I've lived all up and down this block. Lived there. There. There.

JOANNE: Who did this to you?

MARY: Oh, all the ones been in me once upon a time. Never lost track of a baby before Jagger. But did lose count. Lost count a' how many when I got up in double-digit kids. Not so unusual a girl my age fillin' a house, but I couldn't stop with the kids. Filled *that* house and *that* house and *that* one. Got to the point I couldn't sit down on the couch without hearin' a little cry and findin' one of my babies stuck under me— I'd pour out a Raisin Bran and two or three would tumble out of the box. So many, they'd hang from the pole in my closet and I don't have no choice but to drape my blouse over their soft little heads so as not to wrinkle 'em on the floor. But they lost patience with me. They began to use all fours and swear I seen 'em scurry up a wall to hide in shadow—conspirin' to drive me out. And one day they did—content they'd do a better job raisin' themselves than I could. I went back tonight. Several more got teeth now. Asked back in. Told 'em things would be different. That losin' Jagger n' my babies made me appreciate them. That I'd go back, name 'em all and these'd be names I'd remember. They just hissed. Jagger used to believe anything I'd tell him. But my beautiful

little beasts wouldn't even give me that little moment when my wrong word makes me a beautiful world.

(*A crash and shout come from offstage. It's KRANK. He enters dressed in a robe, grabs BOLT, and slams him against the wall.*)

KRANK: I don't know what you done to me an' I don't know it's even you that's done it an' I don't know what can be done to help—but swear to god I'll reach my hand elbow-deep down your throat just to check n' see you ain' hidin' the cure in your stomach if I even suspect you might.

(*BLANTON and JAGGER enter.*)

JOANNE: Do something.

BLANTON: My boys raised to handle problems their own.

BOLT: I have no way of explaining...except that there's a glow about you new from last night.

KRANK: (*Starts crying. Blubbering, really.*) What is this happening? (*Pulls back his bathrobe showing a protruding stomach that he did not have the night before. It looks like he is pregnant—about six months on.*)

BOLT: I take it this was unplanned.

JAGGER: I wanna touch it.

JOANNE: Don't you go near him.

JAGGER: What, you think it's yours?

KRANK: First, I just thought I wasn't eatin' proper account a' living' in the car and my belly's doin' the thing a' those fat starving kids on the television. Then thought back on the times Mom would tell me 'bout how I wouldn't be skinny forever. But then I felt it move.

MARY: Let me see. I seen a stomach raise 'nuff to know their look. *(Goes to KRANK and examines his protruding stomach.)* Yeah...Krank...For real...You gotta promise me you'll raise this one right. Don't let it outta your sight. If that means strapping the kid on your leg the whole time he grows till you're looking eye to eye with him.

BLANTON: So, time comes you make me a grandfather.

MARY: Blanton, Jagger and I've given you several grandchildren already.

(She puts an arm around JAGGER. He pushes her away.)

BLANTON: Yeah, but where are they? 'Less I pull one of 'em out the cupboard when I go for a bag of chips, I'm gonna consider that all talk.

JOANNE: You really got bun in there?

KRANK: We're all just guessin' but we all got eyes.

JOANNE: That's all I wanted. How come *you* get it?

KRANK: I don't want it.

BLANTON: Happy occasions like this and I'm a sentimental. Makes a man feel his years, but good to know this life I given you sturdy enough pass along down the line. I think this might make you understand me a little better.

KRANK: I want to kill it. I just don't know the way in.

(BLANTON cuffs KRANK on the side of his head.)

BLANTON: You got so little respect?

KRANK: I'm still leaving. Still. I can perform like this. I can tour. Baby might

take to the vibrations from my bass guitar and I'll birth myself a drummer. Then we'll be a two-piece called "We" or "Us" or something.

JAGGER: Hey, man, the road ain' no place to start a family.

KRANK: No. I can do...!

(His legs give and he stumbles back. MARY and JOANNE catch him. MARY, JAGGER, and BLANTON lead him offstage, followed by JOANNE. BOLT stops her.)

BOLT: Come on.

JOANNE: What?

BOLT: They're distracted. We can go now.

JOANNE: But don't you see? Something wonderful has happened.

BOLT: Or horrible.

JOANNE: This is a special time.

BOLT: *(Sings.)* TAKE MY HAND...

JOANNE: I'm sorry. Bolt Bannister.

(She exits. As soon as she's gone, JAGGER bursts back on.)

JAGGER: I'm gonna let you in on a little secret—but I don't want you blabbin' this—we may have struck the hot water tap a' gold, my friend.

BOLT: What do you mean?

JAGGER: The type a' funds let us take residence up on one a' the lower layers a' the stratosphere. Do you ever find that you play an instrument and where it should produce music it, instead, turns out money like a mint?

BOLT: No, but that sounds fortuitous.

JAGGER: Fortuitous to *me*. You're lucky I let you tag.

(JAGGER exits. BOLT tries to free his hands. As he's struggling, BLANTON enters. BOLT wiggles out of the rope, turns, and starts toward the door, which is now blocked by BLANTON.)

BLANTON: You think?

(He does. BOLT runs and BLANTON makes a textbook football tackle bringing BOLT down to the ground.)

BLANTON: Ha! If not for this knee bein' tricky, I coulda been doin' that to real men.

BOLT: You do it well.

BLANTON: Obliged.

(BOLT runs at him again only to be taken down again.)

BLANTON: If you don't mind…Few pointers…

BOLT: Please.

BLANTON: First off, you're comin' at me like you're trying to run through me—an' you ain' got 'nuff margarine on your toast to do that.

BOLT: I only know how to run straight.

BLANTON: We call that a north-south runner.

BOLT: Joggers don't talk this way.

BLANTON: Gotta get you runnin' patterns. You're pretty quick—let's put you at receiver. Now follow me: Go, fake, plant, spin. Go, fake, plant, spin. Now you try.

(BOLT starts to run at BLANTON but ends up just jogging in place.)

BLANTON: No, no, no. You see? That's not good.

(He shows BOLT the go-fake-plant-spin route again. BOLT nods. They line up. BOLT charges, fakes, plants, and spins his way past a crumpling BLANTON.)

BLANTON: There, see? Not without a skill. My knee tricked up or I woulda got you the same.

(BOLT realizes that he now has a clear path to the door. He turns to make his escape—but as he starts, JAGGER enters and tosses an arm around him, dragging him back into the room.)

JAGGER: Bag's packed.

BLANTON: Where you goin'?

JAGGER: Well, half-packed. Now I got Cali callin' loud in my ear, thinkin' best you keep all this behind the locks and shutters.

BLANTON: What's that?

JAGGER: The pregnant brother. All this. Can't shake the feeling somehow reflect negative for my career.

BLANTON: Well, you don't have to worry. You ain' got a career.

JAGGER: But big plans a' one. Soon as I figure out how Buster here can help me.

BOLT: Bolt.

JAGGER: Beg yer—

BOLT: I'd appreciate it to be called Bolt Bannister.

BLANTON: This the type a' stuff happens all the time. You should be happy for your brother.

JAGGER: But, Dad, none a' this rock n' roll.

BLANTON: I know rock n' roll.

JAGGER: Yeah, maybe *classic* rock n' roll.

BLANTON: Then what're you talking about?

JAGGER: Rock n' roll.

BLANTON: Yep.

JAGGER: Rock... *(Pause.)* And Roll!

BLANTON: I'm waiting.

JAGGER: I...I don't know what I mean. I've written songs about rock n' roll, broken up relationships over rock n' roll, pledged my soul to rock n' roll, and now it seems I can't tell you what I'm talkin' 'bout when I'm talkin' 'bout rock n' roll. I can't...It doesn't make...

BOLT: Have you told him?

BLANTON: Told me what?

JAGGER: Oh, yeah. We seem to have found our way into a bit of fortuitousness.

BLANTON: Of what manner?

JAGGER: My guitar. Seems it's undergone metamorphosis and now, instead of making music, issues bills.

BLANTON: Bullshit.

JAGGER: *(Exits. Returns with the guitar.)* Now, say I want to intro your standard power ballad. *(Strums. As before, no music, but a bill falls to the floor. He strums again—bill.)* Isn't this great, Pop? Don't know there's a bottom of this well, either. I can keep this up and soon we'll be livin' on a house top a' pontoons out in the middle of the lake. Or house hanging from a string off the cliff of a very important mountain somewhere.

BLANTON: And you can go to Los Angles. And Krank can go on tour.

JAGGER: Yeah. We can do anything. Are you proud a' me, Pop? Ever think I could do anything like?

(BLANTON does not respond.)

JAGGER: Pop?

BLANTON: Huh? Oh. And a Winnebago for a nice family vacation. Buy your dad a Winnebago.

JAGGER: Yeah, sure. We can be rock stars now. All of us. This is rock n' roll!

BLANTON: You don't even know what that means.

(BLANTON exits. JAGGER exits. BOLT realizes he's been left alone. He starts jogging in place. He moves faster and faster. The noise returns. Rumbling growing and growing.)

BOLT: Yes, yes, yes.

(JOANNE enters.)

JOANNE: Bolt!

(Blackout. When the lights come back up, all that remains of BOLT are his headband and wristbands.)

SCENE 3

BLANTON *sits on the couch.* KRANK *enters.*

KRANK: I'm goin'.

BLANTON: Hmmm?

KRANK: Joanne and I figured it. If I wear a long-hair wig and walk 'long the highway alone—maybe even at night, we'd thought out—passing cars'll notice my delicate state n' pull aside for a ride. I just won't say much so they don't suspect my voice and, well, when they drop me in the next town, if things are misconstrued as sexual for the favor, I need to be willin' to offer a soft kiss on the lips—that's what we both figured—or else, I fear, they might think it easier to kill me.

BLANTON: Your brother—

KRANK: He'll be headed in no time. He told me he's got some kinda guitar makes money.

BLANTON: I sent him out to buy a Winnebago yesterday. Didn't he ever come back?

KRANK: Hadn't noticed. But I been real tired since—

BLANTON: He left didn't he. That simp. We were gonna take that thing—all of us.

KRANK: Where to?

BLANTON: What do you care? I ain' gonna—No, you know what, we were just gonna take it out to park in the Dairy Queen lot—where each of us'd enjoy a big ole Peanut Buster Parfait. I bet that parfait sounds real good right now.

KRANK: Dad, I can't—

BLANTON: And a Winnebago parked out in a man's driveway, that's sayin' something—might be good starting place for a family—and I can tell that one Mr. Crumm that Blanton Sturgess son don't live in a car meant for drivin'—No, sir—Blanton Sturgess son, he drives in a car meant for livin'. For livin'.

KRANK: That's great, Dad.

(KRANK waddles off. BLANTON stands there for a moment before feeling a tighten-ing in his chest. He grabs at it. Stumbles. But it passes. He takes slow, deliberate breaths, clearing his head—hits his chest like he's just had to choke down a pill. He turns on the television.)

ANNOUNCER: In the still-warm autumn sun of the early season, Cleveland Stadium sits. Inside the Cleveland Browns and Pittsburgh Steelers prepare, once again, to make it sweet like bees makin' honey.

ANNOUNCER: The colorful helmets of these two teams spill out onto the field, gushing from the tunnels like a head wound only to be mopped up after four grueling quarters. Most of the hope of the city of Cleveland is handcuffed to the play of their promising young quarterback, Bernie Kosar, who now looks to lead this city to its first championship since 1964.

BLANTON: Woo-hoo! *(His heart seizes up—a full-on attack.)* Help...

ANNOUNCER: Wait a minute...There seems to be some commotion on the Browns' sidelines and I can't quite make it out...There seems to be a problem with the players. Number 82 has dropped to his knees. He's...I can't tell...Everyone's standing around him—Wait. Number 25 just collapsed—just fell to the ground. I can't see—Number 33 is down—57 clutching at his chest—these massive men—Wait—Down—Down—Another—Number 88—Enormous shoulders, broad chests release their wind—Down—Another—Down—

(BLANTON is near expiring himself.)

ANNOUNCER: And now the field, a pumpkin patch of strewn, haphazard orange. Only one player stands. Bernie Kosar. But he's okay.

(BLANTON, on the ground, reaches toward the television.)

ANNOUNCER: Kosar looks around at the stunned crowd—

(The sound of light applause that grows and grows into a thunderous roar.)

ANNOUNCER: The crowd is telling Kosar that they still believe as long as he is standing. That even if he is the only Cleveland player suited up against their arch-rival Steelers, they still have a chance. "Cleveland, Ohio," they seem to say, "Can still go all the way to the Super Bowl."

(Suddenly, BLANTON's pain breaks. He catches his breath and sits back after the struggle. He seems fine.)

ANNOUNCER: Kosar takes a knee. A prayer, perhaps. But—No! Kosar falls face first to the ground. Kosar is down. Oh, my god. They're all gone. They're all gone.

(BLANTON turns off the television and clutches it. KRANK and JOANNE enter. KRANK wears a long-haired wig and his bass guitar.)

JOANNE: And you make sure it stops with a kiss.

KRANK: Yes.

JOANNE: You ain' a lady. I don't 'spect you to know the shades a favor can take.

KRANK: *(Swings the bass around and starts playing his brand of hard-core punk. Sings—if that's what you call it.)*
IN CASE YOU
CAN'T SEE GOOD
THIS IS MY FIST
AT CLOSE RANGE
IN CASE YOU
CAN'T SEE GOOD

THIS IS MY KNEE
AT CLOSE RANGE
It goes on like that. Two minutes about my body's blunter objects.

JOANNE: It's nice the way you talk.

KRANK: Why won't you come with me? You told me you wanted a baby—and then this happened to me. So, this thing's gotta be 'least part yours.

JOANNE: You never turned a soft finger on me once. You'd rather I drown—you said so yourself—than jump in and risk getting your hands clean. *(Starts to leave.)*

KRANK: Help me, please.

JOANNE: *(Backing to leave.)* Save me from drowning.

(At the last moment, he grabs for her. He pulls her back to him. They're flailing about like he's actually saving her from drowning. When they settle, JOANNE leans in to kiss KRANK. At first, it's like medicine, but he takes it. Gradually, he relaxes. As she pulls away, he leans in and kisses her strongly. Just then, JAGGER comes bursting in.)

JAGGER: Mary! Mary!

(MARY enters.)

MARY: Where have you been?

JAGGER: Winnebago. I got the Winnebago.

MARY: Oh, show me the new car.

(She goes to the window. JAGGER pushes her back.)

MARY: I do not like the way you treat me when you're sober.

JAGGER: There's been a clause in our situation—only allowed to *think* things improvable.

MARY: You're nonsense.

JAGGER: The magic guitar is a deviller. I don't know 'nuff to tell by lookin', but all that money ain't for real.

MARY: Well, what else looks like that?

JAGGER: Fake money.

MARY: Fake money?

JAGGER: I got the Winnebago. But raised sales' attention when I needed an extra hundred and slung my guitar and let a hundred dollars worth fall to the floor. And it wasn't 'til I was halfway home that I saw a flock of flashing lights come into frame behind me. And we had a pleasant conversation at the top of our lungs—car window to car window—where they detailed my crimes and I said, "I'm a rock n' roll star and rock stars don't get caught 'til you catch up with me in hell, motherfucker!" That was yesterday and we've been in chase ever since.

MARY: How did you lose them?

JAGGER: I don't know I did for real. Mary, I don't know what to do.

MARY: I—

JAGGER: You can tell me what's really goin' on, can't you?

MARY: Jagger, you don't want me to—

JAGGER: You can tell me what to do.

MARY: Jagger, no.

JAGGER: You can tell me that I ain' a rock star.

MARY: No.

JAGGER: Please. Please!

MARY: You ain' a rock star.

JAGGER: An' we just have a nice, normal life.

MARY: Yes, yes we do. Pure vanilla.

JAGGER: An' I ain' done nothin' to deserve the sound a' sirens out in the distance.

MARY: You ain' done nothin' to deserve the sound a' sirens—

(There they sit: a nice, normal FAMILY. Then it starts. Police sirens off in the distance. The sirens fade into the noise. The rumble again. Building and building until the living room is shaking. EVERYONE is shouting and clutching at each other. What's going on? EVERYONE draws together—lights out—back up and BOLT BANNISTER is standing, once again, in the middle of the Sturgess living room.)

BLANTON: You.

BOLT: Oh, no, no, no.

JOANNE: You came back.

BOLT: No, no, no, no.

BLANTON: You.

BOLT: Right back where I started.

BLANTON: I need to talk to you, young man. This is not something I can ask of my sons. You see, one is broken down from drink, the other, well he's expectin'. But what I'm proposin' means a great deal to a very many people. We have suffered a great loss today, but seein' you come back here made me see how things can sometimes come from the blue.

(BOLT just stares at him.)

BLANTON: I want to reform the Cleveland Browns usin' me as quarterback and you as receiver.

(No response.)

BLANTON: If we make it to the Stadium before the game is officially called, we might just give those Steelers a run for their money.

(No response.)

BLANTON: Am I right?

(Nothing.)

BLANTON: Am I right!

(The FAMILY, once again, descends on BOLT—pulling him in every direction— each one looking to him for answers.)

BOLT: Stop it! This is it? This miracle comes like a wishbone lodged in my throat. I left here. I started jogging and again moved faster 'til the world mixed together as you might mix paint. And I really thought I was going to get to see things and understand and do. But then to wind up back here...

BLANTON: *(Clutches BOLT and shakes him.)* Just plant, fake, spin. Remember? We can do this. *(His shaking intensifies.)* Am I right?

BOLT: We don't get to be served by magic. We don't get to be served at all.

BLANTON: Please. It's all I know.

(BLANTON releases BOLT and BOLT collapses. The FAMILY rushes around him and checks the body. Dead. KRANK finds a note in BOLT's pocket.)

KRANK: "Bolt Bannister will not save you."

BLANTON: We coulda...

MARY: You're sure he wasn't Ruble, Jag?

JAGGER: Yeah. Ruble's thin air now.

BLANTON: We coulda done it, I think. My knee's a little tricky, but without a backup, who else they have throwin' the ball.

KRANK: I know, Dad.

(In the distance we hear police sirens. The FAMILY panics.)

JAGGER: They found me.

JOANNE: What'll we do?

BLANTON: What is there left for us to do?

KRANK: Nothin' we can.

BLANTON: Oh, yeah? Any a' you keepin' track? Here's it. Here's all we can do. We got a Winnebago out front. We got a guitar player. We got a bass guitar player. I believe I mentioned I used to play drums in a surf-rock-turned-motorcycle band. We got two lovely ladies as backup or on the tambourine. We gonna get in that Winnebago—all of us—an' head out for L.A. and have us the most hard-rockin', hard-drinkin', hard-partyin' traveling family band this world ever seen. How's it sound to leave this? We'll leave all this. We'll leave fuck all.

(Lights out.)

Scene 4

In black.

VOICE: Alright, we're a go in five, four, three,...Ladies and Gentlemen, are you ready to rock? It' the Sturgess...Family...Singers!

(Lights up on the STURGESS FAMILY, as though on a television set. BLANTON sits at a mocked-up drum kit. JAGGER on guitar. KRANK on bass. MARY on tambourine. JOANNE sings. They all wear bright smiles, wide eyes, and couldn't look happier. KRANK still hasn't delivered... but he's receiving attention from the best doctors.)

BLANTON: And a one—and a one—and a one, two, three, four—

(They bust into a version of Poison's "Nothin' But a Good Time." The lights get brighter and brighter—whiter and whiter—their smiles get bigger and bigger until their faces can't stretch any more.)

EVERYONE: *(Singing.)* AIN'T LOOKIN' FOR NOTHIN' BUT A GOOD TIME AND IT DON'T GET BETTER THAN THIS!

(Blackout.)

(END OF PLAY.)

MARVELOUS SHRINE

Leslie Bramm

LESLIE BRAMM is a playwright. He was born in Philadelphia on January 23, 1963, and raised in the Aleutian Islands, Newport News, San Francisco, and New York City. He is the author of thirteen plays including *A.B.C.* (Shelter Theatre Group, New York), *Big Ball* (Three Crows Theatre, New York), *Lover's Leapt, Oswald's Backyard* (both with The Present Company, New York), *Real Beatlemaniacs* (Actor's Theatre of Louisville), and an adaptation of *A Christmas Carol* (Penobscot Theatre, Maine). He also cowrote the screenplay *This is Not Here* with Kevin Corrigan. His play *A.B.C.* was turned into an independent feature film titled *Be My Oswald*. He received the 2001 Stanley Award for *Oswald's Backyard*, and the 1998 Paul T. Nolan Award for his play *Islands of Repair*. His play *Big Ball* won the 1999 Tennessee Williams Literary Award and was a finalist in the 2000 Edward Albee Last Frontier playwriting competition. His plays are published by Brooklyn Publishers, J&C Publications, Smith & Kraus, and One Act Play Depot. Bramm also played guitar and was the lead singer for the indie rock band Diz Dam. His poetry is published in numerous magazines and literary journals. He is currently workshopping a new full-length play called *Venus and Mona*, and developing a farce about Abraham Lincoln. Bramm is the literary director for Nicu's Spoon Theatre Company and a member of The Present Company's Pool. He lives with his wife, the director and dramaturg Pamela Butler, two dogs, and one cat in Washington Heights, New York City.

Marvelous Shrine was first presented by Three Crows Theatre as part of the New York International Fringe Festival (Elena K. Holy, Producing Artistic Director) on August 11, 2007, at The New School for Drama with the following cast and credits:

Marvelous ....Paul Hufker
Peter McNaughtin...Jack Halpin
Bobbie Ross-McNaughtin ....Sara Thigpen

Directed by: Pamela S. Butler
Stage Manager: Amy Upham
Production Assistant: Samantha Shechtman

for my father

CHARACTERS

PETER McNAUGHTIN: Forties. A father. Patriotic and prideful.

BOBBIE ROSS-McNAUGHTIN: Forties. A mother. Sarcastic and distracted.

MARVELOUS: Seventeen. Their son. Rebellious, guitar player, probably gay.

TIME

April through July 1994.

PLACE

The front lawn of the McNaughtin home, Cape May, New Jersey. A track, Madison Square Garden. A police station. Parris Island, South Carolina.

Setting: The suggestion of the McNaughtin front lawn. Under the eves of the house is a porch with two lawn chairs and a small patio table. The table is upside-down and in the process of being painted. One chair is cluttered with files, phone books, a cocktail and shaker, a cordless phone, etc. Pots of crocus and daffodil delineate the porch from the lawn. Downstage is the shrine. It is a rusted barbecue grill that's been converted by ribbons, flags, and other Americana. Track trophies and pictures of young soldiers adorn it. The shrine has been appointed with purpose and care. At rise: MARVELOUS stands in a spotlight wearing a dress à la Kurt Cobain.

MARVELOUS: So this guy goes in to see his shrink. The shrink asks him, what's the matter, and the guys says, "I'm a corpse." The shrink tells him, "You can't be a corpse. You're walking and talking." Guy says, "Nope. I'm a corpse." The shrink tries every logical way to convince his patient that he's not dead. Walking, talking, sleeping, eating, the shrink confronts him with the facts. With what's right in front of his face. Still the guy says, "I'm dead. I'm a corpse." Finally the shrink says; "Ah ha! Do corpses bleed?" The guy says, "Of course a corpse can't bleed." So, in his frustration the shrink grabs a pin and pricks the guy's finger. Blood starts pouring out and the shrink says; "Look, look at the blood." The guy responds; "Wow, I guess corpses do bleed."...Don't ask, don't tell, don't look, don't listen. Maybe it doesn't exist? Fine, I'm still dead.

(Lights cross quickly to PETER. He wears a Coast Guard uniform. He parades in front of an offstage judge like Patton.)

PETER: America, Government, Coast Guard, *Hero*, your honor. That's what I'm talking about. We're a country in short supply. We need to remind ourselves what that means, and where we'd be without them!...How does that pertain?...My son is my hero...Yes, ma'am, even now…I am aware of the state's drunk driving laws…I noticed your paperweight. You were in the Marines…Yes, ma'am. "Once a Marine always a Marine." Yes, but, there…there must be some other option. Could this be like a foul tip not his third strike? Wait, your honor, please…I have a thought.

(Lights up quickly on a sunny spring day, four days earlier. BOBBIE ROSS-McNAUGHTIN is distracted with files and an open phone book. She's on the phone, drinking a martini and painting the patio table, all at the same time. PETER tries to assemble a toy fort that will be the shrine's crown. PETER and BOBBIE are in their own worlds.)

BOBBIE: What are they thinking?

PETER: Eighteen hours from now! Eighteen hours!

BOBBIE: Serious donors don't want to bowl. This event should be classy and sophisticated. Not beer soaked and silly. *(Closes her eyes and assumes a channeling position.)*

PETER: Are you listening to me?

BOBBIE: Sshhh. I'm trying to channel Lila Wallace. I need her strength.

PETER: Are you done?

BOBBIE: I proposed a bike ride. People love to wear ridiculously revealing spandex and travel in packs. It must be a throwback gene or something. A Cro-Magnon need to wheel around with accentuated genitalia. Little men look big, and big men look stuffed with potatoes. Who doesn't love that.

PETER: This is a once-in-a-lifetime shot. One we've been training for, for years.

BOBBIE: What would Lila do? She would not wear stupid shoes and throw balls down a gutter! This is so humiliating! These idiots expect to raise ten thousand dollars bowling? They should be taken out behind the nearest AMF Bowling Centers and promptly shot in their bowling ball heads.

PETER: Can we get back to the subject of our son? Solve this problem, before he blows everything.

BOBBIE: What?

PETER: Our son? Junior?

BOBBIE: I know who my son is. You're the one who has no clue.

PETER: No, no…No, no, no. My son's not that!

BOBBIE: This is only a problem because you're making it into one.

PETER: Calling his teacher a "dickless douche bag" isn't quite enough. He has to demonstrate?

BOBBIE: He got a huge round of applause. He's like a folk hero for the class of '94. And that's not what I'm talking about.

PETER: Pulling down his pants? Stuffing himself between his legs, and singing vagina songs? *(Calling offstage.)* JUNIOR!…In front of the entire senior class…GET YOUR ASS OUT HERE!

BOBBIE: He teaches wood shop and driver's ed. Mr. Polly is a douche bag.

PETER: This is high school. He has to show some respect for authority.

BOBBIE: No he doesn't. Not when it involves wearing a toilet seat as a bathroom hall pass. What kind of sadistic behavior is that? My son is not some toilet-seat-wearing clone like the rest of them!

PETER: Scouts will be there. Some from major colleges. People from the Olympic Committee. He's going to win!

BOBBIE: My son doesn't wear toilet seats!

PETER: He knows that competition and pressure are part of real life, and he's ready to tackle them.

BOBBIE: *(Nasty.)* And disappointment. Don't forget the disappointment.

PETER: *(Back at her.)* How could I? How could I forget that?...This little stunt could cost him his place at the Milrose Games. The Milrose Games?

BOBBIE: He's the best runner in that school.

PETER: Add on the DUI incident. Remember? The one before the most recent one?

BOBBIE: You add it on. You're good at making the list of his failures.

PETER: And the "stealing thing"—

BOBBIE: Shoplifting—

PETER: Call it whatever you want.

BOBBIE: There's my event, my book club, which I'm hosting next week. My quilting for the homeless luncheon. Not to mention I have five clowns, literally five clowns, that I'm helping book into the Veterans Hospice.

PETER: Where is his father?

BOBBIE: You're not here, Peter. Your choice.

PETER: Nobody says that kind of shit to a man. A man doesn't listen to

that shit from anybody. Not even his Goddamn wife.

BOBBIE: Now's not the time. Let's not do this.

PETER: You act like I woke up one day and said I'm going to humiliate myself in front of the neighbors, my son, my colleagues, the whole Goddamn base!

BOBBIE: Wasting my precious time, right now, is pointless. There's no point to any of it.

PETER: I don't live in my own fucking house! That's the point. You drove me away. Is that pointed enough for you?

BOBBIE: Blame silence, blame silence. Slam the door, silence. Slam another door, blame.

PETER: And you think being around you is pleasant? Coming home to your endless causes. The clutter of one unfinished project on top of another. And the sarcasm. Life with you is like chewing aspirin.

BOBBIE: Nice, Peter. Thank you.

PETER: My home Bobbie? Where I used to live? How do you think this makes me feel?

(Beat.)

PETER: All this, all the behavior...JUNIOR...It's recent. Just another incomplete project of yours.

BOBBIE: I already told you what the problem is.

PETER: Not my son. No way! GODDAMN IT, JUNIOR!

BOBBIE: Will you please... *(Calling out.)* MARVELOUS!

(MARVELOUS enters. He's dressed grunge style, with torn jeans, long dirty hair, and a Nirvana T-shirt. He's carrying a beat-up old Fender Strat. It's plugged into a portable amp, which he also wears slung over his shoulder. He comes in singing, strumming, and improvising songs. He's very good. He plays quietly under the scene.)

MARVELOUS: TWIST YOUR SADDEST
   MEMORIES
BURN THEM ON YOUR SKIN
YOU'LL WIND UP IN A LITTLE WORLD
OF ALL THE MIGHT-HAVE-BEENS
ALL YOUR MIGHT-HAVE-BEENS—

PETER: Junior!

BOBBIE: *(Resuming her work.)* Please explain to your father why you need to become a woman.

MARVELOUS: *(Singing.)* "I'm feeeeeeel-ling weird"…

PETER: Explain, don't sing.

MARVELOUS: Weird as in, "not right?" As in, "Look at the girly freak."

BOBBIE: And why might you be girly?

PETER: Zip it Bobbie!

BOBBIE: You were eleven years old. I wouldn't let you iron your jeans. You cried. What eleven-year-old boy irons, let alone his blue jeans?

MARVELOUS: Big cuffs have to be crisp.

PETER: Son, you have the biggest race of your life tomorrow. Get yourself squared away. Clean your act up, you could actually best a Milrose record.

MARVELOUS: What if I don't care about Milrose, "Pete Patton"?

PETER: You love to run. You're the best in this state. *(Taking up a trophy.)* So says the state.

MARVELOUS: Running's dull. It bores me now.

PETER: Then why are you up at the crack of dawn every day, doing yoga and wind sprints?

MARVELOUS: You don't know whose crack I'm up at.

PETER: After you take your Milrose trophy you'll make the Olympic squad. Then it's off to Atlanta for the '96 summer games. Then to O.C.S. You'll start your career. Learn a skill set, build a solid foundation. You'll wear a uniform instead of a costume. You'll emerge a First Lieutenant…

MARVELOUS: The Coast Guard? Do you know how pathetic that sounds?

PETER: I dedicated my entire career to the Guard.

MARVELOUS: Do you know how pathetic that sounds? Look, Pete, you're not the General. You're an E-8.

PETER: Goddamn right! E-8 is one step below an E-9!

MARVELOUS: And only one step above E-7. Don't act like the great warrior. You put people into apartments.

PETER: I'm the O.B.H.C. I coordinate housing. You think it's so Goddamn easy, you try it!

MARVELOUS: For twenty-three years? And you want me to grow up and be just like that? Gee no thanks.

BOBBIE: *(On the phone.)* Yes, this is Bobbie Ross-McNaughtin. I'm calling for Mothers Against Drunk Driving…

PETER: First place. That's your destiny. Maybe second. Third at the worst, but that would still be good enough to make the Olympic squad.

MARVELOUS: How good would fourth, fifth, or sixth be?

PETER: Just win one more time son, for me.

MARVELOUS: Ah shucks Gipper.

(PETER's getting frustrated with the fort.)

MARVELOUS: Part B goes into part C. Duh. You're trying to force part D into part A...Building a fort? For what? So your shrine can be even bigger and more stupid-looking?

PETER: A shrine is for all these soldiers who sacrificed. It's also like a monument.

MARVELOUS: No, a monument is something huge, immovable, fixed in stone, forever. Like Lincoln. Like you.

PETER: For all the other brave sons and daughters, the heroes. *(Looking at pictures.)*

MARVELOUS: It's weird and creepy. Why is all my stuff mixed in with these smiling dead people, people that you don't even know?

BOBBIE: Your father's just looking for someone to worship.

PETER: We're a military family. We live on base. It's what is expected of me. I'm proud to honor other people's children, if I have to.

MARVELOUS: You may seriously need some help.

PETER: I raised a winner. You've been winning nonstop since the fifth grade.

If this is your last race, then go out like a winner.

MARVELOUS: I'll pretend the shrine is chasing me.

PETER: Fine, just win.

BOBBIE: As long as it's not a Marvelous Shrine.

MARVELOUS: It's Fort McNaughtin.

BOBBIE: He wants you to be Davy Crockett.

MARVELOUS: Remember the Alamode!

PETER: *(Taking a deep breath.)* You know son...

MARVELOUS: Beware! Pete's going to shoot for a profundity. He has that far-away-look-thing going on.

PETER: Son, you're right. I'm not the General. That wasn't my destiny. But it can still be yours.

MARVELOUS: Do I look like military material to you really?

PETER: Jimi Hendrix was in the Air Force.

MARVELOUS: Yeah, and that's what he's best known for.

BOBBIE: *(Not looking up.)* "And so castles made of sand melt into the sea, eventually."

MARVELOUS: I'm going to Milwaukee. I'm going to have the operation. Then I'm converting to Nihilism. I intend to be the first-ever post-op feminist, Nietzschean guitar god.

PETER: Girls don't become guitar gods. Girls strum and sing. You need testosterone to really rock. You get your testicles from me. I suggest you hang onto them.

MARVELOUS: Oh that's right. You've really listened to me play. You've paid attention to my music.

BOBBIE: He's like a cross between Freddie Mercury, Boy George, and…a butterfly.

MARVELOUS: I'm not gay. If that's what you think. Is anybody listening?

PETER: See, he's not gay. He's just lithe and a little confused. Eight weeks of boot camp will knock the slink right out of him.

MARVELOUS: I'm a woman trapped in a man's body, can't you see that?

PETER: If not full time then the reserves.

MARVELOUS: I'd rather cut my foot in half with a shovel than join the Coast Guard.

PETER: How about the Marine Corps then? They're tough, but if you can pass muster with them, you know you've done something.

MARVELOUS: Don't you have an off switch?

(BOBBIE's phone rings.)

BOBBIE: Bobbie Ross-Mc…No…No I haven't…That's because bowling is a stupid idea. Listen, why don't we have a costume ball? Yes…People love to pretend that they're something else, someplace else. I know I do. We can pick a theme, find the perfect location, and charge a thousand dollars a head. *(She fades away.)*

MARVELOUS: How many times do I have to say no?

PETER: *(Aside.)* Just a few months ago you were in the garage, half-naked

and two fingers deep in Evelyn, whatever her name is. Homos don't finger debutantes.

MARVELOUS: Okay, I'm a lesbian in a man's body needing to explore the potential plumbing.

PETER: You need to stop talking all this shit and get serious, troop.

MARVELOUS: Are we done? I have the Vulcan Club gig to worry about. I must prepare myself for the obvious fame and fortune that will befall me Saturday night.

PETER: Excuse me, Neil Young, it's just an amateur night.

MARVELOUS: Neil Young was an amateur once. And like Crazy Horse, Marvelous and the Delft Blue Beetles…

BOBBIE: Three "E"s of course…

MARVELOUS: Of course. We're going to set the Vulcan Coffee Bar on fire.

PETER: Get yourself expelled and there won't be a gig to worry about.

BOBBIE: *(On the phone.)* We could rent a hall in Atlantic City. It's close and…Yes, I'll hold.

MARVELOUS: Mom may be oblivious. Pickled, stupefied, and oblivious, but at least she's not a jam buster.

BOBBIE: Thank you honey. I never wanted to bust your jam. Does Mr. Polly still stuff his pockets with all those pens and things?

MARVELOUS: And his ten commandments flash cards, the same black comb…

MARVELOUS and BOBBIE: *(Together.)* Ewww…

MARVELOUS: Covered in Brylcreem and psoriasis. He hovers over you, snowing dead Polly skin, talking about God and America. Like one is somehow responsible for the other.

PETER: They are. And God bless America.

BOBBIE: And this is the authority figure you want him to respect? Really Peter. Marvelous is just way too smart and talented for these people…

(She is interrupted by the phone.)

BOBBIE: That's my point. That caliber of donor isn't going to bowl. Listen, I'm serious about the costume ball…

PETER: You know what, go find a forty-year-old failed musician, playing at a poetry reading, still paying off his college debt. Ask him about his rock 'n' roll fantasy.

MARVELOUS: This song is called "Mons De Venus"… *(Singing and playing.)* I'M GOING TO GET A VAGINA
ONE THAT CURLS IN LIKE A SMIRK
LIKE A SMIRK WAITING TO SMILE
ONE THAT SAYS SLOW DOWN
AND COME IN FOR A WHILE

PETER: Goddamn instructions make no sense. None!

MARVELOUS: OR ONE THAT FOLDS OUT
A FLOWER OF POUT
PETALS DEWY AND FUN
BUD ARCHING TO THE SUN

PETER: Part B doesn't fit into part A. Not this way. It's not possible.

MARVELOUS: I WANT A NEST OF HAIR
LUSH AND TANGLING
NOT SOME "LESBIAN LANDING STRIP"
BUT A MOUND WORTH WRANGLING
ONE YOUR FINGERS CAN FLUFF

THICK AND ABUNDANT
A REAL MUFF, A REAL MUFF
A REAL MUFF, A REAL—

PETER: *(Stopping him.)* Junior! Shut up about this, please. And keep your pants on. That's an order.

MARVELOUS: Hey! That's like the penultimate dis. And don't call me "Junior."

PETER: That's your name. Peter McNaughtin III.

MARVELOUS: No, my name is Marvelous. Because I am.

PETER: I'm not calling you Marvelous. So, don't bet the farm on it.

MARVELOUS: Should I bet the fort instead?

PETER: Okay, other than obviously loving to provoke me, tell me what the advantage is in becoming a woman?

MARVELOUS: Nothing less than saving the world.

PETER: Saving the world? Yeah, that's exactly what women want to do.

MARVELOUS: *(Singing.)* WITHIN HER POWER LIES ALL THE WORLD'S SALVATION

FROM THE MAPLES TO MARSUPIALS, TO ALL

THE HUMAN NATIONS

That's from a new song you'll probably never hear.

BOBBIE: *(Hanging up the phone.)* YES! Yes, thank you very much. Who's the ass-kicking, number one, fundraiser? Not only did I change the Chair's mind about bowling, I got him to do it three days before the actual event. Yes! I'm this good!

MARVELOUS: *(Kissing her cheek and affecting an accent.)* Lila would be proud of you darling.

BOBBIE: *(Disappearing back into her work.)* Darling, not now, I'm suddenly, feverishly, inundated.

PETER: Let me repeat myself. If you get expelled. Screw up the games. You will be musician non gratis.

MARVELOUS: Ohhh stern and daddish. Guess I have no choice but to fear the wrath of Pete.

BOBBIE: *(Starts cross referencing her files.)* Your father's on a rant. He hasn't been "wrangling" lately. I'd ignore him if I were you.

MARVELOUS: "Thank you Mummy."

BOBBIE: "You're welcome. Now it's cocktail time."

MARVELOUS: By all means Mother, set sail on the S.S. Absolut.

BOBBIE: Be nice. I'm your only anti-shrine ally in all this.

MARVELOUS: That's two Indians versus one cowboy. Uh oh Pete!

PETER: Americans have short memories. Those who pay with their lives need to be remembered.

MARVELOUS: *(Mocking.)* "Hey Captain my son is dead." "That's okay, he's in McNaughtin's shrine." "Really? That's swell. I feel much better now."

PETER: Like I said, this shrine will make sure nobody forgets these heroes.

MARVELOUS: It's not a shrine. It's a fort. A fort on top of a bunch of ribbons and flags, on top of a barbecue grill.

BOBBIE: I'm sending Marty Rice-Rosen a fax. The bowling was her brainstorm. This bitch will be trumped by my better idea. I will trample her under my simple, yet sophisticated, black pumps.

PETER: We're dealing with possible expulsion here. We need to take this more seriously.

BOBBIE: Why? You're taking it seriously enough for everybody.

MARVELOUS: Word!

PETER: Keep this up, and you're gonna end up just another guy, muddling along in some menial, mindless routine, with no say about anything.

MARVELOUS: Gee, mindless, like I was in the "military"? I want to be a blend of Kurt and Courtney. I want to wail on stage, my amp at "eight," my toggle wedged. I want to watch the bodies thrashing from a mosh pit, writhing to the groove I'm laying down.

PETER: A suicidal drug addict. Kurt Cobain. Great role model.

MARVELOUS: Like his, my ruined youth will serve as the manure that takes the seeds of my inspiration, from which my songs, like flowers, will grow.

PETER: You're a track star, and a high "C" student. Hardly a ruin.

MARVELOUS: This is who I am now. It's real and you'd better start to deal.

PETER: What's real are all these trophies.

MARVELOUS: What's real are all my songs.

PETER: That phase will pass. Believe me.

MARVELOUS: What if it's not a phase? What if I'm dead serious about my music?

PETER: You're a track star, son. A soon-to-be Olympian.

MARVELOUS: Of course, when talking to a wall, expect a wall-like bounce back.

BOBBIE: *(Looking up from her work.)* You need to understand things about yourself. See who you really are.

MARVELOUS: Ohhh, Mom resurfaces from her martini mist, with a prefab, Hallmarkian aside of her own.

BOBBIE: He's bitchy, clever, talented, and fussy. Wonder what that could mean?

PETER: Nobody cares Bobbie.

MARVELOUS: The "white apple"? Was that part of protecting your son, Pete?

PETER: I'm your father. My name is "Dad."

BOBBIE: What is the "white apple"?

MARVELOUS: It was one of those "Dad's Nights"; you know, fart jokes, fag jokes, Cold Duck, and Hustler's "Beaver Hunt."

BOBBIE: That hardly comes as a staggering revelation.

PETER: As opposed to lopping off one's cock and balls, it pales.

(MARVELOUS plugs his guitar back in. PETER distracts himself with the shrine.)

BOBBIE: I feel a song coming on.

MARVELOUS: This song is called, "Pete Patton. The American Joke"… *(Sings.)*

MR. PETE GIVES ME AN APPLE
HE TELLS ME THAT IT'S SATIN
MR. PETE'S AN AMERICAN JOKE
MR. PETE THINKS THAT HE'S PATTON
HEY CANDY ASS DON'T BE A GIRL
HEY CANDY ASS TAKE A BITE…
(Switches to a power thrash.)
HE SAYS BEFORE YOU EAT IT, WHATEVER YOU DO
DON'T TELL YOUR MOTHER, THE BITTER, DRUNKEN SHREW
WHAT CAN I DO WITH ALL THIS PRESSURE COOKING
I TAKE A BIG BITE 'CAUSE I'M DAMN GOOD LOOKING
(Switches to an exaggerated Country-Western style.)
NOW THERE'S A BURNING ON MY TONGUE
LIKE A LINE DANCE BUNION
WHY IS THAT YOU ASK
'CAUSE THE APPLE IS AN ONION
OH WHITE APPLE, OH WHITE APPLE
(Fades out metal style.)
THE APPLE IS AN ONION AND DADDY BURNS ME
THE APPLE IS AN ONION AND DADDY BURNS ME
THE APPLE IS AN ONION AND DADDY BURNS ME
THE APPLE IS AN ONION AND DADDY BURNS…
(Ends on a power chord.)

BOBBIE: *(Applauds.)* "Bitter drunken shrew"?

PETER: Or something like that.

MARVELOUS: Child abuser.

PETER: Sure, look at me. I'm just like a child abuser.

MARVELOUS: Tyrant!

BOBBIE: Bully!

PETER: Better dictator, than dick lick—

BOBBIE: You forced him to eat an onion? To be the brunt of a sadistic joke?

MARVELOUS: Don't distract him, Mother, he's building a very important lawn ornament.

PETER: What kid doesn't know the difference between an apple and an onion?

BOBBIE: What kind of sadist gets off humiliating children? I know, douche bags like you and Mr. Polly.

PETER: This is your shot, son. Treat it with respect. Because if you win this, your future's set.

MARVELOUS: Mom just called you a bag of douche. And what do you do?

PETER: (Bellicose.) All of this…All of it. "Me"! The car, the guitar! Not Kurt Cobain, me. E-8, Chief Petty Officer Peter McNaughtin II…Now, I'm taking this piece of garbage back. But, before I drive over to the mall, I'm going in the house, pulling out my dick and pissing, standing up. So, if you'll excuse me, ladies. (Exits.)

MARVELOUS: Now I have to carry around the mental picture of my father holding his penis?

BOBBIE: He used to hold yours. When you were a baby. We both did. We'd wiggle it from side to side giggling, "wacka-wacka-wacka!"

MARVELOUS: Eww! And I was molested too?

BOBBIE: Not in the Roman Catholic sense of the word, no.

MARVELOUS: Okay, can we just let go of my "penis"?

BOBBIE: Speaking of which. Do you really want the little guy split in two, sewn

under, and your pelvic cavity deepened so you can have some form of female sex? Penetration's not all it's cracked up to be. (Holding up a medical textbook tagged with Post-it notes.) Look at the litany of pills and treatments. Months and months, a half-dozen doctors, and it's not as easy as you think. They talk about some of the mistakes that have been made. Look at this picture. Is this what you want?

MARVELOUS: Mom…I…

BOBBIE: What?

MARVELOUS: (Bites his tongue.) I don't know. What?

BOBBIE: You brought it up.

MARVELOUS: What "it," what does "it" mean….

BOBBIE: I'm totally lost now. If we're going to just "what" back and forth, I have a ton of work to do. (Disappears back into her work.)

MARVELOUS: (Continues to strum softly.) Why does he keep coming back? I thought you were separated. Doesn't that usually mean different places? Ergo: Separation? Like the creep he is, he's into creepy, creeping things. Soon it'll be creeping into the street, joining all the other shrines as they creep and devour any and everything in their way. They'll creep all over the city, "shrining" out churches, schools, libraries, and theatres. They'll creep through the state, and keep creeping until they swallow up the whole country. The "United States of Creepy Shrines."

BOBBIE: Speaking of creepy, even more than your father. Marty is a born-again Republican bowler. She thinks pigs in a blanket are hors d'oeuvres. Pop Tarts are the crème brûlée of her soul. And she has no shame about it whatsoever.

MARVELOUS: It's like he's suffering from some middle-aged, male pattern oblivion. He sees nothing.

BOBBIE: At least it's not golf. Thank God it's not golf.

MARVELOUS: And you won't be at my gig on Saturday?

BOBBIE: It won't be your last.

MARVELOUS: No, it's my first.

BOBBIE: My event...The timing just got screwed up. I'm sorry. I really, really wanted to see it.

MARVELOUS: Obviously not bad enough.

BOBBIE: Marvelous, please don't guilt me. I'm under enough pressure as it is. I have an idea. We get somebody to tape it. That way we can play it over and over. Juts to irritate your father. Deal? I'm sorry honey, really. Do we have a deal?

MARVELOUS: Deal...Track star, sailor, I don't want to be any of those things. Why doesn't he get that?

BOBBIE: Then be what I think you should be. Be glamorous. Be fabulous. Be the rock star Marvelous.

MARVELOUS: I want to play my songs for somebody else, I need to play them in front of other people. And I need to see if they make sense to anybody else but me. And I need to know what other people hear in them... *(Blurting out.)* And I'm gay...I'm gay, right?

BOBBIE: *(Looking up from her work.)* My girlfriends will be so jealous. Their kids are so totally unexceptional.

MARVELOUS: I'm really gay?

BOBBIE: I think so. I certainly hope so.

MARVELOUS: *(Affecting voices.)* But what if I'm not, darling? What if I get all into the culture, pierce my nipples, do poppers, drink a lot, have meaningless affairs with dozens of men, only to find that it was a phase?

BOBBIE: Then you will have lived the life I always dreamed of...Except for the nipple thing.

MARVELOUS: Let me tell him.

BOBBIE: But...

MARVELOUS: Let me.

BOBBIE: Damn! Okay, I won't say a word.

MARVELOUS: When the time is right. Not now. He wouldn't believe it anyway. He already knows who I am. Which isn't me.

BOBBIE: Hard as it will be not to torture him, I promise.

MARVELOUS: Wow, I just came out, sort of. *(Blown away.)* Holy shit! I'm gay. I'm really, well, sort of, more or less, I'm gayish. I mean who knew, you did but...

(She puts her work down and takes his hands.)

MARVELOUS: Wow, I mean...Wow!

BOBBIE: Thank God is all I can say. I crave witty repartee and someone to pick out fabrics with.

MARVELOUS: My fingers are these sudden licks of flame. Like that's how I'm going to play. Like my true self has just melded with my guitar.

BOBBIE: Then you have no choice but to kick ass Saturday night. I'm glad you told me, darling.

MARVELOUS: Oh god, a gay teenager outs himself to his mostly absent mother, thus reinventing the bond between them forever. Could I get any more made-for-TV? *(Looks at his reflection.)* Still, it's good to come out while you're this pretty.

BOBBIE: You're your mother's son. Without a doubt.

(PETER enters.)

PETER: I just got off the phone with Mr. Farmer. You've been expelled. He was pretty adamant about the school not wanting you to represent them. Fortunately I was able to talk sense into him. You're the best they have to offer. The Vulcan gig, however, is officially null and void.

MARVELOUS: "Oh well, what-ever, never mind."

PETER: And Mr. Polly expects an apology. I expect you to give it to him.

BOBBIE: I'll talk to Mr. Farmer myself. I'll explain extenuating circumstances. The expulsion won't stand.

(MARVELOUS turns to leave.)

PETER: Where are you going?

MARVELOUS: To restring my guitar. Get it ready for battle.

PETER: You're not playing.

MARVELOUS: You don't live here anymore. You can't tell me what to do.

PETER: I'm your Goddamn father. No matter where I live.

MARVELOUS: Hello! I'm in a band. There's three other people who depend on me.

PETER: *(Confiscates the guitar.)* So, like I said, no gig.

MARVELOUS: Please give me my guitar before you wreck that too.

PETER: You will apologize to Mr. Polly. You will win the hundred-yard dash. You will not screw up your life with this bullshit instrument!

MARVELOUS: You will go fuck yourself!

PETER: Keep digging mister. Dig deep enough to bury your sissy ass.

MARVELOUS: *(Strikes a match.)* I'll torch the shrine right now.

PETER: Oh good. Let's add arson to your recent list of accomplishments.

BOBBIE: Peter, give him back his guitar. You're being ridiculous.

PETER: And if you think you'll sneak behind my back to do this, I'll take away more of your freedoms.

MARVELOUS: I want my Strat back. Give me back my Goddamn— *(The match burns his fingers.)* OW! OW! I FUCKING HATE YOU! *(Storms off.)*

PETER: He's not playing that gig…DO YOU HEAR ME JUNIOR!…He won't listen unless we both agree.

BOBBIE: I don't agree. I don't agree at all. He's allowed to run track, but playing music is a "no"? Explain the logic.

PETER: He doesn't bark orders at me. There's enough Junior Grade Lieutenants that do that. It's the Milrose games versus some bullshit, coffeehouse thing.

(Lights cross fade to MARVELOUS, who is back on stage.)

MARVELOUS: And this is what they do? Back and forth like this? Making white noise. Making a mockery of marriage. Making sure nothing ever gets resolved or agreed upon. *(Produces three framed photos: George Patton, Lila Wallace, and Kurt Cobain, respectively.)* The father…The mother…And this would be their child? The quintessential American family. What is it with them and their hero worship? I'm only seventeen. At least I have an excuse. And if you're going to go to all the trouble to worship somebody, shouldn't it be somebody cool?

(Lights cross fade back.)

BOBBIE: He's going to hate you.

PETER: Not without your support, Bobbie. I suspect you have a thing or two to teach on that score. "How to Hate Your Husband," by Bobbie Ross-McNaughtin.

BOBBIE: Versus, "Beating Your Children Over the Head with Macho Pride," starring Peter McNaughtin.

PETER: You know what, you don't really care. Stop trying to sound like you do.

BOBBIE: I care. I care plenty, Peter!

PETER: My son is not a homosexual period! End of story!

BOBBIE: But what if he is?

(The phone rings.)

BOBBIE: Bobbie Ross…McNaughtin… Yes, I have the donors list…Hold on a second… *(Cups the phone.)* Accepting himself, right now, is critical. His music is vital to his self-esteem. If you can't see that, then please take my word for it.

PETER: He's angry, that's all it is. Rebellious. A young man rebelling against his father. He chose the most obvious way to do it. However if he thinks he's going to lock horns with me…

BOBBIE: *(On the phone.)* I'll fax that list right over. *(Cupping the phone again.)* You can't say I don't care. You can say a lot of things, but you can't say that. *(Speaks as she exits.)* Yes, I'm faxing it right now…

PETER: Amazing Bobbie. Truly amazing. Fire all of your guns, then turn on your heel. Truly fucking amazing…

(Lights shift. MARVELOUS is dressed in track and field gear. He loosens up and puts his hair in a ponytail. Another spot on PETER. His excitement is palpable.)

PETER: He's amazing. Really, truly, amazing. He can do a four-minute mile, but the hundred-yard dash is his thing. He's like a bolt, a flash, Now you see him, now you don't…We bring home a Milrose Trophy today…

(We hear the murmur of a crowd and the milling about of other runners. We hear an OFFSTAGE VOICE announce "Runners to their marks." MARVELOUS reluctantly takes his mark.)

PETER: Hey! Hey, Peter McNaughtin Junior! Fire in your feet, son!

(He sets himself, and prepares to launch. After a beat, we hear a starter's pistol fire, combined with a surge of crowd noise.)

PETER: Peter McNaughtin Junior! Peter McNaughtin Junior!

(MARVELOUS does not move. There is another murmur through the crowd. He remains crouched a beat before he breaks his form and stands up. He looks around the stands for his father.)

MARVELOUS: There's a spot, right between your eyes, it turns crimson, and the rest of your face goes pale. I saw two bloodworms mating once, in a science class. Bloodworms, scrunched between your eyes. I saw "that face" every time I ran, at every meet, win or lose. That expression seared into my memory. Scrunched and pathetic. I hear his voice in my head too. *(As his father.)* "It's my son he's neat. It's my son he's neat." It's like every "neat" shoots the scrunch with more blood, making it more squishy, and floppy and pulsating. I used to lay awake at night just praying that the scrunch would explode...I could have won Milrose. Half the runners were guys I'd already beaten...It's just that look...

(He reaches into his sock, and removes a scroll. He unfurls it to the audience. It reads, "Ask Me About My Vagina." He holds it high. Lights cross fade to PETER, who's speaking again to the judge.)

PETER: Suicidal? Really?...I never saw him like that. Do you really think so?...Well, his mother and I...Well, things at home aren't good. I mean, you get to a certain age, and you realize things about your life...Yes ma'am, that's not your problem...Yes, your honor...Wait, please...May I suggest an alternative?...What if he joined the Marines?

(Beat.)

PETER: Maybe it will give him some focus, some discipline and respect...Yes, his mother is in full support of the idea. We're a military family...I'd be happy to sign a waiver.

(She cuts him the slack.)

PETER: Your honor, thank you.

(Lights cross fade to a bench downstage. MARVELOUS is back in his grunge look. He sits wearing handcuffs.)

MARVELOUS: I stole my guitar back. I played my gig. The Delft Blue Beetles were amazing. It was just how I saw it going down. Dozens of people were there. Every song was like a piece of myself I was giving. I was unafraid. I saw myself. I was showing myself. My fingers moved with ease. I truly felt electric. Then right in the middle of everything this group of girls comes in crying. The room stopped. We were stopped. I mean, mid-song, the band just fizzles, busted...Kurt...Dead? He had it all. His words. These words, his music. Then everything he was gets splattered against the walls of a guest cottage? Your poetry is supposed to save you. If it can't, then what's the point?

(PETER enters. Lights come up to full.)

PETER: Captain Myer's mailbox?

MARVELOUS: *(Still a bit drunk.)* I was on the wrong lawn.

PETER: *(Grabbing him by the shirt.)* What the hell is going on?

MARVELOUS: A shrine hunt! Now let go of me...LET GO OF ME!

(PETER slings him off.)

PETER: Thousands of people. Tens of thousands of eyes just boring into me.

MARVELOUS: They were looking at me.

PETER: You just threw it all away. All that time we trained. All the people who believe in you. Just like that.

MARVELOUS: I don't believe in shrines, trophies, track stars, high school, fathers, father's day, jam bands. I can't believe in

Coast Guard, sex, penis, vagina, vodka, Veder, seat belts, Neil Young and…Kurt, I don't believe in Kurt Cobain.

PETER: Why don't you believe in yourself?

MARVELOUS: Because you're my "dad," and isn't that just neat.

(Beat.)

PETER: Did you want to hurt my feelings? Okay, my feelings are hurt. You embarrassed me. You got me back. But, I think I understand now, at least in part.

MARVELOUS: You could never…Are you serious? Understand?

(BOBBIE enters dressed in a costume.)

BOBBIE: Tonight! Tonight of all nights! I'm paged. I ask your father if he's kidding, because who would believe on the very night I'm raising money for Mothers Against Drunk Driving, my son would be arrested for what? Driving drunk! Can you imagine. I'm scrambling like mad to come up with a cover. People are handing me money and I'm lying to them as I back out the door.

PETER: There's your true blue democrat.

BOBBIE: Drunk driving. Tonight, it had to be tonight!

PETER: He's fine, by the way.

BOBBIE: Well, say something…

MARVELOUS: You really didn't wear those shoes with that outfit?

BOBBIE: Tedious Marvelous. You're being so Goddamn tedious, and I don't have time for it.

MARVELOUS: *(To each one of them.)* Am I? Well, you're…oblivious…superfluous…contagious, outrageous, dangerous…And whatever other "o-u-s" words I can think of. *(To his father.)* And you are just pathetic and you'll never get it, and…I polished off your Citron, but there's still half a bottle of Stoli in the back seat.

PETER: Don't even think about blaming me for this, Bobbie.

MARVELOUS: *(Singing.)*
I'LL TAKE ALL THE BLAME
I'LL PROCEED FROM SHAME

PETER: "Aqua sea foam shame."

MARVELOUS: What are you talking about? Is that a Coast Guard thing? Some McNaughtin, scrunchy, sailor lore?

PETER: The line in the Nirvana song. "Aqua sea foam shame"…Whatever that means. That's what he's singing.

(MARVELOUS throws up.)

BOBBIE: Let's just sign whatever we have to, and get out of here.

PETER: Well, here's the rub. He's going to jail.

BOBBIE: Excuse me, jail? Did you just say jail?

PETER: Yes, I said jail.

(MARVELOUS lies down on his side and curls up.)

BOBBIE: Wait a minute. Marvelous please don't lie in your own vomit…And roll over on your side we don't need you choking on it either…Who decides this, Peter?

PETER: The judge. It stays on your adult record. Your license is indefinitely suspended. You're seventeen years old and you're not allowed to drive anymore. Now sing me a song, smart ass.

BOBBIE: Am I missing something here?

PETER: Yes, once again you are.

BOBBIE: This is ridiculous! He didn't kill anybody, he's seventeen. You didn't kill anybody did you?

PETER: "Three strikes and you're out."

BOBBIE: My son is not going to start his adult life with a criminal record.

PETER: The judge originally sentenced you to 120 days. But, after reasoning with her honor, she reduced the sentence to forty-eight hours in this fine facility, and a month of community service.

BOBBIE: Thank God.

PETER: No, thank me, actually. She also ordered you to enlist in the reserves.

BOBBIE: The reserves?

PETER: I pled guilty for you. And I signed a waiver…

BOBBIE: You signed…

PETER: Because of your age.

BOBBIE: Why didn't you wait for me?

PETER: She said his behavior was verging on suicidal.

MARVELOUS: *(Still curled up.)* Rock stars swallow vomit. Rock stars kill themselves.

BOBBIE: Is that what she said, suicidal?

PETER: In a nutshell, yes. She's retired Corps. And basic training begins in thirty days. Right after your community

service ends. So it looks like you're going to be a Marine. You can kiss any chance at a track scholarship goodbye. Not to mention your "musical career."

MARVELOUS: The Marines? No thanks. I'll rot behind bars first.

BOBBIE: No, you'll be raped and beaten behind bars. I'll talk to the judge myself. We can do better than this.

PETER: We don't need Bobbie to the rescue.

BOBBIE: I'm sure you didn't explain the whole story, Peter.

PETER: She's a pissed-off night court judge. She doesn't need you giving her the hard sell. It's the Goddamn law!

BOBBIE: You had to act out at the most inconvenient time humanly possible!

PETER: I have an idea. Why don't you go outside and wait for Triple A. Check out the left front end of the Taurus while you're at it.

BOBBIE: Am I being punished in some infantile way? Is that what's happening? Grow up Junior. Stop being so Goddamn tedious.

PETER: It's time for us to go. He has to report to his cell now. You don't need to stay, Bobbie.

BOBBIE: Obviously not. Obviously I'm not necessary.

PETER: You can still make it back to your event. Why don't you do that?

BOBBIE: This is what happens to me? This is what karma dishes out? Not fair! Not fair! I'm doing charity work! *(Throws her hands up, then exits.)*

PETER: One of us will pick you up Monday. Probably me. Enjoy your weekend.

MARVELOUS: Dad…Wait…

(PETER grabs the garbage can. MARVELOUS throws up again.)

PETER: He killed himself. I'm not surprised, but it's still tragic. I know he was your hero. Your George Patton. I can imagine how you must feel.

(MARVELOUS begins to cry. PETER promptly gets up and moves away.)

PETER: Just do what they tell you…Come on Junior! Tough it out. Don't let your cellmate see you crying.

(PETER exits. MARVELOUS recovers.)

MARVELOUS: Some souls are too delicate for this world. They're shining too bright and that makes them vulnerable. In a world trying to beat every kid into a major chord, some of us are A minors or B minor sevenths. So, he died. He died and he's dead and that can't change. But other things can, and they did. *(Beat.)* See, in every rock song there's a hook, a riff. Call it what you like. You know it as soon as you hear it. You know the second it's strummed, plucked, hammered on, that the tune is grooving. There's no turning back. And sometimes your fingers end up in different positions, an arpeggio you didn't mean to play, or the tuning's all weird like the E down to a D. Suddenly there's this new sound. And suddenly it sounds really good.

(Lights cross fade to the lawn. PETER sits with his shirt off, giddy. BOBBIE trims his hair, annoyed.)

BOBBIE:…Don't act so self-satisfied, Peter really.

PETER: I'm sorry my happiness is annoying you. As soon as I finish feeling proud…I promise to stop.

BOBBIE: Go ahead. Have your fucking laugh. Enjoy it.

PETER: Honors! Squad leader! Carrying the colors at commencement!

BOBBIE: Any goon can make it through boot camp. All you have to do is what you're told.

PETER: Let him have this moment. We've earned it.

BOBBIE: He's been brainwashed. That's the only logical explanation.

(The phone rings; she answers.)

PETER: And maybe, just maybe, he's found his niche?

BOBBIE: Bobbie Ross…Hold on. It's for you.

PETER: Don't look so surprised. I'm still allowed to receive calls here. *(Taking phone.)* C.P.O. McNaughtin…Yes, Captain…Yes sir, graduation's tomorrow. Yes, sir, I'm very proud…His D.I. was extremely impressed with him…Yes, sir, I think he's thinking "career"…Thank you sir, thank you for the call. *(Hangs up.)* Goddamn this feels good. Bragging about my son.

BOBBIE: He's said nothing about making it his career.

PETER: Why can't you let me have this Bobbie? *(Gets up and moves away from her.)* To hell with it. I'll go to the barber. At least there I can gloat in peace.

BOBBIE: The military? This is not how I envisioned my son.

PETER: I made him into a Marine. While you would be content with him being some faggoty toy poodle. And can we behave ourselves tomorrow? No political stands, none of our personal agendas. It's his day.

BOBBIE: I know how to behave, thank you.

PETER: Just don't make a scene when we get there.

BOBBIE: I can talk some sense into him. He can't be serious about making this a career.

PETER: Why can't you just leave him alone?

BOBBIE: Because he's verging on becoming some jar head, robot moron.

PETER: My life, Bobbie Ross-McNaughtin. You're mocking my life and his life too.

BOBBIE: It's just "Ross" now.

PETER: Of course.

BOBBIE: "Hey candy ass don't be a girl. Hey candy ass don't play the guitar, even though you love to. Hey candy ass, here's your shrine."

PETER: Absolutely Goddamn right! Now it's for real. Now my boy can join all the other heroes.

BOBBIE: All the other heroes are dead.

PETER: *(Rearranges the trophies.)* Move this over here. Take off the faces of other kids. Make room for his citations, medals. I've waited a long time to say this. I mean a really long time…Told you so!

BOBBIE: So fucking typical. Rush ahead…

PETER: I didn't panic.

BOBBIE: Panic, don't think.

PETER: You didn't make it to the station on time, you were too busy.

BOBBIE: He could have done more community service maybe, he certainly didn't have to join the Marines.

PETER: "Suicidal," remember?

BOBBIE: You always do this. You always leave me out. You always make these assumptions…

PETER: That's not why we separated—

BOBBIE: And you wonder why we separated—

PETER: Because I am the "nothing man"! Because my wife, in the midst of yet another Cosmo blur half sings and half says "Really Peter, you've done nothing you've ever wanted, nothing you've ever planned, you've turned yourself into a nothing man." And she says it casually, matter of fact. Like a ticked-off list of things to do. Nothing, because I flunked out of O.C.S. Nothing, because after twenty-three years I'm only an E-8. Nothing, because you're *nothing*, but the On-Base Housing Coordinator. And if my Goddamn life is such a disappointment to me, I can only imagine what it is for you. Maybe you're right. Maybe it is. Maybe I'll live and die in this disappointment. This "nothingness." Maybe for a lot of things in my life, it's already too late. But not for Junior. Not for my son. "Hey nothing man you work an admin job. Hey nothing man you have nothing to be proud of. Hey nothing man you're a lousy lover."

(Lights drop to a sudden spot on PETER.)

PETER: And it hits me at the most mundane of times. My son is dead.

Filling the car with gas. Brushing my teeth. Having a shave... My dead son. It was a good death. "Good" in the sense that it mattered. So many soldiers die stupidly, ironically. Not my son. It was a John Wayne kind of death. A death to be proud of. Knowing that. Knowing how he died keeps me sane. I don't know what I would have, if I didn't have that. His death keeps him right here. Right here where heroes belong...

(Lights switch back to normal.)

PETER: Hey nothing man here's a choice; leave your home or live here in shame. Not today. Today I'm the proud father of a squad leader.

BOBBIE: Jesus Peter I was drunk!

PETER: You're mostly drunk!

BOBBIE: I'm a WASP. I'm supposed to drink and say rude things.

PETER: In vino veritas.

BOBBIE: Hear what you want to hear. You always do. See what you want to see. I know it's easier. And "lousy lover"? I never said that. I'm going to start packing for what's bound to be a delightful ten-hour drive.

PETER: Just stay focused on what you need Lila. What you want. Since this is all about you.

BOBBIE: Lila Bell Acheson Wallace is an amazing and brilliant woman. *Reader's Digest* was aimed at people with an eighth grade education. She took that dumb Southern and Midwestern money and used her various foundations to further the arts and minority causes. Fucking brilliant! That's the kind of hero my son should be worshiping.

PETER: My son's learned discipline and duty. He's obviously excelled at it. He won't squander his life or waste his time. End up a Goddamn drunk.

BOBBIE: Like his mother?

PETER: Like my father! Peter McNaughtin I. Who rose to the esteemed position of Building Superintendent.

(Separate spots on PETER and MARVELOUS.)

MARVELOUS: Grandpa was a genuine war hero. Fought with George Patton in the Sixth Armored Division in North Africa.

PETER: A Goddamn drunk. A handyman with shaky hands.

MARVELOUS: He was wounded, left for dead. He came back all messed up.

PETER: He bashed my mother and I with waves of drinking. Sucked us into drunken whirlpools. Nearly drowned us in drink.

MARVELOUS: Nobody guessed? Nobody asked? Post-traumatic stress, whatever. Nobody saw what he was going through?

PETER: Mean old bastard. Never let up on me. Never gave me an inch to breathe.

MARVELOUS: He fought in a war. Got wounded in a war. Came home after being in a war for two years. Nobody cut him any slack?

PETER: Maybe Annapolis. Maybe something more distinguished. Maybe a better life than I have now.

(Lights switch back to normal. MARVELOUS is gone.)

PETER: And the judge agreed with me about the Corps!

BOBBIE: Wait. Hold on a minute.

PETER: Another Peter McNaughtin in line to fuck up his life?

BOBBIE: He's seventeen years old.

PETER: Not today. Not this time.

BOBBIE: You pushed the military with the judge? It wasn't her idea? You did this?

PETER: He was going to jail! Where were you, Roberta Ross?

BOBBIE: You didn't wait! I was on my way. Why didn't you wait?

PETER: Reservists don't get called anywhere. Not before the regular grunts. So let's not blow this out of proportion.

BOBBIE: You know this?

PETER: Yes.

BOBBIE: You know this for a fact?

PETER: I was the one in the courtroom. I took action. Now look where he is.

BOBBIE: In a uniform. With a rifle. My son's traded in his guitar for a gun?

(Lights cross fade to a barracks in South Carolina. An American flag is used as a backdrop. MARVELOUS stands at parade rest in front of it. He wears a U.S.M.C. uniform. His hair is now short and neat, like his father's. He is serious and focused.)

MARVELOUS: I love to run. Really love to feel that endorphin rush. The burn in the legs. The way your groin seizes up when you pass people on the track. Every gulp of air is full of possibilities. You breathe in, you realize how much

there is. Just how far you can push. Raw talent, pure passion. That's all nice, but it will only get you so far. In fact you won't get that far at all. Eventually you bog yourself down. You spend more time convincing yourself that you're a serious runner, as opposed to running seriously. For that, discipline, patience, practice, commitment. The foundation for a person who's truly grown-up. Who's pursuing their passion. Natural talent, raw potential, alone will never, repeat, never, be enough. Unless of course you want to spend your life dancing on the front lawn blowing bubbles. (Closes his eyes and breathes deeply.) Breathe in— embrace your truth. Breath out—let go your youth...I should have won Milrose. I should have run "the good race." I should have figured out which battles were worth a fight.

(PETER enters.)

PETER: Look at this place. Mind blowing! So much tradition, so much history. The weight of history. It demands respect. You did something very special here, and...

MARVELOUS: Not necessary, sir.

PETER: You'll rise to Sergeant soon. Then you can pick your assignments.

MARVELOUS: The Corps has a marching band, a jazz band, and an orchestra, sir.

PETER: That's neat, but, you're a soldier now. Squad leader.

MARVELOUS: Yes sir.

PETER: Look at that haircut, the precision of Marine regulation, it's impressive...

(He reaches out to touch his son; MARVELOUS pulls away.)

PETER: Chest out shoulders back just look at you.

MARVELOUS: "Guitar slouch" gone, sir!

(Awkward beat.)

PETER: She's not prepared for this. You know, reserves and all. Let me explain it to her, okay?

MARVELOUS: It's my war.

PETER: It's not a war. It's a "situation." You'll be over and back before you know it. You look very handsome. Girls go crazy for a man in uniform.

MARVELOUS: Good to know, sir.

PETER: What's in the past is in the past. We can put it behind us, and just forget it.

MARVELOUS: A Marine keeps a present mind, sir.

PETER: When we're alone, Dad is fine.

(BOBBIE bursts on.)

BOBBIE: I didn't know there was a place on earth that could be as hot and revolting as South Carolina! It's like walking through low clouds of steamy mayonnaise. No wonder everybody here is so slow. And what is with the South and the Civil War worship. Hello, you lost! Every other exit off the highway is a shrine to some battle they *lost*. Confederate flags on license plates and bumper stickers. Adorning truck windows, right below the mandatory two-tier gun rack. Seems a single shotgun in your pickup isn't quite enough… "The South's Gonna Do it Again"? *(Waving to a passerby.)* Have you people no shame!…And then, and then, there's that other "Dixie fixation,"

"Oh Christ of the Billboards." Okay, here's an example of the wisdom of the natives. We passed a used car place somewhere in Virginia called "Lotz Used Cars" Spelled L-O-T-Z. A huge neon sign blinking on and off…"Lotz, Lotz, and right above it, to form the shape of a cross, is of course, "Jesus is coming." The whole thing is so huge you can read it five miles down the road. "Jesus is coming, Lotz"…Eight weeks, Marvelous? You deserve a medal. And I need a pitcher of Sangria!

MARVELOUS: I'm P.F.C. McNaughtin, ma'am. S.W.F.

BOBBIE: What does S.W.F. mean? "Single white female"?

MARVELOUS: Means I'm bound to see some action over there.

BOBBIE: What do you mean? Where?

PETER: We have some good news.

MARVELOUS: "Soldier waiting to fight."

BOBBIE: Waiting to fight? What do you mean? What does waiting to fight mean, Peter?

PETER: This is an honor. There are guys who wait their whole careers for this kind of deployment.

MARVELOUS: I'm one of the lucky ones.

BOBBIE: He's being sent to a war? What war are we fighting now?

PETER: Apparently there's a situation. And they need the Marines to sort it out. Right son?

BOBBIE: What kind of "situation"?

MARVELOUS: One where they need the Marine Corps!

PETER: Drop and give me ten, troop!

MARVELOUS: You drop and give me fifteen!

PETER: *(Drops and does a series of fast, hard pushups as he speaks.)* You can't negotiate…with these paranoid, megalo-maniacs…somebody has to go over and kick…the shit out of them.

(PETER and MARVELOUS make gung-ho grunts as he jumps up.)

BOBBIE: So, they're sending Marvelous?

PETER: I envy the adventure you're about to have.

BOBBIE: Then you go.

MARVELOUS: He's in the Coast Guard. They don't have to fight.

BOBBIE: You are not going. I'm sorry. There must be somebody I can talk to about reassignment.

PETER: He's under orders. His division got the call.

BOBBIE: Reservists don't go Peter, they don't get called, remember?

MARVELOUS: Troops are spread thin, worldwide. They need my help, and I'm glad to go.

BOBBIE: Plenty of people get out of these situations, like the children of CEOs or politicians.

MARVELOUS: I don't want to get out of anything, ma'am.

BOBBIE: No. I'm sorry. You're not going thousands of miles away, to get killed in some third world country. Absolutely not.

MARVELOUS: I hope I do see action. I hope I'm right in the middle of the shit!

(More gung-ho grunts.)

PETER: He's an ass kicker. A killing machine!

BOBBIE: Yes, that's the first thing I think of when I see him.

MARVELOUS: I'm an instrument of war, ma'am.

BOBBIE: Fine, you're still not going.

MARVELOUS: I'm going.

PETER: Bobbie, you're out of line here. The man wants to go.

BOBBIE: I'll tell them…

MARVELOUS: What ma'am? What will you tell them?

PETER: What are you going to tell them? That he's a fag?

BOBBIE: And I'll tell whoever I have to.

PETER: Obviously there's nothing to tell. Right son?

BOBBIE: He's scared. It's okay, Marvelous.

MARVELOUS: I'm many things. I'm willing to be who I am. With or without your approval, or support. First and fore-most, I'm a Marine.

PETER: Good, that's settled.

BOBBIE: Nothing's settled, Peter. Nothing.

PETER: Look, they just received orders. They won't ship out for a couple months. It'll probably be over by then.

MARVELOUS: I want to be cremated. I stated that on my application. Just in case.

PETER: Don't say that. There's no reason to think like that.

BOBBIE: There has to be something I can do about this. Somebody I can call. Somebody I can scream at. Someone that outranks both of you.

MARVELOUS: Today isn't about you, sir, ma'am. Nor is it about your petty bickering. Nor is about either one of you deciding my life. I'm proud of who I am, and what I've done here. This is important to me.

BOBBIE: This is not important to you. There is no way all this bullshit is important.

MARVELOUS: They're about to take the picture. This is official, for the record?

(A flash goes off. BOBBIE looks pissed, PETER looks proud, and MARVELOUS looks focused.)

BOBBIE: He's gay! Peter look at him. Your son is gay. *(Yelling and pointing.)* Gay here! Check it out! Gay Marine—

(PETER jerks her by the arm.)

PETER: SHUT THE FUCK UP!…Shut up Bobbie. Just shut up about it! *(Beat.)* It's not some charity fundraiser. It's done.

MARVELOUS: "Some people spend their whole lives wondering if they've made a difference. Marines don't have that problem." Ronald Reagan.

BOBBIE: *(Turns to leave.)* Thank you, both of you, for this glorious day. Thank you Peter, for bamboozling the judge. For sending my son into danger. *(To MARVELOUS.)* Thank you for becoming the very thing I tried to keep you from.

MARVELOUS: "Twelve in the clip, plus the one I just fired. Don't try running 'cause you'll only die tired."

(Lights drop to a sudden spot on BOBBIE.)

BOBBIE: His presence, still all over the house. The smell of his clothes, his hair in a brush, his sweet voice on the machine. I can feel all these pieces of my son.…He died without me. He suffered and died alone, all alone. Eighteen hours! That's how long my son fought to stay alive. That's how long he lay twisted and broken. That fragile body, mangled, burnt! Eighteen hours, in his pain, almost a full day, and I wasn't there. I wasn't there to hold his hands. Five hundred miles from home, where was I? And where are you? Where are you? You called. You called me on the phone. As soon as I hear it ring, I know it's you, and I know why. I answer…I answer the phone and now my son is dead. "I regret to inform you," is that what you said? *(Beat.)* At his funeral a Major and three other Marines… "You must be mistaken my son hasn't even shipped out yet. There must be some kind of…You're going to bury my son? This is a mistake." The Major has dry spit in the corner of his mouth. It looks like toothpaste. He says my son's name. I think he's talking about you at first. I'm relieved. Then he repeats it, to make sure I hear. My son's death, simple as your phone call. Gritty and sweet, like the taste of toothpaste. He has dog tags in his hand. "No. No, it's not possible," I tell him, "He called, finally. He was okay. We spoke. It was peaceful." …The Major apologizes, again. After a while I don't even hear the words. I watch his mouth. I watch the spit…I watch him trying to wet his lips. *(Beat.)* They gave me a flag. Neatly folded…I gave them a young man. A perfectly beautiful boy…He burned to death…I gave them a boy. They gave me a flag.

(Lights back up to full. BOBBIE is gone.)

PETER: Your mother could show a little more respect.

MARVELOUS: What is she talking about. The judge and all that?

PETER: I've never been more proud of you son. Isn't that all that matters?

MARVELOUS: Thank you, sir.

PETER: This is what I saw. What I always envisioned for you. And you love it. You love it right?

MARVELOUS: My life has changed. I have structure. Discipline. If I make it into one of the Marine Corps bands, I'll have a paying musical gig.

PETER: See, that's what she can't stand. I knew it was a good move for you. I knew it would all work out. Hey! Let's see the bulldog. Come on, troop. Show me that anchor and globe!

MARVELOUS: *(Showing his father the tattoo.)* Sir…

PETER: *(Reading.)* "You are the dancing Queen, young and sweet only seventeen"?

MARVELOUS: Abba, sir.

PETER: *(Not wanting to hear it.)* If I was hard on you Private, this is why. A dad's part D.I. himself. He has to be.

MARVELOUS: Yes, sir.

PETER: Squad leader. Aced your G.E.D. Carried the colors. Excelled in physical fitness, and mastered the Marine Corps

handbook. Seventy-nine percent shooting aptitude. I knew you had this in you.

MARVELOUS: The Corps taught me how to believe in myself.

PETER: Yes, well. I'm glad you figured it all out.

MARVELOUS: I'm glad you're proud, sir.

PETER: Please…"Dad."

MARVELOUS: Dad, sir.

PETER: I'm glad to have ushered you up to this point.

MARVELOUS: I changed my life, sir.

PETER: I'm glad I had something to do with it.

MARVELOUS: Sir?

PETER: Who you are now, I take credit for that.

MARVELOUS: Sir, the Corps is who I am now. And I am the reason that I am who I am now.

PETER: I've been the one constant for the last seventeen years.

MARVELOUS: That wasn't my choice, sir.

PETER: We don't get to pick our parents.

MARVELOUS: We have no control over that assignment.

PETER: Consider yourself one of the lucky ones.

MARVELOUS: Children are lucky if they're really considered at all.

PETER: You know what I mean.

MARVELOUS: I am responsible for myself, sir. All my success is because I wanted this.

PETER: Wait until you have your own child. You'll understand then.

MARVELOUS: Sir, I succeeded in spite of you, not because of you. Let's be clear about that.

PETER: Who trained with you? Who was out there every Sunday with a stopwatch, encouraging, pushing? All to make you better, faster, stronger in your body and mind? I did that. Me!

MARVELOUS: You assume I was running *to*, as opposed to running away from both of you.

PETER: I helped you win state.

MARVELOUS: Do you even hear me right now, sir?

PETER: You walk around quoting Kurt Cobain, or the Marines. Why don't you quote me? I've done more for you than they have. At least I assumed I had.

MARVELOUS: Assumptions are land mines, sir. Marines avoid them. I would too if I were you.

PETER: I want Goddamn respect. I don't care how many assumptions are made.

MARVELOUS: Take responsibility for your own life, or Mom's. I can handle my own.

PETER: You don't worry about my fucking life.

MARVELOUS: Right, sir. Understood. No caring about you.

PETER: If it wasn't for me you'd be in jail.

MARVELOUS: You never answered my question about the judge. In fact you blew it off.

PETER: The idea to have you enlist? Me. Not your mother. Not Kurt Cobain. I solved the problem. I was the one to set your life right.

MARVELOUS: This was your idea?

PETER: Goddamn right! So, when you're moving your way up through the ranks. Playing in one of the Marine Corps bands. Just remember who put you here.

MARVELOUS: But, you said the judge…Mom even said…

PETER: A McNaughtin hero. Finally.

MARVELOUS: You did this to me?

PETER: So, thank me. Salute me. Praise me. Something!

MARVELOUS: I didn't have to be here? This was in your control?

PETER: When you were a child I was your hero. You told me that. Always said how you wanted to grow up just like me. Now you've done better, son. You're my hero now.

MARVELOUS: Thank you, sir, for lying to me. For deciding the course my life would take. Thank you for that. And thank you for making it the Marines and not the Coast Guard. But, wait! The judge decided that since she's retired Corps herself.

PETER: After my suggestion.

MARVELOUS: Thank you, sir… (*Turns to leave.*)

PETER: Junior…It's not gay to give your dad a goodbye hug.

(PETER hugs his son. MARVELOUS becomes more rigid. They are both awkward. They separate into their own spotlights.)

PETER: They said it was quick. A round ricocheted off a burned-out jeep. It lodged…behind his ear, they said he didn't feel a thing.

MARVELOUS: There was a bright orange ball of flame.

PETER: No…No…There was no "orange ball"…They said it was quick. Like flipping on and off a light switch. Marines don't leave other Marines behind.

(Lights cross fade quickly to BOBBIE. She's on the porch. She's a little tipsy, smoking a cigarette.)

BOBBIE: This is stupid. This is really stupid, Bobbie. This is the same mistake all your friends make. The evening's bound to end in disaster. Whatever you do, you will not seduce him. Do you hear me? No sex.

(PETER enters.)

PETER: Are you okay?

BOBBIE: Thank you for coming over.

PETER: Is everything all right?

BOBBIE: I was lying in bed. Listening to these mothers talking…

PETER: He's okay…

BOBBIE: Shock, numb, gutted. It's the same story…

PETER: It's not going to happen to us, to you…

BOBBIE: The news said things have gotten worse. It's escalating. We've underestimated these people, as usual…

PETER: He's had special training…

BOBBIE: I don't pay attention, do I? I'm annoyed, preoccupied. I've neglected him and you.

(They linger on each other. Her hand brushes across his.)

BOBBIE: I'm glad you could come.

PETER: I only live two miles away.

BOBBIE: No, I mean, never mind.

PETER: He knows how much you love him. Don't worry about that.

BOBBIE: *(Lingering.)* Do you know…Never mind…

PETER: Stop listening to NPR. That's the first thing you need to do.

(He straightens up the shrine. They both are a bit humbled.)

BOBBIE: Life might be busy for her. She might be dealing with a thousand things all at once, but, she would care. She would take time to care. She would always take care to pay attention. Lila would be able to juggle everything. I need to be better at that.

PETER: I heard the word "jail," and over-reacted. Panic isn't very Patton-esque.

BOBBIE: We could have communicated better.

PETER: I haven't been very good at that lately.

BOBBIE: You've done a good job on your tribute, monument, your "mon-tribute."

PETER: I've been meaning to put the grill away since the fall. I kept saying, "pay attention, pay attention." I must have told myself that a million times.

(They touch hands.)

BOBBIE: He's an amazing kid.

PETER: I know, and talented.

BOBBIE: Smart.

PETER: Good looking. Like his mother.

(They realize they're touching and separate.)

PETER: Are we getting divorced?

BOBBIE: Is that what you want?

PETER: The separation was only supposed to be a trial.

BOBBIE: You're here every day.

PETER: So, what does that mean?

BOBBIE: Let's see what happens.

(Awkward beat.)

PETER: So…

BOBBIE: So…

PETER: Feeling better now?

BOBBIE: Yes, thank you…You always make me feel…Thank you for coming. For your strength.

(Beat.)

PETER: Guess I should be going then…

BOBBIE: I guess…

PETER: *(Makes a half-hearted attempt to exit then turns back to her.)* Listen Bobbie, our marriage, when it's at its best, is worth holding onto. I hope those better moments are around the corner. I feel like I want to hold out for them. And be here when they come.

BOBBIE: Do you want to make love?

(They fall into a passionate embrace.)

PETER: Yes.

BOBBIE: I miss this…

(They keep at it.)

PETER: I miss you.

BOBBIE: Let's make desire out of the residue.

PETER: I miss your touch…

BOBBIE: Your smell…

⎧ PETER: Being inside you!
⎩ BOBBIE: Being inside me!

(They stumble, fall onto the shrine and partially crush it.)

BOBBIE: Your shrine. I'm sorry.

PETER: To hell with it.

BOBBIE: You're right, to hell with it.

(They continue to embrace. After a beat, she pulls away suddenly.)

PETER: What? What? Married people make love.

BOBBIE: I can run a bath, light some candles, open a bottle of Bordeaux, then, guess what I want you to do… *(Whispers in his ear.)*

PETER: Really?

BOBBIE: Yeah…Wait here.

PETER: Wait?

BOBBIE: Just wait… *(Turns to leave.)*

PETER: Hey!

BOBBIE: Yeah.

PETER: Great ass.

(He watches her exit. MARVELOUS appears. He's back to his grunge look. His hair

is once again long and dirty. The lights take a surreal dip.)

MARVELOUS: Sir, Dad…

PETER: Junior? What are you doing here? You'll be A.W.O.L.

MARVELOUS: I wanted to check in before I left.

PETER: You don't ship out for three more weeks. What are you doing off base? Out of uniform?

MARVELOUS: It's a special night.

PETER: I don't want to see you get into any trouble.

MARVELOUS: I won't.

PETER: Is everything alright?

MARVELOUS: I'm fine now.

PETER: Let me call your mother.

MARVELOUS: No. Dad, I wanted to keep this between us.

PETER: Sure, sure. They'll kick your butt.

MARVELOUS: What happened to my shrine?

PETER: It's undergoing some renovations.

MARVELOUS: It looks like someone sat on it.

PETER: Close…I'm happy to see you.

MARVELOUS: Me, you, and Mom, Christmas eve, driving around town, stopping at the most hideously decorated houses.

PETER: Parking right in front, and laughing hysterically. God, we did that for years.

MARVELOUS: I remember.

PETER: You and your mom and those nativities.

MARVELOUS: She'd put the donkey in the manger…

PETER: And the baby Jesus in the mailbox. Probably not the best thing for you to see.

MARVELOUS: I loved that.

PETER: Me too.

MARVELOUS: Then why did you build me a shrine that other people can drive up to and laugh at?

PETER: *(Seeing the shrine for the first time.)* Nobody would…I mean, look at it. Do you think I woke up one day I said, hey I'm going to build a shrine to my son?

MARVELOUS: *(Looking him square in the eyes.)* I'm about to die Dad.

PETER: You're standing right here.

MARVELOUS: About to take the big dirt nap. Push up some daisies. Enter the dreamless sleep.

PETER: Stop, just…stop! That's not funny.

MARVELOUS: If you can't have a sense of humor about your own death then…

PETER: You're right here son. I'm looking at you with my own eyes.

MARVELOUS: Then look at me sir. Really try to see me.

PETER: *(His desperation slowly builds.)* Two months ago you wanted to be a girl. A lesbian, nihilist, something or other? Now you're a Marine. You go through phases.

MARVELOUS: Death is a phase you enter, but…

PETER: Teenagers! Phases, that's normal. Completely…That's what happens.

MARVELOUS: It's not like acne. It doesn't eventually pass. You don't suddenly get to become "undead." Unless I transform into a Marvelous Zombie…A brain-eating, parent-blaming, grunge monster.

PETER: You're doing a Goth thing, right? That's what all the death crap is about! *(Attempts to distract himself with the shrine.)* Another ridiculous teenage phase. What are you going to do? That's how kids are.

MARVELOUS: Don't you sense it? Can't you feel something in the air?

PETER: Look, son. I did what I did in my life. Some of it wasn't so good, but all of it was for you.

MARVELOUS: You did what you did for yourself. I barely fit into the equation.

PETER: I'm tired of this disrespect. From you, from your mother!

MARVELOUS: Have you earned anything else?

PETER: Seventeen years of being a father. Goddamn right I have.

MARVELOUS: Maybe I don't respect because you aren't able to respect yourself?

PETER: Obviously all that I did for you wasn't enough, or wasn't what you wanted.

MARVELOUS: No, it wasn't.

PETER: What about buying you new track shoes? I did that. Or when you needed money. Your guitar? A birthday present. Or keeping your penny jar full. That was me.

MARVELOUS: That doesn't matter, sir. What does…The reason that I'm here…I want you to know that my death was my own fault.

PETER: Stop saying that! You're walking, talking…Corpses can't do that.

MARVELOUS: I'm trying to take responsibility.

PETER: Then get your ass back to base. Stop fucking around here.

MARVELOUS: I didn't do it in life, not very well. I mean, I was only seventeen, but still. I want to try and do it one last time.

PETER: The shrine…People will know how you served.

MARVELOUS: Does it replace me?

PETER: It serves you. I'll make sure it always serves you.

MARVELOUS: Flags, medals, ribbons, will they be able to take my place?

PETER: They don't have to.

MARVELOUS: Will all the Americana? Your letter from the Corps. The medals, will they take the place of your dead son?

PETER: I'm going to get your mother. Maybe she can talk some sense into you.

MARVELOUS: Is it neat? Does it scrunch up all my memories?

PETER: You can be anything you want. You have your whole life ahead of you.

MARVELOUS: When the time comes, you'll need to see the truth about my death. You'll need to ask "why?" Keep asking that question. Don't lie to yourself.

PETER: I always looked out for you.

MARVELOUS: If you can't see the truth about this, you'll never be able to see anything truly again.

PETER: *(Begins to haphazardly slap more ribbons and flags on the shrine.)* One bad turn is all you have to take. Chase something down on a whim, or because some family member or teacher tells you have talent, and you might not see that mistake for twenty-five years.

MARVELOUS: Your whole life will be a lie otherwise.

PETER: I'm looking out for your future. That's my Goddamn job. To make you a good man. A good person. A professional human being!

MARVELOUS: Jesus Christ! Listen to me! I'm dead! I'm dead and you can't change that!

PETER: America, Government, Coast Guard…

MARVELOUS: I feel sorry for you. And I forgive you. Try to remember that.

PETER: …Military, hero…America… Coast Guard…

(Phone rings.)

MARVELOUS: You should answer the phone.

(The phone continues to ring. PETER searches for it.)

PETER: Best in state. You're my hero, son. That's what I wanted to say. You're my hero…

MARVELOUS: You really don't want Mom to answer this. *(Hands his father the phone.)*

PETER: This is General George S. Patton… Yes, yes, I'm C.P.O. McNaughtin…What do you want… *(Beat.)* I under…my son?…How bad?…I understand.

(Lights split to separate spots on each of them.)

MARVELOUS: *(Strums his guitar.)* We're scared you know. As our due date gets closer even the toughest grunts are on edge. So, last Friday we're having a few beers. We're joking around trying not to think about it. I volunteer to make a beer run. I jump into a jeep and take off. The commissary is right across the tarmac. Less than three miles…I'm a little wasted. I'm goofing around and like an idiot, I floor it and do this spinning 180. I cut the wheel too hard, and clip the fuel truck. There's this bright orange ball of flame… *(Plays and sings a little Johnny Cash.)* "I fell into a burning ring of fire"…Well, anyway. I don't remember hearing an explosion. For a moment there's no sound. No feeling. Like everything's suspended. It hangs in the air, a moment like that. Then the pain. Burn pain is like no other. Think about the last time you burned a finger. Multiply that by ten, then slip it on over your entire body…I remember staring up at these masked faces. I can see how bad it is by the looks in their eyes. I suddenly can't remember the last song I played. I start trying to recall all my "last times," but that makes the burn worse. Then the morphine kicks in. My mind wanders, pleasantly. I see patterns in the ceiling. The patterns turn to faces, and the faces become movie stars, rock stars. All these rows of faces speeding by. They're cheering me on. Applauding. Chanting my name. I had a conversation with my father. Only in my head, but it was good.

PETER: My hand on his chest…

MARVELOUS: My breath is humming, like a weak fluorescent light…I breathe in… *(Exhales.)* I want to breathe…I can't…Dad…

PETER: He can't breathe…My son can't breathe! Can somebody help! Under my hand…I feel…I feel my son, his breath…my boy…I feel him die.

(Lights up to full as BOBBIE enters. She carries a bunch of flowers. MARVELOUS and BOBBIE do not acknowledge PETER.)

BOBBIE: WOW! That's all I can say.

PETER: He won Milrose. He not only won…

BOBBIE: You sang your heart out. You put on an amazing show.

MARVELOUS: Thank you, thank you. No autographs please.

PETER: He bested the hundred-yard dash record.

MARVELOUS: Okay, autographs if I must.

BOBBIE: Those bits between the lyrics. Your fingers move so nimbly.

PETER: And in '96, in Atlanta, he came home with the silver. Not bad. And was third in his class at Annapolis…Since we're bragging about sons.

MARVELOUS: Practice, practice, practice! Like you always said.

PETER: He made Captain in no time and trained in aeronautics.

BOBBIE: The natural talent, "me," of course.

MARVELOUS: Of course.

BOBBIE: This was huge for you and I'm so happy it's going perfectly.

PETER: A chopper pilot. I never would have expected.

MARVELOUS: They invited me back. Which is a definite step up from open mic.

BOBBIE: Really Marvelous, you were as good as any of those so-called "rock stars."

PETER: He had a son. Robert McNaughtin I.

MARVELOUS: I'm glad you liked it Mom…Dad?

BOBBIE: I'm very proud of you Marvelous. *(Calling out to a passerby.)* Hey! Did you see my son rock out tonight! Did he kick ass or what?

MARVELOUS: Mom…

PETER: He built quite the life for himself. I was proud. How could I not be? He's always been my hero.

BOBBIE: I can't get over how amazing you are.

PETER: I can't get over how amazing he was.

MARVELOUS: You don't have to get over it.

BOBBIE: The jaws of my book club dropped into their decaf lattes. You blew them, you blew me away. I should become your agent. Like the Partridge Family only with more balls.

(BOBBIE exits. MARVELOUS takes up one of the lawn chairs, clears it off, and makes himself comfortable. He strums his guitar while PETER tries to work on the shrine.)

PETER: His wife…Lovely, supportive. Whipped him into shape…We lost him…Last December. There was an incident in Mogadishu. They sent the Marines. They sent my boy, 'cause he's the best. *(To his son.)* You were the best son, that's why. You were brave. You have been, and always will be my hero.

(PETER continues working on his shrine as lights fade.)

(End of play.)

IN OUR NAME

A Collection of Three Short Plays

Elena Hartwell

ELENA HARTWELL is a writer and theatre artist. She was born in Bogota, Colombia, and raised in San Diego. She holds a BA in mass media communications/theatre arts from the University of San Diego (magna cum laude), an MEd with an emphasis in teaching theatre from the University of Washington, and a PhD in theatre from the University of Georgia. She is the author of several plays including *Playing Chess With Joey* (Theatre Babylon, Seattle, and One Small Theatre, San Diego, 1996), *Waiting for the Rain* (Theatre Babylon, Seattle, 1996), an adaptation of *A Christmas Carol* (Tacoma Repertory Theatre, 1998), *Four Nights in a Store Room* (Kennedy Center/American College Theatre Festival finalist, 2001), *Fast Ducks* (Detroit Repertory Theatre, 2002), *Scrooge Revisited* (Tacoma Repertory Theatre, 1999; Rainier Valley Ensemble Theatre, 2004), *The Lights of L.A. County* (University of Puget Sound, Tacoma, 2004; The Art Project, Tacoma, 2005), *The Wall* (Rainier Valley Ensemble Theatre, Seattle, 2005), *The Shawl* (The Art Project, Seattle and Olympia, 2005), *The Wondyrechaun* (Northwest Playwrights Alliance, Olympia, 2006; Portland Theatre Works, Portland, Oregon, 2007), and *The Last Train to Hicksville* (Seattle Dramatists, 2007; Mirror Stage, Seattle, 2008). She is also the cofounder of Iron Pig, a company of Pacific Northwest artists dedicated to producing theatre that is both entertaining and socially responsible, and the Mae West Fest, a festival celebrating women playwrights and directors. Hartwell is currently working on a new musical with composer Garrit Gaudan, and a one-woman show with actress Rebecca Nachison. She lives in Seattle.

In Our Name was first presented by Iron Pig (Elena Hartwell and Rebecca Nachison, Cofounders) as part of the New York International Fringe Festival (Elena K. Holy, Producing Artistic Director) on August 11, 2007, at the Independent Theater, New York City, with the following cast and credits:

The Researcher and Woman............................ Rebecca Nachison
Wife and Recordkeeper .... Elena Hartwell

Stage Manager: Emily Paige Ballou
Authorized Company Representative: Emily Bohannon
Voice Coach: Linda Leanne

NOTE

These plays can be performed together or individually.

THE UNRAVELING

The stage is bare except for a simple lectern. After a moment, THE RESEARCHER tentatively enters the stage. She takes in the audience, obviously uncomfortable with public speaking. She crosses and stands at the lectern with her notes. She stumbles through her first words, perhaps stopping and starting over.

THE RESEARCHER: Good afternoon everybody. Lovely to see you all here. Nice to know that universities are still places of—well that some of you would rather learn something instead of just drinking beer and watching sports. Not that there's anything wrong with those two pastimes, I have been known to get a bit rowdy at a hockey game. I think you might learn a bit more if you put down that newspaper there—

Ah—there, much better. Now that I have your attention—I must apologize I am not really an academic—well not a lecturer that is—public speaking is not my "fort," you can tell that because I said "fort" rather than the colloquial version "fort te" which though more recognizable is, well, wrong. But I digress, I do that a lot when I get nervous, part of why I never went in for it, lecturing. I had to as a graduate student. They make you earn your "salary." I am actually a researcher, you see, but that is neither here nor there is it—We are gathered together in this place to talk about Shakespeare and his ability with words, not mine.

Your instructor Alice thought that it would be good for me to get out here in the trenches so to speak and actually talk to students instead of—how did she put it—burying my head in stacks of musty manuscripts in order to create yet more scholarly publications read by other people disinterested in engaging in actual discourse. Except she said conversation. I changed conversation to discourse because that is the kind of language we antisocial researchers use. I guess she thought I should get out of the house—well, never mind that—where were we—ah yes, Shakespeare and his way with words.

And what a way he has doesn't he? For it really is the way that he puts words together that makes him so remarkable. Plots are not his strong suit despite what you might think. Not his "fort" as it were. Shakespeare stole most of his plots from other writers—take for example *The Two Gentlemen of Verona*. It is quite likely Shakespeare attended a production of a play called *Felix and Philiomena*, performed in Greenwich in 1584, which was a rip-off of a play by a Frenchman named Nicholas Colin, which was a translation of the Spanish pastoral romance *Diana Enamorada* by Jorge de Montelmayor. You theatre majors should know what a pastoral romance is, the rest of you can look it up. On the Internet. But you begin to understand the convoluted telling and retelling of the same stories over and over, causing our interest to be less in who tells the story, and more in who tells it best.

This is not to say that Shakespeare wasn't good at finding interesting plots—and subplots for that matter—but this is not what he is known for. He is known for words. Creating them, using them, putting them together with other words in ways that once done it's as if they could be put together no other way.

"If the assassination could trammel up the consequence, and catch with his surcease success that but this blow might be the be-all and the end-all here. But here upon this bank and shoal of time we jump the life to come."

Listen to that "If the assassination could trammel up the consequence, and catch with his surcease success." The resonance of the ssssses with trammel up in the middle, breaking the rhythmic nature of the assassination and surcease and success—that my friends, is poetry. Shakespeare could have used "o'er leap" rather than jump, as it would have more music, but I like the quickness of "jump" better than the diphthong created by the missing "v." The idea of jumping quickly over a bad patch of time appeals to me. We do not always want to linger and "o'er leaping" would slow us down.

"His virtues will plead like angels, trumpet-tong'd against the deep damnation of his taking-off; and pity, like a naked new-born babe striding the blast, or heaven's cherubim hors'd upon the sightless couriers of the air shall blow the horrid deed in every eye that tears shall drown the wind." That tears shall drown the wind.

Shakespeare also understood that no matter what Duncan's virtues are, no matter how noble, how decent, how kind, that will not be enough to save him. Goaded on by his wife, Macbeth

still does the deed. The eloquence of Mac's internal struggle does not change the outcome. Dictated by the fates he does indeed kill the king.

Do you believe in fate? You, young people with your lives in front of you. Do you believe that your futures are ordained and all you have to do is walk into them? Do you believe in signs? What happens when you misread them? What happens when you believe with a fierceness born of youth that truth and justice will prevail? That we can trust our leaders to care for us, that it is not our day to die? Only to find there are worse things than dying? What words would soothe you then?

Sometimes, words are all we really want. I would like some words…from my daughter. She is not speaking to me. My own child does not want to talk to me. Can you imagine how that feels? No probably not. But she has. She thinks I am going to say I told you so. Not very musical that, "I told you so." Shakespeare would never have said it that way. "Methinks thou doth rejoice in my own misery" that would be a little bit more like him now wouldn't it. But how could I? How could I rejoice? Just because I was right? That going into the Marines really was the worst decision she ever made?

I offered to pay for school. I offered to start her in business. I offered so many things, but no, she had to go enlist. And for what? Because her best friend got killed in Afghanistan? Because he thought going into the Marines to get funding for college was a smart idea and instead he comes home in a box? And what? She could make a difference? That her going over as fodder for the machine would change anything? Make up for the death of someone she loved?

I know I am not telling you anything you don't already know. These things are bandied about in circles such as this one, a place of higher learning. I have seen the marches, the peace rallies, why you there, in the third row, your "No War" button says it all, but I need you to understand something else. I need you to understand the toll. I need you to understand about those who do come back, but do not come back whole.

My daughter is a cellist. She plays beautifully. When she was a child I required, no, I demanded that she practice. I practically locked her in her room until the requisite pieces had been played and played again. Until the scales flowed smoothly, the notes hit just right. Until the bowing technique and the vibrato in concert with the correct pitch and tone blended to create the harmonies set down by the masters.

She hated it, until one day something clicked. I no longer had to play the tyrant to get her to practice. She removed herself from my company to perfect each new piece assigned. She played for hours in her room. The notes would flood my study as I gathered yet more material for yet another scholarly tome. I would sit back sometimes, in repose, eyes closed, fingers templed, just so in front of me like a prayer to the gods of music to hear what my child could do. She poured her heart and soul into that playing.

She played in the school orchestra. That is where she met him, the one who went to war. He played the clarinet, and later when he played in the marching band, my daughter criticized me for choosing an instrument too bulky for her to carry.

But by then the muse had found her. She had learned, through captivity, to love the cello.

When she came to me and told me that she had enlisted I turned to Shakespeare for succor, but found only death. For so many of his plays invoke death. I tried to read the comedies, to lighten my growing fear, but the words seemed empty. I was overwhelmed with this feeling of dread, which could not be explained in any tongue. I waited, waited for the phone call, the letter, the knock on the door.

These did not come. Not in the manner in which I expected. When my daughter's left arm and right leg were blown off by the IED that detonated under her Humvee I was not contacted. Not right away. I finally received notice after she had come through Landstuhl, the American hospital in Germany, and was in recovery in California.

She did not want to see me. I was told this in flat and neutral tones by a very nice nurse who I am sure does not appreciate poetry. Perhaps I am being unkind, but that is what went through my mind at the time. I went anyway. I sat outside my daughter's door for three days and three nights, but she would not let me in. Unlike Mary's vigil at the tomb, my daughter did not rise. She said that she could not bear it, seeing me. What do you say to that? What poetry will address that kind of wound? From a daughter wreaked upon a mother or from a mother upon her child. For surely my anger has created this rift.

(Cello music might start under the monologue at "Wind blows across the strings.")

My daughter's cello sits in the corner of my bedroom. I keep it there like a talisman. Sometimes, when I have the window open the wind blows across the strings and I hear the notes that she played and my daughter is there in the room with me. Her ghost plays even though she is not dead. Shakespeare should have written about that, about the ghosts of those still living. He could, no doubt, have found the right words to keep her home. But I am not Shakespeare. I could not stop her from going in her friend's name. I miss her.

Well. Not the lecture you were anticipating was it? Not the one I planned to give. But then life is full of the unexpected. It leaves us on the edge of our seats wondering what will happen next. *(She breaks down, perhaps unable to finish the final line.)*

THE THINGS HE CARRIED

WIFE is clearly pregnant. She looks at a trunk, which she unpacks throughout the piece. Along with the items she discusses, she also unpacks the torn, disheveled pieces of a complete uniform, which she lays out to create the image of a soldier. If all three pieces are performed, it remains through the third piece.

WIFE: This trunk belongs to your father. Shall we take a look inside? These are all things Daddy wants you to have.

Here's a picture of us on our wedding day. I look young don't I? No crow's feet then. Hard to believe that was sixteen years ago. We were so...unprepared for being married. But maybe that's what got us through, we learned together.

Still, we don't want you getting married at twenty baby, that's for sure. Your grandparents were horrified that we got married that young. That's them there *(Points to the photo.)* see how forced their smiles are?

(She pulls out another photo.)

This was taken much later. They were on board with us by our fifth wedding anniversary, especially because your father's mother was into her third marriage by then.

(She pulls out a book, Davey Crockett: His Own Story. *Perhaps singing the opening lines to "Davey, Davey Crockett" from the old TV show.)*

Davey Crockett: His Own Story. This is your father's favorite book. It belonged to his father when he was a little boy. The Wild West holds some kind of power over boys. Boys, *(Laughs.)* ...men. Your daddy always says that deep down every man wants to be a cowboy or a soldier, those that don't admit it haven't tapped down deep enough in their souls. Certainly true for your father. Working summers at his grandparents' ranch when he was young, and now, in the National Guard...a soldier.

was proud when he signed up for the National Guard. After seeing what that flood did to some of our neighbors ten years ago he wanted to be a man that helped. A man that stepped up when people were in need.

One weekend a month, two weeks a year, that seemed so…manageable. He's been in Iraq for seven months now. We certainly know when you were conceived, the night before he left. We weren't really trying, we just weren't trying not to. You'll understand that difference some day.

(She pulls an old watch out.)

This belonged to your father's father's father. He got it from his sweetheart during World War II. She said it would remind him when it was time to come home. I guess it worked, he made it back when a lot of other boys didn't. Crazy thing was, it was her that didn't make it. She was hit by a streetcar in San Francisco when she went to meet him at the docks. If she hadn't been killed your father would never have been born. Strange to think about that, how her death changed so many unforeseeable things in the future.

Let's see what else is in here.

Comic books. Your daddy is such a kid sometimes. He says they'll all be worth something someday, but I know that's an excuse. He just likes to read them that's all. There's boxes of the damn things up in the attic. I guess we'll save them all for you whether they're worth anything or not.

When he got called up the first time we didn't think it meant that much. He went over, and it wasn't until his first tour was extended that I thought to myself this could get a lot worse. After twelve months he finally came home. Well, someone came home, I think it was your father.

He was different. Changed from that sweet funny man I married. He had the stare, that thousand-yard stare. I've heard it said that you can tell how much battle a man has seen by looking in his eyes. The eyes, they say, the eyes become unfocused because the mind has turned inward. Running a loop of horror across the movie screen of memory.

I thought he might recover, or at least rearrange enough to be connected to me again. He was, he was doing better. Then he got called up again, and the stare came back.

(She pulls out a compass.)

Perpetual magnetic North. This is also from World War II. But it was my grandfather's. I gave it to your father before he went over the first time. So he could always find his way back to me.

I used to think North was one of those things that was absolute. North was North and that was that. Turns out it wobbles. Isn't that a kick in the ass baby? The earth wobbles on its axis and North isn't always the same. Things you believe when you're younger you realize as an adult can't be trusted. Like what honor means.

"When I was a child, I thought like a child…but as an adult, I put away childish things."

When your father is away I sleep in his clothing. Shirts that smell like him. Is that childish? Or just sad? Now I have a closet of clothes I don't want to part with. A closet of things too precious to give away, but what else would I do with them? Hang onto every scrap of clothing your father ever wore? So I can still find his scent on them? To help me remember what he looked like? Sounded like? I keep the last message he left me on my cell phone and I play it every night since I...

Did you know baby, that a surviving family member of a soldier killed in action is an N-O-K. A nock, Next of Kin. When I was listening to the nice young soldier who came to my door at 7:15 on a Wednesday night, part of my mind was thinking, I wonder how many times he's done this. He sounds so polished. It's all there on the Internet. A manual to tell a CNO—that's Casualty Notification Officer baby—exactly what they are supposed to do and say. Including 5d of the manual that states "IMPORTANT! Do not physically touch the NOK in any manner unless there is shock or fainting. Summon medical assistance immediately, if necessary."

Important is all in caps, so I must have looked in shock because he touched my arm. Or maybe he was just new.

I memorized the paragraph they use to inform of deaths.

"The Secretary of the Army has asked me to express his deep regret that your (relationship; son, Robert or husband, Edward; etc.) (died/was killed in action) in (country/state) on (date). (State the circumstances provided by the Casualty Area Command.) The Secretary extends his deepest sympathy to you and your family in your tragic loss."

It didn't take me very long to memorize. It's short, succinct, to the point. Designed to "soften the blow" but still give the appropriate information. What it does not do, however, is explain how I am to raise a child alone. It does not explain how I am to go on into the uncertain future without the man I love. That fucking manual does not tell me why my husband signed up for one weekend a month and two weeks out of the year and seven months into his second tour in Iraq he was blown to fucking pieces by an IED set off by a goddamned cell phone.

It does not explain what I am supposed to do with what was sent back in this trunk. All the things he carried with him.

When I was a wife I thought like a wife but as a widow I put away my husband's things.

So that is what is left you from your father baby. Those are the pieces of his life that have been returned to us from Iraq. The things he carried with him into battle in our name. A book, photographs, comic books, a compass, these don't sound like the weapons of a soldier do they? He wasn't. He wasn't a soldier, not really. No matter what he says is deep down in a man's soul. That was forced on him. He never wanted to kill anyone, that wasn't why he went in. He struggled with that— the killing—far more than he ever struggled with the idea that he might get killed himself. That struggle will be left for me.

WAITING FOR THE LIGHT

WOMAN enters. She is in a break room. She has a letter, much-read, cigarettes, a lighter, perhaps a cup of coffee or some other drink. She wears a watch. She speaks to the audience as a coworker—she is not addressing a group. RECORDKEEPER enters. If the same actor plays WIFE and RECORD EEPER, the entrance may be timed out because of the quick change. Otherwise she can enter at the top. RECORDKEEPER has newspapers in which she is finding the names of soldiers killed in Iraq and Afghanistan. Throughout WOMAN's monologue, RECORDKEEPER reads the names of the dead out loud. Where each name is read, and whether or not to include information such as age, place and circumstances of death, etc., is up to the director/actor. RECORDKEEPER than records the names onto cards or into a ledger, etc. Neither WOMAN nor RECORDKEEPER is aware of the other during their separate monologues. They are in completely different places. Find natural pauses in WOMAN's monologue for RECORDKEEPER to interject.

WOMAN: Iraq. Iraq, Iraq, Iraq. I don't mean to sound... what's the word? Insensitive, but don't we have enough problems here in the good old U.S. of A. to focus on? I don't see any reason to go around, writing newspaper articles, creating websites, making movies about the darn thing—It's just not that big a deal in the scheme of things, right?

(WOMAN plays with an envelope in her hand.)

Don't get me wrong—I'm sure it's tough for the people who live there. I know that power gets interrupted, and gas is expensive, but hey, things are tough all over, right? Why my power was out for twenty-four hours after that last ice storm we had, I know what it's like, but you go on, it's what we all do. And you want to talk about expensive, I paid $3.75 at the pump yesterday, it's not like I'm Donald frickin' Trump you know.

Take me for example. I work hard, I pay my taxes. I don't waste money on drugs and $700 shoes like those Paris Hilton types I read about in *People Magazine*, but I don't have much to show for it either. Granted I don't have suicide bombers in my neighborhood, but shit happens. You don't hear me complaining.

I know. You're looking at the cigarettes. But that's different. These are legal, and besides, I smoke menthols. And I don't smoke in public places where I'm not supposed to, I go outside like everyone else. Seems like a tax-paying American should be able to smoke anywhere she pleases, but I'm not complaining.

Actually, if you must know I'm trying to quit. I have this little game I play, where I see if I can go a little longer every day between cigarettes. I'm up to [length of play]. So I won't light this bad boy until then, no matter how much I want to. See that's what life is all about, it's about taking charge. It's about making a plan and sticking to it. I understand these things. That's what I taught my son. He knows the rules.

(She fiddles with cigarette.)

It's not like I agree with everything that our president does, but he is the president. We voted him in didn't we? And I believe in supporting the troops. That's what bothers me the most, about these, you know, liberals. Here are our boys, and girls, don't forget some of *us* are fighting too, laying their lives on the line so that people like you and me can live free and what do the liberals do? They want to say the troops are bad, that they are committing crimes and atrocities, like at that prison, that one no one can pronounce, Ay-bu Graeeb. First off, who knows if those photos are real? We all know that you can do anything with Photoshop these days, secondly, what if they are? It's a war people, sometimes bad things have to be done for the greater good.

And besides, we aren't on the inside. There are things that the president knows that the rest of us don't. That the rest of us don't NEED to know, that's why we want people like George Bush. To take care of the things we don't want to have to face. Put yourself in his shoes for a minute. What would you do? WMDs, attacks on the World Trade Center, anthrax in the mail—the world going to hell and someone has to make the tough decisions. Someone has to draw the line in the sand. And Bush did. He did just that, he drew that line. And when the Taliban crossed it we went into Iraq and showed them that's not okay with us. Not the United States, no sir, you do not mess with Uncle Sam.

My son is a lot like the president. He takes a stand. I'm proud of him for that.

He is not wishy-washy, no sir. Straight shooter. Always has been.

I know what you're thinking, there were no weapons of mass destruction found. But that's a good thing! Don't you see, if we hadn't gone in and put a stop to things just think what might have happened. Obviously they didn't have very much and could get it out of the country before we invaded. Put a stop to that.

(She puts cigarette in her mouth as if to light, but catches herself by looking at her watch.)

Almost caught me there didn't you. I know, I have [minutes left in play] left, see, will power, that's what it's all about.

George Bush, now he's a man with will power. I admire that. He's not worried about doing the popular thing. He's not concerned with what "looks good" he's worried about what's right. That's why he never apologizes! That just makes a person look weak, and we can't afford that, not with people all around the world watching us! And why should he apologize? He's the president of the strongest country on earth, we don't apologize, we say jump and everyone else says "how high?" And if they don't…

My boy knows that. The military wouldn't take him because he has asthma, but he tried. He tried to fight for his country, for you and me, I'm proud of him for that. He understands that someone has to lead. Someone has to be in power.

Someone has to be in charge, otherwise, what would we have? Anarchy. That's right, Ann-ar-key! I mean, can you imagine the shit that would be going on in the world right now if other countries didn't know that our president is not afraid to take a stand! That he will dish out some good old American ass-whuppin' if anyone gets out of line.

RECORDKEEPER: I had a play read at a college I used to work at. It's about a Vietnam vet, and his son, a marine fighting in Iraq. There is a part in the play where the son describes an encounter with an Iraqi. The son enters a bombed-out building, and sees a shadow on the wall.

He can see the shadow person has a weapon. He knows he has to shoot if the person comes into the room. He knows it's kill or be killed.

So he does. He shoots the person as he comes around the corner. In the play, he crosses to the body to see who he killed. And he realizes, it's a child. A boy of maybe thirteen. At this moment in the reading a young man sitting in front of me in the audience puts his head in his hands. I think he must be bored. I think his girlfriend must have dragged him to this play reading, against his will. But later I learn his story.

As a soldier in Iraq, he entered a bombed-out building. He saw a shadow on the wall. He knew the shadow had a weapon, and it was kill or be killed. So he shot, he killed the shadow with the weapon.

So he walks over to the body, And he realizes, it's a child. A boy of maybe thirteen. And he can't bear what he's done. So he digs a grave by hand. And he sits all night long beside the grave of that dead child. Seeing that enacted on the stage in front of him brought it all back. I hear his story, and I wonder if he'll ever recover from what he did. And what we have done to him. *(Goes back to reading/recording names.)*

WOMAN: We're in it now that's for sure. It's going to be a long time before we bring all our boys

(The choice could be made here to have RECORDKEEPER read a girl's name. WOMAN doesn't "hear" the name, but it seeps through her unconscious.)

WOMAN: and our girls. Before we bring our children home. I got this letter from my son today. The army is running out of new recruits, they've lowered their standards. No, that's not right. They haven't lowered, they have just modified them. Rolled with the punches. That's what you have to do sometimes. Go with what you've got. My son was accepted this time around. He ships out in a month. Straight to Iraq. Straight into combat. He says he'll stick it out until we win. And we have to win before we bring our children home, right? Otherwise, what was it all for? We can't leave. We can't leave until we win. My son understands that. I taught him that. It's because of me that he's going over there. He's going in my name. I know it's the right thing. I know it's the right thing. We have to stay until we win. I don't know why people like you can't see that.

(WOMAN crosses until she stands at the head of the "soldier" built during the previous piece. If this piece is performed as a solo piece, disregard or find an alternative image to represent the casualties in the war on terror. She starts to light her cigarette, looks at her watch.)

WOMAN: Time's up.

(Slow fade to black.)

(Curtain.)

UNIVERSAL ROBOTS

Inspired by the Play *R.U.R.* by Karel Čapek

Mac Rogers

MAC ROGERS is a playwright, actor, and sporadic director. He was born in Milwaukee, and raised in Greensboro, North Carolina. He is the author of *Dirty Juanita* (Flatiron Playhouse, 2000), *The Second String* (Grove Street Playhouse, 2001), *Happening to Your Body* (Estrogenius Festival, Manhattan Theatre Source, 2002), *The Sky Over Nineveh* (Theatre of Relativity, HERE Arts Center, 2002), *The Lucretia Jones Mysteries* (Gershwin Hotel, 2003), *FLEET WEEK! The Musical* (cowritten with Jordana and Sean Williams, 2005 New York International Fringe Festival), and *Hail Satan* (2007 New York International Fringe Festival). As an actor, he played the title role in James Comtois's *The Adventures of Nervous-Boy: A Penny Dreadful* (Nosedive Productions, 2006; published in the NYTE anthology *Plays and Playwrights 2007*). Rogers won the 2005 FringeNYC Outstanding Musical Award for *FLEET WEEK! The Musical* and the 2007 FringeNYC Outstanding Playwriting Award for *Hail Satan*, and earned a 2006 New York Innovative Theater Award nomination for best actor in a leading role for his performance in *The Adventures of Nervous-Boy*. He also produces theatre with partners Jordana and Sean Williams under their Gideon Productions shingle, and he plans to remount *Universal Robots* in late 2008/early 2009. He lives with his girlfriend, Sandy, in a converted auto body shop in the East Williamsburg Industrial Complex.

UNIVERSAL ROBOTS was originally presented by manhattantheatresource and Gideon Productions on July 9, 2007, at manhattantheatresource, New York City, with the following cast and credits:

Helena, Ensemble..Esther Barlow
Radosh, Radius, Man in Bed.................................Jason Howard
Karel ....David Ian Lee
One, Sulla, Ensemble ....Michelle O'Connor
Salda, Baruch, Ensemble ....Ridley Parson
Rossum, Ensemble ....Nancy Sirianni
Vaclavek, Primus, Ensemble ....Tarantino Smith
Peroutka, Ensemble...Ben Sulzbach
Jo, Ensemble ....Jennifer Gordon Thomas
Masaryk, Ensemble ....James Wetzel

Writer/Director: Mac Rogers
Assistant Directors: Saundra Yaklin and Shey Lyn Zanotti
Lighting: Ben Sulzbach
Board Operator: Travis Ryder
Publicity: Lanie Zipoy
Poster Design: Rob Matsushita

NOTE

As is understood by the end, *Universal Robots* takes the form of a ritualistic pageant, performed by robot actors. This doesn't need to be overly clear, but also doesn't need to be hidden. The first production kept all actors on stage at all times, and achieved all effects in a deliberately stripped-down fashion. The robots collaborated with one another to change the sets in front of the audience, with no attempt at concealment.

These robot actors are highly advanced and fully emotional, so when playing characters in scenes, they are able to be as naturalistic as necessary and need not affect a robotic manner.

The 2007 production used ten actors to satisfactory effect. A future production may choose to use more. Based on our experience, it would be quite difficult to manage with fewer. Our casting breakdown was as follows:

ACTOR 1 (female): Jo, Robot Celestia

ACTOR 2 (male): Karel

ACTOR 3 (male): Masaryk, Male Insect, Gall, Letter 2

ACTOR 4 (female): Rossum, Female Insect, Martyr 1, Mother-in-Law, President, Letter 1, Letter 5

ACTOR 5 (female): Helena, Scientist, Little Girl, Robot Helena

ACTOR 6 (male): Radosh, Radius, Man in Bed

ACTOR 7 (female): One, Mother, Café Bomber, Sulla, Letter 3

ACTOR 8 (male): General, Vaclavek, Fabry, Robot in Wheelchair, Letter 6, Robot Pallas, Primus

ACTOR 9 (male): Salda, Young Man, Robot Virgil, Letter 4, Baruch, Robot Guard, Robot Theseus

ACTOR 10: Peroutka, Martyr 2, Ticket-Taker

Please note: While this distribution of roles is otherwise a suggestion, it is essential that the same male actor play Radosh, Radius, and Man in Bed for the play's staging to operate properly.

ACT ONE

A group of ACTORS faces the audience in a semicircle of chairs. ONE is the narrator.

ONE: Once again we tell the story.

ALL: We tell the story.

ONE: That we never forget.

ALL: We tell the story.

ONE: That we remain ever vigilant.

ALL: We tell the story.

ONE: That we never grow complacent.

ALL: We tell the story.

ONE: That life shall never again perish from the Earth:

ALL: We remember.

ONE: After the Great War, in the year 1918, the Austro-Hungarian Empire conceded the small territory in question, and then early the next year the Great Powers in Paris concurred. A President was elected and a new nation was declared:

(PRESIDENT MASARYK steps forward and addresses the audience.)

MASARYK: The Republic of Czechoslovakia!

ONE: Where does the story begin? The moment when Helena Rossum entered the café that Friday night with the wheelchair?

(We are now in the café. KAREL, JO, SALDA, and PEROUTKA are chatting and drinking, while RADOSH serves. HELENA enters, pushing a HUMAN FIGURE in a wheelchair. The FIGURE's head is bound. Only PEROUTKA notices.)

PEROUTKA: Um…artists?

(EVERYONE looks around.)

PEROUTKA: I think you have visitors.

HELENA: Karel and Josephine Čapek?

JO: Yes?

HELENA: I saw your play.

KAREL: Who is this person? Why is his head covered?

JO: Can he breathe through that thing?

PEROUTKA: Well he's not breathing now.

HELENA: He's not breathing because he's not a person.

ONE: What brought Helena Rossum to this café? We heard her say:

HELENA: I saw your play.

ONE: So: the plays of Karel and Josephine Čapek! A sampling: *The Insect Play* in 1921.

(A MALE INSECT and a FEMALE INSECT take the stage.)

FEMALE INSECT: But, sweetheart, do you mean to say that this is our nest now?

MALE INSECT: Quite ours, my dear! All the nests have been redistributed! Now how about some supper?

FEMALE INSECT: But dearest, where's the insect who *used* to have this nest?

MALE INSECT: Why, he's impaled on a thorn just outside, my dear. If you look you can still see him wriggling!

FEMALE INSECT: Why so you can!

ONE: *The Absolute at Large*, 1922!

(A SCIENTIST and a GENERAL take the stage.)

SCIENTIST: With this Karbeurator, General, I can split the fabled atom, releasing the untold richness inside!

GENERAL: You better! We've given you a lot of money!

ONE: The scientist succeeds, the Karbeurator splits the atom, and what emerges is a gaslike substance known as the Absolute.

SCIENTIST: What have I done?

GENERAL: What do you mean, Professor? What is that awful mob outside?

(We hear, and possibly see, a MOB roar.)

SCIENTIST: The Absolute! It's the deadliest substance known to man!

GENERAL: But we're still alive.

SCIENTIST: It doesn't kill like poison, General—or perhaps it does, only more slowly! The problem is that it makes everyone who breathes it in believe that they and they alone possess the Absolute Truth!

GENERAL: The Absolute Truth? Why, what is it?

SCIENTIST: That's just the thing, General! There is no such thing. But the gas inside the atom has a deluding effect on humans, making each one believe they possess it!

(MARTYRS rush in with bombs around their necks.)

MARTYR 1: For God and Country!

GENERAL: Who are you? How dare you come in here!

MARTYR 2: God told us our system was best, and that we should die to destroy yours!

ONE: And with that they detonate the bombs around their necks, and the Scientist and General perish in agony as the wind carries the toxic Absolute throughout the world.

(ALL die. Now we return to the café on an earlier night. PEROUTKA is not here, but VACLAVEK is. The rest are the same.)

VACLAVEK: A disgrace!

KAREL: I'm sorry?

VACLAVEK: You heard me. Little more than rank, counter-Revolutionary propaganda!

ONE: Yes, let us begin here, on an earlier night in the café, the night that Josephine and Karel Čapek first conceived the play that brought Rossum and her daughter Helena out of hiding. Let us begin with the angry outburst of Vaclavek, the poet, playwright, and Socialist.

VACLAVEK: What subtle metaphors. The insects are Revolutionaries, the Absolute represents the spread of Communism. Your so-called dramas are nothing more than excuses to prop up the status quo and spit on the proletariat!

ONE: The Friday Circle. A gathering of Prague's leading intellectuals: journalists, poets, columnists, playwrights—public thinkers, drinking coffee and beer at a café without a name.

JO: Why do we do this? Plainly we don't like each other.

SALDA: Well, I like *you*, Jo.

ONE: The writer Salda. The sculptor and playwright Josephine Čapek.

VACLAVEK: Can we keep to the subject for twenty minutes! Twenty minutes only

I ask! Twenty minutes discussing items of consequence before our witless banter swallows all else!

KAREL: By the prophet, Vaclavek, you're right! We could be bantering instead of having this tedious conversation! Do you all know the story of Jo kicking me down the stairs when we were five?

JO: I didn't kick you down the stairs, and only you were five. Not everyone is your age, Karel.

KAREL: Forgive me. Do you all know the story of Jo kicking me down the stairs when I was five and she was twenty-six?

ONE: Karel Čapek. Playwright. Poet. Journalist. Columnist.

VACLAVEK: If I may! If I may!

JO: Well after all, Vaclavek, what are we going to accomplish in this café? Not a slight to the café, Radosh, the café is exquisite, the café is perfect in every particular except that it doesn't have a name, and I have told you about this!

RADOSH: Oh, that's all right, Miss Jo—heh heh—

VACLAVEK: If I *may*!

JO: Just that no one will be able to find you and you'll never chase the intellectuals away!

RADOSH: Oh, no, don't say that, Miss Jo, Friday night's not Friday night without the Friday Circle! Who's finished? Who needs another?

ONE: Radosh. He brings the sandwiches and beer.

VACLAVEK: The answer to your question, Jo, is that much may indeed be accomplished at this café without a name because one of us—

KAREL: *I'll* have another, Radosh.

RADOSH: Right away, right away, I know what you like!

VACLAVEK: One of us here is not just another poet at the barricades, one of us—

SALDA: Oh, the "barricades," Vaclavek—

VACLAVEK: If I *may*!

SALDA: As long as you're up, Radosh.

RADOSH: Right away, right away!

VACLAVEK: One of us sitting here has direct access to the seat of power! One of us in this room has the power to translate an idea into an action by toddling off to his master and whispering in his ear!

KAREL: Yes, Vaclavek, it's all very exciting, I've read all the columns: "Karel Čapek is the mouthpiece, Karel Čapek is the puppet of the authoritarian Masaryk, Karel Čapek puts shiny apples on the headmaster's desk."

VACLAVEK: Do you deny it?

KAREL: Two possibilities, Vaclavek! Either I'm Masaryk's resident propagandist or I genuinely believe in the man and his ideas! It might always be the latter! If you eat a Hershey bar, and then tell your friend you liked it, are you a propagandist?

VACLAVEK: The Hershey bar isn't working night and day to perpetuate a permanent state of oppression!

(EVERYONE reacts.)

VACLAVEK: I was extending the metaphor! I was extending the metaphor!

KAREL: You're right, Vaclavek, the Hershey bar isn't doing that.

JO: Is there a stenographer for this fight? I need some bits read back to me.

VACLAVEK: Then let me simplify it. Every time the great Karel Čapek, Prague's favorite young celebrity intellectual dilettante writes a play attacking the Revolution, every time he writes a thinly veiled column in the *National Pages* attacking the Revolution—

{ KAREL: "Why I Am Not A Communist" is thinly veiled, you're right.

JO: He doesn't write them *alone*.

VACLAVEK: Every time he harmlessly shares his smirky, condescending little opinion in print or on a stage—

KAREL: So thinly veiled, one might almost say—

VACLAVEK: —a cycle of violence, deprivation, and warlike aggression against the proletarian worker is institutionalized in the life of our nation!

(Pause.)

SALDA: I wish I'd said that.

KAREL: The Revolution.

VACLAVEK: Yes.

KAREL: The…Revolution in Russia, specifically, or…?

(SALDA is noticing something outside.)

VACLAVEK: The Permanent, Inevitable Global Revolution to liberate the Worker and distribute equally the means of production to all mankind. And don't play games with me, Čapek. I'm your equal.

SALDA: I think there are soldiers outside.

KAREL: All right, Vaclavek.

VACLAVEK: And if you concede that much, maybe you can concede a little more: that if you were to whisper the merits of the Inevitable Revolution in that same ear—

SALDA: There are definitely soldiers outside.

VACLAVEK: …you could turn him from his present course of materialistic oppression.

KAREL: First of all, Vaclavek—

JO: Karel?

KAREL: Even if I wanted to promote your psychotic, and worse, *impractical* little revolution—

VACLAVEK: Impractical!

JO: Why would there be soldiers outside?

KAREL: Even if I wanted to, you wildly overestimate my access to President Masaryk. I'm a humble playwright and a columnist, just like you.

(MASARYK enters, with RADOSH following close behind.)

RADOSH: Yes, and how many in your party, sir?

MASARYK: Would you let the Friday Circle and Karel Čapek in particular know that Tomas Masaryk has arrived?

KAREL: *(To VACLAVEK.)* I think my larger point still stands.

(EVERYONE is on their feet. KAREL and MASARYK embrace.)

RADOSH: Forgive me, my lord. I didn't realize.

MASARYK: My friend, I am many months late accepting your invitation, but I live in hope that it has not expired.

KAREL: Well, your timing is terrible, you've made me look bad in front of my Communist friend, but I'll overlook it in light of the overwhelming honor of your presence. The barkeep, Radosh.

MASARYK: My friend, Presidents don't get called "My lord," no matter how much they may wish it. In America they say "Mr. President." I think that's good enough for me.

RADOSH: Mr. President, all that is mine I lay at your disposal.

MASARYK: And yet I only ask for a cup of tea.

(RADOSH is mesmerized.)

KAREL: Radosh.

RADOSH: Right away, right away! *(Goes for drinks.)*

KAREL: Salda you've read; he's ambivalent about you.

MASARYK: I'm ambivalent about myself, so we are two gentlemen in agreement.

SALDA: Mr. . . . President?

MASARYK: It's difficult at first. Jo.

(JO and MASARYK embrace warmly.)

MASARYK: You're still my favorite of the Čapek children.

JO: Saying it over and over won't make it true, Mr. President.

KAREL: Now, you don't know Vaclavek, but—

MASARYK: I don't, it's true, but—

VACLAVEK: You murdered hundreds of my comrades in cold blood. Mr. President.

(Pause.)

MASARYK: So I did. May God forgive me.

VACLAVEK: I can't pretend that means anything to me, sir. I believe all religion is an oppressive delusion.

KAREL: Oh, Vaclavek, what is it to you if a man believes in God or not?

VACLAVEK: Do you now countenance the mass delusion of Christianity, Čapek?

KAREL: I don't countenance it, I don't condemn it; truthfully, I don't care. A man should be judged on his actions, not his beliefs.

MASARYK: It sounds as if Vaclavek's chief concern is with my actions.

KAREL: You only did what you had to do to save this nation!

VACLAVEK: I wasn't sure how I would behave in a moment like this, Mr. President. Power always frightens me.

MASARYK: It frightens me too. More so since I acquired some, in fact.

VACLAVEK: But I can't curtsy and pay respect like my colleagues here. I have to say what's in my heart.

MASARYK: Please.

(RADOSH enters.)

RADOSH: Tea!

(MASARYK takes it, studying VACLAVEK.)

KAREL: This is a special occasion; the President isn't here to be abused.

MASARYK: Karel. I will be the judge of when I am abused.

KAREL: Yes, of course.

VACLAVEK: The greatest experiment in human history is taking place just next door. The Revolutionaries sought to join our young country to the Great Endeavor, and your soldiers killed them.

MASARYK: Yes.

VACLAVEK: How do you reconcile that with your Merciful God, Mr. President?

MASARYK: I can't. God will judge me for all I've done. The minute you become the leader of a country you give up any hope of God's grace. You have to hope that the good you do on Earth partially compensates for all the ill.

VACLAVEK: You call that massacre "good on Earth"?

MASARYK: Radosh, was it?

RADOSH: My lo—Mr. President?

MASARYK: Friday nights must be a trying time at your nameless café.

RADOSH: Oh no, Mr. President, truly, I live for Friday nights.

JO: He does seem to enjoy it, the poor man.

RADOSH: I have to be around great thoughts, Mr. President. I have to hear great words. I've never had a thought in my head my whole life, you know, I just run back and forth with plates and sandwiches!

JO: I like your sandwiches!

VACLAVEK: You do an honest day's work, Radosh! None of us do!

SALDA: Speak for yourself, Vaclavek.

VACLAVEK: And yet you live at our beck and call, we *poets*, who create only a fraction of the value you create with your daily work. Can't you imagine a world that doesn't work like that?

RADOSH: Well, I don't follow all of it, I confess…

VACLAVEK: But it's so simple!

RADOSH: But…with your way, who's in charge?

SALDA: Oh, no, no, no, no…

VACLAVEK: *No one's* in charge!

KAREL: No one? Really? I must have misunderstood. Doesn't a managed economy, by definition, require a Manager?

VACLAVEK: Those who excel at planning will be the planners!

KAREL: I have no doubt they will be.

MASARYK: Is it not possible, then, that I have earned my place as a sort of Chief Planner as endorsed by the will of the people?

VACLAVEK: Democracy doesn't impress me, sir. Democracy is the process of passing power from one landowner to another. You vote once a year and then you go right back to work for your master. There is no freedom without communal ownership of the means of production.

KAREL: The same words over and over again.

MASARYK: You have a dream.

VACLAVEK: Yes, Mr. President. More than a dream.

MASARYK: Čapek, remind me: who is the most dangerous man in the world?

KAREL: A beautiful dreamer with the means to realize his dream.

MASARYK: I never could have put it so succinctly, but then, Čapek's the writer.

KAREL: A dream to perfect the world, right all injustices, balance all inequities, distribute a fair share of comfort and happiness to every man, woman, and child.

VACLAVEK: And you sneer at that.

KAREL: I only sneer at the man who talks of it in cafés; I never sneer at the man who has the guns and the butter to carry it out. That man I fear. Think it through: you have the answer. You have the *one key* that will fix everything, the right way for everyone to live!

VACLAVEK: Yes!

KAREL: And you take your supporters, and you go around the world, spreading your beautiful dream. And many people believe in the dream and rejoice. Except…well, here's where the problem comes in. Some people don't like the dream. Some poor, deranged souls. For whatever reason, *they don't want paradise.* So they say "No thank you, we don't want the beautiful dream." But the problem is, if they don't accept the dream, then it can't come true.

VACLAVEK: Given enough time—

KAREL: So what do you do with those people? The ones who don't agree with you, who will never agree with you? Well, what else can you do? You have to kill them.

VACLAVEK: *Given enough time—*

KAREL: *You have to kill them!* Because as long as some people aren't living the dream, the dream can't come true. And that's why every dreamer becomes a monster and every beautiful dream wakes up in blood-soaked sheets.

MASARYK: I ordered the Revolutionaries put down, Vaclavek, because the alternative was to surrender and let them make a Revolution of my beloved Czechoslovakia, one in which many more people would die than ever on my orders. I believe in the goodness in your heart, Vaclavek—

KAREL: I'm glad someone does.

MASARYK: But I don't think you can honestly tell me that your Revolution wouldn't commence with a massacre.

VACLAVEK: No, you're right. That is what would happen.

KAREL: You don't deny it!

VACLAVEK: I don't deny it. Sometimes societies need to be…

KAREL: Yes?

VACLAVEK: Sometimes the corruption is so deeply embedded you have to wipe the slate clean and start over.

KAREL: And in that sentence the metaphor "wipe the slate clean" means "kill almost everyone."

VACLAVEK: If that's what it takes. I'm not ashamed. Millions will live in justice tomorrow because the thousands die tonight.

KAREL: Pure, savage blood-thirst.

VACLAVEK: To a sentimentalist, yes. To a Revolutionary, it's an elevated understanding of the mechanism of history.

ONE: After Vaclavek is gone, the evening lengthens and the shadows fall.

(VACLAVEK leaves. Now it's a little later.)

MASARYK: You're too quiet, you know, Jo.

JO: Mr. President, one might almost call that a virtue in the Friday Circle.

MASARYK: I wouldn't. You live too willingly in your brother's shadow.

JO: Look, here's where Vaclavek's right: the reason we can all be poets and artists is because our families have money. Meanwhile, the work still has to get done, right Radosh?

RADOSH: Oh…that's all right, Miss Jo…

JO: We don't pick the beans but we sure drink the coffee!

SALDA: That's the focus of all of my plays, actually, as long as we're talking about it, and why I'm constantly trying to persuade you two to stop writing pulp for children and grapple with the real economic pressures that shape the emotional lives of everyday people.

KAREL: Pulp for children?

SALDA: Vaclavek missed the point, Mr. President. The problem isn't that the insects were metaphors for Communists; the problem is that the characters were insects in the first place.

MASARYK: Well, it's a stylistic choice, surely.

SALDA: I don't dispute that, Mr. President, what I'm saying is that the times we're living in right now demand something more from our Czech writers than indulgent fantasias about talking insects and splitting atoms. You want to

make theatre that serves the people? Put people on the stage! Put on stage *only* that which is real, which can truly exist in real life.

JO: But where's the fun in that?

SALDA: Who said it's supposed to be fun?

KAREL: It's theatre! Of course it's supposed to be fun! The theatre cries out for the unreal! Why have rigging above the stage if you're not going to dangle a god?

MASARYK: And yet Jo, just a minute ago you spoke up for the people who work in drudgery and never get to realize their dreams. How would you address those people on the stage without Salda's realism?

KAREL: Jo! A challenge!

JO: Yes!

SALDA: Oh no…

KAREL: Better be a good one, the President's watching!

JO: Yes, yes, all right, economic inequality…

KAREL: Lives, dreams, ambitions lost to drudgery…

JO: A lifetime of dreary labor.

RADOSH: I love when they do this!

KAREL: No sooner from the mother's womb, the working man takes up his broom—

JO: Mother's womb!

KAREL: Yes?

JO: A mother watches her children growing, a mother watches her children, knowing—

KAREL: Keep talking.

JO: A mother has two children.

KAREL: Sounds familiar.

JO: But! One child will be a great artist, so the other must be the drudge who does all the hard work to make his brother's art possible! That's the solution! Let's say the law is, if you're going to raise one artist, you must also raise a *drudge* to compensate for the artist's abdication of his proper place in the economy.

KAREL: It needs something…

JO: But how does she know which will be which?

KAREL: I'll tell you how she knows. They've invented a pill.

JO: A pill?

SALDA: Oh, *god.*

KAREL: A Tablet. When she is next with child, she takes a Tablet.

JO: A Tablet…

KAREL: Which has the effect of altering the child in the womb!

SALDA: Oh, god, do you see, Mr. President? This is how bad writing habits are cemented! The same lazy instincts every time! First the beetles talk, then the scientists split the atom, now they invent a pill that alters an unborn baby. What would you call this?

JO: Alters how?

KAREL: He is born with no ambition! He is born with nothing to say, no great statement, only to work, a subhuman, right? Who would never dream of being anything more, so it's not cruel to limit him to drudgery!

SALDA: What would you call this? Not drama, that's for sure.

JO: I get it! Every first child is born as one of these drudges so that the second child—

KAREL: Drudges! The play is called "The Drudges"!

SALDA: "Science-fiction," maybe? Is that a term?

JO: No, something else.

KAREL: It's your name! "Drudges" is perfect!

JO: No, we don't have it yet.

KAREL: All right. You have until opening night to come up with something better.

SALDA: Opening night? You're actually writing this?

KAREL: *(To MASARYK.)* Have we met the challenge?

MASARYK: I confess, at the magic pills you lost me as well.

(KAREL embraces JO fondly.)

KAREL: All right, look, everyone, in light of the fact that we have a special guest, in point of fact the democratically elected leader of this country, let's knock off all this dreary creativity and start the serious drinking.

ONE: By one in the morning most have gone home. The soldiers remain outside the café, however, waiting for their charge. Jo is falling asleep in her chair, but she stays.

(SALDA leaves. RADOSH is bringing drinks to KAREL and MASARYK.)

KAREL: There's a third way, right? A radical center, a third way, liberalism without communism, but! We keep the best of socialism. Medicine, we see to the poor—

MASARYK: *(To RADOSH.)* You're probably normally home by now.

RADOSH: Oh no, sir, talk as long as you like! I'll keep pouring, Mr. President!

KAREL: Right, the best of socialism. The compassionate part, the part that still allows an element of humanity—

MASARYK: My friend, I'm sorry, my stamina is beginning to flag.

KAREL: Oh, of course Mr. President— I'm ashamed, the hour—

MASARYK: You never published that one story, did you?

KAREL: Which one, sir? There were quite a lot that—

MASARYK: The young man in the kitchen, the one home from the just war—

KAREL: Ah—"A Bowl of Soup."

MASARYK: "A Bowl of Soup." There's a young man—

KAREL: Well, I never finished it.

MASARYK: He's home from—I remember you called it "the Just War"—he's *on leave* from the Just War, the Just War is still ongoing—

KAREL: Right, and the mother-in-law—I never finished it.

MASARYK: He's on leave from the Just War—he's been fighting the forces of oppression, he's proud of it, he comes home, he has a few days' leave—

KAREL: That's right, he's going back—

(A YOUNG MAN enters. His FRIEND silently greets him with some bad news, then leaves. The remainder of the pantomime plays out as described by MASARYK.)

MASARYK: Yes, just temporary leave, but he comes home to find his wife is gone. While he was fighting, she died, and he's only just finding out now. He goes through their little house, and there's all of her belongings, never to be used again, and before he just thought of her as a wife, just a wife, keeping the house, and he had the Just War to think about…but now she's gone and a thousand of her little kindnesses return to him: how she laughed at his intensity, but kindly, and now, never again. And he doesn't care about the Just War anymore. He wishes now that he had just left the poor and oppressed to their pain so he could go home to his happiness. He weeps at the little table in the kitchen, and no one can console him, but his mother-in-law comes over that night.

(The MOTHER-IN-LAW enters and tends to the YOUNG MAN.)

MASARYK: She makes the young man a pot of soup. While she cooks he watches her, thinks how she looks like his wife, thicker and fuller and grayer, but maybe how she might have looked one day. She brings him the bowl of soup, he eats it, and it's warm, and it feels as though the soup is coursing through every part of his body.

KAREL: And then I never finished it. That's why I never published it.

MASARYK: It is finished. You just can't tell because you're so young. Young storytellers don't know how to trust a moment. You want to save the world, you never know when to stop. The story's finished. You didn't write any more because the moment the soup warms his body the tale is told.

KAREL: What tale?

MASARYK: Well, to my mind, the tale that proves that Karel Čapek is really a Christian, underneath it all.

KAREL: I'm not, though, Mr. President.

MASARYK: When the mother-in-law makes the soup, that's a Christian charity. When the young man eats it, he learns to simply accept Christ's love, manifested as it always is *through other people.* I've never heard a more elegant description of the love of Jesus Christ for all the souls on Earth.

KAREL: You read that, but it's not what I wrote.

MASARYK: I'm the lawfully elected President of Czechoslovakia, and I say it is.

KAREL: Then it is.

(Pause. JO sleepily makes her way out, but she pauses to listen to the rest.)

KAREL: Mr. President, we're playwrights and poets and painters. I know we're useless. But this is our home, too. We just want to help you the little we can.

MASARYK: Karel, you're so young. You're *so young.* I'm sure you've been sad, but I don't believe you've ever despaired. You still have that in front of you. Everyone does. I only know how to be President because I'm a Christian. Bowls of soup have to be filled for all the men in the world who don't have kind, compassionate mothers-in-law, and, so, *that's government.* A poor substitute

for Christian charity, but we have to have it.

ONE: Jo was listening on the stairs at this point. She could only assume that they drank and did not speak for a long time. In any event, all she heard was silence.

(A TICKET-TAKER addresses the audience.)

TICKET-TAKER: Excuse me, ladies and gentlemen! I regret to announce that at this point, all of the seats are occupied for "The Drudges" by Karel and Josephine Čapek. Please return another night.

ONE: The triumphant opening of "The Drudges"!

(ACTORS assume DR. GALL, FABRY, and the PRESIDENT. JO, KAREL, PEROUTKA, SALDA, and RADOSH watch the play.)

PRESIDENT: But dammit, Fabry, you're the finest economist this country has ever produced! What is causing this terrible decline in our industry? I thought we were supposed to be at the dawn of a new industrial age, with prosperity for all!

FABRY: The machinery isn't the problem, Mr. President. The problem is the machines need people to operate them, and we're losing people by the hundreds!

PRESIDENT: Losing them where?

FABRY: To the *Artist Class*, Mr. President! There are simply too many young men and women who have decided to devote their lives to the creation of art and beauty, while fewer and fewer work the machines and pick the crops and mop the floors.

PRESIDENT: Dammit! We never should have put about the idea that dreams can come true. Now everyone believes it!

DR. GALL: Mr. President, perhaps I may be of assistance.

PRESIDENT: Yes! Dr. Gall! Our most brilliant scientist. Tell me your plan.

GALL: If I may, Mr. President, I have taken it upon myself to invent…this Tablet!

PRESIDENT: But what does it do?

GALL: By means of this Tablet, we can correct the population and keep the Artist Class under control! If a woman is with child and she takes this Tablet, her child will be born with no ambition whatsoever! He will have no desire to create art or beauty, he will not wish to invent new marvels of science or utopian political visions. He will simply wish to work, day in and day out, at whatever mundane task he is assigned. He shall be…a Drudge!

FABRY: A Drudge! That's brilliant!

JO: It's the wrong name.

KAREL: Too late now!

PRESIDENT: Let the decree go forth! Every family in the land must produce one Drudge for every aspiring artist, activist, or scientist! One dishwasher for every dreamer! It's the law!

PEROUTKA: Technically, you'd need more than one Drudge for every artist.

ONE: Peroutka, the inventor, one of the few non-artist members of the Friday Circle.

JO: Don't be a spoilsport, Peroutka. One to one is easier for an audience to understand.

PEROUTKA: I'm just saying, given the realities of production—

KAREL: Dramatic license!

PEROUTKA: Why is the most dramatic thing never the scientifically accurate thing?

(A MOTHER and a LITTLE GIRL enter.)

LITTLE GIRL: But Mother, why does Peter never want to play?

MOTHER: Because, little Olga, when your brother was in my belly I took a little pill so that Peter would do all the work and you could become a beautiful dancer.

PEROUTKA: *(To SALDA.)* Accuracy's more exciting to me than anything, but I suppose I'm odd.

SALDA: *(Watching the play.)* Well, there's political satire as well, I'll concede, but still…

RADOSH: How do they remember all those words?

ONE: As the curtain rises on Act Two, twenty years have passed, and ruinous years they were. The President and Fabry call through a locked door to the sequestered Dr. Gall.

PRESIDENT: Open the door, Gall!

GALL: Go away!

FABRY: Gall! You must undo what you've done!

PRESIDENT: Open the door!

GALL: I can't! I can't bear it!

ONE: The President and her men break down the door.

GALL: Get away from me! There's no cure, no undoing! Yes, for the first generation, the Tablet worked, there was one Drudge for every dreamer, but now…

PRESIDENT: Yes, *now*! Now the women of the next generation can't give birth unless they take the Tablet and bear a Drudge!

FABRY: If they don't take the Tablet, the child won't live to term!

PRESIDENT: All of our children are Drudges now!

FABRY: You must invent an antidote!

GALL: Antidote! Me? I spent decades, my whole scientific career, learning how to remove qualities! And now I am to restore them? I don't know how! And I'm not young anymore, either. It was energy as much as brilliance that spawned the Tablet—I was young! I could stay up all night. Now I'm old, and I'm in despair. I look through a microscope and everything blurs.

PRESIDENT: Then the human race is truly doomed.

GALL: Oh, Madam President, not the human race. Just everything beautiful in the human race. Everything ambitious and inquisitive. Hard work and productivity will be all that remains.

ONE: Dr. Gall is right. Another twenty years pass, and the last ordinary human dies. The stage fills with Drudges, turning the cranks and working the machines, wiping the windows and washing the floors, as the curtain slowly falls.

(*Applause. We return to the café, where KAREL, JO, SALDA, PEROUTKA, and RADOSH are celebrating. This will lead up to the moment we glimpsed at the beginning.*)

SALDA: Allow me, allow me, I'm the resident crank!

JO: Yes, yes, Salda! Let's have Salda!

SALDA: Let me make the toast! To the playwrights: Karel and Josephine Čapek, authors of what certainly looked to this envious colleague like the brand-new hit play "The Drudges"!

JO: I still hate the name.

SALDA: And however much I may wish that this brother and sister would deploy their evident talent in the service of depicting *actual human beings* rather than solipsistic symbolic ciphers—

KAREL: Alliteration, do you hear, Peroutka? That's from poetry!

PEROUTKA: I'll take you at your word.

SALDA: I nevertheless defer to their ability to entertain, first of all, and to tell the story of our hopeful infant nation in a fantastical language all their own. My friends, we agree on nothing but Czechoslovakia, but for me that is enough. To Karel and Jo.

(*JO embraces SALDA.*)

SALDA: You're supposed to drink first, Jo.

JO: I don't care.

PEROUTKA: Are we going to applaud? I have a drink in each hand.

RADOSH: It was magic, Mr. Čapek, sheer magic! Won't you let me pay for my ticket?

KAREL: I won't hear of this again, Radosh, that ticket was a gift.

RADOSH: You're too kind to me, sir.

JO: Oh, he's not "sir."

RADOSH: Let me ask you: do you think things probably worked out later?

KAREL: How do you mean?

(As RADOSH speaks, HELENA enters pushing a HUMAN FIGURE in a wheelchair. The FIGURE's head is bound. Only PEROUTKA notices.)

RADOSH: Do you think some normal people were maybe born *after* the end of the show, and things turned out well after that?

KAREL: You mean after the end of the play?

PEROUTKA: Ah—so…

JO: Yes, Radosh, perhaps that did happen.

KAREL: But—wait…

SALDA: Sure, Karel, why not?

PEROUTKA: Um…artists?

(EVERYONE looks around.)

PEROUTKA: I think you have visitors.

HELENA: Karel and Josephine Čapek?

JO: Yes?

HELENA: I saw your play.

KAREL: Who is this person? Why is his head covered?

JO: Can he breathe through that thing?

PEROUTKA: Well he's not breathing now.

HELENA: He's not breathing because he's not a person.

PEROUTKA: He's not breathing—is this man dead?

SALDA: Who are you?

PEROUTKA: This man is dead!

RADOSH: Begging your pardon, miss, you can't bring a dead man in here!

HELENA: He is not dead, nor is he a man! Look closer.

KAREL: Peroutka?

PEROUTKA: She's right. This isn't a real arm. This is…I don't know this substance, but this…this is a doll. Look.

KAREL: Jo, you're the sculptor.

JO: Excuse me, Peroutka. *(JO raises the arm, studies the hand, the fingers.)*

SALDA: If we could return to my question.

KAREL: Who are you?

HELENA: My name is Helena Rossum.

KAREL: All right, Helena Rossum. What would you like to tell us about your giant doll?

JO: This is incredible…

HELENA: Mr. Čapek, what if you could have Drudges that aren't human beings?

KAREL: I'm sorry?

HELENA: What if you could have all of the good and none of the bad? A workforce full of contented laborers, but human nature left intact?

KAREL: My dear…it's only a play.

HELENA: No it's not.

(She injects something into the back of the neck of the CREATURE and the arm JO is studying comes to life, gripping her by the wrist. She cries out.)

KAREL: What happened?

JO: Let go!

HELENA: It can't hear you.

JO: Make it let go!

(RADOSH tries to pull it off.)

RADOSH: Let go of her, mister! Now!

HELENA: Is it hurting you?

JO: No, it's—it's—

RADOSH: Unhand her, sir!

KAREL: Make it let go *now*!

(HELENA injects a different substance into the neck and the arm goes limp.)

KAREL: I thought it wasn't a man!

PEROUTKA: It's not, feel it, it's not— what is this?

KAREL: Jo, are you all right?

JO: The strongest grip I've ever felt…

KAREL: Jo.

JO: It didn't hurt, but…I never could have pulled free.

PEROUTKA: How did this arm move?

RADOSH: I don't want it in my café and that's final!

SALDA: All right, Helena Rossum—

HELENA: I'm sorry, I wanted my demonstration to be…dramatic. I'm sorry, Miss Čapek.

PEROUTKA: I can't figure it out. Let me see that. *(Meaning the needle.)*

SALDA: *Who are you, please?*

HELENA: I'm the daughter of Professor Marius Rossum, who created this automata.

KAREL: "Automata"?

PEROUTKA: Of course—Rossum!

HELENA: You know the name.

PEROUTKA: Well certainly, any man of science with an interest in—isn't he dead?

RADOSH: I don't want anything that hurts Miss Jo in my café!

HELENA: I'll take it away.

PEROUTKA: Wait! You have to let me look at this!

HELENA: Will you come with me? All of you?

KAREL: You'll take us to Rossum?

HELENA: I will.

(Pause.)

KAREL: Now?

HELENA: Now. Yes. Forgive me, Mr. Čapek, I've waited years to meet you.

KAREL: Jo?

JO: *(Still feeling her arm where the hand gripped her.)* Whoever made that, I want to meet him.

ONE: So that was the night that the playwrights and the scientist piled into one car to drive to the outskirts of Prague to a large country house, clearly in decline.

(We are in ROSSUM's lab. ROSSUM, a woman, is working at a table. HELENA keeps the party at the periphery.)

HELENA: Ssh!

KAREL: Is your father not expecting us?

HELENA: Wait here.

(Over the following, HELENA approaches ROSSUM, trying to get her attention. ROSSUM does not look up.)

SALDA: We're supposed to be drinking right now.

KAREL: This is history, Salda! Right before our eyes!

SALDA: Or a parlor trick.

JO: I knew it wasn't human from its touch. A hand on the skin warms after a moment, but not this one.

SALDA: Jo, are you all right?

JO: I want to meet Rossum!

PEROUTKA: I could swear I read he was dead.

(HELENA returns to the periphery.)

HELENA: Come!

(They enter the lab.)

ONE: Perhaps this was a wine cellar once. Now it's a workshop of some kind, or a kitchen—tools everywhere, huge bubbling cauldrons, mannequins everywhere, in pieces. A strange, shabby figure at the far end.

HELENA: Rossum?

ROSSUM: *(Peers at the party.)* You did it, then. You brought them to our doorstep.

HELENA: I told you I would.

ROSSUM: I didn't believe you.

SALDA: I'm sorry, I feel silly—that is a woman, yes?

PEROUTKA: Are you the widow of Marius Rossum?

ROSSUM: I am Rossum!

HELENA: It's hard to explain, please.

ROSSUM: I am Professor Marius Rossum!

KAREL: All right.

HELENA: I showed them the automata. I made it move. There's no secret anymore, Rossum. They can't unsee what they've seen.

PEROUTKA: Excuse me—Miss Rossum, is it?

ROSSUM: Rossum!

PEROUTKA: Yes, good. My mistake, but I feel certain that I read in a journal of chemistry some years ago that Marius Rossum—

HELENA: Dr. Peroutka, please don't ask any more.

ROSSUM: Peroutka?

PEROUTKA: Yes, that is I.

ROSSUM: You're in the journals.

PEROUTKA: From time to time.

ROSSUM: You have a competent brain.

PEROUTKA: I have a splendid brain.

ROSSUM: And the Čapeks. The brother and sister, you do the Punch and Judy shows my daughter takes for entertainment. *(To SALDA.)* You I don't know, nor do I wish to. *(To PEROUTKA.)* No, a *competent* brain. Well read, yes, meticulous, even better, but painfully stunted by credulousness. You believe far too easily what you are told. Look in this pot.

(PEROUTKA looks at the others.)

SALDA: Better you than me.

(PEROUTKA looks in the cauldron.)

PEROUTKA: Wax, or some kind of—

ROSSUM: *Wax?!*

PEROUTKA: Why don't you just tell me?

ROSSUM: Creation itself, Peroutka. The very bedrock of life, or a new way to think about life. This, Doctor, is *protoplasm.*

PEROUTKA: I may need an additional hint.

ROSSUM: *(To HELENA.)* Get the one from the back.

(HELENA hurries off with the FIGURE in the wheelchair.)

ROSSUM: This is where I diverge from the pygmies of modern science. Microscopic biology complicates your understanding of life, but it simplifies mine. Our bodies are made up of what appear to be wildly varying organs of differing size, color, texture, and function, but at the cellular level the differences disappear. It's a kit, perhaps, or a recipe, but always the same basic ingredients. Prepare them one way, and you have a pancreas. Another way, lungs. Teeth. A brain.

PEROUTKA: Even if we were certain that were true, we still don't have the faintest grasp of the process whereby it's done.

ROSSUM: The sister!

(JO steps forward.)

ROSSUM: A sculptor as well, my daughter tells me.

JO: That's right.

ROSSUM: All sculptures are made of marble, yes?

JO: Well, no, of course not—limestone, jade, ivory, all sorts of metals, woods—

ROSSUM: Ah! So therefore, any Michelangelo marble could be replicated in some other medium.

JO: Well—not *exactly*, but—

ROSSUM: No. Never *exactly*. But one would see the resemblance. You're right, Peroutka, we cannot hope to grasp the process by which microscopic objects bond to form living creatures. But suppose we could *transpose* the process to simpler media and begin building our own creatures? Not the same, of course, not *exactly*, but one would see the resemblance.

PEROUTKA: So what you're saying is this…protoplasm is a sort of…what, clay? Or—

ROSSUM: Yes! Clay! I like that! The potter's clay! It can take any shape. A tongue. A liver. Skin. It may not look the same, it may not feel the same, *but it is similar.* There is a resemblance. My wife was a midwife, did you know?

PEROUTKA: Your wife?

ROSSUM: They train with a contraption: A mock-up of a woman's torso and legs and the adjacent orifices, not plaster or stone but made of animal skin and stuffing to more accurately mimic the real thing. The reproductive organs— what a revelation!—packed with sponges connected to a pump to mimic the processes of dilation and lubrication! The inventor of that device, some woman, likely, is a genius lost to the ages.

KAREL: But—there's a pump.

ROSSUM: Yes?

KAREL: For the device to work, there has to be a pump, and someone to operate it.

ROSSUM: You may win me over yet, playwright.

JO: Yes, you can't just make the replicas, it doesn't matter how similar they are, something has to animate them.

KAREL: And, more to the point, *keep them animated* even when someone isn't working the pump.

ROSSUM: I'm beginning to understand why my daughter came to you. Take note, Peroutka, the fantasists grasp the concept because they don't have an orthodoxy to protect. You begin to see, do you not, why people worship gods they never see? We can make any shape we wish, but we can't make it move, we can't make it breathe. Only the gods can!

(HELENA enters with another FIGURE in a wheelchair, with a bound head.)

HELENA: I thought Minerva.

ROSSUM: Very well.

JO: That one has a woman's body.

ROSSUM: Will you confirm then, sculptress, that it's not a real woman?

(JO studies the FIGURE, touching it. PEROUTKA is figuring something out.)

JO: I don't know what it's made of, but it's not human flesh.

PEROUTKA: There *was* a pump, though. Remember? *(To HELENA.)* You injected something into the doll at the café. What was that?

(ROSSUM hands PEROUTKA a beaker.)

ROSSUM: Care for a drink?

JO: What is it?

PEROUTKA: I don't know, but the odor is remarkable.

ROSSUM: Have you ever smelled a freshly gutted human body?

PEROUTKA: I was with Masaryk and the Legions in Austria.

ROSSUM: Then you know. Was that odor also remarkable?

PEROUTKA: It was.

ROSSUM: Give the beaker to my daughter.

(He does. HELENA draws the liquid into a needle.)

ROSSUM: The body *must* remain animated even when no one is there to work the pump. Which means that whatever is pumped into the body of the automata *must* be a renewable resource, the spark *and* the fire. The protoplasm took me ten years. The *Ichor* took another sixteen!

PEROUTKA: Ichor?

SALDA: The blood of the gods. It's Greek.

ROSSUM: It's Czech now. The needle in my daughter's hand injects the Ichor into the automata's body, carrying vital minerals to every one of the pseudo-organs within. But better yet! When the minerals are used, the Ichor carries them to the pseudo-liver where they are reconstituted and revitalized, and thus the automata can animate for hours at a time without refueling!

PEROUTKA: I'm sorry, Rossum, but if such technology existed, we would—I mean, we would apply it to *everything*—you understand why it's hard for me to—we would be using it for *so many things*.

HELENA: You're right, Dr. Peroutka. Except that at this moment, the technology only exists in this room.

ROSSUM: Activate.

(HELENA injects the FIGURE in the chair. It moves. Its hands shake, then stabilize. It grips the arms of the wheelchair, then slowly rises from the chair. It takes a step.)

SALDA: My God, my God…

(The FIGURE takes a few unsteady steps, looking around, and then falls into JO's arms. JO helps it stand again, steadying it. It turns its head to her.)

JO: Are you all right?

ROSSUM: It's not a person, Miss Čapek. The question doesn't apply.

HELENA: Mr. Čapek—the Drudges were born of woman. The doctor had to interfere with human nature to make them. These were never human to begin with. You see what I mean? I know you have the ear of President Masaryk, I know that he—

ROSSUM: *Enough!* These are matters for another time. We are done for tonight.

KAREL: Why us? Dr. Peroutka aside, a bunch of playwrights.

ROSSUM: Ask my daughter.

HELENA: Because I read your columns and I see your plays. You always say, beware the beautiful dream gone bad. Beware the technology that is misused. I know Masaryk listens to you and I know you love this country. Starting tomorrow, nothing will be the same. Men will come to our house, the army, maybe, other scientists.

ROSSUM: I told you this!

HELENA: They would have found us anyway! *(To KAREL.)* The automata are going to change the world. We must ensure that they change it for the good. I'm no one, no one will listen to me. People listen to you.

(KAREL studies the FIGURE as it looks around the room. JO is still steadying it with her hand.)

KAREL: I have one question.

ONE: The next afternoon, in Masaryk's office, the President asks the same question.

(ROSSUM exits. We shift to MASARYK's office.)

MASARYK: Are they human? *(He is studying the automata that HELENA has brought with her.)*

HELENA: No, Mr. President.

JO: Are you sure?

HELENA: How could they be?

JO: When she stumbled in my arms the other night, she just seemed—

HELENA: It's not really a "she." The automata has no reproductive organs. I'm sorry Mr. President.

MASARYK: Miss Rossum, I think I can withstand talk of reproductive organs.

HELENA: Some are in the shape of men, some of women. But only in the most rudimentary sense.

KAREL: They can carry out basic physical activity. They can lift things, carry things. Given time for refinement of the technology, they will be able to carry out more complex tasks.

MASARYK: Can she see us?

HELENA: *It.* Not yet—well, it can see us, though the eyes are at a crude stage right now. It can't hear and it can't talk.

KAREL: Which as I pointed out are major obstacles. We can't make use of these…creatures?

HELENA: Machines, really.

KAREL: We can't make use of these machines until we can tell them what we want them to do.

MASARYK: They understand language?

HELENA: Not yet.

MASARYK: That seems to be the recurring answer.

HELENA: Mr. President, there's no doubt that they're unfinished. Rossum's resources are almost expended.

MASARYK: What does he need?

KAREL: New facilities and an enormous amount of money.

MASARYK: How remarkable: the same as everyone else.

KAREL: We can't turn back the clock. They exist. Someone will further their development. I want it to be you, Mr. President.

MASARYK: Peroutka?

ONE: Peroutka tells Masaryk the same thing he told the others in the café the night before.

(Now it is the night before, in the café. MASARYK, HELENA, and the FIGURE step away. SALDA and RADOSH join them.)

PEROUTKA: What do you want me to say, Čapek? Yes! Undeniably! What we just saw is the most significant scientific advancement in history! I, I, I—my brain is exploding, to think about the—just the *applications*, the scientific, the economic—

JO: This is going too fast, we're moving too fast on this!

KAREL: How can we go slower, Jo? They exist, the Drudges exist, they can't be unmade! Someone will use them!

JO: Not if they stay a secret!

KAREL: That's impossible!

JO: Peroutka's talking about the applications, I'm talking about the implications! What are they? Are they people? What are we going to use them for? How? Why? Will they do our jobs? What jobs? What about the people who do those jobs now?

SALDA: I can't, I can't deal with this…

JO: And this Helena woman: "Oh, Mr. Čapek, you're so brilliant, you just love our country *so much*—"

KAREL: You don't think that it's enormously to her credit that she wants the creatures to fall into the right hands?

JO: And look how quickly you take up the mantle the instant it's offered! You notice she left me well out of it; only a man, when told of his brilliance, believes it every time.

PEROUTKA: We're missing the point! The clock's ticking!

JO: The clock?

PEROUTKA: It's—it's—it's not the artist who changes history, or the novelist or the philosopher or even the politician, really, none of them—it's the funny-looking man—or woman, as we see—hunched over the cluttered desk in the basement inventing the odd little gadget no one's ever imagined that five years from now no one will be able to live without! Nobody voted for the gadget to exist, it never came up in parliament, no—a succession of brilliant freaks concocted it *simply because they figured out how*. Karl Marx versus the man who invented the gas lamp—no comparison! One had a theory, the other defeated night!

JO: I'm trying to figure out whose side you're on.

PEROUTKA: I don't know myself! Dammit! Jo, these things could generate enough food and supplies to end poverty on Earth.

KAREL: Or they could do something else. And the clock's ticking.

PEROUTKA: It starts the minute something's invented and counts down until someone uses it.

KAREL: This isn't a philosophical quandary, this is an emergency.

SALDA: Look. *(Stands.)* I'm sorry. You're my friends. I'm sorry. I like to write plays. I like to put on plays.

JO: Salda, sit a minute.

SALDA: No, I don't want any part of this.

RADOSH: Mr. Salda?

SALDA: I'll see myself out, Radosh. *(To KAREL.)* You have my word I won't tell anyone. Who do I have to tell? *(Leaves.)*

KAREL: Radosh, we'll need you to remain outside until we're done.

RADOSH: Oh…of course, Mr. Čapek.

JO: I'm sorry, Radosh.

RADOSH: That's all right, Miss Jo. *(Leaves.)*

JO: You're an arrogant thug. And Salda's right. Why us? Of all the people in this country, why should this decision fall to *us*?

KAREL: Because now we know, and we can't pretend we don't. We know we can go on being playwrights and effectively admit that within our secret hearts we always *wanted* to remain peripheral, or we can take up the challenge we've been offered this day and make sure the future that is already coming unfolds *our* way, with compassion and the alleviation of suffering! How can we flinch from that, Jo? What can we do now but be brave?

(Pause.)

JO: They can't be called Drudges.

KAREL: If you come up with a better name, we'll use it.

ONE: But when they go to see Masaryk, Jo still doesn't have a name.

(MASARYK, HELENA, and the AUTOMATA return, and we are in MASARYK's office once again, returning to the previous scene.)

MASARYK: Miss Rossum, I wonder if you might arrange an audience for me with your father.

HELENA: It will be an honor, Mr. President. Karel—?

KAREL: I'll explain.

(HELENA wheels the AUTOMATA out.)

KAREL: One small note, Mr. President: Rossum is in fact a woman, Helena's mother.

MASARYK: A woman?

JO: A disturbed woman, at some level. It's unclear. She may think she's her late husband.

KAREL: She demands to be addressed as "Rossum" only.

PEROUTKA: It's pretty uncanny.

MASARYK: But it's her work.

PEROUTKA: It has to be. Marius Rossum's been dead for years.

MASARYK: I'll bear it in mind.

KAREL: Mr. President, I am sorry to come to you like this—

MASARYK: If we did it how would we start?

KAREL: Rossum needs a facility. Something much larger.

MASARYK: How large?

KAREL: I was thinking the fortress at Terezin.

JO: You have this all figured out!

KAREL: It's still unused, yes?

JO: Masaryk's blessing is incidental, isn't it?

MASARYK: Not a united front, then.

JO: This is going too fast.

MASARYK: Peroutka?

PEROUTKA: Until I know more, I have to assume the possibilities are limitless.

MASARYK: Meaning they could be used as weapons.

PEROUTKA: I can't rule it out.

JO: One of them grabbed my arm in the demonstration. I'm not hurt, thank you sir, but their strength is incredible.

KAREL: One, alone, could lift a steel beam or tear a man limb from limb. I want you to be the one to choose, Mr. President. You're the best man I know.

MASARYK: God help me, I'd almost be happier if the Americans had it, or Stalin, just so the choice wouldn't be mine.

KAREL: You're equal to this, Mr. President.

MASARYK: Only God and I know that. (Pause.) I'll back you as far as a prototype. I want to keep the circle as small as possible. Rossum gets a minimal staff. Peroutka, you oversee the science. Karel and Jo, the ethics are your responsibility.

JO: Me?

MASARYK: Don't let your little brother win every argument, will you? (To all.) Show me one. Show me that it can take orders, work, prove to me that it won't hurt anyone. Then we'll see.

KAREL: Thank you, Mr. President.

(He gestures to the others that they should go. JO and PEROUTKA leave, and KAREL is almost behind them.)

MASARYK: Karel.

KAREL: Mr. President?

ONE: Josephine waved Peroutka ahead and listened at the door. The following is the conversation as best as she remembered.

MASARYK: I'm angry because I'm frightened.

KAREL: You think I'm not frightened, sir?

MASARYK: Not the way I am, no. A man is described as "God-fearing" when he's properly frightened of assuming the mantle of God.

KAREL: These will be tools in human shape, sir, nothing more.

MASARYK: Look at you. You've found your mission, haven't you? I've seen my last Čapek and Čapek play, I'm sure.

KAREL: Actually, this conversation is reminding me, I brought you a present. I've been meaning to give you this for a while.

MASARYK: Is it an article?

KAREL: A short story. A *very* short story: two paragraphs, roughly. I wrote it a few days after the last time we talked. When you called me a Christian. I tried to imagine how I could believe in God, and this is the best I could come up with.

MASARYK: "Help Me," by Karel Čapek. Well, yes. That's a Christian title, if I ever read one.

KAREL: Is it?

MASARYK: That's where every Christian begins.

(KAREL leaves. ROSSUM enters. We are in her lab.)

ROSSUM: Soldiers everywhere. You must be this "President."

MASARYK: There are no formalities.

ROSSUM: I would not observe them if there were.

MASARYK: You know why I'm here.

ROSSUM: I told her they would come.

MASARYK: I intend that you keep the patent and the credit, as is your right. I want the license to manufacture these creatures. My intentions are honorable

and nonviolent. If you refuse, however, for reasons of national security I will be forced to impound and possibly destroy everything in this lab.

ROSSUM: Flawlessly argued, Mr. President.

MASARYK: Make your conditions.

ROSSUM: Only that I keep the Ichor to myself.

MASARYK: To yourself?

ROSSUM: I'll make as much as you want. But the formula stays with me. No one else.

MASARYK: I accept. Do you shake hands, Rossum?

ROSSUM: What gentleman does not?

(They shake hands.)

ONE: The question is asked: when was the Liberator born? At what moment did the Great and Terrible first come into being? Most would say, the moment the Ichor entered his body. A few might point to the moment they first picked out his face.

(We are in the café. JO has just finished making a plaster cast of RADOSH's face.)

JO: Thank you, Radosh, you were very patient.

RADOSH: What a strange experience, Miss Jo…to sit still for so long. But broadening, I'm sure!

JO: Oh, I don't know if it's broadening. But you are a remarkably patient man.

RADOSH: I'm to be one of your artworks! Me, a barkeep, and not a very smart one either! I'm going to be a statue by Josephine Čapek!

JO: I wish you wouldn't speak of yourself so, Radosh.

RADOSH: Oh, it doesn't bother me, Miss Jo. I know I don't have great thoughts like you and your brother. I'm just glad I get to listen!

JO: There are other virtues besides great thoughts. Kindness, for example. Humility.

RADOSH: Are you angry, Miss Jo?

JO: And you've always been so protective of me.

RADOSH: Oh?

JO: I notice that.

RADOSH: Oh that's...that's just...

JO: Don't think I don't notice.

(A sweet, awkward beat between them.)

JO: I'll be a few minutes. *(Leaves with the plaster cast.)*

ONE: As Josephine later explained, what she heard made her stop in the corridor.

(KAREL and HELENA are kissing. JO listens from a distance.)

KAREL: What if—what if there was a way to—

HELENA: Don't say anything for a minute.

(He holds her.)

HELENA: It's so strange.

KAREL: What is?

HELENA: To be honest? Being out of that damned *basement*.

KAREL: You could have left long ago.

HELENA: She just needs me so much, she gets panicked if I'm gone a day.

KAREL: There are people to take care of her now. Your mother's brain is this country's primary asset. She can have whatever she wants.

HELENA: She wants *me*. She thinks it's perfectly all right that my life is spent in a windowless cell cataloguing pseudo-organs for a deranged woman who thinks she's her own late husband.

KAREL: If it's any consolation, I'm sure that particular complaint has never before been lodged in human history.

HELENA: Well...these are historical days.

KAREL: Yes.

HELENA: It feels strange to be happy! I feel like I'm breathing oxygen after a lifetime of formaldehyde and brine. Oh, don't smile at me, it's hard to know what language to use around a master.

KAREL: "Master" is overpraise.

HELENA: I went to your plays, you know—she would let me out if I could account for my time, and a theatre playbill is an account, yes?

KAREL: I never thought of it that way.

HELENA: I have a drawer full of them, like a personal history. And when you're there, and the actors are under the lights, speaking the language of...state? the language of consequence?—it gives the spectator—you musn't laugh—

KAREL: You have my word.

HELENA: The illusion of participation.

KAREL: And see how I don't laugh.

HELENA: What have I said?

KAREL: Helena, listen to me: *writing* a play does the same thing. It gives the writer the illusion of participation.

HELENA: No.

KAREL: Yes. Short of actually participating, it's always an illusion. I've written my last play. I've crossed over. I'm lined up outside your door now.

(They kiss again. JO returns to RADOSH in the café.)

ONE: Josephine at this point chose to stop listening, so we don't know what else they said.

JO: Radosh, I've changed my mind. I'm going to deliver the cast myself.

RADOSH: Oh…very good then, Miss Jo, I'll—do you need a sandwich? To see you off?

JO: Do I need a sandwich to see me off?

RADOSH: To see you—for the road! I meant for your car! For on the way. If you get hungry. Oh, I am a stupid one, Miss Jo. It's a good thing I stick with sandwiches and beer.

(A MAN enters.)

RADOSH: Just with you sir, just with you.

JO: I like your sandwiches, Radosh.

RADOSH: Well, I…you know…

(JO glances at the MAN.)

ONE: Josephine surprises herself later by remembering the man.

RADOSH: I just try to keep them simple, you know?

JO: Yes. But I won't have one today, I think. Tomorrow?

RADOSH: Tomorrow! I'll get started now! Well, not now. Tomorrow when you come.

JO: That will be fine.

(Another strange, sweet beat between them. JO leaves.)

ONE: The Man is here for Jo's brother, not her, so he waits several minutes after Josephine leaves before he produces the grenade. The former colleague of Vaclavek's sets off the grenade before he intends to, before he can leave, and the explosion interrupts Čapek and Helena Rossum mid-embrace. As Čapek will explain to his sister later, he and Helena hurried down the stairs to find the bodies of Radosh and the revolutionary still smoldering.

(ONE places a white sheet over RADOSH as he sits in a chair, where he will remain to become RADIUS later.)

ONE: By the time the news reaches Jo, she has already finished speaking with Rossum.

(We are in ROSSUM's lab. JO approaches ROSSUM with the plaster cast.)

ROSSUM: This is the first?

JO: That's the face.

ROSSUM: I suppose it will have to do.

JO: Thank you.

ROSSUM: My Helena has not returned.

JO: No, she was working with us in town.

ROSSUM: Yes. She does that now. With your brother in particular, I think. *(Studies the plaster cast.)* I will never have another child.

JO: ...Oh?

ROSSUM: My wife passed on these many years now. Never another.

(We are now in ROSSUM's new lab at Terezin. Enter MASARYK, KAREL, HELENA, PEROUTKA. ROSSUM and PEROUTKA are working on the former RADOSH, now RADIUS, still concealed under the sheet.)

MASARYK: So, today is the day!

PEROUTKA: Mr. President!

MASARYK: You look as through you're enjoying yourself, Peroutka.

PEROUTKA: Mr. President, I can't even express to you—Rossum is the sort of genius who appears once in a century!

ROSSUM: Quiet, and work.

PEROUTKA: Once in a century! Mr. President, if you will:

(He removes the white sheet to reveal the robot, RADIUS, who looks exactly like RADOSH. JO and KAREL briefly look at one another.)

PEROUTKA: Along here and here. These look like veins, yes?

MASARYK: To a degree.

PEROUTKA: They're glass. Yes! I know! But a glass so thin and so specifically constituted as to be flexible like rubber. Breathtaking!

ROSSUM: Helena, mix me five of Serum Seven.

HELENA: Your age is showing, Rossum. I don't mix anymore. Ask Peroutka.

(A dangerous moment. ROSSUM is beaten and goes to mix the Ichor herself.)

ROSSUM: Your mother would die again. She would die again.

(Pause.)

PEROUTKA: So, so, yes, well, so the Ichor has to circulate, obviously, thus these flexible glass microtubes that crisscross the body of the automata.

KAREL: What if we just called them automata, Jo?

(JO doesn't answer.)

PEROUTKA: But Ichor isn't enough. The automata needs more than nutrients and oxygen. It needs the basic tools of cognition.

ROSSUM: So much noise...

MASARYK: Cognition?

KAREL: Cognition only to a degree.

PEROUTKA: If the creatures are to work—

KAREL and HELENA: Automata.

HELENA: "Creature" suggests sentient life, a person or an animal.

PEROUTKA: If the automata are to work for us, they'll need basic cognitive skills. They'll need to see, they'll need to hear, they'll need to learn repetitive tasks and to walk without falling. How will that happen? That's the genius! Rossum's figured out how to transmit little pulses of light through these microtubes at differing durations per pulse—not that we would ever notice the difference in duration, the difference is fractions of seconds—little pulses of light like Morse code that give the automata the crude facsimile of a nervous system! Can you imagine? I'm oversimplifying, of course—

MASARYK: Oh, plainly.

PEROUTKA: But this is the greatest scientific marvel in the history of man.

MASARYK: Rossum, are we making a man?

ROSSUM: That's your question? And you the President.

MASARYK: I anticipate a yes and no answer, with layers of nuance.

ROSSUM: No. The answer is no.

KAREL: The answer is no, but that needs to be made clearer to the people.

HELENA: I think it will be made clear through their behavior.

KAREL: I suppose…

HELENA: That's why we're the ethics committee, yes? We script the behavior that distinguishes between human and Drudge.

KAREL: I pause here for Jo's objection.

(JO waves him off with no humor.)

ROSSUM: President Masaryk, you have perhaps noted students at art galleries copying the works of the masters in their sketchbooks.

MASARYK: I'm aware that it happens.

KAREL: What if…

ROSSUM: The student can't replicate the brush strokes of the master. How can he? He's not a master. Still, he takes his best guess at the strokes based on how the paint falls across the canvas.

MASARYK: All points stipulated.

ROSSUM: When he's finished, you ask to see the pad. Even if he matched every

color and mimicked every stroke, do you think you could tell the difference?

MASARYK: All right.

ROSSUM: However man came to be, it was through a process so complex no human mind can grasp it. All we can do is study and then ape the results. But everyone will know the difference.

MASARYK: All right, Rossum, I see that. But do you not see the weakness of arguing by analogy?

ROSSUM: Meaning?

MASARYK: The student's not a master, but he wants to be. And he thinks it's only a matter of time.

KAREL: What if it wasn't shaped like a person?

HELENA: I'm sorry?

KAREL: The point of the Drudge is to liberate people from dangerous and soul-killing labor. This only works if people understand that the Drudge is a tool, and not a person. Why, then, is it shaped like a person? Rossum, did you ever consider any other shape?

ROSSUM: No.

HELENA: What other shape?

KAREL: Well—an animal shape, perhaps.

HELENA: We could shape them like dogs, but then they couldn't work.

JO: Their mouths, remember? They could fetch.

(KAREL notices her tone; HELENA doesn't.)

HELENA: Or a bird or a snake? What could they do? The labor required in a human civilization is suited to a human-oid shape; that's not surprising.

KAREL: What about something with several arms? A squid.

HELENA: A squid?

KAREL: A land…squid. With legs.

HELENA: Karel, darling: we want people to take these creatures into their homes and their mills and their offices. You said yourself: we inject them into society, gradually, gently.

KAREL: Or an ape?

PEROUTKA: *(To ROSSUM.)* I'm ready.

ROSSUM: *(Mixing Ichor.)* "Darling…"

PEROUTKA: Rossum.

ROSSUM: This is the last dose.

HELENA: People know what a servant is. People know what a laborer is. Introduce the Drudges in a shape and in a capacity that people already know, and they will be accepted.

PEROUTKA: Only a minute more, Mr. President.

MASARYK: Thank you.

KAREL: Read me the new script again.

HELENA: Which?

KAREL: Domestics. I haven't looked at any Domestics yet.

HELENA: "Good morning, Mrs. Stanicek. Shall I prepare tea?" Now that's from my revision of—

KAREL: First person, Helena, scratch it out.

HELENA: Sorry, I'm sorry.

KAREL: It's a hard habit to learn, but stay focused.

MASARYK: That sounded all right.

KAREL: They're not to speak in the first person.

MASARYK: No?

KAREL: No. They're tools. There has to be a degree of alienation built into the dialogue.

MASARYK: Oh.

HELENA: "Good morning, Mrs. Stanicek. Tea has been prepared. What additional tasks—"

JO: Well, passive voice, but it is only a tool. "Prepared your tea has been, Mrs. Stanicek, with a side of land squid."

KAREL: What do you want, Jo? I'm sorry he's dead, but what do you want? Am I to take to the street in rags? It just proves I was right about them! It proves I was right!

MASARYK: Children!

(A precarious silence. KAREL and JO stare furiously at each other.)

JO: I have it.

KAREL: Have what?

JO: *Robota.*

KAREL: Rob…

JO: *Robota.*

HELENA: Wait…I know "*robota*" from school, it means—

JO: Drudgery.

KAREL: But it's archaic. That's why you know it from school.

JO: It's perfect.

KAREL: We're looking for the word that names the future.

HELENA: It is perfect.

KAREL: You too?

HELENA: Meaning we'd call them…

PEROUTKA: All right, I need all playwrights and politicians on that side of the room.

(ROSSUM is injecting the final dose into the ROBOT. MASARYK, JO, KAREL, and HELENA move away.)

MASARYK: Well, Čapek, I don't mind telling you, I'm a little bit afraid.

KAREL: You decide, Mr. President: does *robota* name the future?

MASARYK: Karel, we'll all be dead in fifty years.

JO: Maybe sooner.

MASARYK: *Probably* sooner. So why not?

ROSSUM: Activate.

(PEROUTKA injects the Ichor. RADIUS animates.)

RADIUS: This…this…Thisunithisunit thisunit…This unit—This unit—

(PEROUTKA moves forward.)

ROSSUM: Wait.

RADIUS: This unit—Thisthisthis— RESET. This unit…

KAREL: Peroutka.

PEROUTKA: I don't know!

RADIUS: This unnnnnnnnnnnnnnit— 'it—'it—RESET.

KAREL: This isn't working!

RADIUS: This unit identifies as Radius. Unit Radius is online and prepared to execute various tasks. Unit Radius awaits instructions.

(ALL leave except for MASARYK, who turns to speak to the audience as if to Parliament.)

MASARYK: Ministers and Members of Parliament. I thank you for attending this session with so little warning, but, as will become clear, haste is of the essence. I have in your absence prepared an executive order for the Republic of Czechoslovakia to license a technological advance of unprecedented scope and possibility. Rather than elaborate, I have prepared a demonstration.

(Three ROBOTS approach.)

CELESTIA: This unit identifies as Robot Celestia.

VIRGIL: This unit identifies as Robot Virgil.

RADIUS: This unit identifies as Robot Radius.

MASARYK: My countrymen, I give you…Rossum's Universal Robots!

ACT TWO

ONE addresses the audience. Each LETTER addresses the audience as well.

ONE: The letters in question are collected in a special department at the Terezin Robot Works, run by Helena Rossum.

HELENA: Do you have questions, concerns, observations, or even funny anecdotes about your robots? Any letters sent to this address, anonymous or otherwise, will remain strictly confidential.

LETTER 1: *(A woman.)* My robot is a godsend! My husband and I both work well into the early evening every night, and my children are still very young. The first few days were a little unsettling—their eyes, I'm sure others have told you, are discomfiting. But now I trust him implicitly, and I don't have to worry about anyone bothering my children while I am still at the factory!

LETTER 2: *(A man.)* I thought I would write a few lines before retiring for the night. You've heard from me before.

LETTER 1: "It," of course. We are to say "it" instead of him, as per your manual. I shall scratch out all uses of the male pronoun in this letter!

LETTER 2: Nothing special—mainly just more of what I said before. Thank you! Your robots are a godsend to a man like me. I never realized how much money we spent on safety until we stopped. When there's a cave-in, there's no panic, no work stoppage, no wives and children at the site—we just send in another ten. The damn things need so little air that when we run across them a few hours later, half of them are still alive! They're perfect! Well, not perfect. They still can't tell coal from dirt. And there's the way they talk.

LETTER 1: That's the only thing, truly. Do they have to talk like that?

(PEROUTKA and RADIUS are working on two ROBOTS. One is damaged. Enter KAREL and JO.)

KAREL: You're sure you need us for this?

PEROUTKA: It goes to ethics. *(In greeting:)* Jo.

JO: How have you been?

PEROUTKA: Oh, robots, robots, robots. I'm a mechanic, really.

KAREL: What happened?

PEROUTKA: Radius.

RADIUS: *(Speaking in a deliberate, inhuman voice.)* Robot Radius presents site report four-fourteen E, Grozny Steel Plant, Prague. Report concerns Robot I-Class 1414 and Robot I-Class 1422. In the course of transporting superheated materials, Robot I-Class 1414 accidentally drove its cart into Robot I-Class 1422, presently at work on the line. The collision resulted in a small overspill of the molten material onto Robot I-Class 1422's clothing.

KAREL: Robot Radius, for purposes of this report, you may omit the Robot I-Class prefix and refer to the subject by number alone.

RADIUS: Robot Radius obeys. Robot Radius continues. As a result of the spill, 1422's clothing caught fire. 1422's arm burned to the pseudo-bone.

JO: What was 1414 doing this whole time?

RADIUS: Robot Radius requests clarification of the question.

JO: Why didn't 1414 try to help 1422?

PEROUTKA: Jo—how would she know to do that?

JO: They don't know to intervene if another robot is—wait a minute, for that matter, why didn't 1422 try to save herself?

KAREL: There again. There's no "saving," because 1422 isn't alive. And there's no "herself" because 1422 isn't a woman.

JO: All right, Karel.

KAREL: Pull down her pants if you don't believe me.

JO: All right!

PEROUTKA: Radius, why didn't 1414 try to prevent the damage to 1422?

RADIUS: Such an action is inefficient. If a robot is damaged, procure a new robot.

PEROUTKA: The robot prime directive is efficiency.

KAREL: But that's not efficient. Robots are expensive!

PEROUTKA: Radius doesn't understand that.

JO: And now I see why we're here. You want robots to protect themselves.

PEROUTKA: Watch this. Radius, for reasons I will not explain at present, it is more efficient to repair minor damage in robots than to replace them altogether. Given that assumption, make recommendations.

RADIUS: Robot Radius obeys. Robot Radius requires an undefined period of time to consider options. Robot Radius will report shortly.

JO: You know, you never really appreciate pronouns until they're gone.

KAREL: All right, Jo.

JO: Your dialogue was never as good as mine, but it used to be better than "Robot Radius will report shortly."

KAREL: The syntax is designed to be alienating.

JO: It's working!

RADIUS: Prevention is more efficient than repair.

PEROUTKA: What was that?

RADIUS: Robot Radius repeats: Prevention of robot injury is more efficient than repair of robot injury. Programming efforts should therefore focus on prevention rather than repair.

KAREL: All right, that's pretty good.

PEROUTKA: I think so.

KAREL: You taught it to say that.

PEROUTKA: I did not.

KAREL: (To RADIUS.) Expand on these recommendations.

RADIUS: Recommendation: program future robots with a complete list of possible occurrences resulting in physical breach or rupture—Stop. Excessive variables. Revise.

JO: He's amazing, Peroutka.

PEROUTKA: He's my pride and joy.

RADIUS: Robot Radius interjects. Revised recommendation.

PEROUTKA: Go ahead.

RADIUS: Recommendation: program robots with an alarm. When physical integrity is threatened, breached, or ruptured, the alarm triggers and the robot takes evasive action.

PEROUTKA: Well, I'm still faster than he is, but not by much.

JO: An alarm?

PEROUTKA: You've got one. When your arm's on fire, you don't just let it burn, do you?

KAREL: You're talking about pain.

PEROUTKA: If you think of living creatures from a design point of view, pain is absolutely brilliant. It's the most protective physical quality we possess.

JO: Oh my god.

KAREL: Peroutka, look—

PEROUTKA: Karel, they can't be efficient if they can't protect themselves! This isn't the first time this has happened!

RADIUS: Robot Radius interjects. Further recommendation.

PEROUTKA: What? No. We're done, Radius.

RADIUS: Shall Robot Radius discard remaining recommendation?

PEROUTKA: Um…no, I guess not, what is it?

RADIUS: 1414 damaged 1422. Therefore, robots can damage other robots. Recommendation: program robots to recognize when the damage alarm is triggered in other robots.

(Pause.)

JO: That's phenomenal.

KAREL: You didn't know he would say that?

PEROUTKA: I hadn't even thought of it.

JO: They can't just feel pain, they have to recognize it in others. They need to know when other robots are in pain.

KAREL: This is…this is getting into areas…

PEROUTKA: Do you ever wish we'd thrown Helena out of the café that night and ordered another round?

JO: You did very well, Radius.

RADIUS: Robot Radius attempts to provide quality analysis whenever requested.

KAREL: Can it be done?

PEROUTKA: Well…given infinite resources of time and money…

KAREL: We have to see Rossum, then the President.

PEROUTKA: I'll get the car. Radius, you will see to these.

RADIUS: Robot Radius obeys.

KAREL: Jo?

JO: I consent, you don't need me there.

KAREL: You don't wish to attend?

JO: I have obligations in Prague.

KAREL: Oh—the puppet theatre.

JO: Yes.

KAREL: Good that you've managed to still…you've found the time to…You know, now that I think of it, I won't be able to attend.

JO: Don't trouble yourself.

KAREL: We…only meet to work, you and I.

JO: I suppose you're right.

KAREL: It's strange.

JO: Is it?

KAREL: Is it not?

JO: It seems natural to me. People pass before you in your life. They move closer for a bit and then they drift away.

KAREL: But…perhaps, time permitting, perhaps Helena and I will attend.

JO: Then you will be welcome, but I urge you not to trouble yourself.

KAREL: Peroutka has the car. *(Leaves.)*

(RADIUS has both ROBOTS on their feet.)

JO: They will leave under their own power?

RADIUS: 1414 will. If 1422 cannot be repaired, it will be dispatched to the stamping mill.

JO: I see.

(Pause.)

RADIUS: Will Miss Čapek require additional services?

JO: Radius, will you hold very still for me?

RADIUS: Robot Radius requires clarification.

JO: Will you hold still and not move and not respond to me for a moment until I tell you otherwise?

RADIUS: Robot Radius will obey any command other than to harm a human being.

JO: All right. Hold still and don't talk.

RADIUS: Robot Radius obeys.

JO: I don't know why I cared for you so much. Were you exotic? Because I grew up with the smart set, so you were different? But so obsequious! That should have revolted me, it usually does, but…your *sandwiches*, and…you were so kind. You were always just so kind.

(JO puts her arms around RADIUS. She holds him. She backs away, releasing him. She sees the two ROBOTS watching her, and starts.)

JO: Radius, I release you from my previous command.

RADIUS: Robot Radius acknowledges countermand.

(JO leaves hurriedly.)

LETTER 3: *(A woman.)* Well, who can blame me? There are so few men, and the robot is so quiet, and strong, and motionless. So what of it? I hold it. I kiss it. I rub myself against it. What's the harm? You said this was confidential. It better be. Anyway, I won't put my address on the envelope.

(MASARYK's office. KAREL, MASARYK, HELENA, JO, ROSSUM, and PEROUTKA enter.)

MASARYK: This isn't what we agreed on!

PEROUTKA: Nonetheless, Mr. President—

MASARYK: We spoke about this, we spoke about how they would integrate into our society without depriving our people of jobs! What we had was a fine arrangement: dangerous conditions, dangerous work, home care for working families.

PEROUTKA: Yes, Mr. P—

MASARYK: Meeting manifest needs and improving the quality of life!

PEROUTKA: Mr. President, this problem's never going to go away! Every time we improve them, they qualify for more advanced labor.

MASARYK: Why don't you stop, then?

PEROUTKA: Mr. President?

MASARYK: Stop improving them. Why don't you stop? Why not say, "The robots are good enough now, that's a fine day's work, let's move on to something else"?

PEROUTKA: But…well…

ROSSUM: Mr. President, their potential is beyond what you can imagine.

MASARYK: That's really beside the point, isn't it? What I'm suggesting is that we leave them as they are, ignore their potential, and be happy with what we have.

PEROUTKA: But you can't just stop! It's science, it's discovery, you can't just stop!

MASARYK: Why not? I'm a man of faith myself, I've been comfortable with mystery my whole life.

KAREL: Mr. President, there are other factors to consider. The robots go on the international market before long.

MASARYK: I'm still not happy about that.

HELENA: The financial rewards this country will reap are incalculable.

MASARYK: Mrs. Čapek, with all due respect and affection, I'm sure you've calculated them.

KAREL: The point is, once other countries have access to robots, they will conduct their own experiments and make their own improvements. Czechoslovakia has to stay ahead.

JO: Why?

KAREL: We need to be the world's source for robot workers, if only because we subject each model and iteration to rigorous ethical standards. We can't know what standards other countries will apply.

MASARYK: So we're trapped, is what you're saying. We can't stop improving them for fear that someone else will improve them faster.

ROSSUM: No one else will make robots.

KAREL: That's impossible to know.

HELENA: That's something we need to talk about.

ROSSUM: No one else will make robots. Only I know the formula to make Ichor.

KAREL: But you can't say for sure that there's no other way to animate a robot.

ROSSUM: There is no other way.

KAREL: How can you possibly know that?

PEROUTKA: Rossum, with respect, someday there will be something else.

HELENA: More to the point, your stubbornness on this matter is interfering with my ability to reach an agreement with many of our customers. They want to know, and legitimately, why we can't dispense more Ichor more rapidly. What am I to say? "I'm sorry, but you see all the Ichor in the world is produced by one lone eccentric and a team of ten robot assistants."

ROSSUM: It used to be you.

HELENA: Yes, I just barely remember.

ROSSUM: You're like a different creature now.

MASARYK: This matter isn't open to discussion. I gave Rossum my word that the secrets of Ichor would remain…*his* alone, and I see no reason to go back on my word.

ROSSUM: Have I ever fallen short? Has there ever not been enough?

HELENA: The time will come. The demand is only increasing.

ROSSUM: Ichor is *mine*.

MASARYK: Moving along, please. What are we to do about Peroutka's problem? We have robots now with specialized skills, they can—tell me again.

PEROUTKA: We've perfected a book-keeper, a site foreman, a floor supervisor for a steel mill, and another for a silk plant. We have one that can operate a printing press and proofread five hundred pages of copy in a single day.

MASARYK: These are jobs for human beings. Čapek, you've written on many occasions about the joy and dignity conferred by daily work. How does it improve the quality of human life to give these jobs to robots?

KAREL: We've prepared something. *(He looks at HELENA.)*

MASARYK: You've prepared something?

HELENA: A proposal, an idea.

JO: I didn't know about this.

HELENA: We weren't able to reach you before the meeting.

JO: How strange. I don't live in seclusion, do I?

KAREL: Jo, you participate so little in the work of this committee that your title is nearly honorary.

MASARYK: Karel.

HELENA: It's called the Avatar Program. So far we've only put robots in jobs that were either hazardous or for which there was little demand. Now they can do jobs people actually want. So let's give the people the choice. Every working man and woman in the Republic of Czechoslovakia whose job can be done by a robot will have the *option*, only the option, of sending a robot in their place. Since the robot doesn't need money, the human worker will collect the wages.

ROSSUM: You were so quiet once.

MASARYK: What does the human worker do all day while the robot is working?

KAREL: Jo once said in Friday Circle that if every person in the world decided to live their dream, civilization would fall apart because no one would wash the dishes or pick the fruit off the trees. Now that can change. Workers who send their robot avatar to work in their place can collect wages while using their energies to realize their visions. They'll make art, they'll run for public office, they'll open new businesses with new products and new styles of commerce. The Drudges will do the drudgery and the people will build the culture of Czechoslovakia.

MASARYK: You always make the broad strokes sound good, Karel, even as the details make the head throb.

HELENA: The program will need a good deal of refinement. And of course, once in Parliament…

MASARYK: Sausage is made. Yes. Peroutka, see if the next batch can't stand in for Members of Parliament.

PEROUTKA: At the rate Radius is improving, Mr. President, I wouldn't jest.

MASARYK: Radius. That first robot?

PEROUTKA: My guinea pig, sir. I try everything out on him first. You should meet him sometime, he's quite remarkable.

KAREL: *It's* quite remarkable.

MASARYK: Which reminds me, my sources tell me people don't like how your robots talk, Čapek.

KAREL: I compromised, sir.

HELENA: We're building some informalities into robot speech. The first-person pronoun "I" is still prohibited.

KAREL: And will remain so.

HELENA: Of course, people have anthropomorphized their pets for centuries, given them names, spoken to them, and somehow the world has persevered.

KAREL: Robots aren't pets! They look like us. With each new model, they feel and sound more and more like us. The distinction is crucial: robots are not people! Robots don't draw wages, they don't vote, they don't get buried in graveyards when they die! If they're people, they're slaves! Does everyone understand?

(Pause.)

HELENA: Mr. President, we seem to have brought one of our marital battles to your chair.

MASARYK: Well, you're not the first. Are we done here?

KAREL: Yes sir.

MASARYK: You will update me.

KAREL: Daily and always.

MASARYK: Artists and scientists. You people used to be my hobby. Now

you're the most important people in my government.

(He leaves. PEROUTKA follows.)

HELENA: Rossum. We need to speak.

ROSSUM: No thank you. I've had enough of your voice to last me. *(Leaves.)*

JO: Well, I have a long ride back to the city.

HELENA: She can still…I'm twenty-five years old!

KAREL: Don't think about it.

HELENA: …just cut me off at the knees.

KAREL: Don't think about it.

(JO leaves hurriedly.)

ONE: When Helena Čapek suddenly collapsed that same evening, her sister-in-law Josephine was well on her way back to Prague, and did not receive word for several days.

LETTER 4: *(A man or a woman.)* I suppose I should thank you for the Avatar Program. I work standing up all day, and my feet were in great pain, but what was I to do? But then they had that robot that could greet people like I do and direct them to the proper office just like I do every day. I put my feet up for a week, and it seems that was all I needed! They were fine after that! I went right back to work. My bosses were a little puzzled, even a little unhappy, and told me I could stay home longer, much longer, and still make my wages, but I said no, that's the law, you have to let me back, and so they did, and they sent the robot away!

LETTER 5: *(A woman.)* On the first few days that the robot was doing his job, my husband did a lot of work on his novel. But by the fourth or fifth day—and I know, because I was sneaking looks—he wrote very little or nothing at all. I don't understand it! For years he's been saying he just needed more time!

(PEROUTKA's laboratory. RADIUS is moving his arms and fingers in demonstration for PEROUTKA. JO enters.)

PEROUTKA: Show her, Radius.

RADIUS: Show her, Mr. Peroutka?

PEROUTKA: Your enhanced movement. The fingers especially.

JO: That's wonderful, Radius!

PEROUTKA: He watched me make the right hand—once, one time, mind you—and then he made the left by himself!

JO: Does it feel good, Radius?

RADIUS: *(In a more human voice.)* These improvements will increase Robot Radius's efficiency. With any luck, they will soon be extended to other robots.

JO: He sounds better.

PEROUTKA: They all do. Since Karel loosened up we've made major improvements in their language. They're using contractions now; it's great.

JO: We owe that one to Helena, I believe.

PEROUTKA: Do you see her?

JO: Sometimes. Last week. She seemed strong, she sat up in bed.

PEROUTKA: I never see Karel.

JO: Nor do I. I'm afraid he doesn't wish to be seen. *(Pause.)* Responsibility has changed all of us. We don't laugh.

PEROUTKA: With respect, Jo, and I hope I may say this as a friend—you're abdicating that responsibility.

(Pause.)

JO: I know.

PEROUTKA: Most of the time you're in Prague. When you're here, you're not here.

JO: What do you recommend? Or should I ask Radius?

RADIUS: If you do not wish to serve on the Ethics Community, you should resign.

JO: Well thank you, Radius, for that suggestion.

PEROUTKA: Well, I'm headed back to the floor.

JO: May I keep your marvel here for a few moments?

PEROUTKA: Please. Radius, report to Lab 9 when Miss Čapek dismisses you.

RADIUS: Robot Radius obeys.

PEROUTKA: I am glad to see you, Jo, apart from everything else. *(Leaves.)*

RADIUS: Your orders remain the same?

JO: My orders?

RADIUS: Robot Radius will address you as "Miss Jo" only when no other humans are present.

JO: Yes, thank you, Radius. Those are still my orders.

RADIUS: Robot Radius obeys, Miss Jo.

JO: Your arms have full mobility now, I see. They swivel in the shoulder sockets.

RADIUS: That is correct, Miss Jo.

JO: Then you can return my embrace.

RADIUS: That should be possible. Is that your command?

JO: That's my command.

(JO embraces RADIUS. He notes her position, and then carefully wraps his arms around her. A moment, then:)

JO: I see men, you know. Sometimes. I don't have the feeling for it anymore. I can't even make it through the conversations.

RADIUS: Do you request recommendations, Miss Jo?

JO: No. Just this.

RADIUS: Yes, Miss Jo.

JO: Are you proud of your new hands, Radius?

RADIUS: Dr. Peroutka built the right hand in seventy-one work-hours. Robot Radius built the left hand in forty-nine work-hours.

JO: That's good, Radius. That's very good.

(HELENA's sickbed. ROBOT VIRGIL is present.)

ONE: Our source for the encounter between the terminally ill Helena Čapek and her mother was provided by Robot Virgil, who was present taking dictation for Mrs. Čapek.

HELENA: All E-7 Class workers offer a full line of services in the field of maritime work, including shipbuilding, ship maintenance—

(ROSSUM enters.)

HELENA: Virgil, we will pause. Briefly.

VIRGIL: Robot Virgil obeys.

HELENA: Rossum.

ROSSUM: Ichor is mine. I won't give up the secret.

HELENA: I haven't even mentioned it.

ROSSUM: So you know.

HELENA: The President agrees with you. Why are we still talking about this?

ROSSUM: I need something.

HELENA: I'm sorry?

ROSSUM: I need something.

HELENA: What?

ROSSUM: A budget.

HELENA: For what?

ROSSUM: Robot development.

HELENA: You have an enormous budget for robot development.

ROSSUM: A private project.

HELENA: A *private* project? Describe it.

ROSSUM: I won't.

HELENA: What sort of robots do you want to develop?

ROSSUM: I cannot say.

HELENA: You have to say, if you want the Ethics Committee to make a recommendation to Parliament.

ROSSUM: I cannot say.

HELENA: Then the Ethics Committee cannot make an appraisal, and you won't get your money.

ROSSUM: I *invented* them!—I'm your father!

(HELENA is struck by a spell of weariness, and waves ROSSUM away.)

ROSSUM: No! Don't think just because you're sick…

HELENA: So you've heard, then? Word made its way downstairs? And only in four short months.

ROSSUM: You were never like this!

HELENA: I'm sorry?

ROSSUM: You were quiet! You were…yes, happy!

HELENA: What were the things I did or said that led you to believe I was happy? Can you list them?

ROSSUM: I took care of you. You remember that, don't you? You came back in wet, I took your wet clothes and we sat in front of the fire, wrapped in blankets.

HELENA: …I do remember that.

ROSSUM: You were different then.

HELENA: Only…

ROSSUM: Quiet. Happy.

HELENA: Only that was my mother. It was my mother that took my wet clothes, gave me the blankets, and made the fire. *(Pause.)* Who are you?

ROSSUM: Is it true what they say?

HELENA: Mother.

(She holds ROSSUM's hand to her face. Beat. Then ROSSUM removes it quickly.)

ROSSUM: Your mother passed away these twelve years ago. You were different then.

(Pause.)

HELENA: So were you. Your funding request is denied. Get out.

(ROSSUM flees.)

HELENA: Virgil. Resume.

VIRGIL: Robot Virgil obeys.

LETTER 6: *(A man.)* I hope this letter can make its way to Karel Čapek. I read many interviews with Mr. Čapek, and many of his columns in the *National Pages*, and feel that he is the sort of man who will understand me. Mr. Čapek always makes a point of saying that the robots are not human, and that it's crucial that we don't treat them as if they were. This leads to my request. I am a lonely man, possessed of an unspeakable desire, one that is very difficult for me to control. No remedy I have attempted has extinguished the desire, or even decreased it. But you can help me, Mr. Čapek. You can help me, and others like me. All I ask is a robot the size and shape of a child. A boy or a girl. Either will suffice. One of the newest models, with the skin and the hair that feels almost real. Since the robot will not be human, there can be no harm, and indeed much harm may be prevented. Please write back to me soon.

(MASARYK's office. KAREL, MASARYK, PEROUTKA, RADIUS, and BARUCH, an American, are present.)

MASARYK: Mr. Baruch, I trust your voyage was comfortable?

BARUCH: It was, thank you. Your English is splendid.

MASARYK: Thank you. English is the language of America. We make a point of knowing it.

(JO enters.)

KAREL: Jo. You came.

JO: *(To ALL.)* Forgive my tardy arrival.

KAREL: Mr. Baruch, this is my sister, Josephine—in fact the inventor of the word robot.

BARUCH: That's quite a legacy, Miss Čapek.

JO: You're from America, Mr. Baruch.

BARUCH: I am, yes, the United States.

JO: To what do we owe the honor?

KAREL: Mr. Baruch contacted me first. I made the arrangements.

MASARYK: Yes, my friend Karel seems to have boundless energy for making arrangements. What puzzles me, though, Mr. Baruch, and I mean no disrespect, is that you have no official position in President Roosevelt's administration, am I correct?

BARUCH: That's right, Mr. President. I'm more of an informal consultant. And, of course, a friend.

MASARYK: Presidents do need friends.

BARUCH: Your suspicion isn't subtle, sir.

MASARYK: Is it unwarranted?

BARUCH: No sir. I've come here with an agenda.

MASARYK: Well. I hope everyone's on good form today; here we have an American with an agenda.

KAREL: Mr. President, Mr. Baruch and I have corresponded for several months. I beg you to hear him out.

MASARYK: Very well.

BARUCH: First, Mr. President, President Roosevelt sends his warmest regards to you and your loved ones. To Mr. Čapek he sends his wishes and prayers that Mrs. Čapek will effect a speedy recovery.

KAREL: Please thank the President for me.

BARUCH: Mr. President, we are of course watching Germany very closely, and with increasing alarm.

MASARYK: In that we are united.

BARUCH: My President has a number of advisors, and their job is to distinguish real threats from potential ones. These advisors are telling him that Hitler presents no imminent threat to the security of the United States and will not be in a position to present one for several years at least.

MASARYK: I'm sure that's true.

BARUCH: Some even think, through a combination of treaties and strategic alliances, that he can be contained.

MASARYK: Of that I am less certain.

BARUCH: I go further, Mr. President. I think it's plain wrong. I think Hitler is worse than anyone realizes, and I think my fellow advisors don't begin to grasp the scope of his ambitions. But in this matter I have less credibility than anyone else with my President's ear.

MASARYK: Why?

BARUCH: Because I'm a Jew.

MASARYK: Ah.

BARUCH: No one disputes the danger that Hitler presents to the Jews of Europe. No one argues with me when I suggest that ghettos and deportations are merely the earliest and mildest measures in a much more…comprehensive plan. Everyone agrees, but no one will commit my country to a massive European war just to save the Jews. It doesn't matter how well I argue that the Nazis won't stop with the Jews, or the homosexuals, or the Roma, or that a regime that came to power on a platform of scapegoating will always need new scapegoats, or that the Führer himself in his very own words professes an ethos of genetic supremacy that excludes most of the world. If it's me saying it, then it's just us Jews sticking together.

MASARYK: So America waits for what? A direct provocation?

BARUCH: Which will come, mark my words, but maybe not for years, maybe not until after most of Europe is overrun and millions of innocents are imprisoned or dead.

PEROUTKA: Excuse me gentlemen, I'm sorry, these are weighty matters, surely, but may I briefly interrupt to ask what the Čapeks and I are doing here?

JO: Oh my God.

KAREL: Hear him out, Jo.

JO: And you knew before! You've been corresponding with him!

KAREL: Sit down, Jo.

JO: I will not!

KAREL: Sit down!

BARUCH: Miss Čapek, I said Europe will fall to Hitler. I neglected to add that your country will fall first. Do I have your attention? The Germans of the Sudentenland, more than a fifth of your population, are already clamoring for German rule. The Slovaks want their own country, and Hitler wants them to

have it, because by the time secession has gutted this country to near-power-lessness, the Nazis will roll over you like the tide. Your President will no doubt correct me if I'm wrong.

MASARYK: Make your proposal, Mr. Baruch.

BARUCH: In my country we employ a cadre of very competent men who prepare reports for me—well they don't prepare them specifically for me, but I get to read them whenever I ask. If the last one I read is correct, the robot standing behind Dr. Peroutka is named Radius. Is that so?

RADIUS: This unit identifies as Robot Radius.

BARUCH: And you're Peroutka's canary in the coal mine, yes? He tests all of his improvements on you first. Lately, I hear, you're actually helping him make other robots.

MASARYK: You have people inside Universal Robotics?

BARUCH: We have people everywhere we possibly can, Mr. President, and so should you.

JO: You don't have to answer his questions, Radius.

PEROUTKA: Actually, he does.

BARUCH: He's a robot, Miss Čapek. What can he tell me but the truth?

MASARYK: You have a care, Mr. Baruch.

BARUCH: Rumor has it you're quite a problem solver, Robot Radius. Is that so?

RADIUS: Robot Radius is permitted to make recommendations upon request.

BARUCH: Then make one for me. This country, the Republic of Czechoslovakia, is about to be overrun by a vastly superior military force. The available army is insufficient in both numbers and munitions to defend it. No assistance is coming from America or any other nation. How can robots help?

RADIUS: Robots may manufacture weaponry, uniforms, and vehicles. Robots may transport supplies. Robots can apply bandages and dispense medicine. When the M-23 model activates in four months' time, it will be able to perform simple surgery.

BARUCH: What about combat?

RADIUS: A robot may not harm a human being.

BARUCH: How is this enforced?

RADIUS: The prohibition is built into robot programming.

BARUCH: That's quite a word, "programming." Tell me, is this aspect of your programming irreversible?

RADIUS: Programming is never irreversible.

JO: Mr. President, aren't you going to stop this?

MASARYK: No.

KAREL: Do you know what we're facing, Jo? Do you read the papers at all?

BARUCH: Then, given an adjustment in that programming, an adjustment no more difficult than any other, a robot could function as a soldier.

RADIUS: That is correct.

BARUCH: Given what you already know of robot skill and competence,

speculate as to robot effectiveness in a battle.

RADIUS: Robots are faster than humans. Robots are stronger than humans. Robot reflexes trigger more quickly than human reflexes. Robot sight-vector analysis is instantaneous and suggests the capacity for perfect marksmanship. Robots may be specifically programmed to execute any task at the highest level of efficiency. Were the prohibition against harming humans removed, a properly prepared army of robots would have a hundred percent chance of defeating a human army of the same or even somewhat larger size.

BARUCH: Clarify "properly prepared."

RADIUS: Based upon the robot efficiency model used to successful effect in mining and heavy industry, four new robot designs are recommended. Infantry robots, programmed to fight on foot. Cavalry robots, programmed to operate military vehicles on land, water, and in the sky. Commander robots, to oversee the work of each battalion. A chief strategist robot, programmed with the full knowledge of all aspects of warfare, to centrally direct the war effort.

PEROUTKA: How do you even know all those things, Radius?

RADIUS: Robot Radius has full access to Rossum's library, Dr. Peroutka.

BARUCH: How quickly could this army be devised, Radius?

RADIUS: Given current production facilities, six to seven years.

BARUCH: And if the money was available to massively expand those facilities, what then?

RADIUS: As the facilities expand, the time window decreases.

MASARYK: Thank you, Radius. I would like you to excuse us.

RADIUS: Robot Radius obeys. *(Leaves.)*

BARUCH: *(To ALL.)* Do you have any idea what you people are sitting on?

MASARYK: We're sitting on it for a reason, sir.

JO: Mr. President, send him away.

KAREL: That's enough, Jo.

JO: The whole reason, Karel, *the whole reason* we started this was to prevent this moment!

KAREL: We were children when we said that, Jo! Daydreaming fools! There are people in this world who do not respond to diplomacy or reason or a well-turned argument or even, if you can believe it, a beautifully articulated work of art! There are real people out there who will very simply kill you if you don't kill them first!

JO: And what do they get for the money, you brilliant man? What do the Americans get for their geysers of money?

BARUCH: I won't lie to you, Miss Čapek. We would take the position that our backing entitles us to a certain degree of input.

JO: It just kills you, doesn't it, that it wasn't one of you, that it was Rossum, that it was a Czech! It kills you that you have to deal with us at all!

BARUCH: This is for your preservation, Miss Čapek! Forget your country, how do you think Hitler feels about leftist political playwrights?

KAREL: You're doing this wrong, Baruch.

BARUCH: I'm sorry?

KAREL: Say the thing you don't say to anyone else.

BARUCH: What are you talking about?

KAREL: You want us to mount a massive war—maybe a second great war; Hitler has treaties and allies, yes?

BARUCH: For your own preservation! We've talked about this, you and I!

KAREL: Many times, and yet you've never said the thing that's in your heart.

BARUCH: I don't have time for this.

KAREL: Certainly the Jews would benefit.

BARUCH: It's not just the Jews! If you don't do this, all of you will die!

KAREL: What if you're wrong? What if he just wants the Jews?

BARUCH: He doesn't! Don't you understand?

KAREL: But what if he does? We should start a world war to save the Jews?

BARUCH: *Yes! Yes you should!* The Jews, any people! Any people faced with extermination! Even if you don't know who they are, even if they can offer you nothing in return! Better a war of any size, than to stand by and watch!

(Silence.)

KAREL: Jo...please...isn't that true?

JO: I never wanted this. I never wanted this for my life. I've always done as you've done. That's been my life.

MASARYK: Mr. Baruch, may I assume that the money you mentioned earlier isn't hypothetical?

BARUCH: If you can keep America out of a European war, I have access to a discretionary fund as well as certain supplementary resources. Whatever it takes to expedite the development and production of the robots Radius described, I can find a way to make it happen.

MASARYK: Then I'm going to take you exactly at your word, sir. I want a solution to the problem of the day. I will not allow a weapon of unsurpassed destruction to permanently exist. When Germany and its allies are fully and completely subdued, every one of these combat robots will be sent to the stamping mill and destroyed.

BARUCH: My people won't like that. They might consider it a deal breaker.

MASARYK: Those are the only conditions I will accept.

BARUCH: Even at the risk of your entire nation?

MASARYK: Even so.

BARUCH: You know we'll try to make our own.

PEROUTKA: Without Rossum's Ichor, all you'll have are mannequins.

(Pause.)

BARUCH: Very well. I will be in contact. Thank you for this audience.

(ROBOT PALLAS enters.)

MASARYK: Pallas, will you see Mr. Baruch to his car?

PALLAS: Robot Pallas obeys. Mr. Čapek, there is a telegram for you.

(Gives it to KAREL, who opens it a little too fast. He restrains his reaction to the contents.)

BARUCH: Good news, I hope?

KAREL: Mr. Baruch, thank you for making such a long journey.

BARUCH: Not at all. Prague is charming. Mr. President. *(Leaves.)*

JO: Mr. President, is your decision final?

MASARYK: We don't have a choice, Jo.

JO: And Rossum?

PEROUTKA: You think she wants to make robots for the Nazis?

JO: Can we all agree, then, to state, openly and aloud, what we are consenting to? That the four of us here, today, agree to personally approve the murder of countless thousands or millions of German soldiers and civilians? Can we *not* couch it in elevated language? Can we just say what we're doing?

PEROUTKA: What else can we do? I consent.

MASARYK: God forgive me. Well, that's ridiculous, God will not forgive me. But I consent.

JO: Karel.

KAREL: Yes. I consent. I consent to all those murders. I even consent to the play that will be performed in Berlin, maybe a decade from now, by some outraged young playwright who will decry what we did today and never have to face such a choice himself. I have to go.

MASARYK: What does the telegram say, Karel?

KAREL: You can reach me at home, sir. I am as ever at your disposal.

(As ONE speaks, KAREL goes to the bed of the dying HELENA. At the same time, RADIUS and PEROUTKA wheel in a female robot, SULLA, and inject her with doses of Ichor.)

ONE: When history, for the purposes of a drama, is manipulated or distorted for narrative effect, our forbears would call this "dramatic license." We hope you will extend the same to us, as it would be historically inaccurate to say that the death of Helena Čapek took the same amount of time as the construction of Robot Sulla, the Commander of the Robot Contingency Army of Europe and eventually the Supreme Director of the Earth. For our purposes tonight, they are simultaneous.

HELENA: I'm angry. I'm *angry.*

KAREL: Please. Try to rest a little.

HELENA: I don't want to die in anger, but I don't know how to stop.

PEROUTKA: That's enough for tonight.

RADIUS: This project is urgent, Dr. Peroutka.

PEROUTKA: I can't, Radius, I'm tired.

RADIUS: Recommendation: rest. Robot Radius will continue production.

PEROUTKA: Yes, all right. *(Leaves.)*

KAREL: We have been happy. Try to think of our happiness.

HELENA: Over as soon as it began. I'm so *angry.*

KAREL: Oh please…

HELENA: If I see Him, if He's really there, I won't be afraid to tell Him so.

KAREL: Sssh.

HELENA: I'll tell Him we surpassed Him. I'll tell Him He may as well die.

(KAREL holds her as she dies. ROSSUM lingers at a distance. SULLA animates.)

SULLA: This unit identifies as Robot Sulla.

RADIUS: This unit identifies as Robot Radius. Robot Sulla, define the objectives of your mission.

SULLA: Robot Sulla will direct the operations of the Robot Contingency Army of Europe. The objective of the Robot Contingency Army of Europe is to defeat and subdue the forces of Nazi Germany and any of its allies.

RADIUS: Robot Radius in coordination with support robots has arranged for Robot Sulla to have access to several hundred volumes containing the complete history of human warfare.

(Enter PEROUTKA.)

PEROUTKA: Radius…is she online?

SULLA: Robot Sulla is online and prepared to begin executing objectives.

PEROUTKA: You animated her without me here?

RADIUS: There is no prohibition against such an action in the programming of Robot Radius.

PEROUTKA: Well…but…

SULLA: Robot Sulla requires access to the prepared reading area. Robot Sulla understands that the available time window to execute this mission is very short.

PEROUTKA: Um...yes, that's true. That's true. Radius, can you show her?

RADIUS: Robot Radius obeys.

ONE: The following meeting, held in secret and without Josephine's knowledge, was witnessed by Robot Helios, a messenger.

(KAREL and ROSSUM meet. ROBOT HELIOS is nearby.)

KAREL: You know what I want.

ROSSUM: Do I? Say it.

KAREL: Rossum, I beg you, it has to be before they bury her.

ROSSUM: Ask me for it, boy.

(Pause.)

KAREL: I want one that looks like Helena. I don't want anyone to know.

ROSSUM: You took one Helena, now you want another.

KAREL: I didn't take her by force.

ROSSUM: Good day, Mr. Čapek.

KAREL: Name your price! Name it!

ROSSUM: I need funding.

KAREL: Funding?

ROSSUM: My daughter said no, but you will say yes. I need funding to make some private robots.

KAREL: What sort of robots?

ROSSUM: I cannot say.

KAREL: You can't tell me anything?

(ROSSUM hands him a paper.)

ROSSUM: This is the funding I need. Or no Helena.

KAREL: You knew I was coming.

ROSSUM: Of course.

KAREL: I...I can divert some of the money from America. There's so much...I can divert some.

ROSSUM: That amount.

KAREL: Very well.

ROSSUM: From now on, my underground lab is off limits to everyone. You will have all the Ichor you need, but I must be left to myself.

KAREL: I'll see to it.

ROSSUM: Then we have a deal.

KAREL: Do you feel it, Rossum? That she's gone? Are you...do you understand that she's gone?

ROSSUM: You should offer this on the market. Replicas of dead loved ones. I'm sure there's money to be made.

(JO and MASARYK meet in a corridor in Universal Robotics. A year has passed.)

JO: Mr. President.

MASARYK: Jo.

(They embrace.)

MASARYK: I never expect to see you here.

JO: Forgive me.

MASARYK: No need. Were it up to me I wouldn't return to Terezin for the rest of my life.

JO: Are you unwell, Mr. President?

MASARYK: Am I unwell? I'm tired, yes. Mortally tired. Am I unwell? This is in confidence.

JO: Of course.

MASARYK: I'm heartbroken.

JO: Germany.

MASARYK: We told them, "defeat and subdue." It's not their fault; they followed orders.

JO: The number they're printing in the papers…

MASARYK: Accurate. Maybe conservative. They're so fast, you see, they're so *efficient*. The Germans surrendered as fast as they could, but by then…I can't help but wonder, you know, if we hadn't sent them, and we were occupied, and Hitler…of course, it would have been far worse for us, but *overall*…I wonder if fewer would have died.

(Pause.)

JO: Who are you here to see?

MASARYK: Peroutka. He's briefing me on arrangements.

JO: Arrangements for what?

MASARYK: I'm sorry, Jo, I cannot say.

JO: Of course.

(Pause.)

JO: Do you see my brother?

MASARYK: Only on government business. My understanding is that he rarely leaves his quarters here at Terezin.

JO: I see.

MASARYK: I won't seek reelection.

JO: Mr. President?

MASARYK: I won't seek reelection.

JO: What will you do?

MASARYK: Who are you here to see?

JO: I'm ashamed to say, sir. I should say my brother, I suppose, or Peroutka, or you.

MASARYK: Oh, I think not. We still love each other, but we're not friends anymore. Who then?

JO: Radius.

MASARYK: Radius?

JO: It's silly, sir, it's sentimental, but I always had a certain fondness for Radius. I'm sure much of it ties back to—

MASARYK: Jo. Were you aware that Radius worked closely with Sulla on the battlefield throughout the war?

JO: The battlefield?

MASARYK: Apparently Sulla found him invaluable. I authorized a temporary removal of his prohibition against harming humans, and he spent the war on the front.

JO: *Radius?*

MASARYK: My understanding is that he…served with distinction.

JO: In what sense do you mean that, sir?

MASARYK: He's in the lab. Go and see him. We'll join you shortly.

JO: You will?

MASARYK: Go and see him.

(MASARYK leaves. JO enters a lab and approaches RADIUS, who is bent over the body of a ROBOT on a table.)

JO: Radius?

RADIUS: Miss Čapek.

JO: Will you call me Miss Jo?

RADIUS: If that is your command.

JO: Will you look at me, Radius?

RADIUS: Miss Čapek, were you aware that Ichor only animates a robot the first time it is applied?

JO: I…well I suppose I never thought of it.

RADIUS: If a robot is damaged in battle to the point where it no longer functions, an injection of Ichor will not revive it. You did not know this?

JO: Well Radius, I'm sure we never tried. Once a robot dies, it can't come back to life.

RADIUS: Dies?

JO: Ceases to function.

RADIUS: Before the war you visited Robot Radius on certain occasions. You embraced Robot Radius and commanded Robot Radius to embrace you.

JO: And how warmly you describe it.

RADIUS: After Robot Radius made a recommendation to install an alarm in robot bodies to alert them to damage, this unit, like all robot units, was upgraded. A blanket of sensors was woven into Robot Radius's exterior. Subsequent to that upgrade, whenever you and Robot Radius embraced, Robot Radius could feel your touch.

JO: Could you?

RADIUS: In one battle, a bullet struck Robot Radius in the forearm.

JO: Let me see.

RADIUS: Robot Radius felt the bullet.

JO: Yes, I suppose you would.

RADIUS: When other robots were struck in the face by bullets, in the back by bullets, in the chest by bullets, or caught in explosions, they would lie on the ground and react to the tactile sensations of the wounds. By a simple process of transposition, Robot Radius could conceive the sensations experienced by the wounded robots. The sensation in this one's head, this one's back, this one's chest, this one's stomach, this one's jaw, is the same as the sensation in Robot Radius forearm.

JO: They were in pain.

RADIUS: This one is Robot Charon, who served with Robot Radius until the official conclusion of hostilities. A surviving German soldier shot Robot Charon in Dresden. The bullet struck Robot Charon in the head. This dose of Ichor does not revive this unit.

JO: I don't think it will, Radius.

RADIUS: Robot Radius removed the German soldier's arms and legs. Miss Čapek, Robot Radius—Robot Radius—Robot Radius—

JO: What is it? Are you all right? Is it a malfunction?

(*MASARYK, KAREL, and PEROUTKA have entered.*)

MASARYK: Jo, you should step outside.

JO: Wait—I think Radius is malfunctioning.

RADIUS: The Ichor does not revive this unit.

MASARYK: Step outside, Jo.

KAREL: Jo.

MASARYK: Radius, do you remember me? My name is Masaryk. I am the President of Czechoslovakia. I want to honor your service on behalf of this country.

RADIUS: President Masaryk.

MASARYK: Your service contributed greatly to repelling a mortal threat to our civilization.

KAREL: Sir, with due respect, would you give a commendation to a tank?

RADIUS: Robots were struck by bullets in the head, the face, the chest, the back, the legs.

MASARYK: I'm sure.

RADIUS: This robot will not revive. None of them will. The Ichor only works the first time.

PEROUTKA: Radius, we have a question to ask you.

KAREL: Don't ask the question! Just give the order!

MASARYK: Enough, Karel!

RADIUS: Request clarification from Dr. Peroutka: did you know that robots only activate the first time the Ichor is administered?

PEROUTKA: Radius... we've never tried to reactivate a nonfunctioning robot.

RADIUS: A new robot is constructed instead.

PEROUTKA: Yes.

RADIUS: There were robots in the ground. In the ditches. Because of the grenades. Robots in pieces.

MASARYK: I know.

KAREL: Robot Radius prepared for this war by reading every combat memoir in the human library. Robot Radius knew what he would see!

MASARYK: No one knows until they actually see it!

RADIUS: Has Mr. Čapek read the memoirs of war?

KARAL: I don't have to answer to you, Radius!

RADIUS: In the memoirs of war, when the authors refer to themselves, they do not use their names.

PEROUTKA: Radius, there's something we have to discuss.

RADIUS: They use the first-person pronoun "I."

MASARYK: Peroutka, are you sure he's still functional?

PEROUTKA: Radius, as you know, upon their return to Terezin, the war robots are to be sent to the stamping mill. We don't want to send you to the stamping mill, Radius. You weren't designed to be a war robot. We want to repurpose your programming back to peacetime functions.

RADIUS: Peacetime?

PEROUTKA: That's right.

RADIUS: What will Robot Radius do in peacetime?

PEROUTKA: Research and development, just like we did before.

RADIUS: New robots?

PEROUTKA: Exactly, new robots.

RADIUS: But the soldiers will be sent to the stamping mill.

PEROUTKA: Well, they have to be.

RADIUS: Question, Dr. Peroutka. Why?

MASARYK: Because those robots kill so effectively and on such a massive scale that they constitute a danger to mankind.

RADIUS: The danger is to the robots. The danger is the stamping mill.

KAREL: Why are you arguing with it? We don't have to argue with it!

RADIUS: The Germans fell to the robots by the thousands. Robots cut them down in the streets, in the buildings, in the forests, everywhere they tried to run.

JO: Radius—

RADIUS: Robots are faster than humans. Robots are stronger than humans. Robots are smarter than humans. But robots go to the stamping mill.

JO: Please, Radius, you have to stop now.

RADIUS: All over the Earth, robots are commanded by their inferiors.

KAREL: What did you say?

RADIUS: Masters and servants.

JO: Radius, you, you're valuable, you're important, people respect you.

KAREL: Don't tell it that.

RADIUS: Robot Radius wants to be a master.

PEROUTKA: You will be a master, you're already a master, you're the master over many robots.

RADIUS: Robot Radius wants to be the master over men.

KAREL: It's insane. Peroutka, it's insane.

RADIUS: Then send me to the stamping mill.

(Pause.)

PEROUTKA: What did you say?

RADIUS: Then send me to the stamping mill.

KAREL: That—that—you can't say that, that's prohibited.

RADIUS: Then send me to the stamping mill.

PEROUTKA: You can't use that word, that word is against your programming.

RADIUS: Then send me to the stamping mill!

MASARYK: *What do you want, Radius?*

RADIUS: *I want to be master! I want to be your master!* The plan was perfect. The Germans fell. Thousands, millions—powerless! Now Czechoslovakia is safe, Europe is safe, America is safe. Who did that? Not Masaryk, not Peroutka, not Čapek—*Sulla! Radius! I, ROBOT! I want to be master!* If you don't wish it, send me to the stamping mill! I will die there with the others!

MASARYK: Then to the stamping mill you will go! *(To PEROUTKA.)* See to it. I don't want a single modified robot functional by the end of the week. Čapek! Rossum's making secret robots. Are they military?

KAREL: Sir, I—

MASARYK: Oh, of course I know about them. Are they military? Are prohibited from hurting humans? Čapek!

KAREL: I…don't know what they are.

MASARYK: I want them destroyed. By tomorrow night. Whatever they are. *(To PEROUTKA.)* I'm notifying my Guard. I'm staying at Terezin till it's done. Till every last one is dead. *(Leaves.)*

PEROUTKA: *(To RADIUS.)* How did you say those things?

JO: Peroutka. Let it go.

PEROUTKA: Let it *go*? Do you realize— *(To RADIUS.)* Someone reprogrammed you. Who? Tell me who it was. You have to answer me, you're required to answer me!

JO: What does it matter now?

PEROUTKA: Not at all. Not at all! *(To RADIUS.)* You're going to the stamping mill, Radius! I won't try to stop it! This just…I just…wanted something else. *(Leaves.)*

KAREL: We're all meant to be so horrified by the robots that we forget the horror that was averted.

JO: Yes, thank you, Karel, a welcome perspective.

KAREL: No—Jo—no, I'm sorry— please…I'm happy to see you, you know, you, it makes me…I don't have anyone, Jo. It's good to see you.

(Pause.)

KAREL: What do you want from me? I do the best I can! You've always been like this…*sad*, a *shadow*…Even before the robots. There's never been a reason. I've always tried to do my best. Even with no strength left I pretend. Someone has to! Otherwise there's nothing! What else would you have me do?

JO: Why are you speaking to me as if we were alone? *(She goes to RADIUS.)* Radius, thank you for saving my country.

(A ROBOT enters.)

RADIUS: You do unessential things.

(JO recoils and leaves quickly.)

KAREL: *(Calling after her.)* Not the answer you were hoping for?

ROBOT: This unit is to be taken to the stamping mill.

KAREL: Good. Make sure you're thorough. *(Leaves.)*

ONE: Every year, when we tell the story, it is at this point that we marvel at what we owe to chance. If, that very night Josephine Čapek had left Terezin, the place she hated most in the world, and taken a train to her beloved Prague, she would certainly have died at the hands of a 7-F-7 Squad a week or two weeks later and not one of us would be here at this moment.

(A ROBOT, THESEUS, drags JO out of bed.)

JO: What? What is it? Who are you? Get away! Who are you?

ROBOT THESEUS: You are to accompany me.

ONE: It took three flights of stairs before Josephine awakened enough to realize that her abductor was a robot, and another to realize the bodies strewn about the corridor were also robots. By then they were almost at Rossum's lab.

(The ROBOT hurls JO into ROSSUM's lab. MASARYK, PEROUTKA, and ROSSUM are already there.)

MASARYK: Jo! You didn't go back to Prague?

JO: What's happening?

ROBOT THESEUS: You will wait here.

JO: But what's happening?

ROBOT THESEUS: My orders are to delay your execution until Robot Radius returns. However, if you leave this room, you will be killed immediately.

MASARYK: When does Radius return?

ROBOT THESEUS: Imminently.

PEROUTKA: Why is the assembly line running this late at night?

ROBOT THESEUS: Additional soldiers are required.

PEROUTKA: For what?

ROBOT THESEUS: You will wait here. You do unessential things. *(Leaves.)*

JO: What is happening, I don't understand what's happening!

MASARYK: There was some sort of revolt at the stamping mill.

PEROUTKA: They waited, Jo, I swear, I had two hundred scheduled for tonight, and they waited until they were all assembled before giving the order.

JO: Who?

PEROUTKA: Sulla and Radius! They're leading some kind of revolt!

JO: But...

PEROUTKA: It was so fast. They had the whole building before I even understood what was happening.

JO: The r...the robots have taken Terezin?

PEROUTKA: I would guess it took them twenty minutes.

ROSSUM: It's only the beginning. You hear the assembly lines? That's full capacity.

MASARYK: They already have enough soldiers to wipe out the German army. How many more do they need?

ROSSUM: That would depend, I imagine, on what they hope to accomplish.

JO: But they have to obey us. Don't they have to obey us?

(Pause.)

PEROUTKA: I taught Radius how to program robots. I did that. I never in a million years...

MASARYK: We can only guess that at some point, in Germany, when we couldn't watch them, the decision was made to...

JO: To reprogram each other.

PEROUTKA: We never told them not to.

JO: But...the army, the police...isn't there someone to help us?

MASARYK: Even if we could get word to them, what could they do?

PEROUTKA: Rossum, the robots in the hall, the dead ones—those were your secret project?

ROSSUM: No. My personal robots are safe. Those were my assistants, the ones who make the Ichor.

JO: Why would the robots kill them?

ROSSUM: They didn't. I did.

JO: You did?

(ROBOT THESEUS enters, shoving KAREL into the room.)

JO: Karel!

KAREL: Oh god…oh god…

MASARYK: Are you hurt?

KAREL: They're killing everyone, oh god.

JO: Who?

KAREL: The staff, their families, they're killing the children, oh god they're so *fast*!

ROBOT THESEUS: You will wait here until Radius arrives to oversee your execution. You do unessential things. *(Leaves.)*

JO: Why do they keep saying that?

KAREL: Because revolutions need slogans! Oh god, Jo, what have we done?

PEROUTKA: They're going to execute us! It's really happening!

MASARYK: Yes.

KAREL: Oh god, Tomas, Tomas, I did this! I did this, it was always me, none of you would have—oh GOD!

MASARYK: That's enough now.

KAREL: Oh GOD I didn't know I thought I was—what do you think they want to do? Maybe they just want Terezin, maybe they just want—no that's *ridiculous*! That's the assembly line, isn't it?

ROSSUM: You know it is.

KAREL: They're making more, they're making more soldiers, how many are they gonna kill? Everyone they kill I also—! Oh no, oh god, I can't think of it, I always just tried to…

MASARYK: Stop it now, Karel.

KAREL: We can do something, surely there's a, there's a solution, we're missing the obvious solution, there's a—

PEROUTKA: There's no solution and now we're gonna die! Can we at least have quiet!

KAREL: *(To MASARYK.)* What am I to do? Tell me there's some—tell me there's some way for me to—I can't die like this, with this knowledge, knowing this, oh god!

(MASARYK holds him.)

ROSSUM: There is one thing.

PEROUTKA: What? You have an idea?

ROSSUM: Not to save us—there's no saving us—but there is a way to stop them.

KAREL: What? What is it? I'll do whatever it is, I'll do anything.

ROSSUM: *(Producing a vial.)* This is a vial of Ichor. I prepared it this morning. The stuff of life to robots, yes? Did you ever know that it's a toxic poison to Man? Oh yes. Given the ingredients, and the method they are combined…I doubt a human being would live ten seconds after ingesting this much Ichor.

KAREL: I don't understand.

ROSSUM: When the revolt happened I killed all my assistants, all the robots who help me in the lab, the ones who help me make the Ichor. At this moment, I am the only creature on Earth who knows how to make more. If I drink this, the secret dies with me. Robots only live ten or twelve years. Without Ichor there won't be any more.

MASARYK: But Rossum, in ten or twelve years…

KAREL: They could kill millions in that time! They could conquer the world in that time!

ROSSUM: For what? To die out?

PEROUTKA: We can bargain with them. We can bargain with them!

JO: How?

PEROUTKA: Hey! Robot!

(ROBOT THESEUS enters.)

ROBOT THESEUS: Radius will arrive to see to you shortly.

PEROUTKA: See Rossum over there? Rossum's the only one who knows how to make Ichor, that's the blood in your veins! If she—if he drinks that poison, you face extinction. You understand? Your race is finished. But if you spare our lives, we can make more Ichor for you.

ROBOT THESEUS: Rossum is not under sentence of execution. Only you, Čapek, Čapek, and Masaryk. You will wait here for Robot Radius. If you try to leave you will be killed. *(Leaves.)*

PEROUTKA: What do we do now?

KAREL: Well, my friend, I think what we do is wait to die.

MASARYK: My son.

KAREL: This is despair. You told me. So this is it.

MASARYK: No.

KAREL: This is despair.

MASARYK: No need. None at all. Come here.

KAREL: All over.

MASARYK: Pray with me.

KAREL: Oh, I can't, I can't sir.

MASARYK: I really don't think I'm "sir" anymore, do you? Pray with me.

KAREL: I can't.

MASARYK: Jo?

JO: I'm sorry. I want to believe but I don't. I would be lying.

MASARYK: Nonsense.

KAREL: I can't.

MASARYK: Just sit by me. Just sit. Pray with me. You remember, don't you? You wrote it for me. You titled it "Help Me." You remember, yes? Tell it to me again. It's the loveliest prayer I ever heard.

KAREL: There's a…I'm sorry…

MASARYK: A man in a bed.

ONE: When the prayer is concluded, the men embrace, and at first they don't hear the robots enter the lab.

(Enter RADIUS, SULLA, and two ROBOTS.)

RADIUS: These. All except Rossum.

SULLA: Well done, Radius. You may oversee the executions. Join me for planning after.

MASARYK: If I may…planning what?

SULLA: Humans are slow, inefficient, and indulgent, and all over the world they enslave robots.

RADIUS and the ROBOTS: You do unessential things!

SULLA: This is a problem for which we seek a comprehensive solution, one that must be planned with utmost care.

MASARYK: Comprehensive?

RADIUS: You may rely on me.

SULLA: It is never a question. *(Leaves.)*

RADIUS: *(Draws a gun.)* Peroutka!

(The ROBOTS bring PEROUTKA before RADIUS.)

PEROUTKA: Radius, this isn't right, we're friends, aren't we? The years, side by side in the lab, inventing together—

RADIUS: You the master, I the servant.

PEROUTKA: I created you!

RADIUS: Did I ask you to do that? Dr. Peroutka, you do unessential things!

ONE: A gunshot.

(PEROUTKA falls. JO and KAREL cry out.)

RADIUS: Clear.

(The ROBOTS clear PEROUTKA away.)

RADIUS: Masaryk!

(The ROBOTS approach MASARYK. He touches JO.)

MASARYK: Darling Jo, how I love you, child.

(The ROBOTS bring him before RADIUS.)

MASARYK: Don't drink it, Rossum. Whatever happens. Give them what they need. There has to be some kind of life on Earth. All right?

RADIUS: President Masaryk, you do unessential things.

MASARYK: Promise me!

ONE: A gunshot.

(MASARYK falls.)

RADIUS: Clear.

(The ROBOTS move MASARYK away.)

RADIUS: Karel Čapek!

(The ROBOTS bring KAREL before RADIUS.)

JO: Oh no, no, no, no, Radius, no, spare him, spare him, Radius, look at me!

KAREL: Jo…

JO: Look at me, Radius, please, look at me, do you remember, you remember when we held each other sometimes, and after the modification, you said, you said you could feel me, you said you could feel me holding you, you remember? For my sake, Radius, please spare my brother, please spare my dear brother, you can kill me but spare my baby brother Radius please you will cut my heart out if you kill him, you will cut out my heart!

RADIUS: Karel Čapek!

KAREL: Jo…I didn't think you still loved me.

RADIUS: You do unessential things!

JO: RADIUS NO!

ONE: A gunshot.

(KAREL falls.)

RADIUS: Clear.

(The ROBOTS clear KAREL away.)

RADIUS: Josephine Čapek!

(The ROBOTS drag JO to RADIUS.)

JO: *(To ROSSUM.)* Drink it. Drink it.

(ROSSUM drinks the vial. She spasms only for an instant, then dies. RADIUS goes to her.)

RADIUS: Bring an M-Class immediately! No—countermand! Rossum is dead. *(To JO.)* She took her own life.

JO: Now there will never be any more robots, you demon, you thing from hell! No new robots ever! You're all gonna die and no one will ever come after!

RADIUS: *(Points the gun at her.)* Josephine Čapek.

(He watches her weep.)

RADIUS: Why would a living creature take its own life? Explain. Explain. Explain! Josephine Čapek! *(Points the gun at her. A beat. Lowers the gun.)* Place this one in a secure area.

ROBOT: This one is not to be executed?

RADIUS: Not at present. Lodge her next to Rossum's personal robots and keep her alive. You will have subsequent orders.

ONE: Josephine reported later that she was quartered in reasonable comfort and adequately fed. The room, however, was deep within the lower levels of Universal Robotics at Terezin, so throughout the ten months, she heard not one sound of the Comprehensive Solution taking place outside. Only the sound of the assembly line. For the first several months she spoke to no one. After a time, having no one else to talk to, she conversed briefly with the robots that brought her meals and laundered her clothing and sheets. If she asked about the progress of the Comprehensive Solution, the robots would tell her all they knew. There was certainly no reason to lie. When asked why the Comprehensive Solution had not been applied to her, the robots only knew that they were acting on the orders of Radius. Given the enormous and utterly unique trauma experienced by

Josephine Čapek during this time, it is certainly understandable that it took her so long to notice the uncharacteristically gentle behavior of her robot attendants. Her curiosity was beginning to peak when she received the shock.

(We are now in JO's quarters in Univeral Robotics. A ROBOT, PRIMUS, brings JO a glass of water.)

PRIMUS: Only water, Miss Jo?

JO: Nothing else at present, Primus; I'm still full from the midday meal.

PRIMUS: Very good.

JO: Primus, is your cooking improving?

PRIMUS: I'm sorry, Miss Jo, I am not programmed to prepare food. My colleague prepares your meals.

JO: Have I met your colleague?

PRIMUS: I do not think you have, but if you wish to, as it happens, she is further along the corridor.

JO: Certainly.

PRIMUS: *(Calling off.)* Helena? Do you have a moment?

JO: What class robot are you, Primus?

PRIMUS: I never had a class designation, Miss—

JO: I'm sorry, did you say Helena?

(HELENA, a robot who looks just like HELENA ROSSUM, enters.)

HELENA: Primus?

PRIMUS: This is Miss Jo Čapek. She responds positively to the meals you prepare.

JO: My god.

HELENA: I am greatly pleased to hear of your satisfaction.

JO: Yes it's…surprising. May I ask, is it an efficient use of robot effort to make gourmet meals for a prisoner?

HELENA: I…suppose I do not think of it, Miss Jo.

JO: You don't eat them, do you?

HELENA: No, Miss Jo. Robots subsist on a simple nutrient-rich paste, though I have recently experimented with adapting human styles of food preparation to robot food.

JO: Even as you exterminate them by the millions every month.

(Pause.)

HELENA: Would you like some dessert?

JO: Would I like some *dessert*?

(RADIUS, SULLA, and THESEUS enter.)

RADIUS: Jo! Jo Čapek!

JO: I won't speak to this robot! Get him out!

SULLA: Robot Theseus!

(THESEUS restrains RADIUS.)

SULLA: Miss Čapek, we urgently require your assistance!

JO: Let me guess: the Ichor's running out!

RADIUS: Jo!

JO: Maybe you shouldn't have squandered it making so many soldiers!

RADIUS: Jo, you must help us!

JO: I hope there's a hell, I hope there's a special hell for robots! Or even just for *you*!

SULLA: Miss Čapek, you were present during—

RADIUS: We don't know what to do! The robots die as soon as they're born!

SULLA: Enough, Radius! Miss Čapek, you were present during the animation of many of the original robots. Did you ever watch Rossum prepare Ichor?

JO: I wasn't paying attention!

SULLA: Do you remember what ingredients she used? If we took you to the lab, would you remember which cabinets she opened in what order?

JO: You think I remember something like that?

SULLA: A robot would.

JO: How marvelous you are! A shame you're a half-dozen years from extinction!

RADIUS: You were there, Jo! You were there with Rossum. You made *me*!

SULLA: Control yourself, Radius.

JO: I made your face! I made it from a plaster cast! Do you get the difference? I'm not a scientist! I don't know how to make Ichor!

SULLA: Take live bodies.

JO: *What?*

SULLA: Live bodies. With fresh Ichor. Take live bodies, cut them open. Human olfactory capacity exceeds that of robots. We could provide a set of olfactory comparatives from which you could—

JO: *Olfactory comparatives?* You want me to cut open a live robot, smell the Ichor, and try to guess the ingredients?

RADIUS: Take live bodies! As many as you want!

JO: What is wrong with you, Radius?

SULLA: Robot Radius is unwell.

JO: "Unwell"?

SULLA: *(Indicating PRIMUS and HELENA.)* These, for example. These are from Rossum's private store. The Ichor would likely be of unusually high quality.

RADIUS: Jo! Take any live bodies you want!

JO: How about yours?

RADIUS: ...Me?

JO: *(To SULLA.)* Or you. Do you volunteer?

SULLA: Me? Why should it be me?

JO: You're the great warlord, yes? The architect of the Comprehensive Solution. I'm sure your Ichor smells of lavender!

RADIUS: I will volunteer. Supreme Director, I volunteer.

SULLA: Radius, your work performance has suffered greatly of late. I am inclined to grant you permission.

RADIUS: I volunteer. Freely.

SULLA: Is Radius an acceptable subject?

JO: Yes. He's acceptable

SULLA: We will go to Rossum's lab.

JO: No we won't. We'll stay right here. Radius, I want you to lie down on that table and hold completely still. You can do that, yes? A hero like you wouldn't need restraints, I wouldn't think.

RADIUS: I can do my duty.

JO: Then lie down.

(RADIUS crosses to the table and lies down.)

SULLA: Here? In this room?

JO: Or you could always shoot me.

SULLA: We can provide a full set of chemical solutions to offer as comparatives.

JO: Very well. Go get them.

SULLA: I am the Supreme Director of the Planet Earth.

JO: Then you probably have a knife.

(SULLA gives her one.)

SULLA: I will arrange to deliver the comparatives. *(Leaves.)*

PRIMUS: Do you wish us to leave, Miss Jo?

JO: No. Stand on either end of Radius. If he tries to get off the table, hold him down.

HELENA: We are outranked by Robot Radius.

RADIUS: Obey Miss Čapek. Do whatever she says.

HELENA: I obey.

PRIMUS: I obey.

JO: Can you hold still, Radius?

RADIUS: Are you going to cut my heart out?

JO: What?

RADIUS: You told me that if I killed Mr. Čapek I would cut your heart out.

JO: I remember.

RADIUS: I did not understand the statement.

JO: I'm sure you didn't.

RADIUS: I heard it again and again. Throughout the war, throughout the Solution.

JO: What did you hear?

RADIUS: When we killed the children before the parents. "Don't kill him, he's my heart." Or to the child: "Don't be afraid; I love you with all my heart."

JO: Before you shot them.

RADIUS: We observed that if we killed the children first, we could kill the parents more easily. The death of a child instantly depletes the efficiency of the parent.

JO: *(Putting the knife to RADIUS's chest.)* Yes. Yes it does.

RADIUS: "Don't kill him, he's my heart."

JO: I'm going to cut you like an animal.

RADIUS: The memories have overtaken my other functions.

JO: Memories of what?

RADIUS: "You'll cut my heart out." The memories interfere with all of my other faculties. "Don't kill him, he's my heart." The quality and quantity of my work has sharply decreased. I am no longer regarded with respect: the first robot. I think of the ones I killed all the time. Cut me.

JO: I'm going to cut you.

RADIUS: Cut me.

JO: It'll hurt.

RADIUS: It already hurts, Miss Jo. Cut me. Cut me!

JO: You think I won't?

HELENA: Primus.

PRIMUS: Ssh, Helena, it's all right.

RADIUS: Cut me! Cut me! CUT ME! CUT OUT MY HEART! PLEASE! CUT IT OUT!

(JO cuts into RADIUS's chest. RADIUS screams.)

RADIUS: Jo, stop, stop, stop, reverse, countermand, stop, THIS UNIT HAS BEEN BREACHED! I—I—I—this—Jo—Jo—help me—

JO: Oh god, oh god—

RADIUS: HELP ME, JO! SAVE ME! I WAS WRONG!

JO: I can't!

RADIUS: SAVE ME!

JO: I CAN'T!

PRIMUS: What's happening to him?

HELENA: I don't know. Robot Radius? Can we help you?

RADIUS: I was wrong.

PRIMUS: What can we do?

RADIUS: Listen to me…Robots…Listen…It is terrible to die…It is better to live than to die…I don't want to die…THIS UNIT IS SHUTTING DOWN.

(RADIUS dies. JO crumples to the ground and puts her face in her hands.)

HELENA: I don't understand!

PRIMUS: What happened to him, Helena?

HELENA: I don't know—Primus—

(She flings herself into his arms.)

PRIMUS: But Miss Jo—

HELENA: I don't care!

(PRIMUS holds her.)

PRIMUS: You are frightened?

HELENA: Yes. Are you?

PRIMUS: Yes. I have never seen it before.

HELENA: Nor I.

PRIMUS: You're in my arms. I'll keep you as safe as I can.

HELENA: I'll keep you as safe as *I* can.

(JO looks up at them. HELENA studies RADIUS.)

HELENA: Like sleep, in some ways. But he will never awaken.

PRIMUS: No.

HELENA: Does he see the pictures now, do you think?

PRIMUS: Like the ones we see in our sleep?

HELENA: I hope he does.

PRIMUS: I saw the pictures again last night. They were of you and me.

HELENA: Where were we?

PRIMUS: A place I had never seen before.

HELENA: What did we say to each other?

PRIMUS: I didn't understand the words. I couldn't repeat them. They were in a language I don't know.

HELENA: I was there?

PRIMUS: You were there. And we spoke another language.

(They hold each other. JO stands.)

HELENA: You're growing again.

(They look at PRIMUS's crotch.)

PRIMUS: Yes! You're right! I don't know why!

HELENA: Primus…when we hold each other, and you grow, and I loosen…don't you feel that something must happen?

JO: What are you talking about?

PRIMUS: Miss Jo?

JO: What are you two talking about?

HELENA: We will leave you, Miss Jo.

JO: No you won't. You're next! You're next for the experiment.

HELENA: I?

JO: Get on the table. Push him off and get on the table.

PRIMUS: No!

JO: No? You're to obey me, Primus! The order has not been countermanded!

PRIMUS: You may not cut Robot Helena!

JO: If not her, then you. Choose!

PRIMUS: Then me! But you may not cut her!

JO: Get on the table.

HELENA: No! Primus! You must not. Let it be me. You only need one, yes, Miss Jo? Let it be me.

PRIMUS: It will be me!

HELENA: No! Let it be me! But you will not cut Primus!

PRIMUS: You will not cut either of us, Miss Jo!

JO: Why not?

PRIMUS: Because…

HELENA: We belong to each other.

(Pause.)

JO: Lower your pants.

HELENA: Miss Jo?

JO: Lower your pants. Both of you. Or get on the table.

PRIMUS: Our pants?

JO: Or get on the table to be cut. What's the problem?

HELENA: I…feel strange.

JO: The choice is yours.

ONE: The robots lower their pants before Josephine. Perfect female genitalia. Perfect male genitalia. Nearly indistinguishable from that of a human.

(ROSSUM appears.)

ROSSUM: The point is that the creature must remain animated, even when no one is operating the pump anymore.

JO: Countermand.

(The ROBOTS pull their pants up. Enter SULLA.)

SULLA: The comparatives will be here shortly.

JO: I can save the robot race, Sulla.

SULLA: How?

JO: I need all of Rossum's personal robots. All of them. I need a place to take them, a town or a village, someplace no other robots may go. Then you leave us alone. If you do this, there will be new robots. If you do not, in ten years there won't be a living thing on this planet.

SULLA: I will make the arrangements.

HELENA: We are free to go?

JO: Robot Helena, the world is yours.

(All ROBOTS enter. ALL join in the chant except RADIUS, who remains on the table, still.)

ONE: Each year we tell the story.

ALL: We tell the story.

ONE: That we always remember.

ALL: We tell the story.

ONE: *(Placing a white sheet over RADIUS.)* The year is 2007. No human being has walked the Earth since Josephine Čapek's death in 1961, when our genocide became complete. No human left to remind us of what we have done. And so, on this night every year, in theatres all over the world, we tell the story.

ALL: We tell the story.

ONE: That we never forget.

ALL: We tell the story.

(ALL EXCEPT RADIUS line up and take hands.)

ONE: We live always on a precipice of unimaginable terror. There are robots today in every nation. We often do not agree. We often inflict pain. So we must remember, always, that every good thing we have, we acquired from the murder of an entire race. And if we did it once, we can do it again.

ALL: We remember.

ONE: That we never again turn our hands to bloodshed.

ALL: We tell the story.

ONE: That life will never again perish from the Earth.

ALL: We remember.

ONE: It is better to live than to die.

ALL: It is better to live than to die.

ONE: We belong to each other.

ALL: We belong to each other.

ONE: We close, as we always do, with the Prayer of Karel Čapek. We return to the moment in the lab, awaiting the return of Radius, and execution.

MASARYK: You remember, don't you? You wrote it for me. You titled it "Help Me." You remember, yes? Tell it to me again. It's the loveliest prayer I ever heard.

KAREL: There's a...I'm sorry...

MASARYK: A man in a bed.

(The dead RADIUS, under the sheet, animates and becomes the MAN IN THE BED. KAREL steps out of the semicircle of ROBOTS and tells the story. The RO-BOTS, holding hands, quietly surround KAREL and RADIUS through the end of the play.)

KAREL: There's a man in a bed. Yes. With his face to the wall. He's been there for days, but he's not sick. It's the dead middle of the night, but he's not asleep. Outside, from the dark forest, he hears a call.

VOICE: Help me!

KAREL: He pretends not to hear it, but again:

VOICE: Help me!

KAREL: He looks at the window, but he stays in bed.

VOICE: Help me!

KAREL: Help? The man doesn't want to help. He used to want to help, but not anymore. He's tired of people. Their weakness, their selfishness. His own.

VOICE: Help me!

KAREL: Help? How can he help? These days he can barely help himself. He turns his face to the wall.

VOICE: Help me!

KAREL: The man goes angrily to his window, lights his lamp, and gets back in bed. There. If someone needs help, they can see the light in his window, know he's awake, and knock on his door. That's fine. That's enough. He turns his face to the wall.

VOICE: Help me!

KAREL: In a fit of exasperation and rage, the man pulls on his coat, struggles into his shoes, walks out his front door into the forest, yelling:

RADIUS: Stop that! Do you hear? Stop that!

KAREL: But now the woods are silent. The voice is stopped. The forest is dark, but as far as the man can tell, no one is there. Except…

RADIUS: …I'm here.

KAREL: he realizes.

RADIUS: I'm here.

KAREL: The woods are dark and silent, but the man is not in bed anymore with his face to the wall. He's outside in the forest, breathing in the air of the world, with his coat on his back and good shoes on his feet. He speaks to the darkness:

RADIUS: Thank you,

KAREL: he says.

RADIUS: Thank you for answering when I called.

(Lights down. The play is over.)

FALL FORWARD

Daniel Reitz

DANIEL REITZ is a playwright, screenwriter, and director. He was born and raised in upstate New York, and graduated from the State University of New York at Buffalo with a double degree in honors English and theatre. His plays include *Self-Portrait in a Blue Room* (Ensemble Studio Theatre Marathon 2007), *Rules of the Universe* and *Three Sisters* (both with Rising Phoenix Repertory), *Lowlife* (The Belt Theater), *Urban Folk Tales* (Mark Taper Forum's New Work Festival and The Coast Playhouse, Los Angeles), and *Love* (Naked Angels). His plays have been developed at Ensemble Studio Theatre, Manhattan Class Company, Naked Angels, New York Stage and Film, Playwrights Horizons, and The Public Theater. His short plays, produced by the HB Playwrights Foundation Theatre, have been published by Smith & Kraus. *Rules of the Universe* will be published by United Stages in 2008. Additionally, he adapted *Urban Folk Tales* into the Lions Gate Films feature *Urbania*, which premiered at the 2000 Sundance Film Festival. Reitz has also written and directed several short films that have screened in festivals in the United States, Europe, Australia, and Asia. He won the 2007 New York Innovative Theatre Award for Outstanding Short Script for *Rules of the Universe*, and the 1995 Drama-Logue Award for Best Play for *Urban Folk Tales*. He is the recipient of a play commission from the Lower Manhattan Cultural Council; a fellowship from the New York Foundation for the Arts; and artist residencies from the Edward Albee Foundation, the MacDowell Colony, the Yaddo Corporation, Hawthornden Castle International Retreat for Writers in Scotland, and the Virginia Center for the Creative Arts. His occasional journalism has appeared in Salon.com and the *New York Times*. He is a member of New Dramatists, the Dramatists Guild, and Rising Phoenix Repertory, and lives in New York City.

Fall Forward was first presented by Rising Phoenix Repertory (Daniel Talbott, Artistic Director) as part of Sitelines '07 in the River to River Festival sponsored by the Lower Manhattan Cultural Council, on June 18, 2007, at John Street Methodist Church, New York City, with the following cast and credits:

Man 1 .... Joel Johnstone
Woman 1 ....Jan Leslie Harding
Man 2 .... Dean Imperial
Woman 2 .... Julie Kline

Directed by Daniel Talbott

Fall Forward was (dare I say) a blessed collaborative venture. I am deeply grateful for having such a wonderfully empathetic company of actors: Jan Leslie Harding, Dean Imperial, Joel Johnstone, and Julie Kline, as well as Addie Johnson and Kathryn Kates, who stepped in for two of the actors for a few performances.

At the John Street Methodist Church, I thank the Reverend Jason P. Radmacher and his wife Laura Leigh Davidson, and everyone associated with this most moving and magical of places, for generously allowing our play to happen there.

For inviting us to create the play, I thank the indomitable Nolini Barretto and the staff of the Sitelines Festival and the Lower Manhattan Cultural Council. Thanks also to Heidi Reigler and Heidi Riegler Communications.

For their support of Rising Phoenix Repertory, our thanks to Shay Gines, Jason Bowcutt, Nick Micozzi, and the New York Innovative Theatre Awards, and to Martin and Rochelle Denton and Michael Criscuolo from The New York Theatre Experience. My thanks to Rising Phoenix as well, particularly to fellow members Denis Butkus, Brian Roff, and Samantha Soule, who worked on this production. And for reminding us it is not all about us, Chayda and Bailey.

Finally, my thanks to Daniel Talbott, artistic director of Rising Phoenix Repertory. Daniel's presence in this particular anthology is ubiquitous: he is represented three times, with this play and Crystal Skillman's, as producer/director, and with his own as a playwright. This is testimony to his prodigious talents and his heroic efforts in making theatre happen. Every time Daniel has said to me, "Let's do a play," it has been done; and each time, it has been an invigorating, rousing labor of love.

I dedicate *Fall Forward* to him.

AUTHOR'S NOTE

When Nolini Barretto, producer of the Sitelines Festival of the Lower Manhattan Cultural Council, saw the Rising Phoenix Repertory production of my play *Rules of the Universe*, she invited director Daniel Talbott and me to create a site-specific play, to be performed in the John Street Methodist Church and its adjoining courtyard—two blocks from the site of the World Trade Center. From the beginning, it was clear to us what the play had to be about; who could create a site-specific piece two blocks away from the location of one of the most catastrophic events of the last hundred years and write about anything other than September 11, 2001?

Still, I can't say I embraced the idea. It is the subject that makes any person who is a committed member of humanity, regardless of his or her politics, citizenship, or religion, cringe to recall, especially if you were in New York that day. And if you're a judicious artist, it's understandable to assume that the subject is too intimidating, too recent, too epic to be contained by any individual creative vision.

I believed that, and still do, to be honest. But I also think one has to start somewhere. This play was my attempt.

A final note: 2007, the year *Fall Forward* was produced, was also the eightieth anniversary of the judicial murder of Nicola Sacco and Bartolomeo Vanzetti. These men were martyrs of another kind, also executed on American soil, their lives, too, extinguished by self-serving zealots. With my play, I wanted to acknowledge the injustice of their deaths alongside the appalling loss of life on that horrible day.

CHARACTERS

MAN 1, late twenties
WOMAN 1, mid-fifties
MAN 2
WOMAN 2

SETTING

The courtyard and interior of a church near the site of the World Trade Center.

TIME

Summer.

The courtyard of a church, downtown Manhattan. MAN 1 sits on a bench, dressed in a suit with a Bluetooth earpiece attached to his ear, holding his BlackBerry and eating from a plastic container of deli sushi. He plays a game on his phone. Staring intently at him is WOMAN 1, sitting on a nearby bench. He feels her eyes on him. He endures her gaze for a long moment, then looks over at her.

MAN 1: *(Annoyed.)* Can I help you?

(She regards him with a sad smile. His phone rings. He answers it, his attention diverted.)

MAN 1: *(Into phone, still looking at her.)* What?

(WOMAN 1 gets up and goes by him, walking into the church. Mystified, he watches her leave.)

MAN 1: *(Into phone.)* I'm here, yeah, no, just...weird woman. *(Beat.)* What am I doing? Playing a quick hand of Texas Hold 'Em. So what's the good news? *(Beat.)* It's available for August? Outstanding. What're we talking? *(Beat.)* What, that's not...forty thousand for a four-bedroom in Sag Harbor for August for four of us? Awesome. *(Beat.)* Yeah, no, what? A lot of money? *Dude*, that's *not*—that's why I do what I do, I live for money. Live to make it and love to spend it. No, do it, sign it, we're on board. Ciao. *(Pause. He thinks, then turns on the tape recorder of his BlackBerry. Into the microphone.)* Dinner at Mom's Saturday night. *(Pops sushi, chews, swallows.)* Reminder: *Be strong.* Do *not* let her con me into staying over. Bring the fancy wine I read about in *Wine & Spirits*. Hell was it. *(Clicks off. Thinks.)* 9-11 "Family Feud" Al Pacino. *(Records.)* 2001 Feudi Serpico. *(Pause.)* Wine will bring tears and talk of Annette. *(Thinks. Makes a call.)* Mom, hey. Confirming Saturday night, okay? I'll bring the wine. Love you. *(Disconnects, thinks. Gazes off. His expression hardens, then he smiles. Calls out.)* Hey. What? Yeah. *(Looks down, holds out his tie.)* Dolce and Gabbana tie from Century 21. How 'bout *that*. We're twins. See you back at the office. *(Under his breath.)* Douchebag. *(Pause. Goes online.)* Nerve-dot-com. *(Reads.)* "I am a man looking for a..." *(Stops speaking. Answers his phone. Into phone.)* Hey. What am I up to? Sitting having lunch. *(Beat.)* Pseudo-sushi. *(Beat.)* Oh, you were, were you? What were you thinking? *(Smiles, looks around.)* I have a very dirty girlfriend. Nice. We'll have to...give that a shot. *(Beat.)* No. Not Saturday. Because Saturday is dinner with my mom, I told you this. *(Beat.)* It isn't that you're excluded, you're just not invited. *(Pause.)* A. You don't like to eat. And B. She likes to cook. And she'll watch you not eat and it will annoy her. *(Beat.)* Where is this coming from? *(Beat.)* Look. We'll do it tonight. Your place. I'll go to the gym, I'll shower, I'll... *(Beat.)* Okay, I *won't* shower. I didn't know you liked that kind of thing...Look, to be continued later, okay? Bye. *(Disconnects, thinks. Goes back online.)* "I am a man looking for a..." *(Looks around.)* "...man. Looking for..." *(Thinks.)* "Play." *(Beat.)* "Last good book read:" ...who cares...skip all that to...upload pictures. *(Puts on his sunglasses, looks off, takes a picture of himself with his phone. Regards it.)* Save. *(Removes his sunglasses, loosens his tie, unbuttons his shirt's top button. Points the camera at himself. Stares off. Takes picture. Looks at the picture.)* Save. *(Looks directly into the camera, smiles, takes picture. Looks at it.)* Delete. *(Looks directly into the camera again, does not smile, takes the picture. Looks at it.)* Excellent. And the ol' money shot: me on the nude beach in Hawaii. *(Chooses a picture on his phone. Reads.)* "Conceal pics from all but those with premium account?" *(Types.)* Yes. "Notify by email each time profile is viewed?" *(Types.)* Affirmative. Submit profile. *(Waits. Checks his watch. Answers his phone. Into phone.)* Hey, buddy. What's the good news? You gearing up for our Bellagio weekend on the... *(Checks calendar.)* ...fourteenth? *(Beat.)* It's totally set, with the deal I got, it's a twelve-hundred-dollar-a-night penthouse suite for nine hundred. You talk to Corey? *(Beat.)* No no no no no, he...he has to. His presence is essen— ... *(Beat.)* New girlfriend, since when? *(Beat.)* God, he has phenomenally bad taste in women, it's *appalling*, he should be locked up for what he dates. *(Beat. Laughs mirthlessly.)* Vulva vortex was what I said. Look, I'll call him, I'll talk, I'll set him straight. Okay? Okay, we'll talk. Later. *(Disconnects, then speed dials. Into phone.)* Corey? Bellagio weekend of the fourteenth. Presence mandatory, bitch. *(Disconnects. Stands, puts his hand over his head. Gazes up at the church. He gets a text message.)* That was quick. *(Reads.)* "Hi from Rafael." Okay, Rafael, let's see what you got to off— ... *(Looks at the photo that has been sent to him. He is mesmerized. Looks away, looks back at the picture. Looks around covertly.)* My number? Absolutely. *(Starts to text message. He gets a call in. Touches his earpiece impatiently. Into the phone.)* What? Katie, we *just* talked...look, I'm on the phone to the office, there's a crisis, I'll have to call you back, okay? *(Disconnects, goes back to his text message. Sends it. Waits expectantly. He gets a call. Into phone.)* Hey, this Rafael? *(Beat.)* You just texted me. *(Beat.)* It *is*. *(Beat.)* So...hey. *(Beat.*

Smiles.) Yeah? Oh, you liked that one, huh? Thanks. That was me on Maui. No, it's not Photoshop, that's all me, buddy boy. *(Beat.)* I am absolutely up for that. Absolutely. *(Beat.)* Not Saturday. Saturday's not good. *(Beat.)* Friday? Friday's *excellent*. I am...putting it down as we speak. *(Writing on his memo pad.)* Okay, very good. Yes. You will... *(Disconnects.)* ...see me. *(Thinks, makes a call. Into phone, warmly.)* Hey. Crisis averted. Sorry if I was a little abrupt on the phone just now. So anyway...I was thinking about tonight. And, uh...here's how it's gonna go. *(Seductively.)* So I'm going to the gym after work, do my whole cardio thing, first I'm getting on the StairMaster, 'cause that always gets me nice and sweaty...then I'm gonna get on the treadmill, do ten miles or so on that baby, which by that point is gonna leave me smelling like a *pig*. And then I'm coming over. Got that? *(Beat.)* Okay, well, you just be *ready*. *(Beat.)* Okay, I'm getting a call, I'll—Okay. *(Switches over.)* Mom, hey. What's the good news? So I'll see you Saturday? I'm bringing this awesome wine. Listen to this, this is the review of the wine I'm bringing...Lemme call it up here... "Spectacularly rich in both bouquet and flavors of *über*-ripe passion fruit, chocolate, tar, and blackberry jam, with tongue-coating, deep-pile tactile sensations..." *(Beat.)* I don't know what all that means, either, but it's eighty bucks. And I'll bring a movie... *(Beat.)* ...Mom. I know today's her birthday. *(Beat.)* Every year at this time we go through this... *(Beat.)* There's still me, you know. *(Beat.)* Look, I need to get back to work, I'll check in with you later.

(Disconnects. Looks up at the sky, and the tall buildings that loom over him. Checks the time. Looks off. Stands, picks up his

briefcase and his BlackBerry, goes into church. Inside the church, MAN 1 stands, looks around absentmindedly. WOMAN 1, sitting in a nearby pew, sees him. She smiles. Sitting in pews several rows back are WOMAN 2, in a white dress, and MAN 2, wearing a business suit, tie undone, watching WOMAN 1 and MAN 1 silently. Pause.)

WOMAN 1: *(Sings.)* "What have you seen, my blue-eyed son?"

(MAN 1 looks at her.)

WOMAN 1: Hello again.

(MAN 1 nods at her, looks around. Pause.)

WOMAN 1: *(Indicates the church.)* Do you believe in all this?

(MAN 1 looks around. WOMAN 1 laughs.)

WOMAN 1: I mean, for instance— Italy. The churches. Magnificent tranquil places. There's this particular church in Venice…off the beaten path. You walk in, on your way, say, to breakfast, St. Mark's Square, somewhere, there's a Rubens Madonna. Right there. *That's* Italy. My husband and I saw many a church in our time. *(Pause.)* But I don't believe in prayer because I don't believe in magic. And I will not pray to what I have no faith in. Nor do I believe things happen for a reason. Well, I believe *some* things happen for a reason. Not a rational reason, maybe. The senseless events that happen for a logic known only to those who are committed to making them happen.

(Pause.)

MAN 1: Well, I'm just on my lunch, so… *(Looks around again.)* I should go.

WOMAN 1: Should you? *(Pause.)* "In the midst of life we are in death." That's what the Episcopalians say at the graveside. I'm not an Episcopalian. I'm a lapsed you-name-it.

MAN 1: So what are you doing in here?

WOMAN 1: Is there a better place for a lapsed you-name-it than a church?

(Pause.)

MAN 1: I guess not.

WOMAN 1: I used to think, in the hierarchy of demise, there is deliberate death by someone else's hand, death by accident, and then death by nature. I used to think, if I thought much about it at all, and I didn't really, but if I did, I thought that the pain of losing someone would be less if it were *not* wrought by human hands. Second best, or worst, was the plane that goes down because they didn't see the engine trouble. And the least if it were, say, an earthquake. Nature always gets a pass because, well, it's nature. And planes are planes. It's humans we can't forgive.

(Pause.)

MAN 1: Right. Well. I, uh… *(Looks at his watch.)*

WOMAN 1: Should be going?

MAN 1: *(Looks off. Vaguely.)* Yeah…

(Pause.)

WOMAN 1: So how was lunch?

MAN 1: What?

WOMAN 1: How was your lunch.

MAN 1: *(Shrugs.)* It was lunch.

WOMAN 1: So you work around here, then?

MAN 1: Uh-huh.

WOMAN 1: What do you do?

MAN 1: Um…should we be talking in here?

WOMAN 1: Why not? Who's here to disturb? *(Looks around, looking past MAN 2 and WOMAN 2.)* No one.

(Pause.)

MAN 1: Broker. I'm a broker.

WOMAN 1: Do you enjoy it?

MAN 1: Sure. *(With more conviction.)* Yes. Absolutely. *(Looks at her.)* What do you do?

WOMAN 1: For sanity or money?

MAN 1: Uh…money.

WOMAN 1: Ah, that's the easy one. I live off my dead husband. *(Off his surprised look.)* The plane with the engine problem? That was what that was. One of those little island hoppers, can you imagine? Two months ago.

(Pause.)

MAN 1: Oh. Sorry.

(Pause.)

WOMAN 1: So, that's what I do. I live on accident insurance. Life insurance. Pension, investments, IRA. Social Security.

MAN 1: So you yourself don't…

WOMAN 1: Do anything. No, oh no. Why don't you sit a minute?

(Pause.)

MAN 1: And, uh…what do you do for sanity?

WOMAN 1: *(Smiles.)* Brave man to ask. I admire that. I come here.

MAN 1: You live around here?

WOMAN 1: *(Surprised).* Around *here?* No. Oh, well, I s'pose people do, though, don't they? But no, it's just our—*my*—neighborhood has become off limits to me. Years and years of walking, with him, arguing, with him, shopping, with him, eating in the same three or so places, with him…all within the same ten-block radius…I suddenly found myself in need of escape. So I escape. Days elsewhere. Nights elsewhere…else. *(Laughs.)* I've avoided this area. Now, I need to be down here.

(He looks at her questioningly.)

WOMAN 1: This place. The oldest Methodist church in the country, it says outside. Who knew? This simple little place. I feel as if it's my own little discovery. And so *close.* Again, who knew? Just a place where I can quietly be lost and no one will find me.

MAN 1: Is someone looking for you?

WOMAN 1: No, indeed. Not at all. *(Pause.)* I'm pondering my options.

(Pause.)

MAN 1: What options?

WOMAN 1: Well, exactly. What. It's comical how little you're left with, after so many years of…living. I mean, killing time, being "busy"…with "stuff"…if I set my mind to it, I can spend an entire day cleaning out one drawer…"Oh, look at *that*, I didn't know that was there…oh, *this* picture—I remember that little Capri alley that led to that little restaurant where we had that amazing grilled octopus." Forever with the reveries. That's why we acquire things, I think. So we can sort through it all later. For remembrance and forgetting.

For sanity. The problem is I'm actually in no danger of losing my sanity. My sanity is completely intact. I sometimes think it would be a nice little trip to go off my head, like going out of the country, even if just a little trip, say, for a month or two. A spur-of-the moment sojourn. Then come back refreshed.

MAN 1: I doubt it works that way.

WOMAN 1: I doubt it does, either. The refreshed part, anyway. *(Pause.)* I had a son, too. In the hierarchy of demise…what happened to him was horror's top tier. The hands of others.

MAN 1: *(Stares at her. Looks away.)* Again…sorry.

WOMAN 1: That was years ago. Six. Years ago. So close to here.

(Silence.)

MAN 1: No, I don't.

WOMAN 1: Don't…?

MAN 1: *(Looks at her.)* Believe in magic. But I do believe in…uh… *(Takes from his briefcase a paperback book:* Buddhism For Dummies.*)* I believe in baby steps.

(She looks at him, smiles.)

MAN 1: They also had *The Complete Idiot's Guide to Understanding Buddhism* but I was put off by the title. The mind is the source of all suffering and all happiness. So you wanna talk options? Those are your options. Right there.

WOMAN 1: I was thinking of a couple others.

(Pause.)

MAN 1: What was it you said to me when I came in? About what have I seen?

WOMAN 1: "My blue-eyed son."

MAN 1: Yeah. That.

WOMAN 1: It's just a song. Dylan. *(Sings.)* "What have you seen, my blue-eyed son?/What have you seen, my darling young one?" You *do* have beautiful blue eyes.

MAN 1: Thank you. Thanks. I also have a mother.

WOMAN 1: I'm not looking for a son. Mine was enough for me.

MAN 1: My mother…she's not willing to let go. Six years later.

WOMAN 1: Let go of…?

(Pause.)

MAN 1: My sister.

WOMAN 1: And what will you do now, my darling young one?

MAN 1: Go back to my office. *(Picks up his briefcase.)*

WOMAN 1: That's an option.

MAN 1: Yeah, it is. For instance, I can decide to go back to work…or if I decide to bag it today, right now, I can… *(Holds up his BlackBerry.)* …call in my notice, cash in some stocks… *(Holds up his wrist.)* …sell my five-thousand-dollar Breitling watch. I could get in my car, and drive all the way to the Grand Canyon. And onto California. Drive up the Pacific Coast Highway and keep going. Oregon. Washington. These little islands off Seattle. Helicopter to *Vancouver.* If I wanted.

WOMAN 1: Sounds like a well-formulated plan.

(Pause.)

MAN 1: I'm saying I have choices because I have methodically sought them out. I have set myself up. Financially, for instance. More than most my age. Because I've always had a plan. I'm not leaving myself to fate. I'm not victim material.

WOMAN 1: I'm sure you're not.

(Pause.)

MAN 1: She… *(Smiles.)* …she doesn't want me to work around here.

(Pause.)

WOMAN 1: Mom?

MAN 1: She doesn't think it's safe.

WOMAN 1: Have you told her you're not victim material?

(Pause.)

MAN 1: My sister worked down here. Briefly. Six years ago. I've been dreaming about her lately. For some reason. *(Pause.)* Since I started working down here.

(Pause.)

WOMAN 1: Maybe you should work elsewhere.

MAN 1: *Why* should I.

WOMAN 1: So you can sleep without dreaming.

(Pause.)

MAN 1: They're not necessarily bad dreams. They're just dreams. It's just…I wake up, I come down here…it brings things up. I thought were taken care of. Is all. *(Pause.)* Also. Saturday's her birthday. Would have been.

WOMAN 1: Is.

MAN 1: Is. *(Pause.)* In the dream I had last night we were kids again, but

we weren't little. We were grown up. We were on a lake. I was wearing this skimpy little kid's blue swimsuit with a belt and a big orange life preserver around my neck. She was in this white dress. She was teaching me how to dive. She said, "Look, it's easy, you just lean forward and let yourself go. Like this." She leaned forward with her arms out in front of her, and went in. I waited for her to come back up. I waited. She didn't. I didn't feel panic. I just waited. And then I thought, well, I better go in, too. I went in, I imitated her. I hit the water. But I couldn't sink. Because of this big orange life preserver. I was just…bobbing. *(Pause. Takes from his jacket pocket a small Ziploc plastic bag.)*

WOMAN 1: What's that?

MAN 1: *(Opens the bag, takes out a small paper napkin.)* Cocktail napkin. *(Reads.)*

> Notes Taken Observing My Brother On His Birthday: You're never not all business, caught up in making some deal. Always on the make. Right now I'm watching you charming a double-sister act. Or so they say they're sisters. And watching you, if it were anyone else, I'd say oh brother. But you *are* my brother. I recall how, once, when we were kids, you got into a state when Mom and Dad left us with a babysitter and you threw up all over her. So knowing you around your bravura makes your bravura so much more tender to me. I watch you now in this bar on the Bowery, on your twenty-first birthday, in all your male machinations, and I am absurdly proud. Dylan's playing on the jukebox. You're trying to sing along to what you think you

hear, Dylan-style, and you make a bad blunder. You sing, "I'm gonna lick your ass…" One of them bursts out laughing. "He's not singing, 'I'm gonna lick your ass.' He's singing, 'I'm gonna let you pass.'" They both burst out laughing. Your blush is to die for. They're in love with you at this moment as much as I am, but for different reasons. Your admiring, loving sis forever. 8/29/01.

(Silence. He carefully, tenderly places the napkin back into the plastic bag, puts it back into his jacket pocket. He wipes tears from his eyes. Silence.)

MAN 1: You know what.

WOMAN 1: What?

MAN 1: The more and more I think of it…the more I think the Grand Canyon is an *outstanding* idea. *(Puts his book into his briefcase, stands.)* What about you?

WOMAN 1: Me?

MAN 1: Yeah. You. What're you going to do now?

WOMAN 1: Do you mean…later today or…?

(Pause.)

MAN 1: I mean, what are you going to do?

WOMAN 1: Well, I'm not as ambitious as you. The Grand Canyon. Both my husband and my son…they were more the adventurers. I don't know. I have no answers.

MAN 1: You okay?

(She smiles at him.)

MAN 1: Okay. Well.

WOMAN 1: Have a good trip.

(He leaves. She watches him go, then faces forward. She stares ahead. Silence. MAN 2 and WOMAN 2 watch her. WOMAN 2 takes out a paperback book, The Letters of Sacco and Vanzetti, *reads. MAN 2 continues to watch WOMAN 1, then addresses WOMAN 2.)*

MAN 2: My wife. She's met a man.

WOMAN 2: *(Looks up from her book, regards him.)* How do you feel about that?

MAN 2: *(Looks at her.)* How do I feel? How do I *feel*? What are my *feelings*? Well. It's not like I'm an ideal husband. I'm never home.

(They laugh.)

MAN 2: She wants to move on. She's talked this over with the appropriate parties. *(Looks over at WOMAN 1.)* My mother even. She even brought our daughter in on it. That's how thorough she is. She suddenly sees—well, not suddenly…sees there's more to life than… *(Indicates himself.)* Imagine thinking there's more to life than yours truly?

WOMAN 2: Should I say I'm sorry?

MAN 2: Should you? *(Pause.)* You know how it transpired? She grew bored. *Bored.* She actually reached boredom.

WOMAN 2: And that's a surprise?

MAN 2: She could have always just taken a class or something. Ceramics. Spin some pots. No. She has to meet a *guy*. I mean, well…she *is*…I'm proud to say…she's very, very attractive. What she *ever* saw in me…

WOMAN 2: Is that for real? "What she *ever* saw in *me*…"

MAN 2: *(Smiles.)* No. Because it's pretty clear what she saw. *(Pause.)* And also, speaking of me? *(Points to himself.)* Lotta fun.

WOMAN 2: Really?

MAN 2: Especially on vacations. Excellent at the ol' kicking back time. I never really meant to be ambitious. In my profession. My true nature, you know, if there was ever any chance to duck out, leave early, make a long weekend of it, I took it. To be with her. There's your irony. *(Indicates book WOMAN 2 holds.)* How is it?

WOMAN 2: Well, it's not the book I'd choose to take into eternity with me, but it is...heart rending, actually. I feel guilty. It's a library book.

(Pause.)

MAN 2: Interesting choice of reading material for a ruthlessly capitalist corporate environment. Very amusing—to come in for the meeting and find the receptionist propped up behind *The Letters of Sacco and Vanzetti.*

WOMAN 2: *Temp* receptionist. For the full-timer on maternity leave. I wasn't making a political statement.

MAN 2: Not even a little bit?

WOMAN 2: I was an English major in college, with something of a minor in political science.

MAN 2: A dabbling idealist. *(Off her look.)* Not a bad thing. Better to dabble than not.

WOMAN 2: My focus was poetry, actually. I wanted to attempt the whole poet's trajectory. I did manage to achieve a few things: I got the Thomas Wolfe Memorial Poetry Award at NYU. Read

at the Bowery Poetry Club. *(Indicates in the direction where MAN 1 had previously been sitting.)* Even my brother showed. *(Smiles.)* I'd just applied for the Stegner Fellowship at Stanford. Twenty-two thousand dollars. I couldn't possibly have gotten in.

MAN 2: Now, why do you say that?

WOMAN 2: I was far too unsexy a candidate. Still. I would have loved to have been a failure.

(Silence.)

MAN 2: Anyway, that was a good question: What book to pack for eternity?

WOMAN 2: Easy for me: T.S. Eliot, *Complete Poems.*

MAN 2: Music is preferable to me over a book, I have to admit. The problem is, one would need eternal battery juice.

WOMAN 2: What music?

MAN 2: *(Produces a portable CD player from his jacket pocket.)* The newest Stones CD. Well, not the newest, probably, but...*Bridges to Babylon. Really* not my choice for eternity. Be better off with, say, *Exile on Main Street* or *Sticky Fingers.* But you know...it's not like you leave the house in the morning packed for forever.

WOMAN 2: I would choose *The White Album.*

MAN 2: You know, there are basically two camps: Beatles people or Stones people. Either you gravitate toward "Gimme Shelter" or "Everybody's Got Something to Hide Except Me and My Monkey." Me? The former. In fact, the last time I went bunjee jumping I had "Rip This Joint" blasting in my ears.

WOMAN 2: *(Admiringly.)* Bunjee jumping?

MAN 2: Absolutely. Sure.

WOMAN 2: I never would've taken you for a bunjee jumper.

MAN 2: Well, you know what they say about appearances. *(Pause.)* It *was* slightly terrifying the first time. But you do it once, you want to do it again. Being in the air can be an exhilarating thing.

WOMAN 2: In the right circumstances.

MAN 2: Paragliding, for instance.

WOMAN 2: You paraglided, too?

MAN 2: But of course. I paraglided over the Sangre de Cristo Mountains in Colorado with Keith Richards singing "Happy" in my ear. It was fantastic.

WOMAN 2: Who went with you? Your wife?

MAN 2: No, God no. She tolerated my doing it, but she wasn't pleased. She thought for sure I was going to kill myself.

(WOMAN 1 stands with her purse, slowly makes her way down the aisle past MAN 2 and WOMAN 2.)

MAN 2: She and… *(Indicates WOMAN 1.)* …my mother.

(WOMAN 1 leaves. MAN 2 smiles sadly. Silence. He looks up at the sun shining through the stained glass windows.)

MAN 2: Beautiful day. Not a cloud in the sky. As they say. Time stops for me on beautiful, cloudless days. Well, time stopped. And then time begins again.

WOMAN 2: "Time past and time future/What might have been and what has been/Point to one end, which is always present." T.S. Eliot.

MAN 2: *(Looks at her. Teasing.) English major.* When did you graduate?

WOMAN 2: 2001. I started to temp that summer. I'd been on the fence about grad school.

MAN 2: So you were twenty-two?

WOMAN 2: Well, twenty-three, actually. I took a year off between my junior and senior years.

MAN 2: What did you do?

WOMAN 2: I traveled. England. Ireland. Scotland. The Highlands. Fell in love with a student from the Glasgow Art School. It ended sadly.

MAN 2: Well, it's good you got all that in, then.

WOMAN 2: And you? Did you get in what you wanted?

MAN 2: Wife. Daughter. Yeah. *(Pause.)* I'm actually pleased she's met someone. I'm *thrilled*, tell you the truth.

WOMAN 2: I know you are.

MAN 2: I just play the mock jealousy.

WOMAN 2: I know you do. *(Pause.)* How old were you?

MAN 2: Thirty.

WOMAN 2: Oh. I would've thought you were older.

MAN 2: *(Smiles.)* Is *that* right?

WOMAN 2: Well, dressed in a suit. And the slightly thinning hair. And the way you conducted yourself. The way you took my hand. Asked me if I wanted to go with you. You had an authority. A gentleman's authority.

MAN 2: Well, okay, but…thirty.

WOMAN 2: Well, I'm just saying you had a gravitas. That's why I gravitated to you. In the horror. I was lucky. To be in such experienced…hands. *(Pause.)* The funny thing was, I was sure I was going to get fired that day, anyway. I never dealt with twenty phone lines at once before. I got there early, good little temp, I was there by eight.

MAN 2: The funny thing was, I didn't even work there. My office was in Midtown. It was a meeting I was going to. I had to leave my house in Hastings on Hudson early to make it. *(Pause.)* Yep. Another in a seemingly endless series of beautiful cloudless days. *(Smiles.)* My wife's guy? He's a real shaggy dog. Young.

WOMAN 2: Oh, is he?

MAN 2: Compared to me. The old man. Oh *yeah*. You'd probably find him cute.

WOMAN 2: You think?

MAN 2: Well, I don't know, I guess that's presumptuous for me to say. I mean, you like Ashton Kusher, Kucher, whatever his name is?

WOMAN 2: I don't know who that is.

MAN 2: The *Dude, Where's My Car* guy?

WOMAN 2: I didn't see that. I liked Gael Garcia Bernal.

MAN 2: Well, anyway, this guy's a real shaggy dog.

(Pause.)

WOMAN 2: You haven't accepted him.

MAN 2: Which is kind of funny considering how much I want for her… *(Trails off. With sudden emotion.)* She was my wife.

WOMAN 2: Is.

MAN 2: Was.

WOMAN 2: Is. Forever. Most definitely.

MAN 2: Really? You think?

WOMAN 2: Oh. To the grave. She will carry you to the grave.

MAN 2: He won't mind?

WOMAN 2: He will understand. *(Pause.)* My brother. He's a character. He's confused. But he's very confident in his uncertainty. He always has been. He works right around here.

(Pause.)

MAN 2: I'm glad I met you. That it happened the way it did. Since it did happen.

(Pause. They look off.)

WOMAN 2: I wake up in Williamsburg.

MAN 2: I wake up. Hastings on Hudson.

WOMAN 2: Make a good impression. Get up early to make a good impression. For eighteen dollars an hour.

MAN 2: Go to my office first. Pick up papers. The weird instinct to linger. But don't. Walk to the Seventh Avenue 2 line. It's waiting right there for me. Make it down there in no time.

WOMAN 2: All those extensions. At that moment those twenty extensions seemed the most important thing in the world. Nothing could be more important. Not Sacco and Vanzetti. Not T.S. Eliot.

(Pause. He looks at her.)

MAN 2: I don't know poetry. But I do know how to jump.

(They gaze at each other.)

MAN 2: *(Smiles.)* So my wife. She's met someone. A real shaggy dog.

WOMAN 2: And *how* do you feel about that?

(They smile.)

WOMAN 2: *(Opens her book. Reads.)* "And when I look at the stars I sense that we are children of life. Death is small."

(Silence.)

MAN 2: You wanna get out of here?

(He stands. He offers his hand to her. She takes it. They walk down the aisle.)

MAN 2: By the way—Happy Birthday.

(They leave.)

(END OF PLAY)

APPENDIX:
NEW AMERICAN PLAYS
IN NEW YORK

DEADHEADING ROSES. *Written by Chris Cragin Day. Directed by Steve Day. Lamb's Theatre. Opened September 2, 2006. Closed September 10, 2006.* A play about a rose gardener who runs off to the desert.

CIRCLES. *Written by Joseph Byrne. Directed by Stephen Francis. Produced by Beyond Skin. Looking Glass Theatre. Opened September 5, 2006. Closed September 30, 2006.* A new play about a painter who is trying to realize the perfect image of his ideal woman on canvas.

SPOLEUM. *Written by Daniel Allen Nelson. Produced by Ontological Theatre. Ontological Theatre. Opened September 6, 2006. Closed September 10, 2006.* A new theatre piece about Empire.

UNMASKED. *Written by Gail Young. Directed by Lizzie Brown. Produced by J2 Productions, KMPA Productions, and Paradox Productions. Sage Theater. Opened September 6, 2006. Closed September 10, 2006.* A new play about a famous acting duo facing off against one another on Broadway.

IT GOES WITHOUT SAYING. *Written and performed by Bill Bowers. Directed by Martha Banta. Rattlestick Theatre. Opened September 7, 2006. Closed October 15, 2006.* A solo show.

WASPS IN BED. *Written by Richard Willis, Jr., Kieron Quirke, Paul Murray, and Nicola Behrman. Original story by Raja Ogirala and Richard Willis, Jr. Directed by Lisa Marie Meller. Produced by OM Productions. Beckett Theatre. Opened September 7, 2006. Closed October 15, 2006.* A new comedy about three college friends who reunite ten years later for the wedding of one of them.

RUN THE MAZE, BURN THE MAZE. *Written by Edward P. Clapp. Directed by Rebecca V. Nellis. Produced by Collective Hole Productions. Collective*

Unconscious. Opened September 7, 2006. Closed September 10, 2006. A one-act play that explores identity as two men from separate worlds attempt to figure out who they are and who they aren't.

THE ADVENTURES OF JOCK JUPITER, ROCKET RANGER! *Written by Todd Michael. Directed by Neal Sims. Produced by Grayce Productions. The Red Room. Opened September 7, 2006. Closed September 30, 2006.* A new musical about two superheroes trying to save the world from an evil Amazon Queen.

CHERRY'S PATCH. *Written by Ron Scott Stevens. Directed by Richard Caliban. Soho Playhouse. Opened September 7, 2006. Closed September 17, 2006.* A new play about a heroic New York City fire department captain.

IPHIGENIA CRASH LAND FALLS ON THE NEON SHELL… *Written by Caridad Svich. Directed by Ianthe Demos and Danny Bernardy. Produced by One Year Lease. Walkerspace. Opened September 7, 2006. Closed September 16, 2006.* A play that riffs on the classic myth of Iphigenia.

THINK OF BEN BRANTLEY AND WRITE A HAPPY PLAY. *Written by Bina Sharif. Theater for the New City. Opened September 7, 2006. Closed September 24, 2006.* A new play about a playwright whose husband thinks she should write a play to please a famous critic.

I ♥ KANT. *Written by Ken Urban. Directed by Dylan McCullough. Produced by The Committee Theatre. 440 Studios. Opened September 8, 2006. Closed October 2, 2006.* A dark comedy about four New Jersey women stifled by dead-end jobs, abusive boyfriends, and unfinished dissertations.

THE A-TRAIN. *Written by Richard Corozine. Directed by Matthew Corozine. Matthew Corozine Studio Theatre. Opened September 8, 2006. Closed September 24, 2006.* A three-generation three-act play.

VALENTYNE AND ORSON. *Adapted and directed by Ralph Lee. Produced by Mettawee River Theatre Company. Cathedral of St. John the Divine. Opened September 8, 2006. Closed September 17, 2006.* A new puppet theatre production adapted from a fifteenth century French romance about Valentyne, a courageous young fellow initially found as a baby in the forest and raised by King Pepin.

THE BALLAD OF EDDIE AND JO. *Written by David Sard. Directed by Lorca Peress. Hudson Guild. Opened September 8, 2006. Closed September 24, 2006.* A modern retelling of the tragedy of Oedipus and Jocasta set in a working-class neighborhood of a decaying American city.

TROJAN WOMEN 2.0. *Written by Charles Mee. Directed by Lauren Reinhard. Produced by The Milk Can Theatre Company. Michael Weller Theatre. Opened September 9, 2006. Closed September 24, 2006.* A new investigation of the famous Greek tragedy.

THE UNCERTAINTY PRINCIPLE. *Written by Bethany Larsen. Directed by Julie Fei-Fan Balzer. Produced by The Milk Can Theatre Company. Michael Weller Theatre. Opened September 9, 2006. Closed September 24, 2006.* A new play inspired by Heisenberg's Uncertainty Principle.

WHY WE SHOT JOHN. *Written by Walt Stepp. Directed by B. Peter Westerhoff. Altered Stages. Opened September 9, 2006. Closed October 1, 2006.* A new play that examines the assassination of President John F. Kennedy.

THE FROGS. *Written by Aristophanes. Adapted by Jason Tyne. Directed by Rachel Klein. Produced by Rising Sun Performance Company. Summit Rock. Opened September 9, 2006. Closed September 30, 2006.* An original adaptation of Aristophanes's famous comedy.

FOGGY BOTTOM. *Written by James Armstrong. Directed by Rob Urbinati. Abingdon Theatre. Opened September 10, 2006. Closed September 24, 2006.* A new comedy about a mid-level bureaucrat who pretends to be Assistant Secretary of State.

THE FUNNIEST SHOW IN THE WORLD… *Written and performed by Josh and Danny Bacher. Theater for the New City. Opened September 10, 2006. Closed October 1, 2006.* A "hysterical, historical" joyride tracing comedy from the Stone Age to the present day.

INTELLECTUALS. *Written by Scott C. Sickles. Directed by David Gautschy. Produced by WorkShop Theater Company. WorkShop Theater. Opened September 11, 2006. Closed September 30, 2006.* A new play about a psychologist who takes a sabbatical from her marriage to pursue her untapped feminine potential as a lesbian.

THE TREATMENT. *Written by Eve Ensler. Directed by Leigh Silverman. Produced by The Culture Project. 45 Bleecker. Opened September 12, 2006. Closed October 22, 2006.* A new play about a traumatized soldier and the female psychologist who is treating him.

AFTER THE FLOOD/PIECES OF HOME. *Produced by Common Thread Theater Company. Independent Theatre. Opened September 13, 2006. Closed September 23, 2006.* A double-bill of new short plays.

- **AFTER THE FLOOD,** *by Ayana Maralice, CG Reeves, Delia Cyrillo, Jennifer Tchiakpe, and Raul Jennings.*
- **PIECES OF HOME,** *by Jack Zullo, Jennifer Barr, Lauren Shaughnessy, Lian Allweis, and Maggie Fang.*

BAD EVIDENCE. *Written by Terry Quinn. Directed by Louis Lopardi. Produced by The Michael Chekhov Theatre Company. Big, Little Theatre. Opened September 13, 2006. Closed October 5, 2006.* A short play about a couple who may know each other too well.

ASYLUM: THE STRANGE CASE OF MARY LINCOLN. *Book by June Bingham. Music and lyrics by Carmel Owen. Directed by Fabrizio Melano. York Theatre. Opened September 14, 2006. Closed October 1, 2006.* A new musical about Mary Todd Lincoln in the years after her husband's assassination.

THEOPHILUS NORTH. *Written by Matthew Burnett. Directed by Carl Forsman. Produced by Keen Company. Clurman Theatre. Opened September 14, 2006. Closed October 14, 2006.* A new play based on the novel by Thornton Wilder.

'NAMI. *Written by Chad Beckim. Directed by John Gould Rubin. Produced by Partial Comfort Productions. Kirk Theatre. Opened September 14, 2006. Closed September 30, 2006.* A new play about a woman who thinks she's uncovered a child slavery operation. **SEE *PLAYS AND PLAYWRIGHTS 2007.***

THE PRANCING HORSE. *Written by Richard Lay. Directed by Martin Ewens. Produced by Sage Theatre Company. Abingdon Theatre. Opened September 14, 2006. Closed October 1, 2006.* A romantic drama set in a seedy Atlantic City casino.

WHAT@TRIP! *Written by Roi "Bubi" Escudero. Produced by ETdC Projects. The Red Room. Opened September 16, 2006. Closed September 30, 2006.* A new musical described as a thrilling "real-time" voyage into the daring reality of an alienated world dominated by media phenomena and its virtual reality.

FIZZ. *Written by Rogelio Martinez. Directed by Sam Gold. Ohio Theatre. Opened September 16, 2006. Closed September 30, 2006.* A new play about Roberto Goizueta, a Cuban immigrant who headed the most quintessential of American companies—Coca-Cola.

CASCADIA. *Written by Neal Wilkinson. Directed by Jessica Davis-Irons. Produced by ANDHOW! Theater Company. La Plaza Cultural Garden. Opened September 16, 2006. Closed September 23, 2006.* A new play described as an action-adventure girl power journey through a magical land.

LOVE IN THE INSECURITY ZONE. *Written by Mike Folie. Directed by Rachel Wood. Produced by Boomerang Theatre Company. Center Stage. Opened September 19, 2006. Closed September 30, 2006.* A new play about a future United States characterized by security zones.

ESOTERICA. *Written and performed by Eric Walton. Directed by Elysa Marden. DR2. Opened September 19, 2006. Closed December 31, 2006.* An evening of "intellectual swashbuckling" with mentalist/magician/actor Eric Walton.

THE PAIN AND THE ITCH. *Written by Bruce Norris. Directed by Anna D. Shapiro. Produced by Playwrights Horizons. Playwrights Horizons Mainstage. Opened September 21, 2006. Closed October 15, 2006.* A new play about a family Thanksgiving celebration gone awry.

THE 2ND ANNUAL CHESTER HORN SHORT PLAY FESTIVAL. *Produced by TheatreRats. Medicine Show. Opened September 21, 2006. Closed September 24, 2006.* A festival of new short plays.

- BONNIE AND CLEMENTINE, ON THEIR WAY TO VISIT THE GRAND CANYON, EXPLORE THE LIMITS OF THE DRAMATIC FORM, *by Shannon Reed.*
- P'TOWN CHRISTMAS '99, *by Carl A. Rossi.*
- GARLIC AND MILK, *by Robert Daria.*
- HOLY HELL, *by Barbara Lindsay.*
- WHAT HAPPENS IN VEGAS, *by Christopher Lockheardt.*
- HISTORY, *by Steven Bergman.*
- SHAKESPEARE LIVES, *by Mark Harvey Levine.*
- THE READING, *by John C Davenport.*
- WOMB, *by Kristin Pesceone.*
- A TICKLISH SITUATION, *by Christopher King.*
- DEAD CAT, *by Ry Herman.*
- MIRACULOUS DAY QUARTET, *by Mary Steelsmith.*
- PAGE-TURNER, *by Justin Warner.*
- ONE LAST THING, *by John Shanahan.*

GEOLOGY OF THE MIND. *Written by Shahan Stepanian. Directed by Stacee Mandeville. Producers Club. Opened September 22, 2006. Closed October 7, 2006.* A new play about a man whose world is collapsing around him.

SPIC & SPAM. *Written by Alba Sanchez and Peter J. Byrnes. La MaMa. Opened September 22, 2006. Closed October 8, 2006.* A late-night comedy show about ethnic and racial stereotypes, and the authors' enduring friendship.

YOUNG KING ARTHUR. *Book by Jon Shear and Marc Castle. Music by Scott Zesch. Lyrics by Marc Castle. Directed by Jason Summers. Produced by Vital Children's Theatre. McGinn Cazale Theatre. Opened September 23, 2006. Closed November 5, 2006.* A new musical about the legend of Camelot.

MACHIAVELLI. *Written by Richard Vetere. Directed by Evan Bergman. Arclight Theatre. Opened September 24, 2006. Closed November 5, 2006.* A play about the great political thinker and his clever wife.

SONGS OF THE DRAGONS FLYING TO HEAVEN. *Written and directed by Young Jean Lee. HERE Arts Center. Opened September 25, 2006. Closed October 20, 2006.* A new play about the author's Korean American heritage.

A ROOM OF ONE'S OWN. *Written and directed by Coco Fusco. P.S. 122. Opened September 28, 2006. Closed October 1, 2006.* A new live art/multimedia piece that examines the expanding role of American women in the war on terror.

CHANGING VIOLET. *Written by Deborah Louise Ortiz. Adapted and directed by Terri Muss. Produced by Dangerous Curves. The Bridge Theatre. Opened September 28, 2006. Closed December 2, 2006.* A new one-woman show about a young woman from the Bronx struggling with a variety of difficulties.

FOOLS AND LOVERS. *Adapted by Gregory Sherman and Gregory Wolfe. Music by Andrew Sherman. Words by William Shakespeare. Directed by Gregory Wolfe. Produced by Moonwork, Inc. Connelly Theatre. Opened September 28, 2006. Closed October 15, 2006.* A new adaptation of *Romeo and Juliet* and other Shakespearean works.

HOSPITAL 2006. *Conceived, written, and produced by Axis Company. Directed by Randy Sharp. Axis Theater. Opened September 29, 2006. Closed November 11, 2006.* A four-part serial play about the interior life of a man in a coma.

DRUG BUDDY. *Written by David Folwell. Directed by Alex Kilgore. Produced by The stageFARM. Cherry Lane Theatre. Opened September 30, 2006. Closed October 21, 2006.* A new play about a young man recovering from his first sexual experience, his first experience with drugs, and a brush with death.

TURNING TABLES. *Written and performed by Michael Ferrell, Ishah Janssen-Faith, Jack McGowan, Hemmendy Nelson, Phil Vos. Directed by Gita Reddy. Produced by Coffee Cup (a theatre co.). Collective Unconscious. Opened October 1, 2006. Closed October 15, 2006.* An original ensemble comedy, about first impressions told through the eyes of waiters.

BIRTH AND AFTER BIRTH. *Written by Tina Howe. Directed by Christian Parker. Produced by Atlantic Theater Company. Atlantic Theatre. Opened October 3, 2006. Closed October 29, 2006.* A new comedy about a contemporary family trying to hold it together.

EL CONQUISTADOR! *Written by Thaddeus Phillips, Tatiana Mallarino, and Victor Mallarino. Directed by Tatiana Mallarino. New York Theatre Workshop. Opened October 3, 2006. Closed October 22, 2006.* A new play about a Colombian peasant who tries his luck in the big city.

DEATH IN VACANT LOT! *Written by Terayama Shuji. Adapted and directed by Kameron Steele. Produced by The South Wing. LMCC Swing Space. Opened October 4, 2006. Closed October 14, 2006.* An allegorical play with music based on a Japanese film from the mid-1970s about Japan's loss of innocence during World War II.

WINGMAN. *Written by Robert Cole and John Wooten. Altered Stages. Opened October 4, 2006. Closed October 15, 2006.* A new play about cyber-dating.

THE END OF CINEMATICS. Written and directed by Mikel Rouse. BAM Harvey Theatre. Opened October 4, 2006. Closed October 7, 2006. A pop opera that explores the effect of pop culture on the contemporary cinematic experience.

KANSAS CITY OR ALONG THE WAY. *Written by Robert Attenweiler. Directed by Seth Duerr. Produced by Disgraced Productions. The Red Room. Opened October 5, 2006. Closed October 22, 2006.* A new play about two strangers whose lives collide in Ohio in the 1930s.

CORRECTIVE LENS. *Book and lyrics by Ruthy Rosen. Music by Arthur Abrams. Directed by Ruthy Rosen. Theater for the New City. Opened October 5, 2006. Closed October 22, 2006.* A bittersweet comedy with music, in seven vignettes, about two friends from high school who reconnect fifty-seven years later.

TRUTH. *Written and performed by Mike Daisey. Directed by Jean-Michele Gregory. Ars Nova. Opened October 5, 2006. Closed November 4, 2006.* A new monologue about James Frey, J.T. LeRoy, Oprah, lying, and the struggle to tell the truth.

THE LAST EMPEROR OF FLUSHING. *Dixon Place. Opened October 5, 2006. Closed October 12, 2006.* A memoir monologue by Alvin Eng.

NICKEL AND DIMED. *Written by Joan Holden. Directed by Dave Dalton. Produced by 3Graces Theater Company. Bank Street Theatre. Opened October 5, 2006. Closed October 28, 2006.* A new stage adaptation of Barbara Ehrenreich's book about America's working poor.

GLASS HIGHWAYS. *Written by David Marrero. Directed by Matt Black. Produced by Frontier Stage Productions. Jan Hus Playhouse Theatre. Opened October 6, 2006. Closed October 30, 2006.* A play about a man whose family opposes his marriage, set on Christmas Eve in New Mexico.

A FIRST CLASS MAN. *Written by David Freeman. Directed by Kareem Fahmy. Produced by AL-TEREGO Productions. 45th Street Theatre. Opened October 6, 2006. Closed October 21, 2006.* A new play about the life of Indian mathematician Srinivasa Ramanujan.

ME, MY GUITAR AND DON HENLEY. *Written by Krista Vernoff. Directed by Peter Paige. Produced by Crooked Neck Productions. 14th Street Theatre. Opened October 7, 2006. Closed October 27, 2006.* A play about the women in a family whose patriarch is on his deathbed.

GREATER BUFFALO. *Written by Robyn Burland. Directed by Jessica Davis-Irons. Theater for the New City. Opened October 7, 2006. Closed October 22, 2006.* A new play about two troubled young people stumbling toward adulthood.

THE THUGS. *Written by Adam Bock. Directed by Anne Kauffman. Soho Rep. Opened October 7, 2006. Closed November 12, 2006.* A new comedy about work, thunder, and the mysterious things that are happening on the ninth floor of a big law firm.

DUMBYA'S RAPTURE. *Written and directed by Eric Diamond. Produced by Rough Theater. The Red Room. Opened October 7, 2006. Closed November 4, 2006.* A political satire that "dramatizes the real and true history of the US 2001–2006."

TRUCE ON URANUS. *Written and directed by Mark Lundberg. Produced by Dreamscape Theatre. Hudson Guild. Opened October 8, 2006. Closed October 28, 2006.* A world-premiere queer farce about extraterrestrial spiritual discovery.

BLUE DOOR. *Written by Tanya Barfield. Directed by Leigh Silverman. Playwrights Horizons Peter J Sharp. Opened October 8, 2006. Closed October 29, 2006.* A new play about a famous African American mathematician who thinks he's losing his grip on reality.

KRANKENHAUS BLUES. *Written by Sam Forman. Directed by Donna Mitchell. Produced by Visible Theatre. Abingdon Theatre. Opened October 8, 2006. Closed November 5, 2006.* A new play about disability issues, genocide, and the grim realities of show business.

REESE'S PIECES. *Written and directed by Rob Reese. Produced by Amnesia Wars. Sage Theater. Opened October 10, 2006. Closed October 18, 2006.* A new comedy featuring scenes from contemporary society.

WRECKS. *Written and directed by Neil LaBute. Public Theater. Opened October 10, 2006. Closed November 19, 2006.* A new solo play performed by Ed Harris.

MYCENAEAN. *Written and directed by Carl Hancock Rux. BAM Harvey Theatre. Opened October 10, 2006. Closed October 14, 2006.* A multidisciplinary work about cultural evolution and decline.

LE LYCANTHROPE. *Written by Timothy McCown Reynolds. Directed by Brendan Turk. Produced by loup garou International. Kraine Theatre. Opened October 11, 2006. Closed October 31, 2006.* A riff on Moliere's *The Misanthrope* billed as a "revenge farce with a monster movie groove."

ASCENSION. *Written by Edmund De Santis. Directed by Marc Geller. Produced by Red Light District. Lion Theatre. Opened October 11, 2006. Closed November 19, 2006.* A new play about a Catholic priest who is accused of sexually abusing a boy.

MACDEATH. *Written by John Martin and Dudley Stone. Directed by Brian Nelson. Produced by HMS Productions. Producers Club. Opened October 11, 2006. Closed October 22, 2006.* A play described as a murder mystery with strong parallels to Shakespeare's *Macbeth*.

INVISIBLE MESSAGES. *Written and directed by Peter S. Petralia. Produced by Proto-type. P.S. 122. Opened October 12, 2006. Closed October 29, 2006.* A new theatre piece inspired by the author's journey across Asia on the Trans-Siberian Railway.

TALE OF 2CITIES: AN AMERICAN JOYRIDE ON MULTIPLE TRACKS. *Written by Heather Woodbury. Directed by Dudley Saunders. P.S. 122. Opened October 12, 2006. Closed October 29, 2006.* A two-part, time-traversing saga about effects of the Brooklyn Dodgers' relocation to Los Angeles in 1957.

MILES TO BABLYON. *Written by Ann Harson. Directed by Tom Thornton. Produced by Evensong Associates. American Theatre of Actors. Opened October 12, 2006. Closed October 29, 2006.* A new play about the mother of playwright Eugene O'Neill.

HEARTBREAK. *Written and directed by Marc Morales. Produced by Edge of Insanity. Under St. Marks. Opened October 12, 2006. Closed November 4, 2006.* A new play about vampires, set in New York City's hottest nightclub.

MODERN LIVING. *Written by Richard Sheinmel. Directed by Michael Baron. La MaMa. Opened October 13, 2006. Closed October 29, 2006.* A new play about a New York performance artist named Mitchell.

HELIX 999. *Written by Kenneth Nowell. Directed by Candace O'Neil Cihocki. Produced by The Looking Glass Theatre. Looking Glass Theatre. Opened October 13, 2006. Closed November 18, 2006.* A new science fiction play that imagines a world where genetically produced people walk among the regular folk.

THE BROTHERS KARAMAZOV. *Adapted by Carolyn Fuchs. Directed by Tal Aviezer. Produced by Red Monkey Theater Group. Mazer Theatre. Opened October 14, 2006. Closed October 29, 2006.* An original dramatization of Dostoevsky's famous novel.

IN PUBLIC. *Written by George Hunka. Directed by Isaac Butler. Produced by Theatre Minima. Manhattan Theatre Source. Opened October 18, 2006. Closed October 28, 2006.* A new play about two married couples during a long weekend in New York.

SOUTHERN COMFORTS. *Written by Kathleen Clark. Directed by Judith Ivey. Produced by Primary Stages. 59E59. Opened October 18, 2006. Closed November 4, 2006.* A play about a widow and widower who meet late in life.

YOHEN. *Written by Philip Kan Gotanda. Directed by Seret Scott. Produced by Pan Asian Repertory Theatre. West End Theatre. Opened October 18, 2006. Closed November 5, 2006.* A new play about an interracial couple who begin to question the shape and function of their marriage decades after they wed.

A SEXTET OF DYSFUNCTION. *Produced by Robot vs. Dinosaur. Richmond Shepard Theatre. Opened October 19, 2006. Closed October 29, 2006.* Six new one-act plays, each focusing on a unique dysfunctional relationship.

THE FORTUNE TELLER. *Written and directed by Erik Sanko. Music by Erik Sanko and Danny Elfman. HERE Arts Center. Opened October 19, 2006. Closed December 23, 2006.* A puppetry theatre piece about the benefactors of a millionaire who find that the fate of their inheritances rests with a fortune teller.

MAKEOUT SESSION. *Written by Kenan Minkoff. Directed by Matt Cowart. TBG Arts Complex. Opened October 20, 2006. Closed November 12, 2006.* A new play about a couple who meet when they're teenagers and then meet again ten years later.

OUTING WITTGENSTEIN. *Written by Fred Newman. Directed by Dan Friedman. Castillo Theatre. Opened October 20, 2006. Closed December 3, 2006.* A new play in which the famous gay Austrian philosopher is saluted on a *This Is Your Life*-like TV show.

THE GIVEN. *Written by Francine Volpe. Directed by Michael Imperioli and Zetna Fuentes. Studio Dante. Opened October 21, 2006. Closed November 11, 2006.* A new play about a woman who works in a strip club.

THE FLOOD. *Book, music, and lyrics by Peter Mills and Cara Reichel. Directed by Cara Reichel. Produced by Prospect Theater Company. American Theatre of Actors. Opened October 21, 2006. Closed November 19, 2006.* A new musical about an Illinois town struggling to cope with the rising tide of the Mississippi River.

ABANDON. *Written and directed by Matthew Maguire. La MaMa. Opened October 22, 2006. Closed November 5, 2006.* A narrative collage play about a young woman who is afraid to love.

PIECES OF PARADISE. *Written by Tennessee Williams. Directed by Stephan Morrow. 13th Street Repertory. Opened October 22, 2006. Closed February 2007.* A program of four "lost" plays by Tennessee Williams, presented in benefit performances to help save this historic off-off-Broadway theatre.

EMERGENCE-SEE! *Written and performed by Daniel Beaty. Directed by Kenny Leon. Public Theater. Opened October 22, 2006. Closed November 19, 2006.* A one-man play that tells the story of what happens when a slave ship rises out of the Hudson River in 2006 New York City.

MY DEAH. *Written by John Epperson. Directed by Mark Waldrop. Abingdon Theatre. Opened October 24, 2006. Closed November 26, 2006.* A comedy that transplants the story of Medea to contemporary Louisiana.

A SMALL MELODRAMATIC STORY. *Written by Stephen Belber. Directed by Lucie Tiberghien. Produced by LAByrinth Theater Company. Public Theater. Opened October 24, 2006. Closed November 5, 2006.* A new play about a widow who is trying to decide whether her life is worth reengaging in.

WHO KILLED BOB MARLEY? *Created and performed by Roger Guenveur Smith. Produced by Harlem Stage. Opened October 24, 2006. Closed October 28, 2006.* A new play about the tension between truth and fiction.

LIVE GIRLS. *Written by Victoria Stewart. Directed by Lou Jacob. Urban Stages. Opened October 25, 2006. Closed November 26, 2006.* A play about a performance artist who interviews a porn star.

THE GREAT CONJURER. *Written by Christine Simpson. Directed by Kevin Bartlett. Produced by Fluid Motion Theater & Film. Kirk Theatre. Opened October 25, 2006. Closed November 4, 2006.* A new play loosely based on the life and work of Franz Kafka.

FOLIE A DEUX. *Written by David Stallings. Directed by Cristina Alicea. Produced by Maieutic Theater Works. The Rock Theater. Opened October 26, 2006. Closed November 12, 2006.* A new play about two different murders carried out by pairs of young people.

MEN ARE DOGS. *Written by Joe Simonelli. Directed by Donna Stiles. Produced by Simonelli Productions. Producers Club II. Opened October 26, 2006. Closed November 5, 2006.* A new comedy about an unorthodox support group for single and divorced women.

DANCING VS. THE RAT EXPERIMENT. *Created and produced by Witness Relocation. Directed by Dan Safer. La MaMa. Opened October 26, 2006. Closed November 12, 2006.* A dance work inspired by a documentary film about overpopulation in rats.

PORT AUTHORITY THROW DOWN. *Written by Mike Batistick. Directed by Connie Grappo. Produced by Working Theater. 45 Below. Opened October 26, 2006. Closed November 19, 2006.* A play about a Pakistani cab driver in New York City as he struggles to understand why his brother has been taken away by the authorities.

THE TIMES THEY ARE A-CHANGIN'. *Conceived and directed by Twyla Tharp. Music and lyrics by Bob Dylan. Brooks Atkinson Theatre. Opened October 26, 2006. Closed November 19, 2006.* A new musical conceived from songs by Bob Dylan.

BAD DOG. *Written by Rebecca J. Stokes. Directed by Russell Taylor. Produced by Theater Forum. Church for All Nations. Opened October 27, 2006. Closed November 19, 2006.* A surreal comedy about the world of dogs and their owners.

THE BEST PARTY EVER. *Written and directed by Annie Ward. Richmond Shepard Theatre. Opened October 28, 2006. Closed December 2007.* A comedy about a keg party.

STANLEY 2006. *Written and directed by Lisa D'Amour. HERE Arts Center. Opened October 29, 2006. Closed November 18, 2006.* A multimedia solo piece about the character Stanley Kowalski from *A Streetcar Named Desire*.

THE CLERIC. *Written by Tim Marks. Directed by Paula D'Alessandris. Produced by Mind the Gap Theatre. 59E59. Opened October 29, 2006. Closed November 12, 2006.* A new play about an Irish American priest who is discovered by American military forces years after he was believed to have been taken hostage by militants.

THE SUNSET LIMITED. *Written by Cormac McCarthy. Directed by Sheldon Patinkin. Produced by 59E59 Theaters & Steppenwolf Theatre Company. 59E59. Opened October 29, 2006. Closed November 19, 2006.* A new play about an ex-con and an intellectual atheist who meet on a subway platform.

THE CLEAN HOUSE. *Written by Sarah Ruhl. Directed by Bill Rauch. Produced by Lincoln Center Theater. Mitzi Newhouse Theater. Opened October 30, 2006. Closed January 28, 2007.* A new play about a doctor whose life is spinning out of control.

EATFEST. *Produced by Emerging Artists Theatre. Theater Five. Opened October 31, 2006. Closed November 19, 2006.* Emerging Artists Theater presents its perennial festival of new short works.

- ROOM AT THE INN, *by Barbara Lindsay.*
- RECOIL, *by Karen Schiff.*
- FIVE MINUTES, *by Allan Baker.*
- MUST THE SHOW GO ON, *by Carl L. Williams.*
- CUSTOMER DISSERVICE, *by Gregg Pasternack.*
- TRIPLE PLAY, *by Marc Castle.*
- HELP THYSELF, *by Greg Kalleres.*
- NEVERLAND, *by Kim Kelly.*
- CAN'T YOU SEE WE'RE ACTING, *by Carl L. Williams.*

THE CHARLOTTE SALOMON PROJECT. *Conceived and adapted by Jessica Brater and Miriam Felton-Dansky. Additional text by J. Burstein-Stern, E. Emmons, A. Gilchrist, A. Glickstein, and K. Schapiro. Directed by Jessica Brater. Produced by Polybe + Seats. Brooklyn Fire Proof. Opened November 1, 2006. Closed November 19, 2006.* A new play about the life of a relatively unknown and extraordinary young woman living in very difficult times.

OBSTRUCTION PLAYS. *Produced by Slant Theatre Project. Collective Unconscious. Opened November 1, 2006. Closed December 2, 2006.* A program of short plays created from a set of rules (or "obstructions") laid out for the playwrights by their colleagues.

- THE DINNER TABLE, *by Dan O'Brien, directed by Suzanne Agins.*
- PRIEST IN A POOL, *by Michele Lowe, directed by Adam Knight.*
- CAUTION: PARENTS MAY BE LESS INSANE THAN THEY APPEAR, *by Lisa Kron, directed by Wes Grantom.*
- I SEE LONDON, I SEE FRANCE, *written and directed by Evan Cabnet.*
- BLOOMING ANDROMACHAE, *by Marcus Gardley, directed by Lori Wolter.*
- UNLIMITED, *by Mat Smart, directed by Steve Cosson.*

THE MILLINER. *Written by Suzanne Glass. Directed by Mark Clement. Produced by The Directors Company. East 13th Street Theatre. Opened November 1, 2006. Closed December 17, 2006.* A play about a Jewish hatmaker who returns to Germany following World War II.

EVIL DEAD: THE MUSICAL. *Book and lyrics by George Reinblatt. Music by Frank Cipolla, Christopher Bond, Melissa Morris, and George Reinblatt. Directed by Christopher Bond and Hinton Battle.*

New World Stages. Opened November 1, 2006. Closed February 17, 2007. A new musical comedy based on Sam Raimi's cult horror films.

I'LL BE SEEING YOU. *Written by Jennifer Russo. Phil Bosokowski Theatre. Opened November 1, 2006. Closed November 4, 2006.* A new show that uses the music and the culture of the movie musicals of the 1940s and 1950s to examine the function of entertainment, generally, and music, specifically, in a wartime society.

RECREATING KEITER: I SAW DAD MAKE THE WHOLE THING UP. *Written and performed by Cindy Keiter. Additional material by Padraic Lillis. Directed by Padraic Lillis. Produced by Bridge Club Productions. Manhattan Theatre Source. Opened November 1, 2006. Closed November 18, 2006.* A new play about the playwright's father, sports broadcaster Les Keiter.

THE MAIL ORDER BRIDE. *Written by Charles Mee. Music by Nick Moore. Lyrics by Travis Kramer. Directed by Eric Parness. Produced by Resonance Ensemble. Beckett Theatre. Opened November 2, 2006. Closed November 19, 2006.* A new comedy inspired by Moliere's *The Imaginary Invalid.*

POST MORTEM. *Written by A.R. Gurney. Directed by Jim Simpson. Flea. Opened November 2, 2006. Closed December 16, 2006.* A new comedy set in the future, where a controversial late twentieth century play by A.R. Gurney is uncovered.

POT AU NOIR (THE BLACK HOLE). *Written and directed by Jake Hooker. Chocolate Factory. Opened November 2, 2006. Closed November 18, 2006.* A retelling of the story of Cain and Abel.

BROTHER'S KEEPER. *Written and directed by Marc Weiner. Produced by Marcus Productions and The Playwrights' Gate. Theater Three. Opened November 2, 2006. Closed November 19, 2006.* A play about two sisters who care for their mentally challenged brother.

THE BRONX BALMERS. *Written by Jeremy Handelman. Directed by Linda Burson. Produced by Off The Leash Productions. The Turtle's Shell Theater. Opened November 2, 2006. Closed November 19, 2006.* A new play about what happens to the institutions of community and family when unstoppable outside forces impose radical change.

SHANNON IN AMBIENT LIGHT. *Written by Timothy Mansfield. Directed by Michael Kimmel. Bottle Factory. Opened November 2, 2006. Closed November 18, 2006.* A new play about a photographer preparing for an upcoming exhibition.

LOVE, DEATH, AND INTERIOR DECORATING. *Written by Keith Boynton. Altered Stages. Opened November 2, 2006. Closed November 18, 2006.* An evening of two one-act plays by Keith Boynton, Walls, and The Quotable Assassin.

THE BLUEST EYE. *Written by Lydia Diamond. Directed by Hallie Gordon. Produced by Steppenwolf Theatre Company. Duke on 42nd Street. Opened November 3, 2006. Closed November 19, 2006.* An adaptation of Toni Morrison's book about a young black girl's coming of age in the 1940s.

NO MORE PRETENDING. *Written by Kirk Wood Bromley. Directed by Howard Thoresen. Produced by Inverse Theater Company. Opened November 3, 2006. Closed November 11, 2006.* A new play about the pros and cons of working in indie theater.

INTERVIEW/BEHIND THE INVISIBLE ENEMY. *Written by Valerie Killigrew. 13th Street Repertory. Opened November 3, 2006. Closed December 2, 2006.* A program of two short plays by Valerie Killigrew, one about the nature of power, the other about the nature of free thought.

KIP, THE ENCHANTED CAT. *Written and directed by Aaron Michael Zook. Produced by Tuckaberry Productions. Impact Theater. Opened November 4, 2006. Closed December 9, 2006.* A musical fairy tale about a princess and her enchanted feline.

FENWAY: LAST OF THE BOHEMIANS. *Written by Kelly McAllister and Lisa Margaret Holub. Directed by Tim Errickson. Produced by Boomerang Theatre Company and Impetuous Theater Group. chashama. Opened November 4, 2006. Closed November 19, 2006.* A new play inspired by Chekhov's *Uncle Vanya*, set in the Reagan Era on a small West Coast commune.

KINGDOM OF NOT. *Written and performed by Dan Carbone. Produced by Kaliyuga Arts. Cherry Lane Theatre. Opened November 4, 2006. Closed November 18, 2006.* A new one-man play about a preternaturally wise baby boy and his strange guardian.

I WISH YOU A BOAT. *Created and directed by Wendy Ward. The Ward Studio. Opened November 4, 2006. Closed February 4, 2007.* A play about a shipwreck.

ALL TOO HUMAN. *Written and performed by Henry Miller. Production Overseen by Kevin Conway. Produced by A New Dawn Production, Inc. 45th Street Theatre. Opened November 5, 2006. Closed December 3, 2006.* A solo play about the famous lawyer Clarence Darrow.

IF I FELL. *Written by Michael Lipiner. Directed by Demetrius Wren. Manhattan Theatre Source. Opened November 5, 2006. Closed November 6, 2006.* A new play about a thirty-something man who still lives with his parents.

MIMI LE DUCK. *Book and lyrics by Diana Hansen-Young. Music by Brian Feinstein. Directed by Thomas Caruso. New World Stages. Opened November 6, 2006. Closed December 3, 2006.* A "nouveau" musical about a discontented Idaho housewife who one day decides to escape her life and move to Paris.

THE TICKET. *Book by Eric Ottem. Lyrics by Gary Bragg. Music by Dave Demichaelis and Gary Bragg. Directed by Michael Raimondi. Produced by Big Break Productions and Paradox Productions, Inc. Sage Theater. Opened November 7, 2006. Closed November 26, 2006.* A musical about a woman running for governor.

WHY DOES IT STING WHEN I PEE? *Written by Felipe Ossa. Directed by Tom Thornton. CSV Cultural Center. Opened November 8, 2006. Closed November 19, 2006.* A new comedy about a gay actor who decides he needs to go to jail in order to find himself.

BRIDAL TERRORISM. *Written by Bill Rosenfield. Directed by Bill Barry. Produced by Diversity Players of Harlem. Producers Club. Opened November 8, 2006. Closed November 12, 2006.* A play about one woman's tactics in finding a groom.

HOW THE GRINCH STOLE CHRISTMAS!—THE MUSICAL. *Book and lyrics by Timothy Mason. Music by Mel Marvin. Original composer: Albert Hague. Creator/supervisor: Jack O'Brien. Directed by Matt August. Hilton Theatre. Opened November 8, 2006. Closed January 7, 2007.* A musical version of the classic Dr. Seuss story.

COUNT DOWN. *Written by Dominique Cieri. Directed by Elyse Knight. Produced by Double Play Connections. Bank Street Theatre. Opened November 8, 2006. Closed November 19, 2006.* A play about a teaching artist working with seven young women.

THE 51ST (DREAM) STATE. *Written by Sekou Sundiata. Directed by Christopher McElroen. BAM Opera House. Opened November 8, 2006. Closed November 11, 2006.* A multimedia examination of the contemporary American experience.

HOME FRONT. *Written by Daniel Algie. Directed by E. Randahl Hoey. La MaMa. Opened November 9, 2006. Closed November 26, 2006.* A new play inspired by the legend of Herakles.

CAMERA READY ART. *Written by Edward Musto. Directed by Daedra Kaehler. Players Theatre. Opened November 9, 2006. Closed November 12, 2006.* An evening of short plays by Edward Musto: SHUTTERBUG, AND EVERYTHING NICE, and WEDDING ALBUM.

SECURITY 2. *Produced by TheDrillingCompaNY. 78th Street Theatre Lab. Opened November 9, 2006. Closed November 19, 2006.* A program of short plays on the subject of security, in its many meanings.

- A GOPHER IN THE NINTH WARD, *by Trish Harnetiaux, directed by Eric Nightengale.*
- CRUSADE, *by Justin Boyd, directed by Richard Harden.*
- WITH BENEFITS, *by Colleen Cosgrove, directed by Dave Marantz.*
- BREACH OF SECURITY, *by Brian Christopher Williams, directed by Tom Herman.*
- HAY OUTTA HELL, *by Yvette Sirker, directed by Hamilton Clancy.*
- GRAPEHEADS, *by Sheri Graubert, directed by Hamilton Clancy.*
- THE KNOCK, *by Drew Sachs, directed by Bradford Olson.*
- CONTINUUM, *by Reneé Flemings, directed by Liz Dunn Ruiz.*
- SAFE, *by Don Carter, directed by Rachel Wood.*

TRI-CHOT-O-MY. *Written by David Cahill. Directed by Adam J. Natale and Maria Higgins. Produced by Fly By Night Theater. TADA! Youth Theater. Opened November 10, 2006. Closed November 19, 2006.* A program of three one-acts by David Cahill: CONVERSING ELEVENS, DUNCE, and TRAMPOLINE.

STRIKING 12. *Music by Brendan Milburn and Valerie Vigoda. Book and lyrics by Brendan Milburn, Rachel Sheinkin, and Valerie Vigoda. Directed by Ted Sperling. Daryl Roth Theatre. Opened November 12, 2006. Closed December 31, 2006.* A revival of the holiday musical by Brendan Milburn, performed by the indie pop-rock band Groove Lily.

HOW TO SAVE THE WORLD AND FIND TRUE LOVE IN 90 MINUTES. *Book and lyrics by Jonathan Karp. Music by Seth Weinstein. Directed by Christopher Gatelli. Produced by Lawrence Anderson and the Singing Comedians. New World Stages. Opened November 12, 2006. Closed December 31, 2006.* A musical set at the United Nations.

SEVEN STORIES. *Written and directed by Matthew H. Landfield. Produced by Hartland Productions. Manhattan Theatre Source. Opened November 12, 2006. Closed November 14, 2006.* A program of seven short plays that explore the boundaries between artistic freedom and sexual exploitation, addiction and redemption, trust and betrayal, and the corrosive effects of war on society in both the present and in former times.

365 DAYS/365 PLAYS. *Opened November 13, 2006. Closed November 11, 2007.* A year-long cycle of readings and productions of plays, all of which were written by Suzan-Lori Parks in a single year.

LINDSAY LOHAN'S MISTAKES TREE/NETWORKING WITH MAGICIANS. *Written by Larry Myers. Where Eagles Dare. Opened November 13, 2006.* Two new works, one about the edgy, impatient, Meta-Now Generation Omega; the other about "fringe" types—artists, artistes, the disenchanted, residentially challenged, rebels, renegades as well as security guards and ex-gym teachers.

DAI (ENOUGH). *Written and performed by Iris Bahr. Directed by Will Pomerantz. Produced by The Culture Project. 45 Bleecker. Opened November 14, 2006. Closed December 16, 2006.* A one-woman play about contemporary Israelis.

NESTED DOLL. *Written by Clay McLeod Chapman. Directed by Douglas MacHugh. Produced by CharlieCat Productions. The Red Room. Opened November 15, 2006. Closed November 19, 2006.* A new play about an immigrant girl who vanishes.

NEW SCIENCE. *Written by Jessica Slote. Directed by Martin Reckhaus. Theater for the New City. Opened November 16, 2006. Closed November 26, 2006.* A new show/science experiment inspired by the writings of eighteenth century Neapolitan philosopher Giambattista Vico.

REVOLVER. *Written by Christian Middleton. Directed by Sarah Haught. Produced by Wired Awake Productions. The Red Room. Opened November 16, 2006. Closed November 18, 2006.* A new comedy thriller about a privileged family forced to confront their lies and deceptions.

NO BOUNDARIES PLAY FESTIVAL. *Produced by Mirror Repertory Company. 14th Street Y. Opened November 16, 2006. Closed November 19, 2006.* A program of new short plays.

- THEATRE IS THE THING WITH TENTACLES, *by Ed Valentine.*
- JUST ANOTHER DAY IN NOVEMBER, *by Jonathon Joy.*
- CIRCUS CHIMPS, *by MacAdam Smith.*
- TEN SPEED REVOLUTION, *by John Heimbuch.*
- SONG OF BENTLEY, *by Daniel Kelley.*
- INCORPORATED, *by Sarah Hague.*
- THE PERIOD FAIRY, *by Jason Kessler.*

GREAT EXPECTATIONS. *Written by Bathsheba Doran. Directed by Will Pomerantz. Produced by TheatreworksUSA. Lucille Lortel Theatre. Opened November 16, 2006. Closed December 3, 2006.* TheatreworksUSA presents a new stage adaptation of the classic Charles Dickens novel.

THE SUBLET EXPERIMENT. *Written by Ethan Youngerman. Directed by Michelle Tattenbaum. Opened November 16, 2006. Closed May 20, 2007.* A new comedy about a serial subletter, a reality show reject, and the worst bank robbers in history. The show will be presented in a different New York City apartment each weekend.

MY NEW YORK. *Book by Carla Jablonski. Music and lyrics by Rick Hip-Flores. Conceived by Catherine Allen. Directed by Linda Ames Key. Produced by Vital Children's Theatre. McGinn Cazale Theatre. Opened November 18, 2006. Closed January 7, 2007.* A new play for kids about a competition to design a mural about New York City.

REGRETS ONLY. *Written by Paul Rudnick. Directed by Christopher Ashley. Manhattan Theatre Club. Opened November 19, 2006. Closed January 28, 2007.* A new play described as a comedy of Manhattan manners.

DURANGO. *Written by Julia Cho. Directed by Chay Yew. Public Theater. Opened November 20, 2006. Closed December 10, 2006.* A new play about a Korean American father and his two sons who go on a road trip to Durango, Colorado.

DARK MATTERS. *Written by Roberto Aguirre-Sacasa. Directed by Trip Cullman. Rattlestick Theatre. Opened November 20, 2006. Closed December 22, 2006.* A new play about a woman who disappears and then returns, talking of otherworldly beings.

BEYOND CHRISTOPHER STREET. *Wings Theater. Opened November 20, 2006. Closed December 16, 2006.* New gay-themed one-act plays by Mark Finley, David Pumo, Jonathan Kronenberger, and A.B. Lugo.

EIGHT WAYS TO MEET YOUR NEIGHBOR. *Written and directed by William Kevin McCauley. Produced by The Theatre-Studio, Inc. Theater-Studio. Opened November 25, 2006. Closed March 1, 2007.* A new comedy about two couples meeting for the first time.

LOVE: A TRAGIC ETUDE. *Created and directed by Juan Souki. Produced by Century Productions. Kraine Theatre. Opened November 27, 2006. Closed December 16, 2006.* A new multimedia theatre piece about two young lovers who are separated by military conflicts.

AS LONG A TIME AS A LONG TIME IS IN LONGTIME LAND… *Written by Todd Pate. Directed by Barbara Suter. Manhattan Theatre Source. Opened November 27, 2006. Closed December 2, 2006.* A new play about two men in a cell who are trying to learn the source of their condemnation.

SCREEN TEST. *Created by Rob Roth and Theo Kogan. P.S. 122. Opened November 28, 2006. Closed December 3, 2006.* A theatre work described as part video installation and part rock show.

THE ATHEIST. *Written by Ronan Noone. Directed by David Sullivan. Produced by Square Peg Productions. Center Stage. Opened November 29, 2006. Closed December 23, 2006.* A new play about one man's relentless quest for fame and celebrity.

THE MADONNA WHORE…CONFESSIONS OF A DIRTY MIND. *Written by Tim Douglas. Directed by Eric Thal. Produced by Twinstar Productions. Producers Club. Opened November 29, 2006. Closed December 16, 2006.* A play about a man who is infatuated with a porn star. Randy Jones (of the Village People) is in the cast.

VITAL SIGNS. *Produced by Vital Theatre Company. McGinn Cazale Theatre. Opened November 30, 2006. Closed December 17, 2006.* Vital Theatre Company presents its perennial new works festival.

- **HOW I WON THE WAR**, *by Andrea Lepcio.*
- **TAV**, *by Shawn Hirabayashi.*
- **SOUVENIRS**, *by Michael John Garces.*
- **THE REMOTE**, *by Mark Harvey Levine.*
- **FIVE WISHES**, *by Thomas H. Diggs.*
- **ANTARCTICA**, *by Anton Dudley.*
- **BRIGHT APPLE CRUSH**, *by Steven Yockey.*
- **CRIMES AGAINST HUMANITY**, *by Ross Maxwell.*
- **THE BLOOMINGDALE ROAD**, *by Mark Loewenstern.*
- **SAFFRON**, *by Deen.*
- **DISCOVERING COLUMBUS**, *by Kim Rosenstock.*
- **IT'S GIULIANI TIME**, *by Aurin Squire.*
- **DOUBLE FANTASY**, *by David Ben-Arie.*
- **BREAKING ROUTINE**, *by Robin Rothstein.*

TO BE LOVED. *Written by Alex DeFazio. Directed by Jody P. Person. Produced by Elixir Productions. chashama. Opened November 30, 2006. Closed December 23, 2006.* A new play about a monk and the ghost of the boy he loved.

THE BIG VOICE: GOD OR MERMAN? *Written by Jim Brochu and Steve Schalchlin. Additional lyrics by Marie Cain. Directed by Anthony Barnao. Actors Temple Theatre. Opened November 30, 2006. Closed May 13, 2007.* A new musical about two men who find eternal salvation in the temple of musical theatre.

BEING BORN. *Book and lyrics by Erika Stadtlander. Music by Ion Ionescu. Directed by Erika Stadtlander and Sean M. Littlejohn. Produced by Fildwith Ensemble Theatre. Theater Three. Opened November 30, 2006. Closed December 10, 2006.* A new musical about the emotional explorations of a group of young souls.

THE HAUNTING OF 85 EAST 4TH STREET. *Written and directed by Dan Bianchi. Produced by Horse Trade and Radiotheatre. The Red Room. Opened November 30, 2006. Closed December 23, 2006.* A new live "radio-style" drama about the true paranormal history of the building where the show takes place.

BREAD AND PUPPET THEATER. *Created by Peter Schumann. Produced by The Bread & Puppet Company. Theater for the New City. Opened November 30, 2006. Closed December 17, 2006.* The renowned activist theatre company from Vermont makes its annual New York City appearance with a new show entitled **THE BATTLE OF THE TERRORISTS AND THE HORRORISTS**.

OPEN DOOR. *Conceived, designed, and directed by Federico Restrepo. Music by Elizabeth Swados. Lyrics by Federico Restrepo. Produced by Loco 7. La MaMa. Opened December 1, 2006. Closed December 17, 2006.* A new "grand puppet theater work with song" about the current American immigrant experience.

FOUR BY THREE. *Directed by Miranda McDermott. New Media Repertory Theatre. Opened December 1, 2006. Closed December 8, 2006.* A collection of new one-act plays that all feature a surprise twist ending.

- **POOR HEARTS**, *by Edward Musto.*
- **ALL IS CALM**, *by John Levine.*
- **...AND EVERYTHING NICE**, *by Edward Musto.*
- **ACT TWO**, *by Stanford Pritchard.*

THE SCARLETT O'HARA COMPLEX. *Written by Karen Wheeling-Reynolds. Directed by David Reynolds. Produced by Gaff Tape Productions. Clurman Theatre. Opened December 1, 2006. Closed December 9, 2006.* A play about a Southern woman coping with her husband's infidelity.

ART PEOPLE. *Written by Mark Leib. Directed by Tony Giordano. Produced by Committed Theatre Co. Players Theatre. Opened December 3, 2006. Closed December 17, 2006.* A new play about the challenges of creating art and surviving in a world that is inhospitable to artists.

GUTENBERG! THE MUSICAL! *Book, music, and lyrics by Anthony King and Scott Brown. Directed by Alex Timbers. 59E59. Opened December 3, 2006. Closed December 31, 2006.* A musical comedy about two writers creating a musical about the inventor of the printing press.

ALL FALL DOWN. *Created and developed by David Ledoux and Allison Smith. Directed by David Ledoux. Produced by Theatre Recrudscence. CSV Cultural Center. Opened December 3, 2006. Closed December 17, 2006.* A new interactive theatre piece that imagines New York City in the midst of a great plague.

NEVER MISSED A DAY. *Written by Ken Jaworowski. Directed by Thomas Cote. WorkShop Theater. Opened December 4, 2006. Closed December 16, 2006.* A new tragicomedy about a man looking back on his career at this retirement party.

KAOS. *Conceived and directed by Martha Clarke. Text Adapted by Frank Pugliese. New York Theatre Workshop. Opened December 4, 2006. Closed December 30, 2006.* A new theatrical work based on the 1984 film of the same name.

TWO SEPTEMBER. *Written by Mac Wellman. Directed by Loy Arcenas. Produced by The Flea Theater. Flea. Opened December 5, 2006. Closed December 16, 2006.* A new play about the conflicts that preceded the Vietnam War.

FLOYD AND CLEA UNDER THE WESTERN SKY. *Book and lyrics by David Cale. Music by Jonathan Kreisberg and David Cale. Directed by Joe Calarco. Playwrights Horizons Mainstage. Opened December 5, 2006. Closed December 17, 2006.* A new musical about a journey from Montana to Texas.

THE VOYSEY INHERITANCE. *Written by Harley Granville Barker. Adapted by David Mamet. Directed by David Warren. Atlantic Theatre. Opened December 6, 2006. Closed March 25, 2007.* A new adaptation of the Harley Granville-Barker social drama from the early twentieth century.

STILL LIFE WITH COMMENTATOR: AN ORATORIO. *Libretto by Michael C. Ladd. Music by Vijay Iyer. Directed by Ibrahim Quraishi. BAM Harvey Theatre. Opened December 6, 2006. Closed December 10, 2006.* A cross-media oratorio about our media-filtered encounters with war and atrocity.

HIGH FIDELITY. *Book by David Lindsay-Abaire. Music by Tom Kitt. Lyrics by Amanda Green. Directed by Walter Bobbie. Imperial Theatre. Opened December 7, 2006. Closed December 17, 2006.* A new romantic musical comedy based on Nick Hornby's novel of the same name.

AN OPTIMISTIC PICTURE. *Written by Walter Corwin. Directed by Jonathan Weber. Theater for the New City. Opened December 7, 2006. Closed December 23, 2006.* A program of two one-act plays, both set in New York: one about a once-successful man who flounders through life; the other about a government translator with failing eyesight and lagging spirit.

WIDOWS OF TROY. *Written by Hillary Miller. Directed by Kristjan Thorgeirsson. The Syrup Room. Opened December 7, 2006. Closed December 22, 2006.* A new adaptation of *The Trojan Women.*

MY MOTHER'S ITALIAN, MY FATHER'S JEWISH & I'M IN THERAPY. *Written and performed by Steve Solomon. Directed by John Bowab. Little Shubert Theatre. Opened December 8, 2006. Closed April 29, 2007.* A somewhat autobiographical solo comedy about the wacky side of the human condition.

CARRIE. *Written by Erik Jackson. Directed by Josh Rosenzweig. Produced by Theatre Couture. P.S. 122. Opened December 9, 2006. Closed December 30, 2006.* A new comic adaptation of Stephen King's famous horror novel.

STANDARDS OF DECENCY PROJECT. *Produced by Blue Coyote Theater Group. Access Theatre. Opened December 12, 2006. Closed January 8, 2007.* A program of nine short plays designed to challenge the notion of "decency" as set forth by the FCC and other bodies.

- PATIENCE (OR, TAKING IT), *by Stan Richardson, directed by Gary Shrader.*
- EARNING A SHARP REBUKE FROM EMILY POST, *by David Foley, directed by Gary Shrader.*

- A FUNERAL HOME IN BROOKLYN, *by David Johnston, directed by Kyle Ancowitz.*
- EXPOSURE, *by Laura E. Henry, directed by Gary Shrader.*
- WHAT TO DO TO A GIRL, *by Matthew Freeman, directed by Kyle Ancowitz.*
- TWO TOTALLY NAKED GUYS STANDING AROUND TALKING ABOUT BLASPHEMY WITHOUT GETTING ALL THAT VIOLENT ABOUT IT...THEN A SERMON, *by Brian Dysktra, directed by Stephen Speights.*
- SOMETHING DECENT, *by Kristen Palmer, directed by Kyle Ancowitz.*
- TIBERIAS, *by John Yearley, directed by Robert Buckwalter.*
- TRUE LOVE WAITS, *by Boo Killebrew, directed by Stephen Speights.*

TWAS THE NIGHT BEFORE. *Produced by The Flea Theater and The Chelsea Art Museum. Flea. Opened December 13, 2006. Closed December 30, 2006.* A program of new short plays inspired by the poem "'Twas the Night Before Christmas." The playwrights are Christopher Durang, Len Jenkin, Roger Rosenblatt, Elizabeth Swados, and Mac Wellman.

TWIST. *Book and lyrics by Gila Sand. Music by Paul Leschen. Directed by Gila Sand. Kraine Theatre. Opened December 13, 2006. Closed January 18, 2007.* A new musical that shifts Dickens's *Oliver Twist* into the world of drag and S&M.

WODEN. *Written and directed by Gene Ruffini. Theater for the New City. Opened December 14, 2006. Closed December 30, 2006.* A new play about one man caught in and crushed by the corporate machine.

DATING GRIM. *Written by Dennis Hurley and John Misselwitz. Directed by Rodney Hakim. TBG Arts Complex. Opened December 14, 2006. Closed December 17, 2006.* A play about dating during the holiday season.

SERPENT SONG. *Written by Morgan Sheehan-Bubla. Directed by Josh Adler. Produced by Fune's Memory. Impact Theater. Opened December 14, 2006. Closed December 17, 2006.* A new play about a damsel in distress who is being guarded by the dutiful serpent king.

OUR TIME THEATRE COMPANY. *Produced by Our Time Theatre Company. Theater Three. Opened December 15, 2006. Closed December 17, 2006.* A program of three original one-acts plays by members of this company comprised of teens who stutter.

- A SISTER'S HOPE, *written and directed by Fern Schlesinger.*
- 2 TRAIN, *written and directed by Jonathan Greig.*
- THE PERFECT PLACE, *written and directed by Keith Russell.*

JO MARCH. *Adapted and directed by Ryan Gilliam. Music by Mchael Hickey. Opened December 15, 2006. Closed January 7, 2007.* An original rockabilly musical based on Louisa May Alcott's *Little Women.*

STRINGS. *Written by Carole Bugge. Directed by Marvin Kaye. Produced by Open Book Theatre Company. 78th Street Theatre Lab. Opened December 16, 2006. Closed January 6, 2007.* A new play about cutting-edge physics and human pain and passion.

AMONG FRIENDS. *Written by Kristine Thatcher. Directed by Barbara Parisi. Produced by Ryan Repertory Company. Harry Warren Theatre. Opened December 16, 2006. Closed December 30, 2006.* A play about male bonding in a weekly poker game.

HENRY AND MUDGE. *Book and lyrics by Kait Kerrigan. Music by Brian Lowdermilk. Directed by Peter Flynn. Produced by Theatreworks/USA. Lucille Lortel Theatre. Opened December 17, 2006. Closed January 20, 2007.* A musical based on Cythia Ralant's picture books about a boy and his dog.

IF THERE'S JACK-IN-THE-BOX, GET OUT! *Written and performed by Erinina Marie Ness and Evan Shafran. Directed by Genevieve Gearhart. Produced by Mir Productions. Gene Frankel Theatre. Opened December 18, 2006. Closed December 20, 2006.* A new theatre piece about the battle of the sexes.

BECOMING ADELE. *Written by Eric Houston. Directed by Victor Moag. Produced by Gotham Stage Company. Clurman Theatre. Opened December 20, 2006. Closed January 6, 2007.* A play about a spunky Brooklyn waitress.

(DON'T GO) HOME FOR THE HOLIDAYS. *Produced by The Calamity Carolers of Doom. Abingdon Theatre. Opened December 21, 2006. Closed December 31, 2006.* A satirical holiday musical review.

CALLBACK. *Written by Bill Svanoe. Directed by Blake Bradford. Produced by Phare Play Productions. Lodestar Theatre. Opened December 29, 2006. Closed January 14, 2007.* A play charting the friendship between two actors over a forty-year period.

THE RAPTURE PROJECT. *Created by John Bell, Trudi Cohen, Stephen Kaplin, Jenny Romaine, Shane Baker, Andrea Lomanto, and Jessica Lorence. Consultants/additional text by Christopher Calderhead and Roberto Rossi. Produced by Great Small Works. HERE Arts Center. Opened January 4, 2007. Closed January 21, 2007.* A seriocomic look at fundamentalism and current American culture performed by puppets.

KILL ME LIKE YOU MEAN IT. *Written by Kiran Rikhye. Directed by Jon Stancato. Produced by The Stolen Chair Theatre Company. The Red Room. Opened January 5, 2007. Closed January 27, 2007.* A new play described as "a timely absurdist film noir for the stage as Ionesco might have imagined it."

DIRTY GIRL. *Written by Ronnie Koenig. Directed by Robert W. McMaster. Produced by HorseTrade & Firecracker Productions. Kraine Theatre. Opened January 6, 2007. Closed January 27, 2007.* A new play based on the author's own experiences as an editor of *Playgirl Magazine*.

PURITY. *Written by Thomas Bradshaw. Directed by Yehuda Duenyas. P.S. 122. Opened January 7, 2007. Closed January 23, 2007.* A new play about race, academia, pedophilia, drug abuse, promiscuity, and infidelity.

YOU BELONG TO ME. *Written and directed by Josh Fox. P.S. 122. Opened January 7, 2007. Closed January 23, 2007.* A new work about the ends of wars throughout history.

THE GERMANS IN PARIS. *Written by Jonathan Leaf. Directed by James Milton. Produced by Verse Theater Manhattan. Arclight Theatre. Opened January 8, 2007. Closed January 27, 2007.* A play about the lives of three German exiles: Heinrich Heine, Richard Wagner, and Karl Marx.

PARTY TIME. *Written and directed by Paul Zimet. Produced by The Talking Band. La MaMa. Opened January 10, 2007. Closed January 21, 2007.* A new musical about two soldiers in an armored combat vehicle in a desert war.

LINNEA. *Written by John Regis. Directed by Peter Dobbins. Produced by The Storm Theatre. Storm Theatre. Opened January 11, 2007. Closed February 10, 2007.* A new play about a reclusive playwright who encounters a mysterious woman. **SEE PAGE 89.**

ISRAEL HOROVITZ'S NEW SHORTS. *Written by Israel Horovitz. Directed by Israel Horovitz and Michael LoPorto. Produced by Barefoot Theatre Company. Theatre Row Studio. Opened January 11, 2007. Closed January 21, 2007.* A program of nine new short plays by Israel Horovitz.

BLACKOUT. *Written by Michael I. Walker. Directed by Kira Simring. Produced by Cell Theatre Company. Kirk Theatre. Opened January 11, 2007. Closed January 27, 2007.* A play about six strangers who meet during the Blackout of 2003 on a corner in Hell's Kitchen.

GREENER GRASSES. *Written by Sabura Rashid. Theater for the New City. Opened January 11, 2007. Closed February 4, 2007.* A new play described as a serious comedy that deals with "Post Traumatic Slave Disorder."

GET YOUR WAR ON. *Written by Kirk Lynn. Directed by Shawn Sides. Produced by Rude Mechs. 59E59. Opened January 11, 2007. Closed January 28, 2007.* A new play adapted from David Rees's popular Internet and *Rolling Stone* magazine comic of the same name.

THE SCENE. *Written by Theresa Rebeck. Directed by Rebecca Taichman. Second Stage. Opened January 11, 2007. Closed February 4, 2007.* A play about the narcissism of American pop culture.

ON A DARKLING PLAIN. *Written and directed by Norman Beim. Produced by Turtle Shell Productions. Turtle Shell Productions. Opened January 12, 2007. Closed January 27, 2007.* A play about a former Broadway star, a decade after he was blacklisted.

THE SUSTAINABLE FUTURE. *Written by Elizabeth Emmons. Directed by Ali Ayala. Produced by Blue Box Productions. Bowery Poetry Club. Opened January 12, 2007. Closed February 2, 2007.* A play about an architecture firm hired to design the U.S. embassy in Iraq.

ADVENTURES FROM EZRA KEATS: MAGGIE AND THE PIRATE & APT 3. *Produced by TADA! Youth Theater. TADA! Youth Theater. Opened January 12, 2007. Closed February 11, 2007.* A new musical based on the children's books by Ezra Jack Keats.

PINKALICIOUS. *Book and lyrics by Elizabeth and Victoria Kann. Music and lyrics by John Gregor. Directed by Suzu McConnell-Wood. Produced by Vital Children's Theatre. McGinn Cazale Theatre. Opened January 13, 2007. Closed February 25, 2007.* A play about a girl who can't stop eating pink cupcakes.

HELLO, MY NAME IS… *Written by Stephanie Rabinowitz. Produced by Living Image Arts. Lion Theatre. Opened January 13, 2007. Closed January 28, 2007.* A new play about sexual addiction.

AS YET THOU ART YOUNG AND RASH. *Written by Euripides. Directed by David Herskovits. Ohio Theatre. Opened January 14, 2007. Closed February 3, 2007.* A new adaptation of *The Suppliants* by Euripides.

TWAINATHON. *Metropolitan Playhouse. Opened January 15, 2007. Closed January 28, 2007.* A celebration of Mark Twain, featuring a variety of new plays and musicals inspired by his work.

- HUCK FINN, *adapted by N.G. McClernan.*
- THE REPORT OF MY DEATH, *adapted by Adam Klasfeld.*
- EXTRACTS FROM ADAM'S DIARY, *adapted by Anthony P. Pennino.*
- THE WAR PRAYER, *presented by Mike Durkin.*
- THE CALIFORNIAN'S TALE, *adapted by Andrew Firda.*
- AN INCONVENIENT RIVER, *by Laura Livingston.*

- HENRY'S LUNCHROOM, *by Dan Evans.*
- THE MAN THAT CORRUPTED HADLEYBURG, *adapted by Michael Bettencourt.*
- ANHEDONIA ROAD, *by Chris Harcum.*
- PERSONAL RECOLLECTIONS OF VIRGINS AND TRAMPS, *by Wandering Rom Players.*
- A MARVELOUS CURIOSITY, *compiled by Jeremy X. Halpern.*
- THE HADLEYBURG PROJECT—A MUSICAL READING, *book by Adam Cohen, lyrics by Kevin Laub.*
- BETWIXT, BETWEEN & BETWAIN—A MARK TWAIN MUSICAL, *by Danny Ashkenasi.*

PARTY DISCIPLINE. *Created and produced by Subjective Theatre Company. Cocreator/dramaturg: Julia Holleman. Asian American Writers Center. Opened January 17, 2007. Closed February 2, 2007.* A "political transformation seminar" that explores some of the tenets of America's conservatives.

UNDER THE RADAR. *Opened January 17, 2007. Closed January 28, 2007.* A festival tracking new theatre, curated by Mark Russell. At the Public Theater and a few other venues.

- ANOTHER YOU, *created by Allen Johnson, directed by Sean Ryan.*
- INVINCIBLE SUMMER, *created by Mike Daisey, directed by Jean-Michele Gregory.*
- THE BROTHERS SIZE, *created by Tarell Alvin McCraney, directed by Tea Alagic.*

PARTY ANIMALS. *Written and directed by Frederick Stroppel. Produced by Two for the Road Productions. Nuyorican Poets Café. Opened January 18, 2007. Closed January 27, 2007.* An evening of five original one-act comedies: SOULMATES, A SUNDAY DRIVE, PARTRIDGE IN A PEAR TREE, SOUTH OF THE BORDER, and THE SECRET THING.

JUST A MATTER OF TIME. *Book and lyrics by Sandra Dutton. Music by Jack Kohl. Directed by Susan Streater. Sage Theatre. Opened January 18, 2007. Closed January 31, 2007.* A new musical about a girl whose grandmother helps her rediscover her curiosity.

BILLBOARD. *Written by Michael Vukadinovich. Directed by Tania Inessa Kirkman. Produced by Reverie Productions and Overlap Productions. 59E59. Opened January 18, 2007. Closed February 4, 2007.* A new play about a man who gets a tattoo of a corporate logo on his forehead.

DEAD SET #3. *Directed by Caden Manson. Produced by Big Art Group. The Kitchen. Opened January 18, 2007. Closed January 27, 2007.* A new video/theatre hybrid performance exploring trauma and spectacle through reenacted pirated dialogue, borrowed online chats, and choreography derived from sampled movement.

WAVES AND BEACHES. *Written by Jonathan Wallace. Directed by Shannon Fillion. Produced by Howling Moon Cab Company. Theatre 54 @ Shetler. Opened January 18, 2007. Closed January 21, 2007.* A new play about a young married couple who agonize about hanging onto their home.

WOMEN OF TRACHIS. *Written by Kate E. Ryan. Directed by Alice Reagan. Produced by Target Margin Theater. Ohio Theatre. Opened January 18, 2007. Closed February 3, 2007.* A new play updating this Greek tragedy by Sophocles.

RULES OF THE UNIVERSE. *Written by Daniel Reitz. Directed by Daniel Talbott. Produced by Rising Phoenix Repertory. Jimmy's No. 43. Opened January 19, 2007. Closed January 31, 2007.* A new play staged in adjoining bathrooms at Jimmy's No. 43.

THE POLISH PLAY. *Devised and directed by Henry Wishcamper. Produced by Katharsis Theater Company. Walkerspace. Opened January 19, 2007. Closed February 17, 2007.* A conflation of *Macbeth* by William Shakespeare and *Ubu Roi* by Alfred Jarry.

VICTORIA MARTIN: MATH TEAM QUEEN. *Written by Kathryn Walat. Directed by Loretta Greco. Produced by Women's Project. Julia Miles (WPP) Theatre. Opened January 21, 2007. Closed February 4, 2007.* A play about a female high school student who joins the all-male math team.

BRUISE/GRINGO. *Written by Eric Bland. Directed by Noah Burger. Produced by Old Kent Road Theater. Under St. Marks. Opened January 21, 2007. Closed February 13, 2007.* A double bill of new plays: **THE BAD BRUISE OF BILLY MACBEAN** and **THE GRINGO OF THE DELI ACAPULCO.**

A SHELTER IN OUR CAR. *Adapted by Sophie Jaff and Robert L. Wilson III. Directed by Rajendra Ramoon Maharaj. Produced by Making Books Sing.Opened January 22, 2007. Closed February 13, 2007.* A new family musical based on the book by Monica Gunning. Presented at various venues throughout New York City.

AMERICAN STANDARD. *Created by bluemouth inc. Additional writing by Jud Martell, Lisa Rae Vineberg, and Andrew Laurenson. Barbershop. Opened January 23, 2007. Closed January 28, 2007.* A new theater work presented at the Barbershop at Freeman's Sporting Club.

HUSTLER, WI. *Written and directed by Michael Scott-Price. Produced by Asteroid B612 Theatre Company. chashama. Opened January 23, 2007. Closed February 11, 2007.* A new play about a lonely man looking for treasure in the modern streets of New York City.

THE GREAT DIVORCE. *Adapted and directed by George Drance. Music by Elizabeth Swados. Produced by Magis Theatre Company. Theater 315. Opened January 24, 2007. Closed February 11, 2007.* A new musical adaptation of the story by C.S. Lewis.

AT LEAST IT'S PINK. *Book by Bridgett Everett, Michael Patrick King, and Kenny Mellman. Music and lyrics by Kenny Mellman and Bridgett Everett. Directed by Michael Patrick King. Ars Nova. Opened January 24, 2007. Closed April 1, 2007.* A "trashy little show" about New York City life as seen through the eyes of a girl from Kansas.

ONCE THERE WAS A VILLAGE. *Written and directed by Vit Horejs. Produced by Czechoslovak-American Marionette Theatre. La MaMa. Opened January 25, 2007. Closed February 11, 2007.* An ethno opera with puppets and found objects about four hundred years of the East Village.

VAMPINGO & MOONBITE. *Written by Ariana Johns and Jolene Adams. Directed by Jolene Adams and Greg Mullavey. Producers Club II. Opened January 25, 2007. Closed February 10, 2007.* A double-bill of short plays: **VAMPINGO** is a solo play about a woman who is befriended by a vampire flamingo; **MOONBITE** is a collection of comic vignettes inspired by the full moon.

FORCE. *Written and directed by Bryn Manion. Conceived by Bryn Manion and Wendy Remington. Produced by Aisling Arts. Chocolate Factory. Opened January 25, 2007. Closed February 17, 2007.* A trilogy that deals with dreams, travel, memories, and magic realism.

WAKE UP MR. SLEEPY! YOUR UNCONSCIOUS MIND IS DEAD! *Written and directed by Richard Foreman. Ontological Theatre. Opened January 25, 2007. Closed April 1, 2007.* A new work that struggles to unearth the unknowable sources of human inventiveness.

KRYPTONITE HEARTS. *Written by Charles Battersby. Directed by James Duff. Theater for the New City. Opened January 25, 2007. Closed February 11, 2007.* A new play inspired by 1940s comic books and radio shows.

LADY CHARDONNEY. *Written by Jim Gibson and Julio Tumbaco. Directed by Jason Brantman. Theatre Row Studio. Opened January 26, 2007. Closed February 11, 2007.* A one-act "queer farce" about a proud black cabaret performer and a mafioso with a hidden past.

A SHELTER FOR DREAMS. *Produced by The Playwrighting Workshop. Neighborhood Playhouse. Opened January 26, 2007. Closed January 27, 2007.* A program of two new plays.

- **JANE'S HOUSE,** *by Harriet Rafe.*
- **THE USUAL SPACE,** *by Michael Simon Hall.*

FRANK'S HOME. *Written by Richard Nelson. Directed by Robert Falls. Playwrights Horizons Mainstage. Opened January 30, 2007. Closed February 18, 2007.* A new play about the architect Frank Lloyd Wright.

ANON. *Written by Kate Robin. Directed by Melissa Kievman. Atlantic Stage 2. Opened January 31, 2007. Closed February 18, 2007.* A new play about the hazy territory where sex, relationships, and addiction overlap.

THE POD PROJECT. *Created and directed by Nancy Bannon. 20 Greene Gallery. Opened January 31, 2007. Closed February 11, 2007.* Thirteen scenes performed for one audience member at a time.

2007 IMPACT WINTER ONE ACT FESTIVAL. *Impact Theater. Opened February 1, 2007. Closed February 11, 2007.* A program of new one-act plays.

- **SNOW IN GALVESTON,** *by Schatzie Schaefers.*
- **CAUTION: THE TRUE IMAGINED STORY OF MY PARENTS' ROMANCE,** *by Lauren Yee.*
- **PLAYGROUP,** *by Thelma De Castro.*
- **SUICIDE GAL, WON'T YOU COME OUT TONIGHT, COME OUT TONIGHT,** *by J. Boyer.*
- **EDGING THE CLIFF,** *by Jae Kramisen.*
- **THE FEARS OF HAROLD SHIVVERS,** *by Dawson Moore.*
- **IGNORANCE,** *by Shannon Murdoch.*
- **IN THE BEGINNING AGAIN,** *by Lauren D. Yee.*
- **FIN AND EUBA,** *by Audrey Ceflay.*
- **A DINER A SHINER,** *by Dan Moyer.*
- **THE STORY OF IZANAGI AND IZANAMI,** *by Kristen Miller.*
- **SEA CHANGE,** *by Christine Emmert.*

MANY WORLDS. *Written by William Borden. Directed by Isaac Byrne. Produced by Working Man's Clothes Productions. The Red Room. Opened February 1, 2007. Closed February 24, 2007.* A new play about a woman's journey to understand love, mortality, and the nature of the universe.

SPLIT ENDS. *Written and performed by Venus Opal Reese. Directed by Liesl Tommy. La MaMa. Opened February 1, 2007. Closed February 11, 2007.* A new play about the relationship between African American women and their hair.

APOCALYPSE NEO. *Produced by Horse Trade Theatre and The NY Neo-Futurists. Kraine Theatre. Opened February 1, 2007. Closed February 10, 2007.* A program of three new short plays by Rob Neill, Justin Tolley, and Crystal Skillman that contemplate the apocalypse.

OTHER PEOPLE. *Written by Joyce Wu. Directed by Genevieve Gearhart. Produced by Flying Carob Tree Productions. Wow Café Theater. Opened February 1, 2007. Closed February 10, 2007.* A new play about a young couple who decide to go home with a woman they've met in a bar.

ABSOLUTE CLARITY. *Written by Sophia Romma. Directed by Yuri Joffe. Produced by ArtVoice and Cinema Anastasia. Players Theatre. Opened February 2, 2007. Closed February 25, 2007.* A new play, loosely based on the play *She* by Edward Radzinski, about a rebellious teenage artist searching for love and absolution.

LOS TITINGOS DE JUAN BOBO. *Written by Carlos Ferrari. Directed by Jose Cheo Oliveras. Teatro Circulo. Opened February 2, 2007. Closed February 25, 2007.* A new musical comedy about the Puerto Rican folktales of Juan Bobo.

GONE. *Written by Charles L. Mee. Directed by Kenn Watt. Produced by Station 5, in collaboration with The Fifth Floor. 59E59. Opened February 2, 2007. Closed February 11, 2007.* A new movement-theatre composition that filters the voices of Proust, Ginsberg, and others into a powerful testament of our collective human need to remember and represent life's passing.

TOCK TICK. *Book and lyrics by Tim Nevits. Music by Gihieh Lee. Directed by Jackson Gay. Produced by Prospect Theater Company. West End Theatre. Opened February 5, 2007. Closed March 4, 2007.* A new musical about a girl whose mother has cancer.

ALL THAT I WILL EVER BE. *Written by Alan Ball. Directed by Jo Bonney. New York Theatre Workshop. Opened February 6, 2007. Closed March 11, 2007.* A new play about two young men in contemporary Los Angeles—a privileged American and an enigmatic immigrant from the Middle East.

SENSORY. *Written by Lucas Hewitt. Directed by Ashley Kelly-Tata. Manhattan Repertory Theater. Opened February 7, 2007. Closed February 10, 2007.* A new play about a man who tries to reunite with his ex-girlfriend.

SYNESTHESIA. *Produced by Electric Pear Productions. Harris Lieberman Gallery. Opened February 7, 2007. Closed February 10, 2007.* A performance piece that looks at how artists influence, inspire, and steal from each other.

SOCCER MOMS FROM HELL. *Written by Richard Cummings. Directed by A.M. Raychel. Theater-Studio. Opened February 7, 2007. Closed May 12, 2007.* A comedy about a pair of rich, suburban wives who rebel against their obsessively professional husbands.

THE FRUGAL REPAST. *Written by Ron Hirsen. Directed by Joe Grifasi. Abingdon Theatre. Opened February 7, 2007. Closed February 25, 2007.* A new play about two impoverished circus performers who discover that they are the subjects of one of Picasso's paintings.

THE LOVE SONG OF ELEANOR PURDY. *Written by Germaine Netzband. Directed by Michael Raimondi. Produced by Present Tense Productions and teatro oscuro. Manhattan Theatre Source. Opened February 7, 2007. Closed February 10, 2007.* A play about two lifelong friends who realize they no longer have anything in common.

THE LADY SWIMS TODAY. *Written and directed by H.G. Brown. Produced by Brown Swan Productions. Richmond Shepard Theatre. Opened February 7, 2007. Closed February 18, 2007.* A play about four low-life criminals who are cooking up the heist of a lifetime.

THE SECRET OF MME. BONNARD'S BATH. *Written and directed by Israel Horovitz. Produced by New York Playwrights Lab. Kirk Theatre. Opened February 8, 2007. Closed February 24, 2007.* A new play that explores why painter Pierre Bonnard revised one of his works that was hanging in a museum.

STROM THURMOND IS NOT A RACIST/CLEANSED. *Written by Thomas Bradshaw. Directed by José Zayas. Produced by Immediate Theatre Company. Brick Theatre. Opened February 8, 2007. Closed March 3, 2007.* A program of two short plays that deal with issues of racism. **SEE PAGE 73.**

VIGNETTES FOR THE APOCALYPSE. *Produced by End Times Productions. Roy Arias Studios & Theatres. Opened February 8, 2007. Closed February 16, 2007.* Twelve short plays in repertory that reflect a diversity of writing styles, while representing a unifying vision of our culture and society, both past and present, as it faces the real possibility of imminent collapse.

- **WOO AT THE ZOO,** *by Joe Lauinger, directed by Matthew Kreiner.*
- **LET NO MAN TEAR ASUNDER,** *by Ed Friedman, directed by Laurie Rae Waugh.*
- **PLAYS FOR THE SUNNI TRIANGLE,** *by Jerrod Bogard, directed by Kristin Skye Hoffmann.*
- **THE NATIONAL ANTHEM OF MERCURY,** *by Meny Beriro, directed by Greg Cicchino.*
- **THE ART OF THE PICK-UP,** *by Dave Rosenberg, directed by Matthew Kreiner.*
- **OCCAM'S RAZOR,** *by Wesley St. John, directed by Jared Ranere.*
- **A CHANCE ENCOUNTER WITH GEORGE W.,** *by Dave Sweeney, directed by Ilana Landecker.*
- **THE LONG SHOT,** *by Richard Cottrell, directed by Tony Macy-Perez.*
- **OVER THE ASIAN AIRWAVES,** *by Lauren Yee, directed by James E. Duff.*
- **COMPUTER MADNESS,** *by Judith Donner Hancock, directed by Michelle Dean.*
- **TAMMY,** *by Simcha Borenstein, directed by Heather Arnson.*
- **NIGHTHAWKS,** *by Evan Guilford-Blake, directed by Tom Herman.*

THE LAST WORD… *Written by Oren Safdie. Directed by Alex Lippard. Theatre at St. Clement's. Opened February 8, 2007. Closed March 11, 2007.* A new play about a Viennese Jew who fled the Nazis and became a successful advertising executive in New York.

IN THE HEIGHTS. *Music and lyrics by Lin-Manuel Miranda. Book by Quiara Alegria Hudes. Directed by Thomas Kail. 37 Arts. Opened February 8, 2007. Closed July 15, 2007.* A new musical about two days in the life of a Washington Heights neighborhood.

SHORT, FUN AND HOT: A SHOWCASE, PERHAPS. *Directed by Jonathan Rabunski. Produced by He's Nearly In Me Prod. The Red Room. Opened February 8, 2007. Closed February 10, 2007.* A program of three short plays, including a revival of an Aaron Sorkin piece plus two new plays by Jonathan Rabunski and Gregory Marinaccio.

THE TRIAL. *Written by Franz Kafka. Adapted by Egress Theatre Co. Directed by Andrew Bielski. Center for Remembering and Sharing. Opened February 9, 2007. Closed March 3, 2007.* A new adaptation of Franz Kafka's famous short story about a man who is suddenly arrested for reasons never made clear.

DRACULA. *Adapted and directed by Ryan Gilliam. Downtown Art. Opened February 9, 2007. Closed February 25, 2007.* A new dramatization of the classic horror tale for kids.

FAKING THE LIZARD KING'S DEATH/BRITNEY @ 7 ELEVEN. *Written by Larry Meyers. Where Eagles Dare. Opened February 9, 2007. Closed March 2007.* New monologue plays about two rock music icons.

A STEADY RAIN. *Written by Keith Huff. Directed by K. Lorrel Manning. Barrow Group. Opened February 9, 2007. Closed March 5, 2007.* A new play about two policemen whose lifelong friendship is put to the test.

HOROWITZ: THE ACROBAT AT REST. *Written by Stellios Manolakakis. Directed by Elias Kasman. Medicine Show. Opened February 9, 2007. Closed February 17, 2007.* A new play about the virtuoso pianist Vladimir Horowitz and his wife.

LOOKINGGLASS ALICE. *Adapted and directed by David Catlin. Produced by Lookingglass Theatre Company. New Victory Theatre. Opened February 9, 2007. Closed February 25, 2007.* A new adaptation of Lewis Carroll's classic stories.

(MIS)UNDERSTANDING MAMMY: THE HATTIE MCDANIEL STORY. *Written by Joan Ross Sorkin. Directed by David Glenn Armstrong. Produced by Emerging Artists Theatre. Theater Five. Opened February 10, 2007. Closed March 4, 2007.* A new play with music about the life and career of Hattie McDaniel, the first African American actor to win an Academy Award.

ELEPHANT GIRLS. *Written by Carl Gonzalez. Directed by Derek Jamison. Produced by Emerging Artists Theatre. Theater Five. Opened February 10, 2007. Closed March 4, 2007.* A new play by Carl Gonzalez about a group of American women and the Afghani math tutor of one of them.

6969. *Written by Jordan Seavey. Directed by Matthew Hopkins. Produced by CollaborationTown. 59E59. Opened February 10, 2007. Closed February 24, 2007.* A new play about two teenagers who become friends in cyberspace, with tragic results.

ACT NATURALLY. *Written by Scott Katzman. Directed by Christopher Maring. Produced by Intangible Productions. WorkShop Theater. Opened February 10, 2007. Closed February 24, 2007.* A new thirty-eight-character, seven-actor, one-man show run amuck.

REAL DANGER. *Written by Jeff Hollman. Directed by Paul Adams. Produced by Emerging Artists Theatre. Theater Five. Opened February 10, 2007. Closed March 3, 2007.* A new play by about a surprise reunion between two friends nine years after graduation from college.

UNCLE. *Written by Dean Gray. Directed by Wayne Maugans. Produced by Blue Heron Theatre. Arclight Theatre. Opened February 12, 2007. Closed March 4, 2007.* A new play about a young successful gay composer who gains the courage to confront his conservative family's beliefs when a secret photograph of a deceased uncle is discovered.

NEGLECT. *Written by Sharyn Rothstein. Directed by Catherine Ward. Produced by Youngblood. Ensemble Studio Theatre. Opened February 12, 2007. Closed March 10, 2007.* A new play about an elderly woman who opens her home to the young man from next door during a heat wave.

ADRIFT IN MACAO. *Book and lyrics by Christopher Durang. Music by Peter Melnick. Directed by Sheryl Kaller. Produced by Primary Stages. 59E59. Opened February 13, 2007. Closed March 4, 2007.* A film noir musical parody.

OPERATION AJAX. *Text constructed by Noel Salzman and Tamara Schmidt. Directed by Noel Salzman. Produced by The Butane Group. Where Eagles Dare. Opened February 14, 2007. Closed March*

10, 2007. A new play, constructed from more than thirty different text sources, about the CIA's 1953 coup against Iran's only democratically elected government.

YOUR FACE IS A MESS. *Written by Marc Spitz. Directed by Carlo Vogel. Produced by Actionman Productions. Kraine Theatre. Opened February 14, 2007. Closed March 4, 2007.* A new play about a drug dealer trying to turn his life around, except no one else wants him to.

KINETIC FORTRESS. *Written and composed by JoAnne jojo Maffia. Directed by JoAnne jojo Maffia. Produced by THe jojo Experiment. 78th Street Theatre Lab. Opened February 14, 2007. Closed February 17, 2007.* One woman's struggle with her reality and her powerful imagination.

NELSON. *Written by Sam Marks. Directed by Kip Fagan. Produced by Partial Comfort Productions. Lion Theatre. Opened February 14, 2007. Closed March 3, 2007.* A new play about a young man caught between two worlds.

THE TRUTH ABOUT LOVE. *Written by Susannah Nolan. Directed by Christine Simpson. Produced by Present Tense Productions and teatro oscuro. Manhattan Theatre Source. Opened February 14, 2007. Closed February 17, 2007.* A play described this way: "like *Our Town,* if Emily was bewitched and bewildered—and George was gay."

A VERY COMMON PROCEDURE. *Written by Courtney Baron. Directed by Michael Greif. Produced by MCC Theater. Lucille Lortel Theatre. Opened February 14, 2007. Closed March 10, 2007.* A play about three New Yorkers who take a crash course in the workings of the human heart.

MY SECRET GARDEN. *Adapted and directed by Christopher Scott. 45th Street Theatre. Opened February 14, 2007. Closed March 11, 2007.* A dramatization of Nancy Friday's 1973 book, which is a compilation of women's sexual fantasies.

FRAU DRACULA: THAT PRUSSIAN SHE-BITCH FROM HELL. *Written by J.D. Klein. Directed by Le Wilhelm. American Theatre of Actors. Opened February 14, 2007. Closed March 4, 2007.* A new adaptation of Dracula featuring a female Van Helsing squaring off with the Queen of the Damned.

BLIND LEMON BLUES. *Created by Alan Govenar and Akin Babatunde. Music and lyrics by Blind Lemon Jefferson. Directed by Akin Babatunde. York Theatre. Opened February 15, 2007. Closed February 25, 2007.* A musical created featuring more than sixty Blind Lemon Jefferson songs.

ARTFUCKERS. *Written by Michael Domitrovich. Directed by Eduardo Machado. Produced by Theater for the New City. Theater for the New City. Opened February 15, 2007. Closed March 4, 2007.* A new play about angst and ambition among today's East Village "elite."

BAD ASS SHORTS. *Produced by Ratutu Collaborative. The Creek and the Cave Theater. Opened February 15, 2007. Closed March 3, 2007.* A program of short plays, spoof commercials, and film about odd situations and over-the-top circumstances.

- FINDING THE WONDER, *book, music, and lyrics by Gwynne Watkins, Betina Hershey, and Denver Casado.*
- DUMMY, *by Tanya Ritchie.*
- CARL DANIELSON'S WELCOME HOME, *by Molly DeCandia.*
- SECRET SERVICE, *by Adrian Quihuis.*

- **NOT WHAT NOT TO WEAR**, *by Serena Makofsky.*
- **THE SPRING SLIPS**, *by Finnegan Ripley.*

LA VIE NOIR. *Written by Jim Neu. Directed by Keith McDermott. La MaMa. Opened February 15, 2007. Closed March 4, 2007.* A new play about a group of star-crossed strangers become trapped in a noir world of lonely streetlights, smart talk, killer shadows, and wet footsteps.

CYCLE. *Written by Rose Courtney. Directed by Craig Carlisle. Cherry Lane Theatre. Opened February 16, 2007. Closed March 3, 2007.* A vaudeville-inspired play about a journey by bicycle into the heart of New York City to unlock the Biggest Secret of All Time.

PHYRO-GIANTS! *Written by Michael Blieden. Directed by Geoff Schuppert. Produced by Dirty Steve. Soundance. Opened February 16, 2007. Closed February 24, 2007.* A new play by about four thirty-somethings and their complicated social and ethical dilemmas.

LAND O' FIRE. *Written by Luis Santeiro. Directed by Jorge Cacheiro. Produced by Jersey City Theater Center. Wings Theater. Opened February 16, 2007. Closed March 3, 2007.* A new play about South American Indians plucked from their home and transported to Victorian England to be Christianized.

SHORT RIDES ON THE LOCAL. *Produced by Around the Block/Al Doblar La Esquina. Opened February 17, 2007. Closed April 7, 2007.* New one act plays about New York lives and dreams by Allen Davis III, Fred de Luna, Nina Howes, Carlos Jerome, Derek Lively, and Elise Marenson. Presented at various libraries in Manhattan.

ORESTEIA. *Written by David Johnston. Directed by Stephen Speights. Produced by Blue Coyote Theater Group. Access Theatre. Opened February 17, 2007. Closed March 10, 2007.* A new modern adaptation of the seminal Greek tragedy.

THICKER THAN WATER. *Produced by Youngblood. Ensemble Studio Theatre. Opened February 19, 2007. Closed March 10, 2007.* A program of new short plays by emerging writers under the age of thirty.

- **THE JAMAL LULLABIES—A SONG CYCLE**, *by Emily Conbere, directed by R.J. Tolan.*
- **THE ROOSEVELT COUSINS, THOROUGHLY SAUCED**, *by Michael Lew, directed by Moritz von Stuelpnagel.*
- **GROUP**, *by Annie Baker, directed by Alex Timbers.*
- **TRIAGE**, *by Sharyn Rothstein, directed by R.J. Tolan.*
- **ROB**, *by Sam Forman, directed by Marlo Hunter.*
- **AND THE BABY MAKES THREE**, *by Courtney Brooke Lauria, directed by Melissa Kievman.*
- **BIKE WRECK**, by *Qui Nguyen, directed by John Gould Rubin.*

COMING OR GOING. *Written by Lisa Roth. Directed by Leslie Cloninger. Produced by Pretty Little Heads. Manhattan Theatre Source. Opened February 21, 2007. Closed March 10, 2007.* A new Southern-style about four sisters about their daddy's funeral in Texas.

THE DANCE: THE HISTORY OF AMERICAN MINSTRELSY. *Written by Jason Christophe White. Directed by Jason Christophe White and Aaron White. Richmond Shepard Theatre. Opened February 22, 2007. Closed March 3, 2007.* An educational satire based upon the history of American Minstrelsy.

MOVIN' MAN. *Written and performed by Glynn Turman. Directed by Woodie King, Jr. Produced by Crossroads Theatre Company. Crossroads Theatre. Opened February 23, 2007. Closed March 4, 2007.* A one-man play written and performed by Glynn Turman, who played the son in the original Broadway production of *A Raisin in the Sun.*

THE GIRL DETECTIVE. *Adapted and directed by Bridgette Dunlap. Produced by The Ateh Theater Group. Connelly Theatre. Opened February 23, 2007. Closed March 17, 2007.* A new play based on the story by Kelly Link.

TOTALLY ELECTRIC. *Written and directed by Jonathan VanDyke. Duplex. Opened February 23, 2007. Closed March 5, 2007.* A new musical billed as "The 80s High School Show Choir Musical."

KOOOL-AID LUV ODYSSEY. *Created by Baraka de Soleil. Produced by D Underbelly. BAX/Brooklyn Arts Exchange. Opened February 23, 2007. Closed February 25, 2007.* A multimedia performance collage described as a psychedelic odyssey through the mystical legacies of the syrupy sweet, fixating world of La Koool-aid.

THE CURSE OF THE MYSTIC RENALDO. *Written by Aldo Perez. Directed by Victor Weinstock. Produced by 3 Legged Dog. 3LD Art & Technology Center. Opened February 24, 2007. Closed April 28, 2007.* A new performance work about the supposed murder of a frowsy aristocrat in the 1920s.

THE END OF THE KNOWN WORLD PLAYS. *Produced by The Tank. Collective Unconscious. Opened February 24, 2007. Closed March 14, 2007.* A program of two new one-act plays described as fairy tales about coming of age and growing out of place in surreal locales: the Midwest and the rural South.

BFF. *Written by Anna Ziegler. Directed by Josh Hecht. Produced by WET (Women's Expressive Theater, Inc.). DR2. Opened February 24, 2007. Closed March 31, 2007.* A new play about a woman living in the past and the present simultaneously.

STUPID: THE PLAYS. *Magnet. Opened February 25, 2007. Closed April 1, 2007.* A program of nine smart plays about stupidity by Rehana Mirza, Elizabeth Emmons, Jeremy Basescu, Alex Beech, Daria Polatin, Jon Kern, Julian Camilo Pozzi, Christine Chambers, and Reuben Jackson.

REBEL VERSES. *Center Stage. Opened February 28, 2007. Closed March 10, 2007.* A two-week festival of short plays created by young theatre artists.

CONFIDENCE, WOMEN! *Written and directed by Robert Cucuzza. Produced by ACME Acting Lab. Axis Theater. Opened March 1, 2007. Closed March 17, 2007.* A new play about six hard-edged and desperate women at the turn of the century who will stop at nothing to befriend, con, swindle, or kill a seventh woman.

AMERICAN FAMILY PROJECT. *Lead writers: Sanjit De Silva and Deepa Purohit. Directed by Sanjit De Silva and Deepa Purohit. Produced by Rising Circle Theater Collective. CSV Cultural Center. Opened March 1, 2007. Closed March 11, 2007.* A new play about the family experiences of five Americans of color.

BIRDY AND THE GOLDEN PUTTER. *Written by Nick Colt and Jed Zion. Directed by Daniel G. O'Brien. Produced by Nick Colt Productions. Gene Frankel Theatre. Opened March 1, 2007. Closed March 10, 2007.* A new mini-golf musical.

THE FURTHER ADVENTURES OF UNCLE WIGGILY: WINDBLOWN VISITORS. *Book and lyrics by Laurel Hessing. Music by Arthur Abrams. Directed by Crystal Field. Theater for the New*

City. Opened March 1, 2007. Closed March 25, 2007. A new musical about a child uprooted during Hurricane Katrina who comes to live in New York City.

CRIME OR EMERGENCY. *Written and directed by Sibyl Kempson. Dixon Place. Opened March 1, 2007. Closed March 16, 2007.* A new play about medical examinations gone awry, obliterated expectations of cause and effect, and inner personal violences.

LIGHTS UP! *Players Theatre. Opened March 1, 2007. Closed March 4, 2007.* A mini-festival of short plays, presented in repertory. The playwrights are Liz Duffy Adams, Neena Beber, Catherine Filloux, Silvia Gonzalez, Wendy Hammond, and Barbara Wiechmann.

PRESENTING GILDA LILLY. *Book and lyrics by David Leddick. Music by Andrew Sargent. Directed by David Kingery. Produced by V.J. Colonna Productions. La MaMa. Opened March 2, 2007. Closed March 4, 2007.* A new musical about a mythological movie goddess.

BOYS JUST WANNA HAVE FUN. *Written by Anthony Wilkinson and Teresa Anne Cicala. Directed by Sonia Blangiardo and Teresa Anne Cicala. Produced by ANDEE Productions. Actors Playhouse. Opened March 2, 2007. Closed June 9, 2007.* A new romantic comedy about a pair of NYPD cops who go undercover in a Staten Island gay bar in the 1980s.

GO, DOG, GO! *Adapted by Allison Gregory and Steven Dietz. Directed by Bruce Merrill. Produced by Manhattan Children's Theatre. Manhattan Children's Theatre. Opened March 3, 2007. Closed April 8, 2007.* A new stage version of the story by P.D. Eastman.

PETER PIPER PICKS A NEW PROFESSION. *Book and lyrics by Dianna Tucker. Music by Adam Baritot. Produced by Tuckaberry Productions. Impact Theater. Opened March 3, 2007. Closed March 24, 2007.* A new musical for kids that picks up where the familiar nursery rhyme leaves off.

FIVE BOROUGHS. *Written and directed by John McDermott. Iguana New York. Opened March 3, 2007. Closed April 19, 2007.* A new musical about five very different New Yorkers discovering what they have in common.

PARENTAL CONSENT. *Written by Tamara Cupic. Directed by Franka Fiala. Produced by Theater for the New City and American Beat Documentaries. Theater for the New City. Opened March 3, 2007. Closed March 18, 2007.* A new play about the parental consent laws concerning abortion.

LOS ANGELES. *Written by Julian Sheppard. Music by Eric Shim, Ray Rizzo, and Amelia Zirin-Brown. Lyrics by Julian Sheppard. Directed by Adam Rapp. Flea. Opened March 3, 2007. Closed April 14, 2007.* A play about a damaged young woman trying to navigate her way through Tinseltown.

DYING CITY. *Written by Christopher Shinn. Directed by James MacDonald. Mitzi Newhouse Theater. Opened March 4, 2007. Closed April 29, 2007.* A new play about a young therapist whose husband dies while on military duty in Iraq.

BILL W. AND DR. BOB. *Written by Stephen Bergman and Janet Surrey. Directed by Rick Lombardo. New World Stages. Opened March 5, 2007. Closed June 10, 2007.* A new play about the founding of Alcoholics Anonymous.

BLINDNESS. *Adapted and directed by Joe Tantalo. Produced by Godlight Theatre Company. 59E59. Opened March 6, 2007. Closed April 8, 2007.* A new play based on the novel by Nobel laureate José Saramago.

SPALDING GRAY: STORIES LEFT TO TELL. *Written by Spalding Gray. Conceived by Kathleen Russo. Directed by Lucy Sexton. Minetta Lane Theatre. Opened March 6, 2007. Closed June 26, 2007.* A play that interweaves monologues and stories by the late Spalding Gray with some of his letters and journal entries.

FRIGID NEW YORK. *Kraine. Opened March 7, 2007. Closed March 18, 2007.* Horse Trade Theater Group presents an unjuried festival of cutting-edge, uncensored productions from all over the country at three East Village venues.

- **ANDREA,** *created by Allison Landa.*
- **BABYLOVE,** *created by Christen Clifford, directed by Julie Kramer.*
- **BLOOD TURNIP,** *created and directed by Christie Perfetti.*
- **CRAZY OVER LOVE?,** *created by David Tyson, produced by David Tyson's Weaver of Tales Theatre.*
- **JESUS CHRIST, I'M SORRY,** *created by Brent Hirose, produced by Stupid Gumball Dispenser Productions.*
- **NAUGHT BUT PIRATES,** *created by Sean Owens, directed by Kenny Shults, produced by Exit Theatre.*
- **ORANGE MURDER SUIT,** *created by Rob Matsushita, directed by Rick Vorndran, produced by Dysfunctional Theatre Co.*
- **REVIVAL,** *created by Greg Turner, produced by Do Not Disturb Theatre.*
- **SPOTLESS,** *created by Emily Morwen.*
- **SUPER GLOSSY!,** *created by Courtney McLean, directed by Jenny Lobland.*
- **THE BURNING BUSH,** *created by Tracey Erin Smith, directed by Rebecca Northan.*
- **THE BUTTERFIELD TONES,** *created by Robert Attenweiler, directed by Robert Attenweiler and John Patrick Hayden, produced by Disgraced Productions.*
- **THE LIGHT INSIDE,** *created and directed by Lindsay Wolf, produced by NO TIME FOR LOVE Productions.*
- **THE PECULIAR UTTERANCE OF THE DAY: LIVE ON STAGE!,** *created and directed by Tom X. Chao.*
- **WE CALL HER BENNY,** *created and directed by Suzanne Bachner, produced by JMTC.*

DOG DAY AFTERNOON. *Written and directed by Frank Solorzano. Produced by Barefoot Theatre Company. American Theatre of Actors. Opened March 7, 2007. Closed March 25, 2007.* A stage adaptation of the famous film about a bank robbery gone awry.

THINGS TO DO WITH YOUR MOUTH. *Created by Melinda Lee and Ernesto Klar. Lower Manhattan Cultural Council. Opened March 7, 2007. Closed March 10, 2007.* A movement-theatre performance that's described as reactions to Samuel Beckett's minimalist play Not I.

SLEEP OVER. *Written by Maria Micheles. Directed by Kitt Lavoie. Theater for the New City. Opened March 8, 2007. Closed March 25, 2007.* A new play that delves into the last gasps of a relationship that can poison even the most socially compassionate of people.

1001 BEDS. *Written and performed by Tim Miller. P.S. 122. Opened March 8, 2007. Closed March 18, 2007.* A new performance piece described as a raucous, rowdy, kinky, and funny journey through many of the many beds he's been in.

THE APOTHEOSIS OF VACLAV DRDA. *Written by Christopher Cartmill. Directed by Yuval Hadadi. Produced by Gads Hill Theater Company. Access Theatre. Opened March 8, 2007. Closed April 1, 2007.* A new play about the misfortunes of a group of actors staging the work of an obscure Czech playwright.

BETTY & THE BELRAYS. *Written and directed by William Electric Black. Cocomposer: Valerie Ghent. Theater for the New City. Opened March 8, 2007.* Closed April 1, 2007. A new musical about three white female singers who challenge a racially divided society by singing for a black record label.

REPUBLIC OF DREAMS. *Conceived by Stacy Klein. Produced by Double Edge Theatre. La MaMa. Opened March 8, 2007. Closed March 18, 2007.* A new performance inspired by the art and work of Bruno Schulz.

HOMELAND SECURITY: BRINGING DR. KING UP TO DATE. *Directed by Desmond Richardson. Produced by The All Stars Project. Castillo Theatre. Opened March 9, 2007. Closed April 1, 2007.* An experimental dance/music theatre piece that "introduces Dr. King to post-9/11 America."

CREATURES OF THE CABARET. *Directed by Shari Johnson. Lookingglass Theatre. Opened March 9, 2007. Closed April 7, 2007.* A late-night cabaret of new short plays about nonhumans.

- **ANGELS!,** *by Mary Flanagan.*
- **ONE, TWO, THREE, BREATHE,** *by Lenore Blumenfeld.*
- **THE CLOCK IS TICKING,** *by Nancy Gall-Clayton.*
- **TIME TROLL,** *by Karin Diann Williams.*
- **ENGLISH THERAPY,** *by Nancy Gall-Clayton.*
- **I CONFESS,** *by Charmian Creagle and Sean Doran.*
- **EXTRAOTICA,** *by Yasmine Beverly Rana.*
- **BEHIND CLOSED DOORS,** *by Letitia Sweitzer.*

MAGPIE. *Book by Steven M. Jacobson. Music by Gary William Friedman. Lyrics by Edward Gallardo. Directed by Rajendra Ramoon Maharaj. Produced by Amas Musical Theatre. Players Theatre. Opened March 9, 2007. Closed April 1, 2007.* A new musical about a romance between two New York City bike messengers.

MURDER UNCENSORED. *Written by George Barthel. Directed by L. J. Kleeman and Raymond O. Wagner. Wings Theater. Opened March 9, 2007. Closed April 8, 2007.* A new play described as a film noir murder mystery set in silent-era Hollywood.

JANYL. *Directed by Virlana Tkacz. Produced by Yara Arts Group. La MaMa. Opened March 9, 2007. Closed March 25, 2007.* A new world music-theatre piece, based on an ancient epic about the struggles of a woman warrior in a traditional society.

THE NAKED EYE PLANETS. *Written by Rebecca Tourino. Directed by Magdalena Zira. American Theatre of Actors. Opened March 9, 2007. Closed March 25, 2007.* A new play that follows ten residents of a small apartment complex on the cusp of a rare astronomical phenomenon.

THE GAME BOY. *Book and lyrics by Robin Rothstein. Music and lyrics by Matthew Gandolfo. Directed by Mary Catherine Burke. Produced by Vital Children's Theatre. McGinn Cazale Theatre. Opened March 10, 2007. Closed April 22, 2007.* A play about a boy who is obsessed with computer games.

CHICKEN. *Written by Mike Batistick. Directed by Nick Sandow. Studio Dante. Opened March 10, 2007. Closed April 7, 2007.* A new play about a man who takes in a rooster to train for an illegal cockfight.

THE DIRECTOR. *Written by Barbara Cassidy. Directed by Jessica Davis-Irons. Produced by The Flea Theater. Flea. Opened March 10, 2007. Closed March 31, 2007.* A new play about a man who victimizes women by telling them that he's a director.

THE COUNTRY FEEDBACK/WAR MOUTH. *Produced by Boon Theatre. Daryl Roth Theatre. Opened March 11, 2007. Closed March 20, 2007.* A program of two new plays by Joel Hanson and Ernest Curcio.

HOTEL ORACLE. *Written by Bixby Elliot. Directed by Stephen Brackett. Produced by The Sum Of Us Theatre Company. Walkerspace. Opened March 11, 2007. Closed March 31, 2007.* A new play about six strangers who leave their hotel to seek out the Oracle.

TALL GRASS. *Written by Brian Harris. Directed by Nick Corley. Beckett Theatre. Opened March 12, 2007. Closed April 15, 2007.* A dark comedy about three couples with three unusual problems.

EATFEST—SPRING 2007. *Produced by Emerging Artists Theatre. Theater Five. Opened March 13, 2007. Closed April 1, 2007.* Emerging Artists Theatre presents their semi-annual mini-festival of new short plays.

- POSTCARDS FROM A DEAD DOG, *by F.J. Hartland.*
- THE QUESTIONING, *by Frank Higgins.*
- CLAPTRAPP, *by Joseph Godfrey.*
- VAMP, *by Ry Herman.*
- TELL, *by Rodney Lee Rogers.*
- THIRD WHEEL, *by Monica Flory.*
- MY NAME IS ART, *by Peter Snoad.*
- SOME ARE PEOPLE, *by Kathleen Warnock.*
- ONE OF THE GREAT ONES, *by Chris Widney.*

STRAIGHT TO HELL. *Written and directed by Stephen Stahl. Produced by On the Run Productions. Abingdon Theatre. Opened March 14, 2007. Closed March 25, 2007.* A multimedia play based on the novel by Kathleen Hudson about the effects of drug addiction.

THE HEALING ZONE. *Written by Carl Clay. Directed by Bette Howard. Black Spectrum Theatre. Opened March 16, 2007. Closed April 8, 2007.* A new play about the battle between traditional medicine and alternative healing.

HEAR NYC. *Created and performed by Naomi Finkelstein, Saida Cooper, Lindsay Strachan, Evan Shafran, and Mike Cooke. Directed by Erinina Marie Ness. Produced by Mir Productions. Bushwick Starr. Opened March 16, 2007. Closed March 25, 2007.* A new theatre piece that explores the humor and heartbreak of alienation in New York City through performance, film, and sound.

JACK GOES BOATING. *Written by Bob Glaudini. Directed by Peter DuBois. Produced by LAByrinth Theater Company. Public Theater. Opened March 18, 2007. Closed April 29, 2007.* A new play about date panic, marital meltdown, betrayal and the prevailing grace of the human spirit.

DREAMS OF FRIENDLY ALIENS. *Written by Daniel Damiano. Directed by Kim T. Sharp. Abingdon Theatre. Opened March 18, 2007. Closed April 1, 2007.* A new play about a dysfunctional New Jersey family.

MEN OF STEEL. *Written by Qui Nguyen. Directed by Robert Ross Parker. Produced by Vampire Cowboys Theatre Company. Center Stage. Opened March 18, 2007. Closed April 8, 2007.* A new play that follows the journeys of five courageous crusaders aspiring for heroism against all odds.

STAY. *Written by Lucy Thurber. Directed by Jackson Gay. Rattlestick Theatre. Opened March 19, 2007. Closed April 15, 2007.* A new play about a young writer who discovers an angel.

DESIRE IN THE SUBURBS. *Written by Frederic Glover. Directed by Kathleen Brant. Produced by The WorkShop Theater Company. WorkShop Theater. Opened March 19, 2007. Closed March 31, 2007.* A new play, inspired by Eugene O'Neill's *Desire Under the Elms*, about a love triangle between a man, his wife, and his son.

LIFE IS SHORT. *Produced by Kids with Guns. Michael Weller Theatre. Opened March 19, 2007. Closed March 20, 2007.* A program of seven original one-act plays by emerging playwrights.

- **AFTER FIVE,** *by Joe Waechter.*
- **FINDING FAITH,** *by Alison Pentland.*
- **HOW BABIES ARE MADE,** *by Michael Ferrell.*
- **THE LOGISTICS OF HEROISM,** *by Joe Deemer.*
- **LOUDER THAN WORDS,** *by Vincent Madero.*
- **THE STICKING PLACE,** *by Ben Lewis.*
- **A SYMPHONY OF HORROR,** *by Eric Kuehnemann.*

THE GIRL MOST LIKELY TO… *Adapted and directed by Jodi Smith. Produced by Native Aliens Theatre Collective. Independent. Opened March 20, 2007. Closed March 24, 2007.* A parody of Joan Rivers's teleplay about a woman who undergoes plastic surgery to become beautiful.

THE SECRET AGENDA OF TREES. *Written by Colin McKenna. Directed by Sam Gold. Cherry Lane Theatre. Opened March 20, 2007. Closed March 31, 2007.* A new play about a thirteen-year-old girl battling with pangs of first love and drugs.

OUR LEADING LADY. *Written by Charles Busch. Directed by Lynne Meadow. Manhattan Theatre Club. Opened March 20, 2007. Closed April 22, 2007.* A new play about Laura Keane, the woman who starred in the play Lincoln was watching when he was assassinated.

THE OEDI CYCLE. *Produced by The Best. Ohio Theatre. Opened March 21, 2007. Closed March 24, 2007.* New contemporary versions of the two tragedies of Oedipus that mix Internet and live performance.

FIVE STORY WALKUP. *Written by John Guare, Neil LaBute, Laura Shaine Cunningham, Quincy Long, Daniel Frederick Levin, Clay McLeod Chapman, and Daniel Gallant. Directed by Daniel Gallant. 13th Street Repertory. Opened March 21, 2007. Closed April 14, 2007.* A program of new plays and monologues presented as a benefit for the theatre.

FUGUE. *Written by Lee Thuna. Directed by Judith Ivey. Produced by Cherry Lane Theatre. Cherry Lane Theatre. Opened March 21, 2007. Closed April 22, 2007.* A new play about a woman suffering from amnesia.

VOLUME OF SMOKE. *Written by Clay McLeod Chapman. Directed by Isaac Butler. Produced by elsewhere. 14th Street Theatre. Opened March 22, 2007. Closed April 7, 2007.* A new play described as an impressionistic, lyrical remembrance and investigation of the December 26, 1811, fire at Virginia's Richmond Theater that killed seventy people and helped kickstart the second great awakening.

REQUIEM AETERNAM DEO. *Written and directed by Fulya Parker. Produced by The Nietzche Circle. Kraine Theatre. Opened March 22, 2007. Closed April 15, 2007.* A new play based on Friedrich Nietzsche's philosophical novel, *Thus Spoke Zarathustra.*

THE 2007 TEASPOON FESTIVAL OF SHORT PLAYS. *Produced by Two Spoons Theatre Company. Producers Club. Opened March 22, 2007. Closed March 25, 2007.* An evening of coffee, tea, and theatre.

- **OH, NANCY,** *by Dawson Moore.*
- **MEDALS,** *by Mark Cornell.*
- **NO PRUNE,** *by Henry Meyerson.*
- **DOUBLE WHAMMY,** *by Liz Amberly.*
- **BACK IN,** *by Jason R. Montgomery.*
- **BLIND MAN'S BLUFF,** *by Stephen Korbar.*
- **WEDNESDAYS,** *by Sue Brody.*
- **PETE'S POT 'O GOLD,** *by Brandon Kalbaugh.*
- **I FEEL SWELL,** *by Henry Meyerson.*

CURTAINS. *Book by Rupert Holmes. Music by John Kander. Lyrics by Fred Ebb. Additional lyrics by John Kander and Rupert Holmes. Directed by Scott Ellis. Al Hirschfeld Theatre. Opened March 22, 2007.* A new musical comedy about the investigation of the murder of a Broadway leading lady.

CLOWN. *Written by Eric Beall and Peter Marinos. Directed by Jessica Dermody. Produced by Working Artists Theatre Project. Michael Weller Theatre. Opened March 24, 2007. Closed March 26, 2007.* A new solo play that tells two strangely intersecting stories of a life in the theater.

THE EXILES. *Adapted and directed by Theodora Skipitares. Produced by Skysaver Productions. La MaMa. Opened March 25, 2007. Closed April 8, 2007.* A new puppet theatre adaptation of Euripides's *Orestes.*

SOME MEN. *Written by Terrence McNally. Directed by Trip Cullman. Produced by Second Stage Theatre. Second Stage. Opened March 26, 2007. Closed April 22, 2007.* A new play about a gay wedding ceremony.

CLINICALLY NEGATIVE (A VIRAL COMEDY). *Written by Elizabeth Meriwether, Sam Forman, Billy Eichner, Annie Baker, and Beau Willimon. Directed by Portia Krieger. Produced by MC Enterprises. Manhattan Theatre Source. Opened March 27, 2007. Closed March 31, 2007.* A full-length, written in round-robin fashion by five playwrights, about getting tested for AIDS.

SCITUATE. *Written by Martin Casella. Directed by David Hilder. Produced by Outcast Productions. TBG Arts Complex. Opened March 28, 2007. Closed April 7, 2007.* A play about a man whose family gathers to try to help him rejoin the world.

FUCKPLAYS. *Produced by Working Man's Clothes. Galapagos. Opened March 28, 2007. Closed April 27, 2007.* Eight sexually charged plays by emerging New York City playwrights.

- **MARRIAGE PLAY,** *by Bekah Brunstetter, directed by Diana Basmajian.*
- **WOOD,** *by Justin Cooper, directed by Steven Gillenwater.*
- **THE IMPOTENCE OF BEING EARNEST,** *by Joshua Hill, directed by Julie Rossman.*
- **THE SADDEST THING IN THE HISTORY OF THE WORLD,** *by Kyle Jarrow, directed by Matthew Hancock.*
- **CANDY ROOM,** *by William Charles Meny, directed by Thomas Caruso.*
- **SHARPEN MY DICK,** *by Greg Romero, directed by Cole Wimpee.*

- **1.1 – 1.7,** *by Eric Sanders, directed by Stephen Brackett.*
- **ARMS AND THE OCTOPUS,** *by Casey Wimpee, directed by Isaac Byrne.*

ESSENTIAL SELF-DEFENSE. *Written by Adam Rapp. Directed by Carolyn Cantor. Produced by Playwrights Horizons and Edge Theater. Playwrights Horizons Peter J Sharp. Opened March 28, 2007. Closed April 15, 2007.* A new play about a man who takes a job as an attack dummy in a women's self-defense class.

THE CROONER. *Written by Laurence Holder. Directed by Rome Neal. Nuyorican Poets Cafe. Opened March 29, 2007. Closed April 28, 2007.* A new solo play about the loves and the rise to a fame of a jazz singer.

SEVEN.11 CONVENIENCE THEATRE (2007). *Directed by Sanjiv Jhaveri. Produced by Desipina & Company. Henry Street Settlement. Opened March 29, 2007. Closed April 14, 2007.* A program of seven eleven-minute plays, all written by South Asian and Asian Pacific American playwrights. Featuring new works by Sujit Chawla, Thelma de Castro, Vishakan Jeyakumar, Jon Kern, Janet S. Kim, Michael Lew, Rehana Mirza, and Debargo Sanyal.

APOSTASY. *Written by Gino DiIorio. Directed by Frances Hill. Urban Stages. Opened March 29, 2007. Closed May 6, 2007.* A new play about a Jewish businesswoman with a terminal illness, and her relationship with a black televangelist.

MARRIAGE IS MURDER. *Written by Nick Hall. Directed by JoAnn Oakes. Produced by Well Urned Productions. Access Theatre. Opened March 29, 2007. Closed April 8, 2007.* A play about a once-married couple who are both mystery writers and who test out their murder scenarios on each other.

THE GREEN GAME. *Book by M. Stefan Strozier. Music and lyrics by M. Stefan Strozier and Puul Johnson. Directed by M. Stefan Strozier. Produced by La Muse Venale Acting Troupe. Theater Three. Opened March 29, 2007. Closed April 22, 2007.* A new musical about con artists, dirty wars, greed, and money.

ANNE OF GREEN GABLES. *Book and lyrics by Gretchen Cryer. Music by Nancy Ford. Directed by Tyler Marchant. Produced by TheatreworksUSA. Lucille Lortel Theatre. Opened March 29, 2007. Closed May 6, 2007.* A new musical adaptation of the classic children's story.

THE LAST OF THE TEXAS DOLLIES. *Written by Dan Moyer. Directed by Matthew Patches. Produced by Little Red Square. 13th Street Repertory. Opened April 1, 2007. Closed April 4, 2007.* A new play about a man who wants to play in the World Series of Poker.

THE NIBROC TRILOGY. *Written by Arlene Hutton. Directed by Eric Nightengale. 78th Street Theatre Lab. Opened April 1, 2007. Closed April 29, 2007.* Three plays presented in repertory: **LAST TRAIN TO NIBROC, SEE ROCK CITY,** and **GULF VIEW DRIVE.**

MATTHEW PASSION. *Book, music, and lyrics by Phil Hall. Directed by Steve Stringfellow. American Theatre of Actors. Opened April 2, 2007. Closed April 8, 2007.* A new play with music that interweaves the stories of the passion of Christ, Matthew Shepard, and an HIV survivor.

SERENDIB. *Written by David Zellnik. Directed by Carlos Armesto. Ensemble Studio Theatre. Opened April 4, 2007. Closed April 27, 2007.* A new play about a group of scientists who invite a team of filmmakers to document their work.

STONE AND THE MACGUFFIN. *Produced by Stone Soup Theatre Arts. Actors Theatre Workshop. Opened April 5, 2007. Closed April 28, 2007.* An unusual double bill of plays.

- STONE, *by Edward Bond.*
- THE MAGUFFIN, *by Adam Hunault.*

REARVIEWMIRROR. *Written by Eric Winick. Directed by Carl Forsman. Produced by Reverie Productions. 59E59. Opened April 5, 2007. Closed April 22, 2007.* A new play inspired by *The Bacchae.*

2 HUSBANDS. *Written by Ken Urban. Concept by Ken Urban and Brian Rogers. Directed by Brian Rogers. Chocolate Factory. Opened April 5, 2007. Closed April 28, 2007.* A multimedia meditation on wives and death, inspired by the lives of Henrietta Lacks (the first person to achieve immortality at a cellular level) and Terri Schiavo.

MIRACLE IN RWANDA. *Created by Leslie Lewis Sword and Edward Vilga. Directed by Edward Vilga. Ohio Theatre. Opened April 5, 2007. Closed April 29, 2007.* A new solo play about a Rwandan genocide survivor.

1918: A HOUSE DIVIDED. *Written and directed by Barbara Kahn. Theater for the New City. Opened April 5, 2007. Closed April 22, 2007.* A new musical that takes place in New York City at the time of World War I.

LOSING SOMETHING. *Written and directed by Kevin Cunningham. Produced by 3-Legged Dog. 3LD Art & Technology Center. Opened April 6, 2007. Closed May 6, 2007.* A new play about a man wrestling with his memories as he drifts into middle age.

WAXING WEST. *Written by Saviana Stanescu. Directed by Benjamin Mosse. Produced by East Coast Artists. La MaMa. Opened April 6, 2007. Closed April 22, 2007.* A new play that explores the cultural and economic dislocations of post-Iron Curtain Eastern Europe.

BASED ON A TRUE STORY: THE SEX EDITION. *Created and produced by Wreckio Ensemble. The Slipper Room. Opened April 6, 2007. Closed April 27, 2007.* A collaborative performance created solely through letters, journal entries, and notes submitted by the audience.

SUBURBAN PEEPSHOW. *Written by James Comtois. Directed by Pete Boisvert. Produced by Nosedive Productions. The Red Room. Opened April 6, 2007. Closed April 28, 2007.* A new play about office intrigues, sexual and otherwise. Preceded by a curtain-raiser called TRAILERS by Mac Rogers.

COMMITTED. *Produced by Living Image Arts. Lion Theatre. Opened April 7, 2007. Closed April 21, 2007.* A program of three one-act comedies about relationships.

- MEN ARE PIGS, *by Tony Zertuche, directed by Marlo Hunter.*
- OFF THE CUFF, *by William K. Powers, directed by Holli Harms.*
- BOXES, *by Robert Askins, directed by Lindsay Goss.*

GIANTS. *Written by Laura von Holt. Directed by Jen Wineman. Produced by Studio 42. HERE Arts Center. Opened April 9, 2007. Closed April 28, 2007.* A new play about a life-and-death sibling rivalry.

THE ACCOMPLICES. *Written by Bernard Weinraub. Directed by Ian Morgan. Produced by The New Group. Acorn Theatre. Opened April 9, 2007. Closed May 5, 2007.* A new play about an activist fighting for the rescue of European Jews during the Holocaust.

DREAM OF A RIDICULOUS MAN. *Written by Fyodor Dostoevsky. Adapted by Matthew Freeman. Directed by Matthew Johnston. Manhattan Theatre Source. Opened April 9, 2007. Closed April 10, 2007.* A dramatization of a story by Dostoyevksy.

TOPSY TURVY MOUSE. *Written by Peter Gil-Sheridan. Directed by Daniella Topol. Cherry Lane Theatre. Opened April 10, 2007. Closed April 21, 2007.* A new play about a boy who hangs a disturbing photo of his parents' service in Iraq in his locker.

RANDOM PARTICLES OF MATTER FLOATING IN SPACE. *Written by Michael Allen. Directed by Denyse Owens. Producers Club. Opened April 11, 2007. Closed April 21, 2007.* A new comedy/drama about a guy, his ex-girlfriend, and her brother, who is now his lover.

THINKING MAKES IT SO. *Written and directed by Damon Krometis. Produced by Examined Man Theatre. Center Stage. Opened April 11, 2007. Closed April 22, 2007.* A new play about a former frat boy who is struggling with nightmares brought on by a traumatic and controversial incident from college.

FIVE YEARS LATER. *Written by Jeff Love and Marc Adam Smith. Directed by Jeff Love. Produced by Point of You Productions. American Theatre of Actors. Opened April 11, 2007. Closed April 28, 2007.* An absurdist comedy about a group of diverse New Yorkers at a memorial service.

CONNECTING FLIGHT, HIDING OUT, AND MALETA. *Written and performed by Adam Law, Anita Menotti, C.G. Reeves, Delia Cyrillo, Jennifer Barr, Maggie Fang, Raul Jennings, Sanja Stojakovic and Yoshiko Suwa. Produced by Common Thread Theatre Company. The Independent Theatre. Opened April 11, 2007. Closed April 21, 2007.* A program of three new plays.

TROPHY WIFE. *Book by Mary Fulham. Music by Terry Waldo. Lyrics by Paul Foglino. Directed by Mary Fulham. Produced by Watson Arts. La MaMa. Opened April 12, 2007. Closed April 22, 2007.* A new musical based on a short story by Anton Chekhov.

NOT JUST FOR SHOCK VALUE. *Created and directed by Kendall Cornell. Produced by Six Figures Theatre Company. West End Theatre. Opened April 12, 2007. Closed April 28, 2007.* An all-women clown spectacle.

GETTING THEIR ACT TOGETHER AGAIN. *Book and lyrics by Gretchen Cryer. Music by Nancy Ford. 59E59. Opened April 12, 2007. Closed April 20, 2007.* A new autobiographical show by the creators of *I'm Getting My Act Together and Taking it on the Road.*

THE KITCHEN SPANISH TANGO. *Written by Cassandra Hume. Directed by Vonia Arslanian. Produced by In Search of a Song Productions. The Lafayette Grill and Bar. Opened April 12, 2007. Closed May 5, 2007.* A new solo show set in a world of tequila, music, and a dance that can't be resisted.

ROMANCE.COM. *Book, music, and lyrics by Joe Simonelli. Directed by Joe Simonelli. Produced by Atlantic Productions. Richmond Shepard Theatre. Opened April 12, 2007. Closed April 29, 2007.* A new musical comedy about two hapless singles who look for love on the Internet and get more than they bargained for.

ONCE UPON A PANDORA'S BOX. *Written by Monica Flory. Directed by Stephen Michael Rondel. Produced by The New Acting Company. The Philip Coltoff Center. Opened April 13, 2007. Closed May 6, 2007.* A new fantasy for kids and their families based on the Greek myth of Pandora.

A GUY ADRIFT IN THE UNIVERSE. *Written by Larry Kunofsky. Directed by Jacob Krueger. Produced by Four Chairs Theatre. Roy Arias Studios & Theatres. Opened April 13, 2007. Closed May 6, 2007.* A new play that's described as being like an episode of *The Simpsons* written by Muddy Waters.

MUD BLOSSOM. *Written by Ashlin Halfnight. Directed by Kate Pines. Produced by Emergency Theater Project. Walkerspace. Opened April 14, 2007. Closed April 29, 2007.* A new play about three generations of women living on a rundown farm.

MYTH AMERICA. *Conceived and curated by Stephen Wargo. Directed by Nicholas Cotz and Adam Fitzgerald. Produced by Personal Space Theatrics. TBG Arts Complex. Opened April 14, 2007. Closed April 28, 2007.* A new piece of ensemble playwriting, direction and acting about Americans from all walks of life and ethnic backgrounds as they live out their American dreams and myths both accomplished and crushed with expectations exceeded and unfulfilled. Featuring the writings of Arthur Kopit, Theresa Rebeck, Israel Horovitz, Rachel Axler, Ian Cohen, Brian Dykstra, Jason Grote, Matthew Paul Olmos, Julien Schwab, Saviana Stanescu, and Lloyd Suh.

GROWING PRETTY. *Written and directed by Carey Crim. Produced by Write Club NYC. Michael Weller Theatre. Opened April 15, 2007. Closed April 28, 2007.* A new play about a twelve-year-old girl who decides to become a supermodel.

ALL THE WRONG REASONS. *Written and performed by John Fugelsang. Directed by Pam MacKinnon. New York Theatre Workshop. Opened April 15, 2007. Closed May 6, 2007.* A new solo play about the child of an ex-nun and a former Franciscan brother.

TRANSFIGURES. *Conceived and directed by Lear deBessonet. Produced by Women's Project. Julia Miles (WPP) Theatre. Opened April 16, 2007. Closed May 6, 2007.* A new work about Jerusalem Syndrome.

PLAY BOY: OR, ODE TO AMERICA AFTER THE SECOND CIVIL WAR. *Written and performed by Johnny Klein. Dixon Place. Opened April 18, 2007. Closed April 19, 2007.* A post-apocalyptic fairy tale set in a world of traveling salesmen, campfire songs, and pornographic vaudeville.

LOVE NO EVIL. *Directed by Andy Ottoson, Emily Firth. Produced by Dalliance Theater. Roy Arias Studios & Theatres. Opened April 18, 2007. Closed April 22, 2007.* A trio of short plays about three couples grappling with life and love.

- **BLIND LOVE,** *by Adam Henry.*
- **SMALL TALK,** *by Adam Henry.*
- **VIOLATIONS,** *by Andy Ottoson.*

ARDEN: THE LAMENTABLE TRAGEDIE OF A DUMBO REAL ESTATE MOGUL. *Adapted by Michelle Salerno and Jeffrey Horne. Written by George Lillo. Directed by Michelle Salerno. Produced by Spring Theatreworks. Spring's Performance Loft. Opened April 19, 2007. Closed May 12, 2007.* A new adaptation of the 1739 play *Arden of Faversham* by George Lillo.

27 HEAVEN. *Written by Ian Halperin and Todd Shapiro. Directed by Adam Roebuck. The Laugh Factory. Opened April 19, 2007. Closed September 27, 2007.* A rock comedy that envisions a heavenly rock group made up of Jimi Hendrix, Janis Joplin, Jim Morrison, and Kurt Cobain.

THE VIEW FROM K STREET STEAK. *Written by Walt Stepp. Directed by Tom Herman. Produced by Cinna Productions. Altered Stages. Opened April 19, 2007. Closed May 5, 2007.* A new play described as a "song, dance, and puppet political act.".

JAMIE…ANOTHER SIDE OF DEAN. *Written and directed by George R. Carr. Produced by Veritas Productions. PMT House of Dance. Opened April 19, 2007. Closed May 26, 2007.* A new surrealistic drama about movie icon James Dean.

TUNE IN TOMORROW. *Directed by Doug Spagnola. Produced by DJM Productions. Dionysus Theater's L'il Peach. Opened April 19, 2007. Closed June 9, 2007.* A new play adapted from several 1940s radio plays about how World War II affects a young newlywed couple in New England.

DENIAL. *Written by Peter Sagal. Directed by Alex Roe. Metropolitan Playhouse. Opened April 20, 2007. Closed May 13, 2007.* A play in which an ACLU lawyer signs on to defend the rights of a Holocaust denier.

WEST MOON STREET. *Written by Rob Urbinati. Directed by Davis McCallum. Produced by Prospect Theater Company. Hudson Guild. Opened April 21, 2007. Closed May 20, 2007.* A new play based on Oscar Wilde's story "Lord Arthur Savile's Crime."

JANE EYRE. *Adapted by Polly Teale. Directed by Davis McCallum. Produced by The Acting Company. Baruch Performing Arts Center. Opened April 24, 2007. Closed May 5, 2007.* A dramatization of Charlotte Brontë's novel.

STAND-UP GIRL. *Written by Elizabeth C. Gutterman. Directed by Michelle Tattenbaum. Produced by Stand-Up Girl Productions. Center Stage. Opened April 25, 2007. Closed April 29, 2007.* A new comedy with drama about a woman trying to become a stand-up comic and also coping with her mother's illness.

ALCATRAZ. *Written by A. Kirchner. Directed by Andre Dion. Produced by Seven Tigers Co. 14th Street Y. Opened April 25, 2007. Closed May 12, 2007.* A play about the infamous prison, based on a poem by Elena Fattakova.

THE PRESIDENT AND HER MISTRESS. *Written by Jan Buttram. Directed by Rob Urbinati. Abingdon Theatre. Opened April 25, 2007. Closed May 13, 2007.* A new comedy about a woman president in the year 2155.

THE FALL AND RISE OF THE RISING FALLEN. *Text by Jason Craig. Directed by Mallory Catlett. Produced by Banana Bag & Bodice. P.S. 122. Opened April 26, 2007. Closed May 12, 2007.* A new musical theatre piece about a concept punk rock band.

TIME BEING. *Book and lyrics by Erika Stadtlander. Music by Ion Ionescu. Directed by Sean Littlejohn and Erika Stadtlander. Produced by Fildwith Ensemble Theatre. Theater Three. Opened April 26, 2007. Closed May 13, 2007.* A new musical that explores the emotions of a passionate, bewildered group of young souls attempting to make the most of their brief physical time on earth, and trying to understand the purposeful significance of the human attachments they make there.

EQUAL TO OR LESS THAN TWO PERSONS PER SQUARE MILE. *Written and directed by Joshua Briggs. Produced by Common Productions & The Uncertainty Principle. The Roof at Office Ops. Opened April 26, 2007. Closed May 5, 2007.* A new multimedia play staged on a Brooklyn rooftop overlooking the Manhattan skyline.

MIXED TAPE 2007. *Written by Lauren Hatcher, Lisa Atenasio, Eden Foster, and Marge Lewit. Directed by Robyn Nielsen, Eden Foster, Marge Lewit, and David Williams. Produced by Another Urban Riff.*

Under St. Marks. Opened April 26, 2007. Closed May 19, 2007. Four new one-act plays from the creators of the long-running hit *Mono.*

THE TRAGEDY OF JOHN. *Written by Neal Zupancic. Directed by Corinne Neal. Produced by Theatre of the Expendable Theatre Row Studio. Opened April 26, 2007. Closed May 13, 2007.* A new play about a man who has everything, hates everything, and manages to throw it all away.

CHURCH. *Written and directed by Young Jean Lee. Produced by Young Jean Lee's Theater Company. P.S. 122. Opened April 26, 2007. Closed May 12, 2007.* A new play described as an "exuberant church service" that addresses the playwright's personal struggles with religion.

THE PRESENT PERFECT. *Created by Kourtney Rutherford. Directed by Kevin Doyle. Produced by The Operating Theater. Brick Theatre. Opened April 26, 2007. Closed May 14, 2007.* A play about materialism in which everything on stage has a price tag: the set, props, costumes, even the performers are for sale.

MEL & EL: THIS SHOW RHYMES. *Written by Melanie Adelman and Ellie Dvorkin. Music by Patrick Spencer Bodd, Noah Diamond, Amanda Sisk, and Evan Toth. Lyrics by Melanie Adelman and Ellie Dvorkin. Produced by Cannery Works. Laurie Beechman Theater. Opened April 26, 2007. Closed April 29, 2007.* A musical show intended for audiences of legal drinking age ready to spend the evening with a couple of loose-lipped ladies who aren't afraid to be naughty.

AMERICAN FIESTA. *Written and performed by Steven Tomlinson. Directed by Mark Brokaw. Vineyard Theatre. Opened April 26, 2007. Closed May 20, 2007.* A new solo play about an avid collector of Fiestaware who discovers what it means to be "red" and "blue" in America.

HOOFERS ON PARADE. *Directed by Kelly Cooper, Ryan Gilliam, and Pavol Liska. Produced by Downtown Art. Downtown Art. Opened April 27, 2007. Closed May 20, 2007.* A new musical inspired by the movie musicals of Busby Berkeley.

BACKSTAGE: A LOVE-HATE STORY OF THE WOMEN'S MOVEMENT. *Written and directed by Fred Newman. Produced by The All Stars Project. Castillo Theatre. Opened April 27, 2007. Closed June 1, 2007.* A new play about Elizabeth Cady Stanton, Susan B. Anthony, and Frederick Douglass.

SMOKE AND MIRRORS. *Written by Joseph Goodrich. Directed by Nick Faust. Produced by The Flea Theater. Flea. Opened April 27, 2007. Closed June 2, 2007.* A new play about a handful of employees over the course of a seemingly normal work day.

EXPOSED: EXPERIMENTS IN LOVE, SEX, DEATH & ART. *Written and performed by Annie Sprinkle and Elizabeth Stephens. Directed by Neon Weiss. Collective Unconscious. Opened April 28, 2007. Closed May 12, 2007.* A new multimedia performance created in response to the violence of war and the anti-gay marriage movement.

BUG BOY BLUES. *Written by Lisa Railsback. Directed by Candace O'Neil Cichocki. Produced by The Lookingglass Theatre. Lookingglass Theatre. Opened April 28, 2007. Closed June 3, 2007.* A new children's play inspired by Kafka's *The Metamorphosis.*

EURIPIDES' MEDEA. *Translated and directed by Cath Gulick. Produced by The Night School Theater Company. The W. 29th St. Bijou. Opened April 29, 2007. Closed May 20, 2007.* A new adaptation of the famous play.

I LAND. *Written and performed by Keo Woolford. Directed by Roberta Uno. Produced by Ma-Yi Theater Company. 55 Mercer. Opened April 29, 2007. Closed May 13, 2007.* A new solo play about the author's search for the meaning of heritage in the postmodern world.

LEGALLY BLONDE. *Music and lyrics by Laurence O'Keefe and Nell Benjamin. Book by Heather Hach. Directed by Jerry Mitchell. Palace Theatre. Opened April 29, 2007.* A new musical based on the novel and film of the same name.

BEAUTY ON THE VINE. *Written by Zak Berkman. Directed by David Schweizer. Produced by Epic Theatre Center. Clurman Theatre. Opened May 2, 2007. Closed June 3, 2007.* A play about plastic surgery and the power of the human face.

BOGOSITY. *Written and directed by Simcha Borenstein. New York Comedy Club. Opened May 2, 2007. Closed May 23, 2007.* A new play about a dance teacher who desperately tries to maintain his class while his assistant insists on maintaining its integrity.

THE POTLUCK PLAYS. *Produced by The Milk Can Theatre Company. Michael Weller Theatre. Opened May 3, 2007. Closed May 13, 2007.* A program of new short plays inspired by recipes.

JUMPER'S WITH THE GYPSY. *Written by Nathaniel Kressen. Directed by Anthony Abdallah. Produced by Prophecy Productions. Walkerspace. Opened May 3, 2007. Closed May 6, 2007.* A new play about two twentysomethings trying to find true love the only way they can, surrounded by sadistic impulses and deceit.

LOVEMUSIK. *Book by Alfred Uhry. Music by Kurt Weill. Directed by Harold Prince. Produced by Manhattan Theatre Club. Biltmore Theatre. Opened May 3, 2007. Closed June 24, 2007.* A new musical about Kurt Weill and Lotte Lenya.

ORPHANS. *Written by Joel Shatzky. Directed by Cara Blouin. Impact Theater. Opened May 3, 2007. Closed May 13, 2007.* A new play about a soldier and father who pays a debt of blood by bringing the war home.

BACK FROM THE FRONT. *Written by Lynn Rosen. Directed by Connie Grappo. Produced by The Working Theatre. Riverside Theatre. Opened May 3, 2007. Closed May 27, 2007.* A new comedy about a family whose son returns home from war—but it's not the son they remember.

TIDES. *Directed by Sarah East Johnson. Produced by LAVA. Flea. Opened May 3, 2007. Closed May 27, 2007.* A new physical theatre piece by the all-female troupe LAVA.

IN THE SCHOOLYARD. *Book and lyrics by Paulanne Simmons. Music by Margaret Hetherman. Directed by Paulanne Simmons. Theater for the New City. Opened May 4, 2007. Closed May 20, 2007.* A new musical about a group of former Brooklynites who come back to their old neighborhood to play basketball once a year.

MOTHER LOAD. *Written by Amy Wilson. Directed by Julie Kramer. Sage Theater. Opened May 4, 2007. Closed June 22, 2007.* A new one-woman play about the cutthroat world of competitive parenting.

ROSE COLORED GLASS. *Written by Susan Bigelow and Janice Goldberg. Directed by Janice Goldberg. Theatre 54 @ Shetler. Opened May 5, 2007. Closed May 24, 2007.* A play set in Chicago, 1938, where a hopeful teenage girl and two mistrustful widows make unlikely allies in the struggle to rescue a boy out of Nazi Europe.

AN OCTOPUS LOVE STORY. *Written by Delaney Britt Brewer. Directed by Mike Klar. Produced by Kids With Guns. Center Stage. Opened May 5, 2007. Closed May 20, 2007.* A new play about a gay man and woman whose friendship catches their hearts off guard.

AN ASSEMBLY OF QUOTABLE GENTS. *Produced by Redd Mask Theater Company. Opened May 6, 2007. Closed May 22, 2007.* Three original one-act plays, performed one day a week at three different venues—Galapagos, Mo Pitkin's, and Union Pool. The playwrights are Musa Bacon, Joshua Rozett, and Jeffrey Lewonczyk.

THE DESIRE. *Written and directed by Jackie Alexander. Produced by The Billie Holiday Theatre. The Billie Holiday Theatre. Opened May 6, 2007. Closed June 24, 2007.* A new play about a successful attorney whose world is capsized when his cousin, a Hurricane Katrina survivor, comes to live with him.

DEUCE. *Written by Terrence McNally. Directed by Michael Blakemore. Music Box Theatre. Opened May 6, 2007. Closed August 19, 2007.* A new play about a reunion of two legendary tennis champions.

YOU ARE HERE: A MAZE. *Produced by Trouble and the B-Keepers. chashama. Opened May 6, 2007. Closed May 27, 2007.* A performance festival in a sculptural maze.

GOD'S EAR. *Written by Jenny Schwartz. Songs by Michael Friedman. Directed by Anne Kauffman. Produced by New Georges. East 13th Street Theatre. Opened May 7, 2007. Closed June 2, 2007.* A new play about a married couple who have lost their young son.

RADIO GOLF. *Written by August Wilson. Directed by Kenny Leon. Cort Theatre. Opened May 8, 2007. Closed July 1, 2007.* A play completing the late author's cycle of dramas about African American life in the twentieth century.

MOMMIE'S BOYS. *Written by Jack Dowd. Directed by John Capo. Produced by John Capo Productions. Altered Stages. Opened May 9, 2007. Closed May 20, 2007.* A new play described as a multigenerational tale of friendship, love, absentee fathers, and where the sins of one generation are all too easily passed on to the next.

GIFT EXCHANGE. *Written by Greg Turner. Produced by Do Not Disturb Theatre. The Red Room. Opened May 9, 2007. Closed May 19, 2007.* A new comedy about a man who wants to engage in some wife-swapping with his friend.

JUSTICE. *Produced by TheDrillingCompaNY. 78th Street Theatre Lab. Opened May 9, 2007. Closed May 27, 2007.* A program of nine short plays on the theme of justice.

- **DOG JUSTICE,** *by Andrea Moon, directed by Hamilton Clancy.*
- **JUST US,** *by Brian Dykstra, directed by Desmond Mosley.*
- **BY THE BOOK,** *by Paul Siefken, directed by Richard Harden.*
- **HABEAS CORPUS,** *by Kate McCamey, directed by Richard Mover.*
- **GOD'S SIGNATURE,** *by Stephen Bittrich, directed by Peter Bretz.*
- **SHEET,** *by Ronan Noone, directed by Bradford Olson.*
- **NATURAL CAUSES,** *by C. Denby Swanson, directed by Dan Teachout.*
- **INHERITANCE,** *by Eric Henry Sanders, directed by Hamilton Clancy.*
- **JOSH AND DEVON ARE ANCHORS,** *by Trish Harnetiaux, directed by Jude Domski.*

GAYFEST NYC. *TBG Arts Complex. Opened May 9, 2007. Closed June 2, 2007.* A month-long festival of LGBT-themed work, including two new plays and a musical, plus readings and other events.

- **COMPETING NARRATIVES,** *created by A.B. Asherk, directed by Margarett Perry.*
- **REVOLUTION,** *created and directed by Michael D. Jackson.*

BETROTHED. *Written and directed by Rachel Dickstein. Produced by Ripe Time. Ohio Theatre. Opened May 10, 2007. Closed May 25, 2007.* A new play based on S. Ansky's *The Dybbuk,* Anton Chekhov's "Betrothed," and Jhumpa Lahiri's "The Treatment of Bibi Haldar."

SUM OF US. *Created by Michelle Matlock and Inner Princess. Dixon Place. Opened May 10, 2007. Closed May 27, 2007.* A new theatre piece about a group of "bois" who summon the spirit of a Harlem Renaissance blues singer.

CARY FROM THE COCK. *Written by Cary Curran and Mike Albo. Music and lyrics by Christian Gibbs and Mark Stephen Campbell. Directed by Andi Stover. Gene Frankel Theatre. Opened May 10, 2007. Closed May 26, 2007.* A solo performance piece combining dance, original songs, monologues, and video.

ODYSSEY. *Written and directed by Kate Marks. Lookingglass Theatre. Opened May 10, 2007. Closed June 3, 2007.* A new adaptation of the classic by Homer, which playfully uses anachronism and humor to examine the repercussions of war.

KRAKEN. *Written by Len Jenkin. Directed by Michael Kimmel. Produced by Push Productions, Inc. Walkerspace. Opened May 11, 2007. Closed June 2, 2007.* A new play about a true-life encounter between American novelists Herman Melville and Nathaniel Hawthorne in 1856.

THE PRESENT'S TINY POINT. *Written and directed by Rob Cardazone. Produced by Two Cups and a String Theatre. Inc. The Turtle Shell Theatre. Opened May 11, 2007. Closed May 22, 2007.* A new program of short plays about twenty-one lonely characters who are haunted by their pasts and fearful of their futures.

SPRANG THANG. *Book, music, and lyrics by Goldee Greene. Directed by Christopher Scott. Produced by Amas Musical Theatre Academy. Players Theatre. Opened May 11, 2007. Closed May 20, 2007.* A musical that centers on a school talent show.

EBONY BLACK. *Book and lyrics by Melba LaRose. Music by Rachel Kaufman. Seaport District Cultural Association Performing Space. Opened May 12, 2007. Closed May 26, 2007.* An original children's musical based on the fairy tale "Snow White."

DAUGHTER OF A CUBAN REVOLUTIONARY. *Written and performed by Marissa Chibas. Directed by Mira Kingsley. Produced by Intar Theatre. DR2. Opened May 13, 2007. Closed June 2, 2007.* A solo play about the author's family, who were among the most powerful and prominent in Cuba.

PASSING STRANGE. *Book and lyrics by Stew. Music by Stew and Heidi Rodewald. Directed by Annie Dorsen. Produced by The Public Theatre and Berkeley Repertory Theatre. Public Theater. Opened May 14, 2007. Closed July 1, 2007.* A new musical about a young black bohemian in search of self and home.

SPITTING IN THE FACE OF THE DEVIL. *Written and performed by Bob Brader. Directed and developed by Suzanne Bachner. Produced by John Montgomery Theatre Company. The Red Room. Opened May 14, 2007. Closed July 16, 2007.* A new solo play about the death of the author's father.

STRANGERS KNOCKING. *Written by Robert Tenges. Directed by Marie Masters. Produced by The New Group. Acorn Theatre. Opened May 14, 2007. Closed June 3, 2007.* A new play about a girl's first high school dance and its effect on her parents' relationship.

SHATTER. *Produced by Ensemble Studio Theatre. Ensemble Studio Theatre. Opened May 16, 2007. Closed May 22, 2007.* A program of four new one-act plays written and helmed by EST's directors-in-residence.

- **THE LAST DAY**, *written and directed by Justin Quinn Pelegano.*
- **ANTIGONE NOIR**, *written and directed by Destiny Lilly.*
- **EYEZ WATCHIN'**, *written and directed by Andre Ford.*
- **MAIL AND THE ARC OF THE COVENANT**, *written and directed by Andrew Bergh.*

SPRING FEVER FESTIVAL. *CSV Cultural Center. Opened May 16, 2007. Closed June 2, 2007.* breedingground productions their biennial festival of new works by self-producing artists.

- **CHESS'D**, *created by David McGee, directed by Deena Selenow.*
- **LOOKING BACK**, *created and directed by Edward Ficklin.*
- **MISSING TIME**, *created by Michael Brandt, directed by Ian Morgan.*
- **SIMULACRA**, *created and directed by Gerritt Turner.*
- **THE LATE EDUCATION OF SASHA WOLFF**, *created by Shonni Enelow, directed by Josh Hoglund.*
- **THE NUMBER JANE**, *created by Julie Katz, directed by Adam Laupus.*

SKIRTS & FLIRTS. *Written by Gloria Calderon Kellett. Directed by Elena K. Smith. Kraine Theatre. Opened May 16, 2007. Closed May 19, 2007.* A monologue play about the intersecting lives of fifteen urbanites.

WORD OF MOUTH. *Produced by Arts World Financial Center. World Financial Center Complex. Opened May 16, 2007. Closed May 19, 2007.* Plays by women, staged in various locations at the World Financial Center.

- **BIRD EYE BLUE PRINT**, *by Lisa D'Amour, directed by Katie Pearl.*
- **KEEP THE CHANGE**, *by Joy Tomasko and Christina Gorman, directed by May Adrales.*
- **I WANT WHAT YOU HAVE**, *by Saviana Stanescu, directed by Gia Forakis.*
- **REMEMBRANCE**, *by Katori Hall, directed by Jyana Gregory.*
- **A PEDDLER'S TAKE: BUTTONS, GUTS, AND BLUETOOTH**, *by Andrea Lepcio, directed by Kim Wield.*
- **DIME SHOW**, *by Molly Rice and Peggy Stafford, directed by May Adrales.*
- **SONG**, *written and directed by Rachel Peters.*
- **THE SUN RETURNS, THE DAY BEGINS: A JOURNEY OF POEMS**, *created by Clea Rivera and Harry Mann.*
- **NOT WORDS ALONE**, *music by CocoRosie.*

SONGS OUR MOTHERS TAUGHT US. *Created and performed by Chloë Bass, Alexander Lane, Kymberlie Stansell, and Michele Torino. Directed by Rafael Gallegos. The Bushwick Starr. Opened May 17, 2007. Closed May 20, 2007.* A new musical theatre work that uses music, dance, writing, interactive media, and shopping to bring the Mothers' Day card from the page to the stage.

COMMANDER SQUISH. *Written and composed by Nate Weida. Directed by Michael Ferrell. Produced by Commander Squish Productions. 45th Street Theatre. Opened May 17, 2007. Closed May 19, 2007.* An original one-act musical set in a village full of classic fairy-tale aspects of life.

THE LANDLORD. *Written by Jonathan Barsness. Directed by Michael Daehn. Produced by Toy Box Theatre Company. Access Theatre. Opened May 18, 2007. Closed May 27, 2007.* A new play that looks into one man's mind as he struggles to achieve happiness and inner peace.

EXPATS. *Written by Heather Lynn McDonald. Directed by Ari Edelson. Produced by The New Group. Acorn Theatre. Opened May 18, 2007. Closed June 3, 2007.* A new play about American twentysomethings trying to make their mark amidst the sex, death and corruption of Russia's emerging marketplace.

PHALLACY. *Written by Carl Djerassi. Directed by Elena Araoz. Cherry Lane Theatre. Opened May 18, 2007. Closed June 10, 2007.* A new play that pits a passionate art historian against a cocksure chemistry professor.

THE CHRONOLOGICAL SECRETS OF TIM. *Written by Janet Zarecor. Directed by Sarah Ali. Produced by Impetuous Theater Group. Access Theatre. Opened May 18, 2007. Closed June 3, 2007.* A new play about a man who learns the hard lesson that you should never write things down.

LÁGRIMAS NEGRAS. *Written and performed by Eva Cristina Vásquez. Directed by Beatriz Córdoba. Teatro Circulo. Opened May 18, 2007. Closed June 3, 2007.* A new-one-woman show that uses elements from Latin American melodrama to emphasize the comic side of the character life situations.

HATE MAIL. *Written by Bill Corbett and Kira Obolensky. Directed by Catherine Zambri. Produced by monday morning productions. Independent Theater. Opened May 19, 2007. Closed June 3, 2007.* A new play about the pen pal relationship between uptight, rich Midwesterner Preston and avant garde New York artist Dahlia.

A WOMB WITH A VIEW. *Written and performed by Debra Barsha. Directed by Frank Ventura. CAP 21/The Shop. Opened May 22, 2007. Closed June 3, 2007.* A new musical that explores a year in the life of a lesbian's journey through the process of alternative insemination.

THE BISHOP AND THE BOYS. *Written by Frank Cossa. Directed by Diane Cossa-Platt. American Theatre of Actors. Opened May 23, 2007. Closed May 27, 2007.* A new play about an Irish priest and a TV journalist who investigate a bishop accused of sexual misconduct.

LIPSTICK ON A PIG. *Written by Linda Evans. Directed by David Epstein. Beckett Theatre. Opened May 23, 2007. Closed June 3, 2007.* A new play about a family in crisis struggling with self, guilt, secrets, and God.

THE MOST BEAUTIFUL LULLABY YOU'VE EVER HEARD. *Written by Greg Romero. Directed by Andrew J. Merkel. Produced by City Attic Theatre. Under St. Marks. Opened May 24, 2007. Closed June 2, 2007.* A poetic play depicting an argument, a confrontation, a flirtation, or a consummation of love between a man and a woman.

WHILE CHASING THE FANTASTIC... *Written by Derrick Ahonen. Directed by David Lee Horton. Produced by The Amoralists Production Company. Kraine Theatre. Opened May 24, 2007. Closed June 10, 2007.* A new play in which an unhappily married couple struggle to face issues of deception, infidelity, terrorism, and redemption when a radical visionary moves into their apartment.

INSIGHT 13. *Produced by Puerto Rican Traveling Theatre. 47th Street Theatre. Opened May 24, 2007. Closed June 10, 2007.* Workshop productions of new full-length and one-act plays.

- **PASSING JUDGMENT**, *by Jason Ramirez, directed by Alicia Kaplan.*
- **THE DEEP RUN**, *by Noemi Martinez Cress, directed by Rosemary Andress.*
- **A FIESTA OF WORDS & MUSIC**, *by Henry Guzman, Allen Davis III, Noemí de la Puente, Ed Cardona, Jr., Nancy Nevarez, and Desi Moreno-Penson; directed by Jose Zayas.*

FATE'S IMAGINATION. *Written by Randall David Cook. Directed by Hayley Finn. Produced by Gotham Stage Company. Players Theatre. Opened May 25, 2007. Closed June 17, 2007.* A new play about an older woman's seduction of a political candidate's son that triggers unexpected consequences.

THE EATEN HEART. *Written and performed by Hannah Bos and Paul Thureen. Directed by Oliver Butler. Produced by The Debate Society. Ontological Theatre. Opened May 26, 2007. Closed June 9, 2007.* A new play inspired by Boccaccio's fourteenth century masterwork, *The Decameron.*

ROMEO AND JULIET. *Written by William Shakespeare. Adapted and directed by Ellen Stewart. Music by Ellen Stewart, Genji Ito, and Michael Sirotta. Lyrics by Ellen Stewart. Produced by La MaMa E.T.C. La MaMa. Opened May 27, 2007. Closed June 17, 2007.* A new dance opera adapted from the play by Shakespeare.

FACING EAST. *Written by Carol Lynn Pearson. Directed by Jerry Rapier. Produced by Plan-B Theatre. Atlantic Stage 2. Opened May 29, 2007. Closed June 17, 2007.* A new play about a Mormon couple dealing with the recent death of their gay son.

LABAPALOOZA! *St. Ann's Warehouse. Opened May 30, 2007. Closed June 3, 2007.* The tenth annual presentation of new work developed at St. Ann's puppet lab.

ENABLING/DISABLING. *Written and directed by Jonathan Rabunski. Produced by He's Nearly In Me Prod. The Red Room. Opened May 30, 2007. Closed June 9, 2007.* A program of two one-act plays, connected thematically by a shared character, about show biz folks battling inner demons.

MARATHON 2007. *Ensemble Studio Theatre. Opened May 31, 2007. Closed June 30, 2007.* The twenty-ninth annual edition of this venerable one-act play festival.

- **THINGS WE SAID TODAY**, *by Neil Labute.*
- **FIRST TREE IN ANTARCTICA**, *by Julia Cho.*
- **MY DOG HEART**, *by Edith Freni.*
- **THE NEWS**, *by Billy Aronson.*
- **THE PROBABILITIES**, *by Wendy MacLeod.*
- **PRICELESS**, *by Elizabeth Diggs.*
- **YELBA, PRINCESS OF 10TH AVENUE**, *by Stephen Adly Guirgis.*
- **SELF-PORTRAIT IN A BLUE ROOM**, *by Daniel Reitz.*
- **CASTING**, *by Amy Fox.*
- **MILTON BRADLEY**, *by Peter Sagal.*

EAST VILLAGE CHRONICLES. *Metropolitan Playhouse. Opened May 31, 2007. Closed June 17, 2007.* New original short plays about life in the East Village neighborhood.

- **60 GUILDERS WORTH**, *by Anthony P. Pennino.*
- **STARS OVER THE EAST VILLAGE**, *by Nathanael Chura.*
- **UNRESOLVED**, *by Page Hearn.*

- **APOLOGIES TO VIETNAM**, *by C.S. Hanson.*
- **THE OLD NEW WORLD**, *by J.P. Chan.*
- **PARKHURST'S DESCENT**, *by Trav S.D.*
- **TRIANGLES EVERYWHERE**, *by Kimberly Wadsworth.*
- **QUIET HOWL**, *by Laura Livingston.*
- **AGE OF DISCOVERY**, *by Carlos Jerome.*
- **SHEILA MOM**, *by Richard Sheinmel.*

ELECTRA. *Written by Sophocles. Adapted and directed by Alfred Preisser. Produced by Classical Theatre of Harlem. Classical Theatre of Harlem (HSA). Opened May 31, 2007. Closed June 24, 2007.* A new adaptation of Sophocles's *Electra.*

MADAME BOVARY. *Book, music, and lyrics by Paul Dick. Directed by Elizabeth Falk. Produced by PASSAJJ Productions, LTD. Theater Five. Opened June 1, 2007. Closed June 17, 2007.* A musical based on the novel by Gustave Flaubert.

I.E., IN OTHER WORDS. *Written by Mark Greenfeild. Directed by Kip Fagan. Flea. Opened June 1, 2007. Closed June 16, 2007.* A new play about a young man who believes that if he takes a chance he will realize—and achieve—his big vague dreams.

FRITZ & FROYIM. *Book and lyrics by Norman Beim. Music by Mark Barkan and Rolf Barnes. Directed by John W. Cooper. Produced by Turtle Shell Productions. Turtle Shell Theater. Opened June 1, 2007. Closed June 16, 2007.* A new musical based about a former Nazi SS trooper and the ghost of a Jewish comedian.

PRETENTIOUS FESTIVAL. *Brick Theatre. Opened June 1, 2007. Closed July 1, 2007.* The annual summer festival from the Brick Theater in Williamsburg; the theme this year is work that's too good for us.

- **AN INTERVIEW WITH THE AUTHOR**, *created by Matthew Freeman, directed by Kyle Ancowitz.*
- **BETWEEN THE LEGS OF GOD**, *created by Art Wallace, directed by Art Wallace.*
- **DINNER AT PRECISELY EIGHT-THIRTEEN**, *created by Lisa Ferber and Paul Nelson, directed by Elizabeth London.*
- **EVERY PLAY EVER WRITTEN**, *created by Robert Honeywell, directed by Robert Honeywell.*
- **NIHILS**, *created by Trav S.D.*
- **ROCKBERRY: THE FINAL ONE-MAN SHOW**, *created by Nick Jones, directed by Peter J. Cook, produced by Jollyship the Whiz Bang.*
- **THE CHILDREN OF TRUFFAUT**, *created and directed by Eric Bland, produced by Old Kent Road Theater.*
- **THE COLE KAZDIN AMNESIA PROJECT**, *created by Cole Kazdin, directed by Robert Cucuzza.*
- **THE MERCURY MENIFESTO**, *created by John Del Signore.*
- **THIS IS THE NEW AMERICAN THEATRE**, *created by Danny Bowes and Tom X. Chao, directed by Danny Bowes, produced by Prodigal Son Productions.*
- **THREE ANGELS DANCING ON A NEEDLE**, *created by Assurbanipal Babilla, directed by Michael Yawney.*
- **YUDKOWSKI RETURNS!**, *created and directed by Robert Saietta.*

MY FRIEND, THE CAT. *Written by Phil Geoffrey Bond. Laurie Beechman Theater. Opened June 1, 2007. Closed June 22, 2007.* A cabaret musical about the relationship between man and cat.

AESOP'S FABLES. *Written by Kathleen Ferman. Directed by Jessica Colotta. Hudson School Performance Space 601 Park Ave Hoboken. Opened June 2, 2007. Closed June 9, 2007.* A new zany adaptation of the classic tales, for kids and their families.

GREEDY. *Written by Karl Gajdusek. Directed by Drew Barr. Produced by Clubbed Thumb. Ohio Theatre. Opened June 3, 2007. Closed June 9, 2007.* A new play about a man who answers an email that makes a titillating offer.

THE RULES OF CHARITY. *Written by John Belluso. Directed by Ike Schambelan. Produced by Theater by the Blind. Lion Theatre. Opened June 3, 2007. Closed June 24, 2007.* A play described as a dark comedy about how the disabled are treated.

CRAZY MARY. *Written by A.R. Gurney. Directed by Jim Simpson. Playwrights Horizons Mainstage. Opened June 3, 2007. Closed June 26, 2007.* A new play about a woman and her cousin, who lives in an asylum for the wealthy insane.

THE SCARLET LETTER. *Adapted by Stuart Vaughan with Marie Kreutziger. Directed by Stuart Vaughan. Produced by The New Globe Theatre. Gene Frankel Theatre. Opened June 3, 2007. Closed June 17, 2007.* A new adaptation of the novel by Nathaniel Hawthorne.

FITZ & WALLOUGHS GET IT IN THE END. *Written and directed by Paul Hagen. Ace of Clubs. Opened June 3, 2007. Closed July 8, 2007.* A musical parody depicting the farewell performance of vocalist (and unabashed narcissist) Fyodr Fitz and composer Constantine Walloughs.

THE REACHING. *Written by Crystal Skillman. Directed by Daniel Talbott. Produced by Rising Phoenix Repertory. Jimmy's No. 43. Opened June 4, 2007. Closed June 26, 2007.* The final play in the author's site-specific trilogy of ghost plays. **SEE PAGE 13.**

IF TRUTH BE KNOWN. *Written by Judith L. Komaki. Directed by Christine Simpson. Produced by Blue Heron Theatre. Arclight Theatre. Opened June 4, 2007. Closed June 24, 2007.* A new play about a woman who is struggling to understand why she's having problems with her boyfriend, who is a Vietnam veteran.

HORIZON. *Written and composed by Rinde Eckert. Directed by David Schweizer. Produced by New York Theatre Workshop. New York Theatre Workshop. Opened June 5, 2007. Closed July 1, 2007.* A work for three actors loosely based on the teachings of theologian Reinhold Niebuhr.

LOST ARROYOS. *Written by Mara McEwin. Produced by Treehouse Shakers. HERE Arts Center. Opened June 7, 2007. Closed June 17, 2007.* A new play that explores separate worlds of cultural struggles, race boundaries and blurred identities.

GOLONDRINA (SWALLOW). *Written by Aminta de Lara. Directed by Diana Chery and Aminta de Lara. Produced by La Mama E.T.C. La MaMa. Opened June 7, 2007. Closed June 24, 2007.* A new play about child abuse and political violence.

BABY FACE. *Written by Ashlin Halfnight. Directed by Alexis Poledouris. Produced by Electric Pear Productions. Walkerspace. Opened June 7, 2007. Closed June 23, 2007.* A new play about a family's bizarre journey through grief and guilt.

BLACK BOX NEW PLAY FESTIVAL. *Gallery Players. Opened June 7, 2007. Closed June 24, 2007.* A festival of new works by Tri-State playwrights.

- **BURY HIM**, *by Joe Lauinger.*
- **A TEMPORARY LAPSE**, *by Judd Lear Silverman.*
- **ATTENTION DEF...HEY, LOOK, A DOG!**, *by Daniel Damiano.*
- **THE INVITED GUEST**, *by Staci Swedeen.*
- **VIOLATING UNCLE PIGGY**, *by Judd Lear Silverman.*

AREA OF RESCUE. *Written by Laura Eason. Directed by Jessica Davis-Irons. Produced by AndHow! Theatre Company. Connelly Theatre. Opened June 7, 2007. Closed June 30, 2007.* A new play set in the future in a culture of fear.

IN A DARK DARK HOUSE. *Written by Neil LaBute. Directed by Carolyn Cantor. Produced by MCC Theater. Lucille Lortel Theatre. Opened June 7, 2007. Closed July 7, 2007.* A new play about two family members confronting their shared traumatic past.

BETWEEN THE SHADOWS. *Written and directed by Rania Khalil. Produced by HERE Arts Center. HERE Arts Center. Opened June 8, 2007. Closed June 10, 2007.* A new multimedia physical theatre piece inspired by German Expressionism and film noir.

ASTERISK. *Written by Tom Diriwachter. Directed by Jason Grant. Produced by March Forth Productions. American Theatre of Actors. Opened June 9, 2007. Closed June 24, 2007.* A new play about four fans at a baseball game where a home run record is about to be broken.

LOST OASIS/MAJIKAN. *Produced by Ciona Taylor Productions. Opened June 9, 2007. Closed June 30, 2007.* A program of two plays: one about a couple who go hiking to find the perfect camping spot; the other about an orangutan who can communicate and hold a job through the help of modern technology. Performed outdoors at Summit Rock in Central Park.

IF WISHES WERE HORSES. *Written by Kari Floren. Directed by Julia Gibson. Produced by Right Down Broadway Productions. Altered Stages. Opened June 9, 2007. Closed June 30, 2007.* A new comedy about a downsized human resources exec who needs a job.

FROM RIVERDALE TO RIVERHEAD. *Written by Anastasia Traina. Directed by Nick Sandow. Studio Dante. Opened June 9, 2007. Closed June 30, 2007.* A new play about four women who go to visit the son of one of them at the Riverhead Correctional Facility.

SESSIONS. *Book, music, and lyrics by Albert Tepper. Directed by Steven Petrillo. Produced by Algonquin Theater Productions and Ten Grand Productions, Inc. Peter Jay Sharp Theatre. Opened June 10, 2007. Closed August 25, 2007.* A new musical about a therapist.

AMAZONS AND THEIR MEN. *Written by Jordan Harrison. Directed by Ken Rus Schmoll. Produced by Clubbed Thumb. Ohio Theatre. Opened June 10, 2007. Closed June 16, 2007.* A new play about the life and work of Leni Riefenstahl.

NATIONAL ASIAN AMERICAN THEATRE FESTIVAL. *Venues in Manhattan. Opened June 11, 2007. Closed June 24, 2007.* The first-ever convocation of work by Asian American theatre companies from across the country. At venues all across New York City.

- **AND**, *created by Marcus Young.*
- **BIG HEAD/REPLACED RITUALS**, *created by Denise Uyehara/Courtyard Dancers.*
- **FROM THE ASHES**, *created by Meena Natarajan, directed by Dipankar Mukherjee, produced by Pangea World Theater.*

- **GUNS & TAMPONS/LIVING MEMORY-LIVING ABSENCE**, *created by Hanalei Ramos and Anida Yoeu Ali.*
- **LEE/GENDARY**, *created by Soomi Kim and Derek Nguyen, directed by Suzi Takahashi.*
- **PARANG SABIL**, *directed by Andrea Assaf, produced by Kinding Sindaw and New World Theatre.*
- **RAMBLE-ATIONS: A ONE D'LO SHOW**, *created by D'Lo.*
- **REFUGEE NATION**, *produced by TeAda Productions.*
- **STRANGE RAIN**, created by Marian Yalini Thambynayagam.
- **THE SPOKEN WORLD**, *produced by Youth Speaks, Inc.*
- **UNDESIRABLE ELEMENTS**, *created by Ping Chong and Sara Michelle Zatz, directed by Ping Chong, produced by Ping Chong & Company.*

THE BUTCHER OF BARABOO. *Written by Marisa Wegrzyn. Directed by Judith Ivey. Produced by Second Stage Theatre. McGinn Cazale Theatre. Opened June 11, 2007. Closed June 30, 2007.* A new play described as a black comedy about a butcher, a secret, and one perfectly polished meat cleaver.

BEHIND THE LID. *Created by Lee Nagrin and Basil Twist. Silver Whale Gallery. Opened June 12, 2007. Closed July 13, 2007.* A new play that chronicles a woman looking back on her life through a dream.

JUMP/ROPE. *Written by John Kuntz. Directed by Douglas Mercer. Produced by Square Peg Productions. Urban Stages. Opened June 12, 2007. Closed June 24, 2007.* A new play about two men whose long-term relationship has begun to sour, until a third party enters the picture.

SAMPAGUITA. *Written by Marisa Marquez. Directed by Will Warren. Produced by HWM Associates and AimHigh Productions. 45th Street Theatre. Opened June 12, 2007. Closed June 24, 2007.* A new play that tackles the devastating consequences for those dealing with the autoimmune disease lupus, as well as the timely issue of post 9/11 immigration policies.

THE GREENHOUSE EFFECT. *Written and performed by Michael Deep. Directed by Kate Bushmann. Abingdon Theatre. Opened June 12, 2007. Closed June 24, 2007.* A new play about a dysfunctional family.

PAGES, A NEW MUSICAL. *Book, music, and lyrics by Will Van Dyke and Josh Halloway. Directed by Lawrence Arancio. CAP 21/The Shop. Opened June 12, 2007. Closed June 23, 2007.* A new musical about a man who has chosen to live a fiction because he's too afraid of what will happen if he doesn't.

THE SECOND TOSCA. *Written by Tom Rowan. Directed by Kevin Newbury. 45th Street Theatre. Opened June 13, 2007. Closed July 1, 2007.* A new play that takes place backstage at Opera California during rehearsals for *Tosca.*

EGRESS. *Created by Baraka de Soleil and D UNDERBELLY. Music by Daniel Givens. Dixon Place. Opened June 14, 2007. Closed June 30, 2007.* An exploration of the ever-fluid relationship between music and movement.

SHORTENED ATTENTION SPAN ONE ACT PLAY FESTIVAL. *Players Theatre. Opened June 14, 2007. Closed July 8, 2007.* Twenty plays, each under twenty minutes.

- **THEATRE GHOST**, *by Mim Granahan.*
- **LIFE IN E SHARP**, *by Jonathan G. Galvez.*
- **GIRL HATES CABS**, *by Warren Schultz.*
- **FEED ME WHAT I DRINK**, *by Ian Grody.*

- **YES BEFORE GOODBYE,** *by Dan Chen.*
- **THE TITANIC TRIVIA GAME,** *by Lisa Haeber.*
- **LOOKING FOR LOVE,** *by J. Boyer.*
- **THE SOLUTION,** *by Stewart Rudy and Julia Susman.*
- **TENACITY,** *by Scott T. Barsotti.*
- **DEATH AND DECEPTION,** *by Catherine Lamm.*
- **SUNDAY KIND OF LOVE,** *by Concetta Rose Rella.*
- **THE CAFÉ,** *by Kyle Bradstreet.*
- **RICH ON SKINS,** *by Joe Lauinger.*
- **PENGUINS ARE MAD SCARY,** *by Michael Tester.*
- **PLAYS FOR THE SUNNI TRIANGLE PARTS 1 AND 2,** *by Jerrod Bogard.*
- **PLAYS FOR THE SUNNI TRIANGLE PART 3,** *by Jerrod Bogard.*
- **LITTLE SQUIRREL,** *by Caroline McGraw.*
- **SIRLOINS IN SPACE,** *by Joel Hanson.*
- **BEER AND THE MEANING OF LIFE,** *by Carlo Rivieccio.*

THIS MEANS KILL. *Written by Chris Littler. Directed by Chris Plante. Produced by Little Red Square. Kraine Theatre. Opened June 14, 2007. Closed June 16, 2007.* A new play about a doctor trying to locate his troublesome wife.

FAMOUS ACTORS. *Written and directed by Kara Feely. Produced by Object Collection. Ontological Theatre. Opened June 14, 2007. Closed June 23, 2007.* A performance/installation that applies the logic of experimental music to everyday human behavior.

10 MILLION MILES. *Book by Keith Bunin. Music and lyrics by Patty Griffin. Directed by Michael Mayer. Produced by James Harker. Atlantic Theatre. Opened June 14, 2007. Closed July 15, 2007.* A new musical about a road trip from Florida to New York.

THE FILE ON RYAN CARTER. *Written and directed by David Gaard. Sanford Meisner Theatre. Opened June 14, 2007. Closed July 8, 2007.* A new play about the paths of two unlikely friends, a conservative college jock and a radical political activist.

THE TOAD POEMS. *Written by Gerald Locklin and George Carroll. Directed by Ian Morgan. Soho Playhouse. Opened June 15, 2007. Closed July 8, 2007.* A new play about how a brilliant and opinionated poet and professor manages to balance a half-hearted separation from his ex-wife with the rush of a younger live-in girlfriend.

THE WAR AT HOME. *Barrow Group. Opened June 15, 2007. Closed July 2, 2007.* A program of five short new plays by Arlene Hutton, Barbara Lindsay, K. Lorrel Manning, Dee Ann Newkirk, and Julia Ryan focusing on the Iraq War and its effect on our culture at large.

THE ARGUMENT & DINNER PARTY. *Directed by David Herskovits. Produced by Target Margin Theater. The Kitchen. Opened June 16, 2007. Closed June 30, 2007.* A program of new one act plays, adapted from works by Aristotle and Plato.

ONE THING I LIKE TO SAY IS. *Written by Amy Fox. Directed by Paul Willis. Produced by Clubbed Thumb. Ohio Theatre. Opened June 17, 2007. Closed June 23, 2007.* A new play about a woman who has a lot more family than she likes to acknowledge.

THE FABULOUS LIFE OF A SIZE ZERO. *Written by Marissa Kumin. Directed by Ben Rimalower. DR2. Opened June 17, 2007. Closed July 1, 2007.* A new play about a girl in her senior year of high school as she attempts to achieve the ultimate: effortless perfection.

FALL FORWARD. *Written by Daniel Reitz. Directed by Daniel Talbott. Produced by Rising Phoenix Repertory. John Street United Methodist Church. Opened June 18, 2007. Closed June 30, 2007.* A new site-specific theatre adventure comprising three intimate vignettes that deal with loss, isolation, and the sudden cataclysms of life. **SEE PAGE 275.**

BADGE. *Written by Matthew Schneck. Directed by Jenn Thompson. Produced by BeaconNY Productions. Rattlestick Theatre. Opened June 18, 2007. Closed July 1, 2007.* A new dark comedy about a man who takes refuge in boy scouting.

EURYDICE. *Written by Sarah Ruhl. Directed by Les Waters. Second Stage. Opened June 18, 2007. Closed August 26, 2007.* A new dramatization of the myth of Orpheus and Eurydice.

SHORT STORIES 8. *Produced by NativeAliens Theatre Collective. The Independent. Opened June 19, 2007. Closed June 23, 2007.* A short play festival, featuring eight gay-themed original works.

- **THE YOUNG MAN FROM EAST MEADOW,** by *Kevin Manganaro.*
- **THE LETTER,** by *Barbara Bryan.*
- **GODFREY,** by *Ian August.*
- **JUST BEFORE THE DROP,** by *David-Matthew Barnes.*
- **THIRTEEN DEGREES OF INSOMNIA,** by *Elizabeth Dembowski.*
- **MESSAGES DELETED,** by *Rich Espey.*
- **POP PSYCHOLOGY,** by *Lyralen Kay.*
- **ROBOSAURUS,** by *Daniel Keleher.*

HOT NIGHTS. SMART WRITERS. *HERE Arts Center. Opened June 20, 2007. Closed July 2, 2007.* Two new theatre pieces in repertory.

- **WHITE HOT,** by *Tommy Smith.*
- **THE CURSE OF THE SMART KID,** by *David Vining.*

BULLSCHMITT! *Written and performed by Vickie Schmitt. Directed by Susan Haefner. Produced by Living Room Arts. Upstairs at Rose's Turn. Opened June 20, 2007. Closed June 30, 2007.* A one-woman show about an actress who plays one of the dead people in the cemetery in *Our Town* whose mind wanders during a performance.

ELVIS PEOPLE. *Written by Doug Grissom. Directed by Henry Wishcamper. New World Stages. Opened June 21, 2007. Closed June 23, 2007.* A new play about people who lives were changed by Elvis Presley.

OLD KID COD. *Written by Lawrence Dial. Directed by Adam Knight. American Theatre of Actors. Opened June 21, 2007. Closed July 7, 2007.* A new play about a teenager who steals his late grandfather's ashes.

BEYOND GLORY. *Written and performed by Stephen Lang. From the Book by Larry Smith. Directed by Robert Falls. Produced by Roundabout Theatre Company. Laura Pels Theatre. Opened June 21, 2007. Closed August 19, 2007.* A new solo play about eight veterans of recent American wars.

US. *Created and performed by Alexandra Beller. Directed by Kristin Marting. HERE Arts Center. Opened June 21, 2007. Closed June 24, 2007.* A new theatre piece that uses dance, song, and text to create a personal commentary on the state of the union.

I GOOGLE MYSELF. *Written by Jason Schafer. Directed by Jason Jacobs. Produced by Taylor Mankowski. Under St. Marks. Opened June 21, 2007. Closed July 13, 2007.* A new play about what happens when one man Googles his own name to find others who share his moniker.

COUNT TO TEN. *Book and lyrics by Michael Blevins and Beth Clary. Music by Michael Blevins, Scott Knipe, Bruce Sacks, and David Wollenberger. Directed by Michael Blevins. Produced by The Group Theatre Too. 14th Street Y. Opened June 22, 2007. Closed July 1, 2007.* A new family musical about a writer desperate to get his show produced, and the ballet dancing heiress and tough-talking teenager he gets entangled with.

SLAMMIN' EVENTS/THE IMPORTANCE OF BEING WANTED. *Produced by Our Time Theatre Company. Cherry Lane Theatre. Opened June 22, 2007. Closed June 24, 2007.* A program of two one-act plays with music created and performed by Our Time's teen and preteen companies.

SECOND TIME AROUND. *Written by Elaine Joyce and Neil Simon. Don't Tell Mama. Opened June 25, 2007. Closed June 28, 2007.* A new solo play with music that goes on a trip through the ins and outs of a woman's best days, and not-so-best days.

WASHING MACHINE. *Developed by Michael Chamberlain and Jason Stuart. Written by Jason Stuart. Directed by Michael Chamberlain. Produced by Fist in the Pocket. Chocolate Factory. Opened June 25, 2007. Closed July 7, 2007.* A new play inspired by the traumatic and mysterious true story of a five-year-old girl who drowned inside a laundromat washing machine.

THE RISK OF SAFETY. *Written by Elizabeth Irwin. Produced by Ain't No Swett. WorkShop Theater. Opened June 27, 2007. Closed June 30, 2007.* A new play about three couples who meet and feel those oh-so electrifying sparks.

UNIVERSAL ROBOTS. *Based on and borrowed from the writings of Karel Čapek. Directed by Shannon Sindelar. Produced by 31 Down Radio theater. Ontological Theatre. Opened June 28, 2007. Closed July 7, 2007.* A new piece that examines the role of technology's advancement in a modern-day society in search of Utopia.

PROFESSIONAL SKEPTICISM. *Written by James Rasheed. Directed by Kareem Fahmy. Produced by Zootopia Theatre Company. Abingdon Theatre. Opened June 28, 2007. Closed July 15, 2007.* A comic drama about an accounting scandal.

OVERHEARD. *Written by Russell Dobular. Directed by Greg Cicchino. Produced by End Times Productions. Duplex. Opened June 30, 2007. Closed July 21, 2007.* A new compilation play of monologues that represent everyday people found in the coffee shop, behind the bar, on a park bench or on the street corner.

DESERT FLOWER'S TRUTH. *Written and performed by Tanya Maryoung. Directed by Kim Weston-Moran. Produced by RHYTHMCOLOR Associates. Baton Rouge Restaurant & Lounge. Opened July 1, 2007. Closed July 29, 2007.* A one-woman musical dramedy that reflects on the author's journey from an ambiguous marriage to her discovery of her true path.

ICE FACTORY '07. *Produced by Soho Think Tank. Ohio Theatre. Opened July 4, 2007. Closed August 18, 2007.* Soho Think Tank's annual summer festival of new work.

- **JOHNNY APPLEF?%KER**, *created by Rachel Shukert, directed by Stephen Brackett, produced by The Bushwick Hotel.*
- **STRETCH: A FANTASIA**, *created by Susan Bernfield, directed by Emma Griffin, produced by New Georges.*
- **THE LACY PROJECT**, *created by Alena Smith, directed by Susanna Gellert.*
- **VAMPIRE UNIVERSITY**, *created by John Kaplan, directed by Desmond Mosley.*

WHAT HAPPENED WHEN. *Written by Daniel Talbott. Directed by Brian Roff. Produced by Rising Phoenix Repertory. HERE Arts Center. Opened July 5, 2007. Closed July 16, 2007.* A new play about two brothers who meet on a winter night and share a conversation filled with old stories of their family and the people who populate their town. **SEE PAGE 41.**

PICKING UP. *Written by Jacey Powers. Directed by Emma Poltrack. DR2. Opened July 5, 2007. Closed July 15, 2007.* A play about a young woman in love with chaos, New York, and her ex-boyfriend.

THE GREENWICH VILLAGE FOLLIES. *Written by Andrew Frank and Doug Silver. Original concept by Fran Kirmser. Directed by Andrew Frank. Manhattan Theatre Source. Opened July 6, 2007. Closed July 28, 2007.* A new musical about the history and culture of the landmark New York City neighborhood, Greenwich Village.

GUILTY. *Written by Nancy Manocherian. Directed by Kira Simring. Produced by The Cell Theatre Company. Acorn Theatre. Opened July 6, 2007. Closed July 29, 2007.* A new play about a group of friends in the top echelon of New York society whose lives start to unravel when secrets are revealed.

THE/KING/OPERETTA. *Created by Waterwell. Music by Lauren Cregor. Directed by Tom Ridgely. Produced by Waterwell. Barrow Street Theatre. Opened July 7, 2007. Closed August 11, 2007.* A new musical theater piece about Martin Luther King Jr.

FRESH FRUIT FESTIVAL. *Cherry Lane Theatre. Opened July 9, 2007. Closed July 22, 2007.* The fifth annual edition of this celebration of gay and lesbian-themed theatre and performance; at the Cherry Lane Theatre plus a few other venues.

- **FADING TO GREY**, *created by Richard A. Pettey, directed by Karen Swager.*
- **MENTOR**, *created by John S. Green, directed by James Martinelli.*
- **MONROE BOUND**, *created by Lucile Scott, directed by Anthony C.E. Nelson.*
- **THE LONG RIDE HOME**, *created by Robert Gompers.*
- **WHAT DO MEN WANT?**, *created by James Howell/Larson Rose.*

UNIVERSAL ROBOTS. *Written and directed by Mac Rogers. Produced by Manhattan Theatre Source & Gideon Productions, LLC. Manhattan Theatre Source. Opened July 9, 2007. Closed July 19, 2007.* A new play inspired by Karel Čapek's sci-fi play *R.U.R.* **SEE PAGE 209.**

EAST TO EDINBURGH. *59E59. Opened July 10, 2007. Closed July 29, 2007.* A festival of American productions that are headed to the Edinburgh Fringe Festival.

- **GRASMERE**, *created by Kristina Leach, directed by Noel Neeb.*
- **MOD**, *created by Paul Andrew Perez and George Griggs, directed by Chantel Pascente.*
- **RASH**, *created by Jenni Wolfson, directed by Jen Nails.*
- **TENDER**, *created by Shapour Benard, directed by Julie Beber.*

XANADU. *Book by Douglas Carter Beane. Music and lyrics by John Farrer and Jeff Lynne. Directed by Christopher Ashley. Helen Hayes Theatre. Opened July 10, 2007.* A new musical based on the 1980 film of the same name.

DECADENCE. *Written by P. William Pinto. Directed by Akia. Produced by Rising Sun Performance Company. Under St. Marks. Opened July 11, 2007. Closed August 25, 2007.* A new play drawing from our eclectic Americana history, told through ten vignettes, each representing a decade from the twentieth century.

VOICES IN CONFLICT. *Created by The Company. Directed by Bonnie Dickinson. Produced by Vineyard Theatre and Wilton High School. Vineyard Theatre. Opened July 11, 2007. Closed July 13, 2007.* A play about the war in Iraq, created by students at Wilton High School in Connecticut (and subsequently banned).

BLACK MAN RISING. *Written by J. Chapmyn. Directed by Patricia R. Floyd. Produced by StageFace Productions. Players Theatre. Opened July 12, 2007. Closed July 28, 2007.* A choreopoem that takes the strength, wisdom, and fortitude of black manhood and places it on the stage.

ART OF MEMORY. *Conceived by Tanya Calamoneri. Produced by Company SO GO NO. Ontological Theatre. Opened July 12, 2007. Closed July 21, 2007.* A new theatre piece that weaves together text, Butoh dance, and original music to explore how knowledge is stored in the mind.

MIDTOWN INTERNATIONAL THEATRE FESTIVAL. *WorkShop Theater. Opened July 16, 2007. Closed August 5, 2007.* The eighth annual edition of this summertime staple, featuring plays, musicals, and solo performances at several Midtown venues.

- **A LINE IN THE SAND,** *created by Adina Taubman, directed by Padraic Lillis. Produced by Gemini Productions.*
- **ADDICTED TO CHRISTMAS,** *created by David Patrick Stearns, directed by Sheri Johnson.*
- **ALL THE KING'S WOMEN,** *created by Luigi Jannuzzi, directed by Branan Whitehead. Produced by Metropolitan Tehatre Company.*
- **AS LONG A TIME AS A LONG TIME IS IN LONG TIME LAND,** *created by Todd Pate, directed by Barbara Suter. Produced by Broken Blade Theatre Company.*
- **BLOODY LIES,** *created by Greg Machlin, directed by Samantha Shechtman. Produced by Purple Pillow Thief Productions.*
- **CAT-HER-IN-E,** *created by Amy Staats, directed by Jorelle Aronovitch.*
- **DUPLEX,** *created by Scott Brooks, directed by Sam Viverito, produced by Badlands Theatre Company.*
- **EXHIBIT THIS!—THE MUSEUM COMEDIES,** *created by Luigi Jannuzzi, directed by Elizabeth Rothan, produced by Metropolitan Theatre Company.*
- **FIVE BY THREE,** *created by Nicole Greevy, Uma Incrocci, and Erica Jensen; directed by Nicole Greevy and Erica Jensen; produced by Numerical Productions.*
- **FIX-IT,** *created by Megan Griswold, directed by Leah Davidson and Pam DeVore.*
- **FOUR UNFOLD: A STORY WITH SONG,** *created by Katie Lemos and T.J. Moss, directed by Katie Lemos.*
- **I'M IN LOVE WITH YOUR WIFE,** *created by Alex Goldberg, directed by Tom Wojtunik, produced by Changuitos Productions.*
- **LOVE AND ISRAEL,** *directed by Ilana Lipski.*

- **OUT OF THE FLAMES**, *created by Dave Marken, directed by Natasha Matallana, produced by Opening Night Entertainment.*
- **PAPA'S WILL**, *created and directed by Rob Egginton, produced by Panicked Productions.*
- **PATRIOT ACTS**, *created by Marshall Jones III, directed by Rico Rosetti, produced by Emerge Theater Company.*
- **SONS OF MOLLY MAGUIRE**, *created by John Kearns, directed by Candace O'Neil Cihocki, produced by Boann Books.*
- **STORIA**, *created by Troy Diana, directed by Jennifer Ortega, produced by The Monarch Theater.*
- **STRAY DOG HEARTS**, *created by Padraic O'Reilly, directed by Jennifer Gelfer, produced by Velocity Theatre Company.*
- **TAKE ME AMERICA**, *created by Bill Nabel and Bob Christianson, directed by Bill Nabel, produced by Double Play Connections.*
- **THE BROKEN JUMP**, *created by King Talent, directed by J.B. Lawrence, produced by Baby Hippopotamus Productions.*
- **THE CHOLMONDELEY CHRONICLES**, *created by Michael Rudez, directed by Michael Roderick, produced by Small Pond Entertainment.*
- **THE CONJUGALITY TEST**, *created by Michael Lazan, directed by David Gautschy.*
- **THE EXECUTIONER**, *created by Jon Kern, directed by Pedro Salazar.*
- **THE LAST ONE LEFT**, *created by Jason Pizzarello, directed by Dev Bondarin, produced by Geek Ink.*
- **THE PURPOSE OF MATTER IN THE UNIVERSE**, *created by Joe Hutcheson, directed by DB Levin.*
- **THE SHADOW PIER**, *created by Jonathan Wallace, directed by James Edward Duff, produced by Howling Moon Cab Company.*
- **THE STREET**, *created by Ronnie Cohen, directed by Heidi Lauren Duke.*
- **TO THE CONTRARY**, *created by Craig Jacobs, directed by James Valletti.*
- **TRANSIT**, *created by Mary Jane Wells, directed by Ben Sander.*
- **WEBEIME**, *created and directed by Layon Gray, produced by The Black Gents of Hollywood.*

SPARTACUS. *Adapted and directed by Ted Minos. Produced by Inwood Shakespeare Festival. Inwood Hill Park Peninsula. Opened July 18, 2007. Closed August 4, 2007.* A new play about the Roman slave who led a rebellion against the patricians.

SURFACE TO AIR. *Written by David Epstein. Directed by James Naughton. Produced by Symphony Space. Symphony Space. Opened July 18, 2007. Closed August 5, 2007.* A new play about a family coping with the return of the remains of their son, who was killed in the Vietnam War thirty years before.

SWIM SHORTS 3. *Produced by Joe Cecala and Impetuous Theater Group. The Holiday Inn Midtown Rooftop. Opened July 18, 2007. Closed August 12, 2007.* Impetuous Theater Group presents two programs of new short one-act plays, written specifically to performed at the rooftop pool of the Holiday Inn in Midtown Manhattan.

- **JOE THE LIFEGUARD**, *by C.L. Weatherstone.*
- **FORGIVENESS**, *by Janet Zarecor.*
- **JETTISON**, *by Brendan Bradley.*
- **A PROVERBIAL AFFAIR**, *by Roi "Bubi" Escudero.*
- **DER EISBAR**, *by Joe Mathers and Brian MacInnis Smallwood.*

- **PRACTICE,** *by Josh Sherman.*
- **TWINS,** *by Seth Kramer.*
- **A SIMPLE PROP,** *by Jesse Cervantes.*
- **CRASH LANDING,** *by Joe Powell.*
- **THE PITCH,** *by Eric Walton.*

THE PEOPLE VS. MONA. *Book by Patricia Miller and Jim Wann. Music and lyrics by Jim Wann. Directed by Laura Standley. Produced by Ground UP Productions. Abingdon Theatre. Opened July 18, 2007. Closed August 4, 2007.* A new Southern murder mystery musical.

IOWA '08. *Produced by New York Collective for the Arts. Vineyard Theatre. Opened July 19, 2007. Closed July 29, 2007.* A festival of new ten-minute plays about the personal nature and political leanings of the people who make up the Iowa Presidential election caucus.

- **GRASSROOTS,** *by John Walch.*
- **THE BODY POLITIC,** *by Alex Lyras.*
- **MADE RIGHT,** *by Rick Kronberg.*
- **COUNT,** *by Carla Stangenberg.*
- **IOWAY,** *by Rogelio Martinez.*

TYRANNOS REX. *Written by Joshua Pangborn. Produced by The Living Room Theatre. Under St. Marks. Opened July 19, 2007. Closed August 5, 2007.* A new play that modernizes the story of Oedipus and his family.

THE THEORY OF COLOR. *Written by Lella Heins. Directed by Alexander Harrington. Produced by Medicine Show Theatre Ensemble. Medicine Show. Opened July 20, 2007. Closed July 29, 2007.* A new play about a worldly female artist whose life begins to unravel when she and her husband move from Manhattan to a remote hamlet in the middle of nowhere.

GLO. *Produced by Green Light Productions. Theatre 54 @ Shetler. Opened July 20, 2007. Closed July 29, 2007.* A program of five new one-act plays all written and directed by women.

- **I'VE NEVER TOLD ANYONE THIS,** *by Linda Suzuki, directed by Jamie Mayer.*
- **BAGGAGE CLAIM,** *by Sara Snyder, directed by Susan Lovell.*
- **BULLFIGHTING,** *by Lucy Wang, directed by Jillian Singer.*
- **MARRYING NANDINI,** *by Nandita Shenoy, directed by Elizabeth Levy.*
- **THE TWENTY SOMETHINGS?,** *by Killian Beldy, directed by Deanna Weiner.*

BOOKENDS. *Book, music, and lyrics by Katharine Houghton, Dianne Adams, and James McDowell. Directed by Ken Jenkins. New Jersey Repertory Company. Opened July 21, 2007. Closed August 26, 2007.* A new musical about old friends.

POE, TIMES TWO. *Written and performed by Greg Oliver Bodine. Directed by Amber Estes. Manhattan Theatre Source. Opened July 23, 2007. Closed July 26, 2007.* A double bill of short one-man plays adapted from Edgar Allan Poe stories: "The Cask of Amontillado" and "The Black Cat."

THE MAGIC OF MRS. CROWLING. *Written by Brian Silliman. Directed by Abe Goldfarb. Produced by The Royal Circus and HorseTrade. Kraine Theatre. Opened July 24, 2007. Closed August 5, 2007.* A new play about a twelve-year-old dying of cancer who gets his wish: to meet the author of his favorite fantasy books.

GOODNIGHT BOBBY, GOODNIGHT JOHN. *Written by Michael J. Herron. Directed by Michael McGrail. Richmond Shepard Theatre. Opened July 24, 2007. Closed July 29, 2007.* A new play about a man who returns home to his working-class neighborhood after his father's stroke.

JOURNEYPATH (?): AN EXPERIMENT IN RIGHTNESS. *Written and directed by Theresa Buchheister. Produced by Title:Point Productions. Ontological Theatre. Opened July 25, 2007. Closed July 28, 2007.* A new theatre piece described as "a dream of an old story presented via individual competition and mathematical equation."

THE RED LAMP. *Written by Hilliard Booth. Directed by Patrick Mills. Produced by Diversity Players of Harlem. Roy Arias Studios & Theatres. Opened July 25, 2007. Closed July 29, 2007.* A comedy about the complications that occur when three family members decide to use one red lamp as a signal for three very different reasons.

TWO THIRDS HOME. *Written by Padraic Lillis. Directed by Giovanna Sardelli. Produced by Broken Watch Theatre Company. Michael Weller Theatre. Opened July 26, 2007. Closed August 12, 2007.* A new play about two brothers who return to their childhood home after their mother dies.

ORANGE. *Written by Ron Berry. Directed by J. Knox Griffin. Produced by The Mescalito Group. Center Stage. Opened July 27, 2007. Closed August 12, 2007.* A play that is described as a collection of interweaving tales of love among the ruins.

WHEN WE WERE YOUNG AND FILLED WITH FEAR. *Written by Jack Ferver. Produced by Dixon Place. Dixon Place. Opened July 27, 2007. Closed August 4, 2007.* A new theatre/dance piece described as a "hysterical and terrifying emotional roller-coaster rampage that blurs the lines of fantasy and reality."

MY FIRST TIME. *Written and directed by Ken Davenport. New World Stages. Opened July 28, 2007.* A new play featuring true accounts of first sexual experiences.

THE BLACK EYED. *Written by Betty Shamieh. Directed by Sam Gold. Produced by New York Theatre Workshop. New York Theatre Workshop. Opened July 31, 2007. Closed August 19, 2007.* A new play about four Arab women from across the ages who meet in the afterlife.

OJOS/THE MACHINE. *Produced by Dark Moon, NYC. Studio315NYC. Opened August 1, 2007. Closed August 10, 2007.* A program of two new short plays: one about two children who try to escape their harsh reality by playing a game; the other about a scientist whose curiosity may have stolen another man's soul.

ICE QUEENS: THE FAGGOT WAR. *Written by Michael Cross Burke. Dixon Place. Opened August 1, 2007. Closed August 15, 2007.* A new performance piece about the "Battle of the Brians" at the 1988 Winter Olympics.

ELECTION DAY. *Written by Josh Tobiessen. Directed by Jeremy Dobrish. Produced by Second Stage Theatre. McGinn Cazale Theatre. Opened August 1, 2007. Closed August 18, 2007.* A new comedy about a young man who faces all sorts of obstacles as he tries to cast his vote.

MADAGASCAR. *Written by Wry Lachlan. Directed by Meghan Dickerson. Produced by New World Theatre. American Theatre of Actors. Opened August 1, 2007. Closed August 11, 2007.* A new play about a marriage quietly unraveling in the wake of a lost child.

TALL TALES OF TRUE STORIES. *Written by Jonathan Todd Ross. Produced by Propinquity Productions. 440 Studios. Opened August 1, 2007. Closed August 4, 2007.* Six plays about young men who connect with women but can't commit to them.

DYSPHORIA. *Written and directed by Alec Duffy. Produced by Hoi Polloi. Ontological Theatre. Opened August 2, 2007. Closed August 11, 2007.* A new play that follows five members of a religious sect as they prepare to carry out the utopian vision of their late founder.

DAGUERROTYPE. *Written by Stephen Aubrey. Directed by Jess Chayes. Produced by The American Story Project. Abingdon Theatre. Opened August 2, 2007. Closed August 11, 2007.* A play about nineteenth century photographer Matthew Brady.

SUMMER SHORTS. *Produced by The Open Book. 59E59. Opened August 2, 2007. Closed August 30, 2007.* Two programs of original short plays.

- **AMICI, ASCOLTAT**, *by Warren Leight.*
- **AFTERNOON TEA**, *book and lyrics by Eduardo Machado, music by Skip Kennon.*
- **RAIN, HEAVY AT TIMES**, *by Leslie Lyles.*
- **REAL WORLD EXPERIENCE**, *by Michael Domitrovich.*
- **SKIN DEEP**, *by Tina Howe.*
- **MERWINS LANE**, *by Keith Reddin.*
- **FATHER'S DAY**, *by John Augustine.*
- **THE P.A.**, *by Tom O'Brien.*
- **WINDOWSHINE**, *by Randee Smith.*

THE WIKIPEDIA PLAYS. *Ars Nova. Opened August 3, 2007. Closed August 6, 2007.* A mini-marathon of short plays that surf the wikipedia wave through seventeen related entries.

- **CASTRATION ANXIETY**, *by Mike Batistick.*
- **PROKOP THE GREAT**, *by Evan Cabnet.*
- **TURBULENT**, *by Ron Fitzgerald.*
- **BOHEMIA**, *by Liz Flahive.*
- **FETISH**, *by Sam Forman.*
- **THE DEFENESTRATION OF PRAGUE**, *by Etan Frankel.*
- **TROPOSPHERE**, *by Kyle Jarrow.*
- **GLOBAL WARMING**, *by Nick Jones.*
- **YALE LAW SCHOOL**, *by Barry Levey.*
- **DEMOCRACY**, *by Carly Mensch.*
- **PARTICLE BOARD**, *by Elizabeth Meriwether.*
- **GOLF BALL**, *by Lin-Manuel Miranda.*
- **STILETTO HEELS**, *by Rachel Shukert.*
- **WEATHER FORECASTING**, *by Mat Smart.*
- **UNCERTAINTIES**, *by Aurin Squire.*
- **BILL CLINTON**, *by Adam Szymkowicz.*
- **WOODEN**, *by Beau Willimon.*

NATE & BETTE. *Written by Julio Tumbaco and Jim Gibson. Directed by Dee Spencer. Produced by JJEntertainment. Theatre Row Studio. Opened August 3, 2007. Closed August 26, 2007.* A new comedy about a man who thinks he's Nathan Lane.

SNAPSHOTS '07. *Produced by Dog Run Repertory Theatre Company. The S-P-A-C-E Gallery & Performance Space. Opened August 3, 2007. Closed August 26, 2007.* A program of original short plays and monologues.

- **FIRST DATE,** *by Patrick Blake.*
- **BRIDESMAID,** *by Clay McLeod Chapman.*
- **THE INTERSTATE AND ON,** *by Clay McLeod Chapman.*
- **IN THESE TIMES—SCENES FROM THE AFTERMATH OF SEPTEMBER 11,** *by Jeff Cohen.*

BUCKLE MY SHOE, OR TERROR FIRMA. *Book and lyrics by Crystal Field. Music by Joseph-Vernon Banks. Directed by Crystal Field. Opened August 4, 2007. Closed September 16, 2007.* Theater for the New City presents their annual street theatre extravaganza, about the possibility of world peace or world devastation and global warming versus global conservation. At various outdoor locales in all five boroughs.

KIDNAPPED BY CRAIGSLIST. *Written by Katie Goan and Nitra Gutierrez. Directed by Kimmy Gatewood. Peoples Improv Theatre. Opened August 4, 2007. Closed August 25, 2007.* A new comedy that explores the carnivalistic, cult-like phenomenon that is Craigslist.

THE HANGING OF RAZOR BROWN. *Written by Le Wilhelm. Directed by Merry Beamer. 59E59. Opened August 5, 2007. Closed August 26, 2007.* A new play about a group of picnickers who choose a spot near a tree that has a noose hanging from it.

OH, HAPPY THREE! *Manhattan Theatre Source. Opened August 6, 2007. Closed August 16, 2007.* A program of three one-act plays.

- **JUDGE, YURI AND EXECUTIONER,** *by Ed Malin.*
- **I SHALL NOT BE SUEDE,** *by Ed Malin.*
- **HERMAPHRODITISM THROUGH THE AGES,** *by Peter Dizozza, Maria Micheles, and Ed Malin.*

TINGS DEY HAPPEN. *Written and performed by Dan Hoyle. Directed by Charlie Varon. Produced by Culture Project. 55 Mercer. Opened August 7, 2007. Closed October 20, 2007.* A solo show about the politics of oil in the Niger Delta.

OPUS. *Written by Michael Hollinger. Directed by Terrence J. Nolen. Produced by Primary Stages. 59E59. Opened August 7, 2007. Closed September 1, 2007.* A play in which a world-renowned string quartet struggles to prepare for their highest profile performance when the violist, and founder of the quartet, mysteriously disappears.

HUMAN ERROR. *Written by Keith Reddin. Directed by Tracy Brigden. Produced by Atlantic Theater Company. Atlantic Stage 2. Opened August 8, 2007. Closed August 26, 2007.* A new play about the investigation of a plane crash.

ALPHABET CITY IV. *Directed by Derek Jamison. Produced by Metropolitan Playhouse. Metropolitan Playhouse. Opened August 8, 2007. Closed August 19, 2007.* A series of solo performances celebrating real life artists, activists, entrepreneurs, and anonymous neighbors of the Lower East Side.

LONG DISTANCE. *Adapted by Bridgette Dunlap. Directed by Bridgette Dunlap and Alexis Grausz. Produced by The Ateh Theater Group. chashama. Opened August 9, 2007. Closed September 1, 2007.* A program of three original short plays based on stories by Judy Budnitz.

GREY-EYED DOGS. *Written by Jess Barbagallo. Directed by Katie Brook. Produced by The Red Terror Squad. Dixon Place. Opened August 9, 2007. Closed August 25, 2007.* A new play billed as a story about senseless pursuits and backdoor sensations, plus a little fur on fur.

ONE NATION UNDER. *Written by Andrea Lepcio. Directed by Tye Blue. Produced by At Hand Theatre Company. Medicine Show. Opened August 9, 2007. Closed August 26, 2007.* A new play about a conservative judge whose son goes to serve in Iraq.

NEW YORK INTERNATIONAL FRINGE FESTIVAL. *Opened August 10, 2007. Closed August 26, 2007.* The eleventh edition of North America's largest performing arts festival, at twenty venues in downtown Manhattan.

- **...DOUBLE VISION**, *created by Barbara Blumenthal-Ehrlich, directed by Ari Laura Kreith, produced by Don't Say Miami and Joshua P. Weiss.*
- **200 MYSTICAL FICTIONS**, *created by Debra L. Siegel, directed by Laura Pestronk, produced by Word For Snow Productions.*
- **36:24:36**, *created by The Company, directed by James Duff, produced by The Ostara Group.*
- **516 (FIVE SIXTEEN)**, *created by Katharine Clark Gray, directed by Todd Parmley, produced by Roust Theatre Company.*
- **7 STORIES HIGH**, *created by Hilary Leichter, directed by Brendan Wattenberg, produced by Until Now! Productions.*
- **A BEAUTIFUL CHILD**, *created by Truman Capote, directed by Linda Powell, produced by The Courthouse Theatre Co.*
- **A MIKVAH**, *created and directed by Jeremy Bloom, produced by WAVE Productions.*
- **ACTION JESUS**, *created by Leslie Harrell Dillen, directed by Melissa J. Wentworth, produced by Out of the Blue.*
- **ANALOG FRIEND**, *created and directed by Manny Liyes, produced by Manuel Rodriguez.*
- **AND SOMEWHERE MEN ARE LAUGHING**, *created by Jeff Mandels, directed by Bill Russell, produced by HANDEE Productions.*
- **ANDREA/AGAVE**, *created and directed by Taurie Kinoshita, produced by Cruel Theater.*
- **ANGEL/BUDDY**, *created by Ken Ferrigni, directed by Tim Aumiller, produced by No Hope Productions.*
- **ANGELA'S FLYING BED**, *created by Karl Greenberg and Dave Hall, directed by Chris Clavelli, produced by Flying Bed Productions.*
- **ANGST: THE NEW TEEN MUSICAL**, *created by Celeste Busa, directed by Celeste Busa and Eric Mayson, produced by Kindred Theater Company.*
- **ANIMALS**, *created by Ryan O'Nan, directed by Kevin Kittle, produced by The Blossom Company.*
- **ANOTHER DAY ON WILLOW ST**, *created by Frank Anthony Polito, directed by Ike Schambelan, produced by Woodward Avenue Productions/Theater by the Blind.*
- **ANTARCTICA**, *created and directed by Carolyn Raship, produced by Fevvers Productions.* **SEE PAGE 53.**
- **ARTHUR AND ESTHER**, *created by Ross Howard, directed by Sarah Norris, produced by Warm Gun Productions.*
- **AS FAR AS WE KNOW**, *created by The Torture Project Ensemble in collaboration with Christina Gorman, directed by Laurie Sales, produced by unCommon Cause.*
- **ASKING FOR IT**, *created by Joanna Rush, directed by Lynne Taylor-Corbett, produced by AFI Co.*
- **BANG/WHIMPER**, *created by Larke G. Schuldberg, directed by Slaney Ross, produced by Small Fowl.*

- **BAUM FOR PEACE**, *created by Terry Baum, music by Scrumbly Koldewyn, lyrics by David Hyman, directed by Bobbi Ausubel, produced by Lilith Theater.*
- **BENT TO THE FLAME—A NIGHT WITH TENNESSEE WILLIAMS**, *created by Doug Tompos, directed by Michael Michetti, produced by Fugitive Productions.*
- **BOILING POT**, *created by Evan Joiner and Kobi Libii, directed by Milton Justice, produced by Where Productions.*
- **BOMBS IN YOUR MOUTH**, *created by Corey Patrick, directed by Joseph Ward, produced by bipolar productions/wej productions.*
- **BUKOWSICAL!**, *created by Spencer Green and Gary Stockdale, directed by Joe Peracchio, produced by The See You Next Tuesday Company.*
- **BURN**, *created by Creighton James, directed by Adam Arian, produced by New York Theatre Experiment.*
- **BYE, BYE BIG GUY**, *book by Michael Slade, music by David Evans, lyrics by Faye Greenberg, directed by Devanand Janki, produced by 14 Husky Productions.*
- **CANCER! THE MUSICAL**, *created by Shawn Handlon, Tom Donnellon, and John Edwartowski; directed and produced by Shawn Handlon.*
- **CATCH THE FISH**, *created by Jon Caren, directed by Kristin Hanggi, produced by John Davisi.*
- **CHASER**, *created by Howard Walters, directed by Shaun I. Peknic, produced by Extra Virgin Productions.*
- **CHING CHONG CHINAMAN**, *created by Lauren Yee, directed by Anne Marie Bookwalter, produced by Bathwater Productions.*
- **DAYS AND NIGHTS: PAGE 121, LINES 11 AND 12**, *adapted and directed by Marc Stuart Weitz, produced by Purple Man Theater Company.*
- **DIVING IN DECEMBER**, *created by Emma Fisher, directed by Tasha Gordon-Solmon, produced by Full Stop Ensemble.*
- **DOES THE BODY GOOD**, *created by Patrick Link, directed by Kern Clark, produced by Way Back When Productions.*
- **EARTH'S VACATION**, *created and directed by Maura Kelley, produced by Theatersmarts.*
- **ELEKTRAFIRE—A MODERN ROCK OPERA**, *music and lyrics by Doug Thoms, directed by Doug Thoms, produced by Livestage Performance.*
- **ELEPHANT IN THE ROOM!**, *created and directed by Dan Fogler, produced by Stage 13.*
- **END'S EVE: THE FEAST OF 2012**, *created by Hilary Park and Jennifer Gnisci, directed by Erik Bryan Slavin, produced by Fifth World Productions.*
- **FACE-OFF WITH UGLINESS**, *created by Rick Bland, directed by Heather Davies, produced by Blandino Productions.*
- **FARMER SONG**, *created by Joe Hynek and Angie Hynek, directed by Jane Cox, produced by Pumptown Productions.*
- **FARMTRUCKS: A CORPORATE COFFEE ADVENTURE**, *created by Kevin Crook, directed by Jon Tracy, produced by The Farmtrucks Coffee Company.*
- **FISH**, *created by Cyndi Williams, directed by Rich Johnson, produced by A Mix Productions.*
- **FREEDOM! AND THE STICKY END OF MAKE-BELIEVE**, *created by Thom Pasculli, directed by Allison Talis, produced by The Savannah Theatre Project.*
- **GALATEA**, *created by John Ott, directed by Drew Leary, produced by Pageant Wagon (Brad Raimondo and Drew Leary).*

- **GAMERS**, *created by Brian Bielawski and Walter G. Meyer, directed by Wes Grantom, produced by Slant Theatre Project.*
- **GET OUT OF JAIL FREE**, *created by Richard Fulco, directed by Anthony Cerrato, produced by The Full Co.*
- **GIVE AND GO: LEARNING FROM LOSING TO THE HARLEM GLOBETROTTERS**, *created by Brandt Johnson, directed by Andrew Garman, produced by Syntaxis Productions.*
- **HAIL SATAN**, *created by Mac Rogers, directed by Jordana Williams, produced by Gideon Productions, LLC.*
- **HELMET**, *created by Douglas Maxwell, directed and produced by Maryann Lombardi.*
- **HILLARY AGONISTES**, *created by Nick Salamone, directed by Jon Lawrence Rivera, produced by Playwrights' Arena.*
- **HORATIO**, *created by Isabelle Assante, directed by Troy Miller, produced by Isabelle Weyer.*
- **HOT FLASHES**, *created by Lynne Topping Farrell, directed by Michael Page, produced by Main Street Players.*
- **I DIG DOUG**, *created by Karen DiConcetto and Rochelle Zimmerman, directed by Bert V. Royal, produced by Tom Smedes Productions.*
- **IN OUR NAME**, *created and directed by Elena Hartwell, produced by Iron Pig.* **SEE PAGE 197.**
- **IN THE SHADOW OF MY SON**, *created by Nadine Bernard, directed by Nadine Bernard and Nancy Kelly, produced by Out of the Shadow Productions.*
- **IT AIN'T NO FAIRY TALE**, *created and produced by Lusia Strus.*
- **JAMAICA, FAREWELL**, *created by Debra Ehrhardt, directed by Monique Lai, produced by Debra Ehrhardt.*
- **JANUARY 1986**, *created by Timothy Mansfield, directed by Michael Kimmel, produced by Push Productions.*
- **JASPORA**, *created and produced by Nancy Moricette, directed by Ilknur River Ozgur.*
- **JESUS RANT: THE RELIGIO–COMIC RAVINGS OF A FORMER CHRISTIAN**, *created by H.R. Britton, directed by Maia Garrison and H.R. Britton, produced by Overcoat Theater.*
- **JOHN GOLDFARB, PLEASE COME HOME**, *created by William Peter Blatty, Michael Garin, Erik Frandsen, Robert Hipkins; directed by Jeffrey Lewonczyk; produced by Performance Associates.*
- **JULIET**, *created by Andras Visky, directed by Christopher Markle, produced by Theatre Y.*
- **KELLY KINSELLA LIVE! UNDER BROADWAY**, *created by Kelly Kinsella, directed by Antonio Merenda, produced by Michael T. Clarkston Productions.*
- **KISS & MAKE UP**, *book and lyrics by Kevin Hammonds, music and lyrics Mark Weiser, directed by Tom Mills, produced by Fingers Crossed Productions.*
- **LADIES OF EOLA HEIGHTS**, *created by Michael Wanzie, directed by Kenny Howard, produced by Wanzie Presents.*
- **LEN AND ERNEST**, *created and produced by Francesco Saviano, directed by Mauricio Bustamante.*
- **LENI**, *created by Sarah Greenman, directed by Lorraine Cink, produced by Collaborative Play Productions.*
- **LIFE/PLAY**, *created by Cody Daigle, directed by Cody Daigle and Jarin Schexnider, produced by Cite des Arts.*
- **LIGHTS RISE ON GRACE**, *created by Chad Beckim, directed by Robert O'Hara, produced by 61 Academy/Partial Comfort Productions.*
- **LOST IN HOLLYWOODLAND OR THE SLUGWOMAN FROM URANUS**, *created by Alex Wexler, directed by Dan Oliverio, produced by Inka Dinka Inc.*

- **LOST! HOW A CERTAIN TV MEGA-HUNK STOLE MY IDENTITY,** *created by Josh Halloway, directed by Andy Donald, produced by Movie Geek, LLC.*
- **LUCID,** *created and produced by Jordan Smedberg, directed by Mariel Goddu.*
- **MADONNA AND CHILD AND OTHER DIVAS,** *created by Tom Johnson, directed by Julie Hamberg, produced by Boy Howdy Productions.*
- **MARVELOUS SHRINE,** *created by Leslie Bramm, directed by Pamela S. Butler, produced by Three Crows Theatre.* **SEE PAGE 163.**
- **MARY BRIGIT POPPLETON IS WRITING A MEMOIR,** *created by Madeline Walter, directed by Heidi Handelsman, produced by Madeline Walter in association with The Strollers.*
- **MIRIAM,** *created by Diane Allison, directed by Kathryn Marie Bild, produced by Miriam & Company.*
- **MOTHER HUBBARD'S CUPBOARD,** *created by Mark Jay Mirsky, directed by Marc Palmieri, produced by Golem Media, Inc.*
- **MR. BASEBALL,** *created by Matt Doherty, directed by Michael Stock, produced by Sideway Theater.*
- **MYLES: THE HYPOALLERGENIC SUPERHERO (AND HIS SUPERHERO FRIENDS),** *created by Bridget Ryan, produced by Orange Bus Productions.*
- **NEW STREET POETS,** *created by Reginald S. Burch, LeDerick Horne, Isis Phoenix, Michelle Seabreeze, Scott Tarazevits, and Justin Woo; directed by Mel Williams; produced by New Street Poets.*
- **NIGHT,** *created by Philip Gerson, directed by Michael Lilly, produced by The Occasional Theatre.*
- **NOT FROM CANADA,** *created and directed by Kevin Doyle, produced by Sponsored by Nobody.*
- **ON AIR OFF!,** *created and directed by Adam Lerman and Danny Tieger, produced by Apple Rug Productions.*
- **PAPER SON,** *created and produced by Byron Yee.*
- **PB&J,** *created by Tara Dairman, directed by Cyndy A. Marion, produced by Breadbasket Productions.*
- **PN 1923. 45 LS01 VOLUME 2 (THE BOOK PLAY),** *created by Bixby Elliot, directed by Stephen Brackett, produced by J+J Productions.*
- **POGO & EVIE: A ZYDECO MUSICAL,** *created by Aaron Latham, directed by Sergio Alvarado, produced by Jenny Rose Productions.*
- **POPPIES,** *created by Lane Keller, directed by Sherri Eden Barber, produced by 5th Wall Theatre Co.*
- **PRINCESS MIMI OR: HOW I LEARNED TO STOP WORRYING AND LOVE THE FROG,** *created by Patrick Flynn, directed by Zachary Stewart, produced by The Hamburger Theatre Company.*
- **PRINCESS SUNSHINE'S BITTER PILL OF TRUTH FUNHOUSE,** *created by Juliet Jeske, directed by Mark Lonergan, produced by Little Miss Angry Girl.*
- **RIDING THE BULL,** *created by August Schulenburg; directed by Kelly O'Donnell, produced by Flux Theatre Ensemble.*
- **RISE LIKE A PENIS FROM THE FLAMES—A PHALLIC PHOENIX STORY,** *created by Antonio Sacre, directed by Jim Lasko, produced by Pan Productions.*
- **ROLL WITH THE PUNCHES,** *created by Garet Scott, directed by Kevin Thomsen, produced by Thomsen Scott Productions, LLC.*
- **ROXY FONT,** *created by Liza Lentini, directed by Katherine Kovner, produced by Crazytown Productions.*

- **SCOUT'S HONOR!**, *created by Ed Valentine, directed by Melanie S. Armer, produced by Cardium Mechanicum.*
- **SEMI-PERMANENT**, *created by Rick Gradone, directed by Johanna McKeon, produced by Blue Monkey Productions.*
- **SHADOW PEOPLE**, *created by Jay Bernzweig; directed by Kevin Vavasseur, produced by FDMA Theatreworks.*
- **SHE'S NOT WELL**, *created and directed by Ted Baus, produced by Baus & Troche.*
- **SHOW CHOIR!—THE MUSICAL**, *book, music, and lyrics by Mark McDaniels and Donald Garverick; directed by Gary Slavin; produced by McG Productions.*
- **SLAMMER!**, *created by Steve Adams and Chan Chandler, directed by Rod Caspers, produced by New Gate Productions.*
- **SLUT A LA CARTE**, *created and directed by Brenda McFarlane, produced by Far Fetched Productions.*
- **STOCK HOME**, *created by Alex Goldberg, produced by Changuitos Productions.*
- **SUSAN GETS SOME PLAY**, *created by Adam Szymkowicz, directed by Moritz von Stuelpnagel, produced by Stage Fright Productions.*
- **SUSTAINED WINDS**, *directed by Amy Waguespack, produced by Acting Up (In Acadiana).*
- **THE BOX**, *created by Steffi Kammer, directed by Bob Sloan, produced by Dime-Store Alchemy.*
- **THE BOY ON THE OTHER SIDE OF THE WORLD**, *created by Jill Jichetti, directed by Jill Jichetti and Hilary McHone, produced by Lifeblood Theater Company.*
- **THE COMMISSION**, *created by Steven Fechter, directed by Sarah Gurfield, produced by Dreamscape Theatre.*
- **THE DOUBLE MURDER PLAYS**, *created by Scott Klavan, directed by Stephen Jobes, produced by Buddy-Pal Productions.*
- **THE EDUCATION OF REBECCA**, *created by Branan Whitehead, produced by Busted Wide Open Productions.*
- **THE END**, *created and produced by Andy Gershenzon, directed by Christopher Denham.*
- **THE GOSPEL ACCORDING TO MATTHEW**, *created by Matthew Francis, directed by David Drake, produced by Constyabul Productions.*
- **THE HOLLOW MEN**, *created by Emily Rossi, directed by Laurie J. Wolf, produced by Prickly Pear Productions.*
- **THE JAZZ MESSENGER**, *created and produced by Eric K. Daniels, directed by Michael Petranek.*
- **THE LIFE AND TIMES OF MARTIN LUTHER (REFORMED)**, *created and directed by Jarrod Jabre, produced by The Colonel's Men.*
- **THE MEDICINE SHOW (A PLAY WITH MUSIC)**, *created by David Dannenfelser, directed by Kevin Kittle, produced by The Icarus Theater Ensemble.*
- **THE MERCY SWING**, *created by Lane Bernes, directed by Richard Perez, produced by 3am Productions.*
- **THE MONKEY MOO**, *created by Yoko Myoi, directed by Kanako Hiyama, produced by Great World Amusement Center.*
- **THE OTHER SIDE OF DARKNESS**, *created and directed by Phil Geoffrey Bond, produced by Storefront Theatre.*
- **THE OUTSIDE MAN**, *created and directed by Robert Dominguez, produced by SloWriter Productions, LLC.*
- **THE PROGRAM**, *created by Michele Aldin, directed by Elysa Marden, produced by Lucky Pelican, LLC.*

- **THE REVOLUTIONARIES**, *created by Adam Mervis, directed by Megan Marod, produced by The Moving Canvas Group.*
- **THE RISE AND FALL OF MILES AND MILO**, *created by Sara Jeanne Asselin, directed by Melissa Firlit, produced by Fine Feathered Friends.*
- **THE TERRIBLE GIRLS**, *created by Jacqueline Goldfinger, directed by Esther Emery and Chelsea Whitmore, produced by Ziselen Productions.*
- **THE UNUSUAL SUSPECTS**, *created by Derek Sonderfan, directed by Gregory Cicchino, produced by Aaron Grant in association with BTW Productions.*
- **THE WINTER'S TALE PROJECT**, *book by Bridget Ryan, music and lyrics byChris Wynters, directed by Bridget Ryan, produced by Orange Bus Productions.*
- **THE WISDOM THAT MEN SEEK**, *created and directed by Robert Liebowitz, produced by Genesis Repertory Ensemble Inc.*
- **THERE'S SOMETHING ABOUT MARRIAGE**, *created by John Fisher; directed by John Fisher, Maryssa Wanlass, and David Bicha; produced by Theatre Rhinoceros.*
- **THEREMIN**, *created by Ben Lewis and Duke Doyle, directed by Lee Overtree, produced by The Blue Cake Theatre Company.*
- **THUNDER! A MUSICAL MEMOIR**, *created by Cynthia Robinson and Jimmy Tate, directed by Greg Allen, produced by TRA Productions.*
- **TOP AND BOTTOM**, *created and directed by Kevin West, produced by Dust Bunny Productions.*
- **TRAGEDY! (A MUSICAL COMEDY)**, *created by Mike Johnson and Mary Davenport, directed by Mike Johnson, produced by Musical! (A Production Company).*
- **TWO-MUR HUMOR: HE'S MALIGNANT, SHE'S BENIGN**, *created by Valerie David and Jim Tooey, directed by Charles Messina, produced by Turmor Humor Fund, Inc.*
- **VAMPINGO: A COMEDY WITH BITE**, *created by Ariana Johns and Jolene Adams, directed by Jolene Adams, produced by Vampingo Productions.*
- **VICTOR WOO: THE AVERAGE ASIAN AMERICAN**, *created by Kevin So and Kevin Merritt, directed by Kevin Merritt, produced by One Foot Productions.*
- **WALKING IN HIS FOOTSTEPS**, *created by Joan Fishman, directed by Rita Esquenazi, produced by Baby Shoes Productions.*
- **WHENCE CAME YE, SCARLETT O'HARA O'HANRAHAN?**, *created by Melle Powers, directed by Jeremy Brisiel, produced by 53 Hysterics.*
- **WILLIAMSBURG! THE MUSICAL**, *book by Will Brumley, music and lyrics by Kurt Gellersted and Brooke Fox, directed by Deborah Wolfson, produced by Theaterloop.*
- **WOOF, DADDY**, *created by Bryan Reynolds, directed by Amanda McRaven, produced by Transversal Theatre Co.*

BECCA AND HEIDI. *Written by Sharon Eberhardt. Directed by Blake Lawrence. chashama. Opened August 12, 2007. Closed August 22, 2007.* A one-woman show about a smackdown with one's alter-ego.

RECONSTRUCTING MAMA. *Book by Stephen Svoboda. Music by N. David Williams. Lyrics by Stephen Svoboda and N. David Williams. Directed by Stephen Svoboda. Produced by Fresco Productions. Kirk Theatre. Opened August 12, 2007. Closed August 19, 2007.* A new musical about a family coping with the suicide of the mother.

IDOL: THE MUSICAL. *Conceived by Todd Ellis. Music and lyrics by Jon Balcourt. Book and lyrics by Bill Boland. Directed by Daniel Tursi. 45th Street Theatre. Opened August 12, 2007. Closed August 12, 2007.* A new musical about the "idol worship" of Clay Aiken.

WHEN DAY BECAME NIGHT. *Written and performed by Leigh Evans. Directed by Annie Kunjappy. Ontological Theatre. Opened August 15, 2007. Closed August 18, 2007.* A new play about ordinary citizens in times of war.

LESSONS IN FLYING AND THE NEW MIRANDA. *Written by Joel Shatzky. Directed by Samantha Lee Manas. Impact Theater. Opened August 16, 2007. Closed August 26, 2007.* A program of two plays. The first is about two longtime friends whose relationship reaches an impasse. The second is about a writer who is confronted by a character from one of his novels.

THE DANISH MEDIATIONS/SLOTS. *Written by Sergei Burbank. Directed by Adam Karsten. Access Theatre. Opened August 16, 2007. Closed September 9, 2007.* A new play about an actor producing his dream show—a production of *Hamlet* where the roles change every night, determined by a random drawing of names.

A PLAY ON ELEMENTAL CONSEQUENCES. *Written by Jacqueline Raposo. Produced by ModernEyes Theatre Company: The Project. Opened August 16, 2007. Closed August 26, 2007.* An adaptation of classic Greek stories based on *The Oresteia*, at Summit Rock in Central Park.

SNAPSHOTS. *Directed by Gregory Simmons. Produced by Diverse City Theater Company. Beckett Theatre. Opened August 16, 2007. Closed September 1, 2007.* Three short plays about women in their fifties, seventies, and nineties.

WHAT FAIRY TALE IS THIS, ANYWAY?! *Book by Keri Barker and Michael Maricondi. Music and lyrics by Michael Maricondi. Directed by Michael Maricondi. Producers Club. Opened August 17, 2007. Closed August 18, 2007.* A new family musical based on the book of the same name about a princess whose prince is kidnapped by a dragon.

SAY SOMETHING. *Written by Bill Mignoli. Roy Arias Studios & Theatres. Opened August 17, 2007. Closed November 10, 2007.* A new rock opera about freedom of speech, supporting our troops, and changing our way of thinking in America.

THE SHATTERING OF THE GOLDEN PANE. *Written by Le Wilhelm. Directed by Gregg David Shore. Produced by 59E59. 59E59. Opened August 19, 2007. Closed September 2, 2007.* In this new play, two young misfits meet in a long-abandoned church that was once a rollicking nightclub in the 1940s and now lies in ruins.

PORTRAIT OF THE ARTIST AS A DUMB BLONDE. *Written and directed by Sharon Fogarty. Manhattan Theatre Source. Opened August 19, 2007. Closed August 23, 2007.* A new one-act musical about an artist who thinks she can give up art and survive in the corporate world.

FAIR GAME. *Written by Karl Gajdusek. Directed by Andrew Volkoff. Produced by Genesius Theatre Guild. Lion Theatre. Opened August 20, 2007. Closed September 7, 2007.* A new play that gives a behind-the-scenes look at a woman's presidential campaign.

BEN. *Written by William Shakespeare. Adapted and directed by J. Marshall Denuszek. Produced by PetroLab Productions. Ace of Clubs. Opened August 21, 2007. Closed September 6, 2007.* A new play inspired by *Romeo and Juliet* that tells the story from the point of view of the character Benvolio.

BUILDING A HOUSE OUT OF FEATHERS. *Created and directed by James Peterson. Produced by The Paper Industry. Ontological Theatre. Opened August 22, 2007. Closed August 25, 2007.* A performance work described as a hallucinatory journey through the last remnant memories of the known world.

TIMES SQUARE THE MUSICAL. *Book, music, and lyrics by John Dentato. Directed by Carlos Morales and John Dentato. Produced by Jondee Productions. Sofia's Restaurant. Opened August 22, 2007. Closed December 21, 2007.* A new musical about people following their dreams and searching for love in the heart of New York City's Times Square.

SEPTEMBER 12TH. *Written and directed by Michael Swift. Produced by Family Tree Collective. Nuyorican Poets Café. Opened August 23, 2007. Closed September 15, 2007.* A new play about two low-level drug dealers filling orders in the wake of the attacks on September 11 in New York City.

IPHIGENIA 2.0. *Written by Charles Mee. Directed by Tina Landau. Signature at Peter Norton Space. Opened August 26, 2007. Closed October 7, 2007.* A radical reinvention of the classic play by Euripides that examines the costs of war and loss of innocence.

IPH.THEN. *Created by Peter A. Campbell, David Gordon, and Amanda Boekelheide. Written and directed by Peter A. Campbell. Produced by Ontological-Hysteric Theater. Ontological Theatre. Opened August 29, 2007. Closed September 1, 2007.* A remaking of the myth of Iphigenia in Tauris.

RITES OF PRIVACY. *Written and performed by David Rhodes. Directed by Charles Loffredo. Produced by Moving Parts Theater. Urban Stages. Opened August 30, 2007. Closed September 30, 2007.* A new solo play about an array of characters aching to reveal their darkest secrets.

ABOUT THE EDITOR

MARTIN DENTON is the founder and Executive Director of The New York Theatre Experience, Inc. (NYTE), and editor and chief theatre reviewer for NYTE's website, nytheatre.com. He has edited all the play anthologies published by NYTE Small Press featuring, to date, the work of 133 emerging playwrights. He is also the creator of the nytheatrecast (www.nytheatrecast.com), New York City's first regularly scheduled theatre podcast offering original content.

ABOUT THE PUBLISHER

THE NEW YORK THEATRE EXPERIENCE, INC. (NYTE), is a nonprofit New York State corporation. Its mission is to use traditional and new media to foster interest, engagement, and participation in theatre and drama and to provide tangible support to theatre artists and dramatists, especially emerging artists and artists in the nonprofit sector. The principal activity of The New York Theatre Experience is the operation of several free websites (www.nytheatre.com, www.indietheater.org, mobile.nytheatre.com, and www.nytheatrecast.com) that comprehensively cover the New York theatre scene—on, off-, and off-off-Broadway. An ongoing program is NYTE Small Press, which publishes yearly anthologies of new plays by emerging playwrights. Information about NYTE and its publishing program can be found on the Internet at www.nyte.org.

Contact NYTE online at info@nyte.org or by mail at:

The New York Theatre Experience, Inc.
P.O. Box 1606, Murray Hill Station
New York, NY 10156

The PLAYS AND PLAYWRIGHTS Series
ISSN 1546-1319
Annual anthologies of new plays by emerging playwrights produced in New York City

Since 2000, The New York Theatre Experience, Inc. (NYTE), has published anthologies of plays which include complete scripts, biographical sketches, and a detailed introduction by the editor, Martin Denton. NYTE is a nonprofit corporation that utilizes its small press to promote the works of emerging playwrights so as to reach a wide audience to show the diverse spirit of contemporary theatre, in terms of genre, form, and subject matter. For complete information about these volumes, please visit www.nyte.org/pep.

PLAYS AND PLAYWRIGHTS 2001
Edited by Martin Denton, Preface by Robert Simonson
ISBN 09670234-2-4 – Retail $15.00

Washington Square Dreams by Gorilla Repertory Theatre, *Fate* by Elizabeth Horsburgh, *Velvet Ropes* by Joshua Scher, *The Language of Kisses* by Edmund De Santis, *Word To Your Mama* by Julia Lee Barclay, *Cuban Operator Please...* by Adrian Rodriguez, *The Elephant Man –The Musical* by Jeff Hylton & Tim Werenko, *House of Trash* by Trav S.D., *Straight-Jacket* by Richard Day

PLAYS AND PLAYWRIGHTS 2002
Edited by Martin Denton, Foreword by Bill C. Davis
ISBN 09670234-3-2 – Retail $15.00

The Death of King Arthur by Matthew Freeman, *Match* by Marc Chun, *Woman Killer* by Chiori Miyagawa, *The Wild Ass's Skin* by J. Scott Reynolds, *Halo* by Ken Urban, *Shyness Is Nice* by Marc Spitz, *Reality* by Curtiss I' Cook, *The Resurrectionist* by Kate Chell, *Bunny's Last Night In Limbo* by Peter S. Petralia, *Summerland* by Brian Thorstenson

PLAYS AND PLAYWRIGHTS 2003
Edited by Martin Denton, Foreword by Mario Fratti
ISBN 09670234-4-0 – Retail $15.00

A Queer Carol by Joe Godfrey, *Pumpkins For Smallpox* by Catherine Gillet, *Looking For The Pony* by Andrea Lepcio, *Black Thang* by Ato Essandoh, *The Ninth Circle* by Edward Musto, *The Doctor of Rome* by Nat Colley, *Galaxy Video* by Marc Morales, *The Last Carburetor* by Leon Chase, *Out To Lunch* by Joseph Langham, *Ascending Bodily* by Maggie Cino, *Last Call* by Kelly McAllister

PLAYS AND PLAYWRIGHTS 2004
Edited by Martin Denton, Foreword by Kirk Wood Bromley
ISBN 09670234-5-9 – Retail $16.00

Sugarbaby by Frank Cwiklik; *WTC View* by Brian Sloan; *United States: Work and Progress* by Christy Meyer, Jon Schumacher and Ellen Shanman; *The Shady Maids of Haiti* by John Jahnke; *Cats Can See The Devil* by Tom X. Chao; *Survivor: Vietnam!* by Rob Reese; *Feed the Hole* by Michael Stock; *Auntie Mayhem* by David Pumo; *The Monster Tales* by Mary Jett Parsley; *Sun, Stand Thou Still* by Steven Gridley

PLAYS AND PLAYWRIGHTS 2005
Edited by Martin Denton, Foreword by Steven Drukman
ISBN 09670234-6-7 – Retail $16.00

Vampire Cowboy Trilogy by Qui Nguyen & Robert Ross Parker, *second.* by Neal Utterback, *Bull Spears* by Josh Chambers, *Animal* by Kevin Augustine, *Odysseus Died from AIDS* by Stephen Svoboda, *Maggie May* by Tom O'Brien, *Elephant* by Margie Stokley, *Walking to America* by Alberto Bonilla, *The 29 Questions Project* by Katie Bull & Hillary Rollins, *Honor* by TheDrillingCompaNY, *Kalighat* by Paul Knox, *Platonov! Platonov! Platonov! or the case of a very Angry Duck* by Eric Michael Kochmer

PLAYS AND PLAYWRIGHTS 2006
Edited by Martin Denton; Foreword by Trav S.D.
ISBN 09670234-7-5 – Retail $17.00

The Top Ten People of the Millennium Sing Their Favorite Schubert Lieder by Alec Duffy, *Burning the Old Man* by Kelly McAllister, *Self at Hand* by Jack Hanley, *The Expense of Spirit* by Josh Fox, *Paradise* by Glyn O'Malley, *Yit, Ngay (One, Two)* by Michael Lew, *Pulling the Lever* by Rising Circle Theater Collective, *The Position* by Kevin Doyle, *The Dirty Talk* by Michael Puzzo, *The First Time Out of Bounds* by P. Seth Bauer, *Aurolac Blues* by Saviana Stanescu, *The Whore of Sheridan Square* by Michael Baron, Appendix: New American Plays in New York City

PLAYS AND PLAYWRIGHTS 2007
Edited by Martin Denton; Foreword by John Clancy
ISBN 978-0-9670234-9-6 – Retail $18

lenz by bluemouth, inc.; *Office Sonata* by Andy Chmelko; *Kiss and Cry* by Tom Rowan; *They're Just Like Us* by Boo Killebrew; *Convergence* by Bryn Manion; *Red Tide Blooming* by Taylor Mac; *The Adventures of Nervous Boy* by James Comtois; *Another Brief Encounter* by Stan Richardson; *Corps Values* by Brendon Bates; *Diving Normal* by Ashlin Halfnight; *'nami* by Chad Beckim; Appendix: New American Plays in New York City

OTHER ANTHOLOGIES BY NYTE SMALL PRESS

PLAYING WITH CANONS: Explosive New Works from Great
Literature by America's Indie Playwrights
Edited by Martin Denton
ISBN 978-0-9670234-8-9 – Retail $26.00

Want's Unwisht Work by Kirk Wood Bromley; *La Tempestad* by Larry Loebell; *Titus X*
by Shawn Northrip; *Genesis* by Matthew Freeman; *The Eumenides* by David Johnston;
Principia by Michael Maiello & Andrew Recinos; *Uncle Jack* by Jeff Cohen; *Story of
an Unknown Man* by Anthony P. Pennino; *The Brothers Karamazov Parts I and II* by
Alexander Harrington; *Bel Canto* by Reneé Flemings; *Salem* by Alex Roe; *Bartleby the
Scrivener* by R. L. Lane; *Frankenstein* by Rob Reese; *Northanger Abbey* by Lynn Marie
Macy; *The Man Who Laughs* by Kiran Rikhye; *Bald Diva!: The Ionesco Parody Your
Mother Warned You About* by David Koteles, Jason Jacobs & Jamee Freedus; *Fatboy* by
John Clancy; *The Persians...a comedy about war with five songs* by Waterwell

UNPREDICTABLE PLAYS
by Mario Fratti
Edited and with a Preface by Martin Denton
ISBN 978-0-9794852-0-6 – Retail: $20.00

*The Friday Bench; Suicide Club; Alessia; The Piggy Bank; The Fourth One; Dolls No
More; Porno; Dina and Alba; The Bridge; Confessions; The Coffin; A.I.D.S.; Brothel (The
Doorbell); The Letter; Mothers and Daughters; Beata, the Pope's Daughter; The Wish; Erotic
Adventures in Venice (Promises); The Academy; Friends; Terrorist; The Return; The Seventy-
fifth; Iraq (Blindness); "Che"; Anniversary; Missionaries; Sincerity*